THE EDGE

Copyright © 1983, 1986, 1990 by Howard E. Ferguson

All rights reserved. No part of this book may be used or reproduced in any manner whatsoever, including photocopying or recording, or by any information storage or retrieval system, without written permission from the publisher, except in the case of brief quotations embodied in critical articles and reviews.

Published by Getting the Edge Company,
800 Playhouse Square Plaza, 1220 Huron Road,
Cleveland, Ohio 44115-1712, (216) 241-3000

Library of Congress Cataloguing in Publication Data

The Edge: the guide to fulfilling dreams, maximizing success and enjoying a lifetime of achievement / [compiled] by Howard E. Ferguson; foreword by Joe Paterno; research committee chairman, John Cvetic; research committee, St. Edward High School wrestling team, coaches and alumni; contributing author, Gary Schwab.
     p.   cm.
Includes biobliographical references
ISBN 0-940601-04-4
   1. Sports—Quotations, maxims, etc. 2. Sports—Psychological aspects—Quotations, maxims, etc. 3. Success—Quotations, maxims, etc. I. Ferguson, Howard E. II. Schwab, Gary.
GV707.E29   1990   89-81379
796'.01—dc20   CIP

First Printing	**- 1983**
Second Printing	**- 1986**
Revised Edition	**- 1990**
Second Printing, Revised Edition	**- 1991**

Printed in the United States of America

Third Printing, Revised Edition - 1993
Fourth Printing, Revised Edition - 1994
Fifth Printing, Revised Edition - 1994
Sixth Printing, Revised Edition - 1995
Seventh Printing, Revised Edition - 1996

THE EDGE

The Guide to Fulfilling Dreams,
Maximizing Success and
Enjoying a Lifetime of Achievement

by Howard E. Ferguson
Wrestling Coach
St. Edward High School
Lakewood, Ohio

Foreword by Joe Paterno

Research Committee Chairman:
John Cvetic, Lakewood, Ohio

Research Committee:
St. Edward High School Wrestling Team,
Coaches and Alumni

Contributing Author
Gary Schwab
Executive Sports Editor
Charlotte Observer
Charlotte, North Carolina

Getting the Edge Company
Cleveland, Ohio

Jim Heffernan Wins a State Title

John Cvetic Wins A State Title

ABOUT THE AUTHOR

Who is Howard Ferguson and why has he written this book?

Good questions.

Howard Ferguson is the head wrestling coach at St. Edward High School in Lakewood, Ohio, a Cleveland suburb. In the 15 years he has been head coach, St. Edward's has won:

- 14 consecutive Sectional Tournaments
- 13 straight District Tournaments
- 11 Class AAA State of Ohio Championships
- 7 National High School Championships
- 82 Tournament Championships in a row

Ferguson is also a successful businessman. He's the founder and president of his own real estate company, which was the first in Ohio to convert apartment complexes into condominiums. With a small staff of five full-time employees and five part-time sales people, Professional Investments of America has, to date, converted 45 apartment buildings into condominiums.

Howard has also been a Certified Public Accountant, a leading salesman for a national real estate company, and a highly successful YMCA wrestling coach, achieving a 138-2 won-loss record over eight years.

In each of his endeavors, Howard has set goals and reached them.

Another area in which Ferguson has succeeded, and what may be his most important accomplishment, is in the relationships he has had with his athletes. He is more than just a coach who wants to win matches. Howard Ferguson provides his student-athletes at St. Edward with the unique opportunity to become the best person they can possibly be — in sports and in life. He is a friend who puts the time and effort into helping each one of them take advantage of every opportunity.

Howard knows that kids see through a lot of things. They can tell whether a coach cares more about them personally or about his won-loss record. Howard's concern for his student-athletes as people first is best illustrated by the numerous wrestling alumni, who have been furthering their wrestling and academic careers in some of the nation's leading colleges and universities.

Ferguson understands motivation. He has not achieved the success he has because he knows so much more than anyone else about selling real estate or about wrestling. His success comes from motivating himself and the people he associates with — and from working harder than the other guy.

Ferguson sets the example. When his team runs 13 miles in pre-season practice, he runs right with them. A life-long philosophy is "the harder I work, the luckier I get."

"When I first started in real estate, I really had no long-range goals," Ferguson recalls. "There was a sales contest every month and I just wanted to win every one. I loved the competition. I wasn't even close to being the best salesman the company had, but my game plan was simple. If the other salesmen worked eight hours a day and I worked 16, they had to be twice as good as me to beat me."

His wrestling teams reflect that philosophy. Where other teams might run 30 minutes after practice, St. Ed's runs 33 minutes — just to get the edge.

One of the St. Ed's wrestlers explained why Howard Ferguson always makes the extra effort in coaching. He said simply, "Because he loves us."

Several years back, Howard Ferguson began collecting messages from successful people, explaining their achievements. Whenever he received a new message, he would share it with his wrestlers as a means of motivation. He gathered so many messages, the idea of a book was born.

It started with a dream, then Ferguson set up a game plan to write a motivational book and followed that up with hard work until it was completed.

In six years, 20,000 copies of **THE EDGE** were sold from Ferguson's house. No major book publisher financed the book. No bookstores bought hundreds of copies at a time. The books were sold one by one by word of mouth.

Ferguson's work was not finished. He learned a lot during those six years, and he wanted to share it with others. So he went back to the drawing board. He contacted the new superstars in sports, and in other fields, to get additional messages of how to be the best you can be. Letters and phone calls poured in from all over the country.

The result of this hard work is the book you're reading. It has new motivational messages, plus expanded commentary from Howard based on his past five years of experience. Also, a chapter was added on cigarettes, alcohol, steroids and street drugs like cocaine, crack and marijuana. It's titled, "Why And How To Say No" — a subject about which he feels very strongly.

Howard is a perfect example of "living your dreams." This book started as an idea that became a dream. The dream was to publish a motivational book that could help others achieve the kind of personal and professional success that Howard discovered. The dream did not die when the book was completed and sold. It continues today with this new, updated edition. Never let your dreams die. Live your dreams, for what else is there in life? Dream some more. Live these new dreams. Howard did. So can you. This is what this book is all about.

— Joe Paterno
Head Football Coach
Penn State University

HOWARD E. FERGUSON
1938 – 1989

Howard E. Ferguson, "Ferg," was many things to many people: an exceptional father, a loyal friend and relative, a motivating coach, an honest business associate, a patient teacher. But more than anything else, Howard Ferguson was an inspiration. Through example he taught us the importance of living life to the fullest, being the best we can be and yet still taking the time to reach out to others. At his funeral more than 1,200 friends and fans stood and applauded Howard — a tribute to both the man and his achievements.

One of Ferg's dreams was to publish a book of quotes that exemplify his philosophy of life. THE EDGE is the realization of that dream.

Howard Ferguson will be dearly missed. However, through THE EDGE, his inspiration will live forever — and the world will be better for it.

DEDICATION

**I DEDICATE THIS BOOK
AND ALL THE THOUGHT THAT WENT INTO IT
TO MY TWO DAUGHTERS
LEE AND JACKIE**

People are inspired by different things and/or different people for different reasons. For me, it was a desire to be someone special to my two daughters — to be able to stand for principles that would be important to them and to be the type of person they could be proud to call their father.

Lee's goal is to become an attorney and is presently attending Law School at Cleveland State University. Jackie is working with young people in the field of Experimental Education, and someday plans to expand her work to include Special Education students.

I have been blessed with many great friends, business associates, employees, coaches and wrestlers. The cornerstone that has kept us together over the years has been loyalty. No one has been more loyal to me than Lee and Jackie. For their loyalty, friendship and love, I thank them from the bottom of my heart, and to them I dedicate **THE EDGE**.

— Howard Ferguson

CONTENTS

1. **CHARACTER**
2. **SET GOALS**
3. **PREPARATION**
4. **PREGAME**
5. **THE GAME**
6. **OVERTIME**
7. **POST GAME**
8. **THE GAME OF LIFE**

CONTENTS

1. CHARACTER
    Honesty — Loyalty — Respect — Unselfishness 1-3
    Self-Understanding and Evaluation 1-11
    Stand for Something — Have The Courage of Your Convictions 1-17
    Class 1-23

2. SET GOALS
    Desire — Determination — Dedication 2-3
    Enthusiasm — Love Your Sport 2-15
    Commitment to Excellence 2-21
    Courage to Succeed 2-29

3. PREPARATION
    Hard Work — Sacrifice 3-3
    Discipline — Organization — Consistency 3-13
    Change Your Weakness Into Your Power 3-21
    Practice it the Right Way 3-27

4. PREGAME
    Faith 4-3
    Positive Mental Attitude 4-11
    Confidence 4-17
    Inner Arrogance 4-23
    Have Fun 4-29

5. THE GAME
    Don't Apologize for Trying to Win 5-3
    Don't Be Afraid to Fail 5-13
    Leadership — Teamwork 5-17
    Concentration — Poise 5-29
    Go For It 5-39
    Extra Effort 5-49
    Welcome Competition — Challenge Yourself 5-55

6. OVERTIME
    Condition 6-3
    Thrive on Pressure 6-7
    Mental Toughness 6-13
    Don't Quit 6-21
    Pride 6-29

7. POST GAME
    Are You Strong Enough to Handle Success? 7-3
    Are You Strong Enough to Handle Critics? 7-13
    Are You Strong Enough to Handle Adversity? 7-19
    Accept Responsibility — Don't Make Excuses 7-31
    Perseverance — Persistence 7-39

8. THE GAME OF LIFE
    Leave Something Behind 8-3
    Don't Forget About Your Education 8-9
    Common Sense 8-17
    The Same Principles Apply 8-21
    The Challenge Never Ends 8-29
    Why and How to Say No 8-35

INDEX OF SPECIAL MESSAGES

WHAT IS CLASS	1-1
THOMAS JEFFERSON — A PHILOSOPHY OF LIFE	1-9
THE MAN IN THE GLASS	1-15
COMMITMENT TO EXCELLENCE	2-1
THERE IS GREATNESS ALL AROUND YOU — USE IT	3-1
WHETHER YOU THINK YOU CAN OR YOU CAN'T YOU'RE PROBABLY RIGHT	4-1
FAITH — A CREED FOR THOSE WHO HAVE SUFFERED	4-7
TRYING TO WIN IS EVERYTHING	4-9
PARADOXICAL COMMANDMENTS OF LEADERSHIP	5-1
WHAT IT TAKES TO BE NUMBER ONE	5-9
WINNERS VS LOSERS	5-11
THE WINNING EDGE	5-52
DON'T QUIT	6-1
ARE YOU STRONG ENOUGH TO HANDLE CRITICS?	7-1
ARE YOU STRONG ENOUGH TO HANDLE SUCCESS?	7-10
PRESS ON	7-43
THE BRIDGE BUILDER	8-1
LITTLE EYES UPON YOU	8-7
THE SAME PRINCIPLES APPLY	8-27

INDEX OF SHORT STORIES

HELEN KELLER	1-9
GALE SAYERS	1-25
SHELLEY MANN	2-9
GLENN CUNNINGHAM	2-9
JACKIE ROBINSON	2-33
DAN GABLE	2-35
ROCKY MARCIANO	3-25
JACK McKINNEY	4-15
EARL RED BLAIK	5-27
BJORN BORG	5-36
CHARLEY BOSWELL	5-61
WILLIS REED	6-18
LOU GEHRIG	6-19
ABRAHAM LINCOLN	6-25
ROCKY BLEIER	6-27
TED WILLIAMS	6-33
SATCHEL PAIGE	6-34
ROLF BENIRSCHKE	7-28
FLOYD LAYNE	7-29
ROY CAMPANELLA	7-36
CARL JOSEPH	7-37
JOHNNY UNITAS	7-45
TERRY FOX	8-6
RICH MAUTI	8-6
TOMMY CHAIKIN	8-51

INTRODUCTION

The whole idea is to somehow get an edge. Sometimes it takes just a little extra something to get that edge, but you have to have it.
— Don Shula, NFL Coach

The Edge. It's something you must have if you are to be successful in athletics — and in life. All great people have it. So can you.

Being successful by being the best you can be is what this book is all about. We aren't offering any pie-in-the-sky promises or candy-coated lines of encouragement. This is not a "How to Become a Great Athlete in 30 Days" book, because 30 days of dedication and hard work are just not enough to be the very best you can be. Your drive towards success must be a sustained and continuous effort.

We will tell you to dream of becoming a great person — then warn you that you need to do more than just dream to reach that goal.

OUR SUCCESS FORMULA

We have only one secret to offer. Our sure-fire success formula can be boiled down to six key words: HARD WORK MAKES DREAMS COME TRUE. That's how you can get The Edge.

We know this may not be what you want to hear. We would like to tell you how to become an overnight sensation — but we can't. Success knows no shortcuts.

We also can't promise you that if you read this book and follow what we tell you to do, that you'll become a professional athlete. There are so few spots available on professional rosters with hundreds of people waiting to fill each spot.

By reading this book, you may not become as good a golfer as Curtis Strange, or as good a baseball player as Don Mattingly, or as good a tennis player as Steffi Graf. What you will be able to do is become the best athlete and the best person that you can be. You won't have to wonder how good you might have become, because you'll know.

This book is geared toward athletics, but it's about all of life's endeavors. It's about succeeding in the classroom, in business and in your personal life.

MAKE SUCCESS YOUR TOP PRIORITY

If you decide to put a high priority on success, you will have to learn to compete. The trouble in America today, in business as well as in sports, is that too many people are afraid of competition. The result is that people have come to sneer at success if it requires hard work, training and self-sacrifice.

To succeed, you have to go out and make your own luck. To do that, you have to work harder than your opponent — you have to get the edge.

No matter what stage of athletic development you are in, you need to get an edge over your competition. If you're working on skill, you want to be able to perform the skills of your sport better than your opponent. If you're working on strength, you want to be stronger than the opposition. If you have physical limitations, your edge will come by out-conditioning your opponent.

THE EDGE GIVES YOU THE CONFIDENCE TO SUCCEED

Our coaching philosophy is based on our wrestlers getting the edge. Other teams might run 30 minutes after practice, so we run 33 minutes. Other teams might practice six days a week, so we have practice every day. We have no magic formula, just hard work. When it's time for our wrestlers to perform in a meet, they take with them a supreme confidence, an edge, that they are going to win — and they usually do.

We love to get people to believe in themselves. That's our most important priority — self-confidence — because 95% of the people in this world do NOT believe they have as much talent or ability as other people.

It's not talent, looks, intelligence or athletic ability that causes you to believe in yourself.

It's asking yourself this very simple question, "Am I doing the very best I possibly can? And doing it every day?"

The most important thing that we can do as coaches is to get people to believe in themselves and care about each other.

At St. Edward High School, we say that when you bring a group of people together, it's a start. When you get a group of people to stay together, it's progress. And when you get a group of people to work together, it's success.

How do you get a group to work together? Heck, we don't know. We're not that smart. Except this — get them to like one another, believe in each other, and feel secure within the group.

When you feel secure, it's easy to look for the good qualities in other people. If you don't believe in yourself, you're constantly looking for the negative things in other people.

We did not invent this philosophy. Read this book and you'll find out many others believe in it also. Why? Because it works.

A PERSONAL SUCCESS STORY

This book was written by a man who once had a very poor self-image.

I believe that I was born with the worst inferiority complex in the state of Ohio. I went around telling myself I didn't amount to anything. That I had no brains. That I didn't have what it took. That I was literally a worm. And, after a while, I became aware of the fact that people were agreeing with me. A worm who couldn't even speak. Not that other worms do, but this one sure couldn't. Whenever I opened my mouth, nothing came out. When it did, it was a long time coming. I was labeled a "stutterer" — a word that, even to this day, I have a very difficult time saying or writing.

It's a fact that people will take you for your own deep, unconscious self-appraisal. What you think of yourself will ultimately be transmitted to them, and they, too, will agree with what you think you are.

One day I was on the third step from the top of the field house at Bowling Green State University, when I decided I was going to get rid of this inferiority complex. I was going to talk and try to live — not like a worm — but like a man. However, I didn't know how to do it! There wasn't anyone around there to tell me. I began to read and apparently I just stumbled on the right kind of reading.

I read everything Thomas Jefferson and Ben Franklin ever wrote. I read everything Dr. Norman Vincent Peale wrote. I read everything written by Sir Winston Churchill, Vince Lombardi and Jack Kennedy.

When I ran out of good reading material, I formed a research group and started writing letters. We wrote to the greatest athletes in the world, the coaches who consistently won, presidents of corporations, colleges, universities and countries. We wrote to everyone that was a winner. The replies came. The response was fantastic. If for some reason someone didn't write back, we called him or her on the telephone. If our call was refused, we wrote another letter.

Gradually, we put it together between the covers of a book and called it **THE EDGE**. This book grew out of my own personal experience, and we felt everything we put in the book would help anyone, because it worked with me. Now, don't get me wrong. I haven't mastered this positive self-image business completely. That's one of the reasons I wrote **THE EDGE**, and why I read a page or two every night.

ASK THE EXPERTS THEMSELVES FOR THEIR SECRETS

The best way to find out about success secrets is to go right to the source. This is why we contacted famous athletes, coaches, sports administrators and team owners, as well as many successful personalities outside the world of sports, such as politicians, writers, poets, entertainers, members of the news media, religious leaders and military generals.

In addition to these personal messages, we spent thousands of hours reviewing every sports book, sports magazine and motivational film we could find to make this book more complete and more valuable for you.

The result of this effort is **THE EDGE**. It's a guidebook to success. Read the book through once; then go back and read each message again. Consider the source. Study them and see if they make sense to you. See where they fit into your overall personal game plan.

Remember, these personal messages were volunteered by successful people — people who have the edge. They responded to our requests because they felt strongly about their messages and wanted to share them with you.

You will find that many of these messages are very similar. All of them are pointing you in the same direction.

The most prevalent thoughts we received formed these success formulas:

    Desire + Sacrifice + Discipline = Preparation
    Preparation + Success = Confidence
    Mental Toughness + Pride = Perseverance

IF YOU ARE PREPARED, HAVE CONFIDENCE AND PERSEVERE, YOU WILL ALWAYS HAVE THE EDGE.

If you have the EDGE, you will always succeed.

Eventually.

— Howard Ferguson

1
CHARACTER

- Honesty – Loyalty – Respect – Unselfishness
- Self Understanding and Evaluation
- Stand for Something
- Have The Courage of Your Convictions
- Class

What is Class?

Class never runs scared. It is sure-footed and confident in the knowledge that you can meet life head-on and handle whatever comes along.

Jacob had it. Esau didn't. Symbolically, we can look to Jacob's wrestling match with the angel. Those who have class have wrestled with their own personal "angel" and won a victory that marks them thereafter.

Class never makes excuses. It takes its lumps and learns from past mistakes.

Class is considerate of others. It knows that good manners are nothing more than a series of petty sacrifices.

Class bespeaks an aristocracy that has nothing to do with ancestors or money. The most affluent blueblood can be totally without class while the descendant of a Welsh miner may ooze class from every pore.

Class never tries to build itself up by tearing others down.

Class is already up and need not strive to look better by making others look worse.

Class can "walk with kings and keep its virtue, and talk with crowds and keep the common touch." Everyone is comfortable with the person who has class—because he is comfortable with himself.

If you have class, you don't need much of anything else. If you don't have it, no matter what else you have—it doesn't make much difference.

> Fame is a vapor, popularity is an accident, money takes wings. Those who cheer you today may curse you tomorrow. The only thing that endures is character...
>
> O. J. Simpson, NFL Halfback,
> Sports Broadcaster, and Actor

> Somebody will always break your records. It is how you live that counts.
>
> Earl Campbell, NFL Fullback

HONESTY — LOYALTY — RESPECT — UNSELFISHNESS

The quotation on fame was sent to us by O.J. Simpson. When we asked for some of his thoughts on motivation and his success as an athlete, he did not choose to talk about his All-American days at Southern Cal, nor did he reminisce about his record-breaking career as a running back in the National Football League.

His message was that some day, no matter how many honors and trophies come your way, your athletic playing career will end. Time is something that not even the swiftest of running backs can elude.

One day, even if you are O.J. Simpson, the cheering of the crowds will stop, as will the headlines in the newspapers and the television interviews. And then, you will no longer be the "Juice," jutting your way through defenses on Sunday afternoons; you will no longer be a superstar.

"The only thing that endures is character," Simpson tells us. While the end of your athletic career may be a long time away, the time to build character is right now. Just as the building that stands the test of time must have a strong foundation, so must you. If you don't start out with that foundation — character — you will have a hard time reaching your goals. If you are able to reach them without character, the satisfaction you feel will be fleeting.

It's very interesting that when we asked one of the National Football League's most recent premier running backs for his message on success, it came back on the same subject — character. Earl Campbell tells us that, "It's how you live that counts."

Before you ever begin to think of yourself as a great athlete, become a great person — feel good about yourself. If you want others to respect you, you must respect yourself first. To get the edge, develop your character.

A solid character foundation includes:

HONESTY — It's just as easy to be honest as it is to be dishonest — both are habit forming. Self-honesty is necessary if you are going to be a great athlete; honesty with others is necessary if you are going to become a leader. It's a quality you must have in sports, and for the rest of your life, if you are to succeed.

LOYALTY — The first quality that I look for in an employee, friend, wrestler or assistant coach is loyalty. He can be an outstanding worker or the greatest wrestler, but if he isn't loyal, I don't want him around. I need a 100 percent commitment — 100 percent of the time.

RESPECT — As you work to reach your goals, remember that others also have goals and are also working hard. Respect people for what they are and for the stand they have taken — even if you don't agree. Respect other people's property. Respect your opponent. Don't fear him, but be aware of his ability, and understand that he is also trying to win. Finally, respect your parents. When you get a little older and a little wiser, you will grow to understand and appreciate them more.

UNSELFISHNESS — Always think of the consequences before you talk or act. What you say or do affects others. Think about it. You'll live a much happier and richer life, if you make an attempt every day to say or do something nice, for someone who may never be able to repay you.

CHARACTER

JOHN WOODEN
College Basketball Coach

Be more concerned with your character than your reputation, because your character is what you really are, while your reputation is merely what others think you are.

JOHN W. GALBREATH
Major League Owner

If I build a building, it's going to stand for 100 years. You see, that's a philosophy, a way of life, just like building your character.

LOU HOLTZ
College Football Coach

The answers to three questions will determine your success or failure. 1.Can people trust me to do my best? 2.Am I committed to the task at hand? 3.Do I care about other people and show it? If the answers to these questions are yes, there is no way you can fail.

THOMAS MACAULAY
English Writer/Statesman

The measure of a man's real character is what he would do if he knew he would never be found out.

WOODY HAYES
College Football Coach

In picking an assistant coach, the first thing I was interested in was the man's character.

MIKE REID
Professional Golfer

Never do anything to compromise your integrity. Anything worth achieving is worth an honorable and honest effort. There are no short cuts to becoming a champion. You will never take any trophies or medals with you when you leave this life, but your character will be with you always. Be true to yourself, and keep in perspective the fact that even if you can't be the world's best athlete in your chosen sport every day…you can be your best person every day.

HENRY WARD BEECHER
American Clergyman

A man's character is the reliability of himself. His reputation is the opinion others have formed of him. Character is in him; reputation is from other people.

CALVIN HILL
NFL Fullback

A football player must be dependable and consistent, regardless of the time and place. Be it the opening kickoff or the final two minutes…character, as much as physical ability, is vital.

THEODORE ROOSEVELT
Twenty-Sixth President

I care not what others think of what I do, but I care very much about what I think of what I do. That is character!

TOM PAGNA
College Football Coach

Character represents the sum total of a personality— what one is, what one has done and will do. It further reflects itself in actions. Great character has no facades. It shines with honesty, respect, true humility, and an inner faith that knows we are but the recipients of a great gift.

J. HAWES
American Clergyman/Author

A good name is seldom regained. When character is gone, all is gone, and one of the richest jewels of life is lost forever.

PETE CARRIL
College Basketball Coach

Winning takes character. Workers get the most out of themselves. When a body has limited talent, it must muster all its resources of character to overcome adversity.

ARISTOTLE
Greek Philosopher/Scientist

Character is that which reveals moral purpose, exposing the class of things a man chooses or avoids.

PHILLIPS BROOKS
American Episcopal Bishop

Some day, in years to come, you will be wrestling with the great temptation, or trembling under the great sorrow of your life. But the real struggle is here, now, in these quiet weeks. Now it is being decided whether, in the day of your supreme sorrow or temptation, you shall miserably fail or gloriously conquer. Character cannot be made except by a steady, long-continued process.

HONESTY

GEORGE WASHINGTON
First President

I hope I shall always possess firmness and virtue enough to maintain what I consider the most enviable of all titles, the character of an honest man.

JOHN MADDEN
NFL Coach and Sports Broadcaster

You have to hear things you really don't want to hear; you must look at things you really don't want to see. That's a tough attribute, because honesty isn't always saying things on the plus side; you've got to be able to say the negative things too.

BENJAMIN FRANKLIN
American Inventor

Avoid dishonest gain; no price can recompense the pangs of vice.

ALBERT SCHWEITZER
French Clergyman/Physician

Truth has no special time of its own. Its hour is now—always.

DON SHULA
NFL Defensive Back and Coach

Some clubs want to win so much they'll do anything to get it. Our approach has been just the opposite. We've tried to do things the right way. And the right way is the rules and regulations and they are precisely what we go by. I may not like all of them, but once they are in, we play by them.

WILLIE SHOEMAKER
Professional Jockey

The best thing you can do is tell the truth, no matter what it is. It may hurt a bit sometimes, but I think in the long run a guy is going to be better off if he knows the truth.

GIB SHANLEY
Sportscaster

I would like to impress upon young people the importance of honesty and integrity. If they have both, they'll never want for anything in life. The other less important things—the material things—will follow.

CONRAD HILTON
Hilton Hotels Corporation Chairman

Some things that I have strictly adhered to are: to have integrity, to never deceive anybody, to have my word good. Under no circumstances deviate from that.

ROY L. SMITH
American Clergyman

The man who cannot believe in himself cannot believe in anything else. The basis of all integrity and character is whatever faith we have in our own integrity.

LENNY WILKENS
NBA Guard and Coach

Young athletes, like all young people, must realize that the future holds extraordinary challenges for everyone and they must accept those challenges as a part of life. Honesty and integrity are most important. Never compromise on what you know is right.

WILLIAM SHAKESPEARE
English Dramatist/Playwright/Poet

This above all: to thine own self be true,
And it must follow, as the night, the day,
Thou canst not then be false to any man.

HARRY TRUMAN
Thirty-Third President

It isn't polls or public opinion of the moment that counts. It is right and wrong and leadership. Men with fortitude, honesty and a belief in the right make epochs in the history of the world.

JOHN F. DODGE
American Manufacturer

There is no twilight zone of honesty—a thing is right or it's wrong—it's black or it's white.

LOYALTY

WOODROW WILSON
Twenty-Eighth President

Loyalty means nothing unless it has at its heart the absolute principle of self-sacrifice.

PAUL BROWN
NFL Coach, General Manager and Owner

I'll never forget something the Dean of Women at Miami of Ohio once told me: "The eternal verities always prevail, you'll never lick them. That is loyalty, honesty, sincerity, discipline, dedication...all the things which are worthwhile. They can never be licked, they'll always be with us."

JOHN WOODEN
College Basketball Coach

No building is better than its structural foundation, and no man is better than his mental foundation. When I prepared my original Success Pyramid years ago, I put industriousness and enthusiasm as the two cornerstones with loyalty right in the middle of the pyramid—loyalty to yourself and to all those dependent upon you.

BUM PHILLIPS
NFL Coach

Loyalty, up and down the line. That's one quality an organization must have to be successful.

FRANK MC GUIRE
College Basketball Coach

I have been telling high school and college athletes that they should all have a goal and that goal is to seek perfection in whatever they are doing. In order to do this, it takes many hours of hard work and endurance. There is no short cut on this tough road to success. The young man must be loyal to what he is doing and to all concerned (coaches, parents and himself). I consider this one of the greatest characteristics.

ELBERT HUBBARD
Wayne State University Dean

An ounce of loyalty is worth a pound of cleverness.

FRANK ROBINSON
Major League Outfielder and Manager

When I was traded to Baltimore, the ballplayers immediately accepted me. It was a great feeling. Nobody acted like he was better than anyone else. That's the way the Orioles' organization is, like a family. They will always be something special to me and I will always be loyal to them.

EARL WEAVER
Major League Manager

I'm a firm believer in loyalty. One of my most difficult decisions as a manager was trading Frank Robinson to the Dodgers. I loved that guy for the way he played baseball. Another time we had a player who was having his problems. He wasn't having a good year and was shaky in the field but heck, the year before with a man on third and less than two outs, he got the runner in 19 times in a row. I owed this guy something so when the money was on the line in September, he played.

RESPECT

WILLIAM HAZLITT
English Essayist, Journalist, Critic and Painter
Where you cannot drive you can always persuade. A gentle word, a kind look, a good-natured smile can work wonders and accomplish miracles. There is a secret pride in every human heart that revolts at tyranny. You may order and drive an individual, but you cannot make him respect you.

JESS BELL
Bonne Bell Cosmetics, Inc. President
When I think about young people, high school students, the one word that comes to my mind is respect. So few of them have respect for other people, respect for property, respect for the law, for their country and most importantly, respect for their own bodies: drugs—booze—cigarettes—over-eating and total disregard for fitness.

Take care of yourself. Your health is your most important possession. By taking care of yourself, respect your body because it's the only one you are ever going to have. Exercise every day for the rest of your life. Stick to good health habits; the bad ones will go away. Life is a constant battle. It really is a matter of the survival of the fittest.

DENIS POTVIN
NHL Defenseman
Respect the people close to you who've given you support in unrelenting ways to help you achieve your sought-after goal. They were unquestionably the fuel that propelled your drive.

REGGIE JACKSON
Major League Outfielder and Sports Broadcaster
I believe it is very important to show respect toward individuals who live up to their obligations and responsibilities, whether or not you like the individuals involved. Respect is a virtue which goes far beyond the emotion of liking.

HERBERT N. CASSON
American Writer
In handling men, there are three feelings that a man must not possess—fear, dislike and contempt. If he is afraid of men he cannot handle them. Neither can he influence them in his favor if he dislikes or scorns them. He must neither cringe nor sneer. He must have both self-respect and respect for others.

CALVIN MURPHY
NBA Guard
I judge a person's worth by the kind of person he is in life—by the way he treats his fellow man, by the way he wants to be treated, and by the way he respects people around him.

JIM BROWN
NFL Fullback and Actor
One thing I learned in football is that you must have respect. It is not so important that people like you, but it is an absolute must that you have their respect.

MONTE CLARK
NFL Offensive Tackle and Coach
Over and over, it has been made crystal clear to me that the basics of life are important—love of God, family and friends; a commitment to integrity so that you will be respected and respect yourself; a commitment to leadership so that by your own actions, others will respect you.

UNSELFISHNESS

RALPH WALDO EMERSON
American Writer/Poet

You cannot do a kindness too soon because you never know how soon it will be too late.

FRANK LAYDEN
NBA Coach and General Manager

When I was coaching, the one thought that I would try to get across to my players was that everything I do each day, everything I say, I must first think what effect it will have on everyone concerned.

CHARLES KINGSLEY
English Novelist/Poet

Never, if possible, lie down at night without being able to say: I have made one human being, at least, a little wiser, a little happier, or a little better this day.

HENRY WARD BUCHER
English Clergyman/Reformer

What I spent I had; What I kept I lost; What I gave I have.

BOB ANDERSON
English Poet

There's nothing so rewarding as to make people realize they are worthwhile in this world.

GERRY FAUST
College Football Coach

I have a rule that I never treat anybody any different than I'd want to be treated myself. And I think that's really important. Take a little time to say, "How would I want to be treated in this situation?" If you do something the way you want to be treated, you'll do it the right way 99 percent of the time.

WILLIAM SHAKESPEARE
English Dramatist/Playwright/Poet

'Tis not enough to help the feeble up, but to support him after.

SAM RUTIGLIANO
NFL and College Football Coach

You cannot live a perfect day without doing something for someone who will never be able to repay you.

WALT MICHAELS
NFL Linebacker and Coach

I'll tell you one thing I'm not going to do. I'm not going to give up on the New York Jets. We've got good people here. We've got good guys. I'm not going to let them quit on themselves. It's my job to make them feel good about themselves—and that's exactly what I'm going to do.

JOHANN GOETHE
German Novelist/Playwright/Poet

If I accept you as you are, I will make you worse; however, if I treat you as though you are what you are capable of becoming, I help you become that.

CHARLES W. ELIOT
American Chemist and Educator

If I had the opportunity to say a final word to all the young people of America, it would be this: Don't think too much about yourself. Try to cultivate the habit of thinking of others; this will reward you. Selfishness always brings its own revenge. It cannot be escaped. Be unselfish. That is the first and final commandment for those who would be useful and happy in their usefulness.

RALPH WALDO EMERSON
American Writer/Poet

There is a time in every man's education when he arrives at the conviction that envy is ignorance; that imitation is suicide; that he must take himself for better, for worse, as his portion; that though the wide universe is full of good, no kernel of nourishing corn can come to him but through his toil bestowed on that plot of ground which is given to him to till.

Thomas Jefferson— A Philosophy of Life

In matters of principle, stand like a rock; in matters of taste, swim with the current. Give up money, give up fame, give up science, give up the earth itself and all it contains, rather than do an immoral act. And never suppose, that in any possible situation, or under any circumstances, it is best for you to do a dishonorable thing. Whenever you are to do a thing, though it can never be known but to yourself, ask yourself how you would act were all the world looking at you, and act accordingly.

He who permits himself to tell a lie once finds it much easier to do it a second and third time, till at length it becomes habitual; he tells a lie without attending to it, and truths without the world believing him.

Helen Keller— Character in Action

"Character cannot be developed in ease and quiet. Only through experiences of trial and suffering can the soul be strengthened, vision cleared, ambition inspired and success achieved."

You, no doubt, know the story of Helen Keller. Born perfectly healthy, she was left completely blind and deaf when she suffered an illness at the age of 18 months. For five years she was isolated from the world, alone in the darkness. Then, with the help of Anne Sullivan, a special teacher, Helen fought back against her handicap.

"Face your deficiencies and acknowledge them. But do not let them master you," she said.

Helen Keller didn't shut herself off. She learned to communicate. She graduated from Radcliffe University and went on to take an honored place in society. She never pitied herself; she never gave up. She explained:

"The marvelous richness of human experience would lose something of rewarding joy if there were no limitations to overcome. The hilltop hour would not be half so wonderful if there were no dark valleys to traverse."

Do not let what you cannot do interfere with what you can do.
John Wooden, College Basketball Coach

SELF-UNDERSTANDING AND EVALUATION

From 1960 to 1975, John McKay's Trojans of Southern California were ranked among the top college football teams in the country, winning the National Championship four times. But his message here tells us he didn't judge himself by national championships. Instead, he judged himself by simply asking, "Did I do my best?"

John Wooden's college basketball record at UCLA was even more impressive. During a twelve-year span, his Bruins won 10 NCAA Basketball Championships. With a record like that, you know his teams were consistently doing the things that they could do best. His philosophy to his players was to focus on what they could do, and not to worry about what they couldn't do.

Once you begin to develop your character, you must make an honest self-evaluation. This can be difficult. Look in the mirror and ask yourself, "What do I see?" You can fool others — your coaches, teammates as well as your family and friends — but you should not fool yourself. Being honest with yourself is a big step in growing up.

We really determine how successful we will be by what we do — not by what our competition does. We coach only one wrestling team in the country — St. Edward High School in Cleveland, Ohio — and whether we win or lose depends on how well we coach, regardless of who the competition is.

Our philosophy is a simple but effective one. We do not waste time and/or energy worrying about whether we are going to win or lose. We concentrate on preparing ourselves to become the very best athletes we can be — both mentally and physically. We strive to gain the edge over our opponents in every possible manner: In strength, in technique, in conditioning and mental toughness. When we do this, we feel so confident that we expect to win. And we do.

After a game, ask yourself if you have put out 100 percent, a very high standard that is seldom, if ever, reached. Don't fool yourself. No one is perfect; we all have faults. The only real losers in life, and in sports, are those who refuse to admit their faults.

You must recognize your weaknesses before you can even begin to think about correcting them. Find out where you made a mistake to determine where you need help. If you lie to yourself or aren't open-minded enough to admit what you're doing is wrong, you'll never correct it.

This honest self-evaluation is necessary for you to pick the right sport to participate in. You'll want to choose a sport that you not only love, but one in which you can eventually excel. It's a shame to see someone work hard and sacrifice, but fail only because of choosing the wrong sport.

Don't let what you can't do stop you from doing something that you can do well. Don't pick a sport because it's popular in high school. Tennis and golf may not draw big high school crowds, but Steffi Graf and Curtis Strange aren't doing badly.

Be honest. And be realistic. Pick a sport in which you can be rewarded for all your hard work and effort. It isn't good enough just to say, "I did my best," if you have chosen the wrong sport for you. Your best may not be good enough. If it isn't, you had better pick another sport or be satisfied with mediocrity.

I am a big believer in the "mirror" test. By that I mean that you shouldn't worry about the fans or the press or trying to satisfy the expectations of anyone else. All that matters is if you can look in the mirror and honestly tell the person you see there that you've done your best.

John McKay, NFL and College Football Coach

SELF-UNDERSTANDING AND EVALUATION

CHUCK KNOX
NFL Coach

Look for and recognize mistakes. This means being honest with yourself and if there is a doubt in any area, go back and check it.

ELROY HIRSCH
NFL Halfback and College Athletic Director

Every athlete should seriously consider the job he has done after every practice or every game. He should go into the locker room and look into a mirror and ask himself one question, "Did I do the very best possible job I could do?" If the answer is, "Yes," he has done his work well. However, if he has doubts—if he can say to himself, "If I had only tried a little harder, I would have made that tackle," or, "If I had only given a little extra effort, I could have intercepted that pass"—then he has not done his job. He must be totally honest with himself in this self-assessment.

THOMAS CARLYLE
Scottish Historian/Social Critic

The greatest of all faults is to be conscious of none.

HALE IRWIN
Professional Golfer

I'm trying to never get mad at outside influences—the gallery, a bad bounce, the weather. I'm pointing the finger at myself. It's taken time for me to get to know my game and myself, but I'm getting there. If some problem or anxiety is bothering me, I try to bring it out, dissect it logically and deal with it. That's why I'm playing better. I'm more comfortable with myself. I'm more me.

EDWARD F. BENSON
English Author

How desperately difficult it is to be honest with oneself. It is much easier to be honest with other people.

DON SCHOLLANDER
Swimmer—Five Time Olympic Gold Medalist

Before you decide how you want to live your life, you must look at yourself and attempt to know yourself.

HAVELOCK ELLIS
British Literary Critic and Writer

Men who know themselves are no longer fools; they stand on the threshold of the Door of Wisdom.

JOE NAMATH
NFL Quarterback and Sports Broadcaster

You must be honest with yourself. If your best isn't good enough, then you've got to find something else to do—another sport where your best will be good enough.

PAUL WESTPHAL
NBA Guard

The key to any game is to use your strengths and hide your weaknesses. More than anything I'm the best judge of what I can do and what I can't do.

JAMES A. FARLEY
American Political Leader

The best advice I can give to any young man or young woman upon graduation from school can be summed up in exactly eight words, and they are—be honest with yourself and tell the truth.

ROY SMALLEY
Major League Shortstop

I've worked hard and I've learned a lot from Rod Carew and Gene Mauch, who know a lot about hitting. I've also learned what works for me, and how to operate within my own limitations and capabilities.

DAN HAMPTON
NFL Defensive Tackle/End

I'm basically trying to do a lot better—in football, in life, in being around people. In football, I'm checking my limits. I want to see where those limits are. I can be a lot better today than I was yesterday, and I can be a lot better tomorrow than I am today. You can fake out fans, your coach, your wife, your mom and dad, but you can't fake out yourself. They say runners search for the perfect race. I search for perfect exhaustion.

HOWARD COSELL
Attorney, Sports Broadcaster and Author

Victory on the scoreboard is a nice thing, but it is not the ultimate victory. The ultimate victory in competition derives from the inner satisfaction of knowing that you have done your best and that you have gotten the most out of what you had to give. Always be honest with yourself.

LIN YUTANG
Chinese Author/Philologist

Sometimes it is more important to discover what one cannot do, than what one can do.

CLOYCE BOX
OKC Corporation Chairman of the Board

Stay with the things that you can do the best. Too many people waste time trying to do things that they can't do.

DANIEL M. GALBREATH
Major League President

It is important for the individual to be totally honest with himself in order to assure the individual of a quality of life which will best enable him to do the best he can. We really shouldn't expect more out of ourselves than we were created to do. We shouldn't expect to be luckier than the next guy or pray for the breaks of the game to go our way, but merely hope that we are able to do the very best we can and reach our maximum level of productivity.

GEORGE MATTHEW ADAMS
American Columnist and Newspaper Executive

Everyone knows that weeds eat out the life of the garden and of the productive fields. The gardener and farmer alike each has to keep the weeding process alive.

It's like that in the building and developing of character. No one knows our own faults and tendencies better than we do ourselves, so it is up to each one of us to keep the weeds out, and to keep all growth vigorous and fruitful.

DON MAYNARD
NFL Wide Receiver

It's the old story. You might be able to fool your coaches, or your teammates, or your opponents. But, you can never fool yourself in anything. I believe that the more critical you are of your own performance—the higher standards you have—the better you become at what you do.

JOHN DEWEY
American Philosopher/Educator

To find out what one is fitted to do and to secure an opportunity to do it is the key to happiness.

SYDNEY J. HARRIS
Newspaper Columnist

Ninety percent of the world's woe comes from people not knowing themselves, their abilities, their frailties, and even their real virtues. Most of us go almost all the way through life as complete strangers to ourselves—so how can we know anyone else?

KYLE ROTE, JR.
Professional Soccer Player

I realized early that I may never become adept at controlling the ball with my feet. Therefore, I would have to make up for it in other ways such as speed, willingness to make contact, the ability to leap into the air and hustle.

EARL WEAVER
Major League Manager

I had to admit that I wasn't good enough for the majors. It broke my heart, but I learned to judge a ballplayer's capabilities the hard way—by having to recognize my own incapabilities.

NOLAN RYAN
Major League Pitcher

The tendency of a fastball pitcher is to muscle up and do what he needs to do. He winds up lunging and losing his rhythm to muscle the ball in there. Everybody has limits. You just have to learn what your own limits are and deal with them accordingly.

BILLIE JEAN KING
Professional Tennis Player and Sports Broadcaster

I don't think that it is fair to think that one sport is greater than another. Athletes are not objective about their sport nor are artists about their art. It's impossible. Some people say that the older athletes are better, or that baseball or football is the toughest. No way. It depends on the person, their body type, their capacities, their mentality. Certain people belong in certain sports. Certain sports are made for certain people—every athlete must find the sport for which he or she is best suited.

WILLIE STARGELL
Major League First Baseman and Coach

Be honest and work hard to get what you want. Don't take short cuts; you only cheat yourself in the long run. Success is not measured by money or fame, but by how you feel about your own goals and accomplishments and the time and effort you put into them.

MARK SULLIVAN
American Journalist and Author

To find a career to which you are adapted by nature, and then to work hard at it, is about as near to a formula for success and happiness as the world provides. One of the fortunate aspects of this formula is that, granted the right career has been found, the hard work takes care of itself. Then hard work is not hard work at all.

BRUCE BOCHTE
Major League First Baseman

In each person, there exists an automatic mechanism—let's call it a trigger—that fills the body, the mind, the spirit with enthusiasm, drive, determination, zest, power, enjoyment. To trigger this mechanism is to put oneself in motion, in action effortlessly, easily, without pain or reluctance.

The trigger in my life has been sports, particularly baseball. But triggers come in different forms: music, science, mechanics, cooking, art, reading, gardening, making friends, woodworking, walking, sewing, studying, sailing, thinking and on and on. The important thing is to search and find the trigger in your own self, to know what makes you go.

BILL WALTON
NBA Center

I was very self-conscious about my height, about my size, about being too thin and things like that. I tended to limit myself to just playing basketball. I finally got to the point where I said, "Hey, this is me. I'm this way and I'm going to make the best of my life, and I'm not going to let other people's hang-ups about me restrict my life."

DICK WILLIAMS
Major League Manager

Nothing comes easy in life, but if you believe in yourself, are honest in your self-appraisal, are able to take constructive criticism and are prepared to give 100 percent total effort in everything you do—you will always be able to hold your head high.

GORDIE HOWE
NHL Right Wing

You have to learn to respect, love and enjoy your work. Winning is of the utmost importance, but my son, Marty, taught me a lesson that effort is the key in his thinking. After losing a game by a 2-1 score, he was singing to himself during his shower and someone questioned his feelings of happiness. He simply related, "I feel badly about the loss, but I feel in my mind that the game I played tonight was the greatest effort of my career so far." The inner self-pride is a great asset. You find that you have peace of mind and can enjoy yourself, get more sleep, and rest when you know that it was a total 100 percent effort that you gave—win or lose.

JOHN HAVLICEK
NBA Forward

If you are honest with yourself and can look into a mirror and believe that you have given 100 percent, you should feel proud. If you cannot, then there is more work to be done. In some cases, successful people never reach the point of feeling they have given 100 percent. Therefore, the task and work is endless and the desire to reach the 100 percent level will always push them to greater heights.

The Man in the Glass

When you get what you want in your struggle for self
    And the world makes you king for a day,
Just go to the mirror and look at yourself
    And see what that man has to say.

For it isn't your father or mother or wife
    Whose judgment upon you must pass.
The fellow whose verdict counts most in your life
    Is the one staring back from the glass.

You may be like Jack Horner and chisel a plum
    And think you're a wonderful guy.
But the man in the glass says you're only a bum
    If you can't look him straight in the eye.

He's the fellow to please—never mind all the rest,
    For he's with you clear to the end.
And you've passed your most dangerous, difficult test
    If the man in the glass is your friend.

You may fool the whole world down the pathway of years
    And get pats on the back as you pass.
But your final reward will be heartache and tears
    If you've cheated the man in the glass.

I have carried the above poem since I was a sophomore in high school. The meaning to me is that we must make the best of the ability God has given us. We have to do the things that are right rather than those that make us look good or make us popular. When all is said and done each day and we put our head on the pillow, it's just us and God, and we can't fool either one.

HERB SCORE   Major League Pitcher, Sports Broadcaster

STAND FOR SOMETHING

Howard Cosell has been both highly praised and highly criticized. The standard line on the former ABC sports announcer was that you either loved him or hated him — there was no in-between.

Cosell has always been a man without gray areas or in-betweens. He has always stood for something, regardless of whether it was popular or not. He promoted honesty in sports journalism; his method was to "tell it like it is."

The most boring and useless people in the world are those who are too afraid to stand for something. These people play it "safe" all the time. They're afraid of taking any risks. They're "fence-sitters" because they sit on the fence and watch other people stand for something they believe in.

Other equally useless people are those who are "two-faced" or wishy-washy. These people are also afraid of standing for something. They can't be trusted because they keep switching sides when it's convenient for them.

You not only have the right to be heard as an individual, you have the obligation. Never try to be somebody else; you must always be yourself. Your dreams, commitment, drive and pride must come from within. Therefore, your first responsibility is to yourself. Nobody can do a better job being you than you, so don't try to be someone else.

Don't be afraid to take a stand. Don't be afraid to speak up. Consider whether something is right or wrong, not whether it's popular. You can't make any useful contribution to society unless you do.

> Stand for something. Don't quest for popularity at the expense of morality and ethics and honesty. Daniel Webster taught this country that what is popular is not always right, and that what is right is not always popular.
>
> Howard Cosell, Attorney, Sports Broadcaster and Author

HAVE THE COURAGE OF YOUR CONVICTIONS

No man is more respected in the game of college football than Joe Paterno, the head coach at Penn State. His message during his coaching career has always been "education first, football second."

In his quote, Paterno is telling you to be your own person. If you don't want to drink, don't drink. If you don't want to smoke, don't smoke. The same goes for using drugs, lying, cheating and other negative things.

Make your decision now. Will drugs, alcohol and cigarettes help you in reaching your goals in athletics and in your life? That answer is a simple no. They can only do you great harm, so eliminate them from your life.

We're asking you to have the courage of your convictions. Follow your commitment to excellence and avoid anything that stands in your way. If you don't, you're only fooling yourself; and hurting yourself.

Associate with people of good qualities; it's better to be alone than in bad company. If your friends have lower standards than you do, pull them up to your level; don't drop down to theirs.

Will those friends of yours who are always after you to compromise your convictions be around when you're in trouble? If they have no convictions, will they have a strong character? Will they be loyal? Think about it.

Have the courage to take a stand. Dare to be different. Dare to be great!!!

> We need people who influence their peers and who cannot be detoured from their convictions by peers who do not have the courage to have any convictions.
>
> Joe Paterno, College Football Coach and Athletic Director

STAND FOR SOMETHING

ADLAI STEVENSON
Governor of Illinois, Presidential Candidate
All progress has resulted from people who took unpopular positions.

SIDNEY POITIER
Actor
I think the way I want to think. I live the way I want to live.

JOHN MC ENROE
Professional Tennis Player
I enjoy competition and I was brought up to try to win every point. I just can't be what you call a crowd-pleaser. I have to be me.

TUG MC GRAW
Major League Relief Pitcher
I'm an emotional ballplayer and unless I express that emotion—right then and there—I can't perform, I can't handle the pressure. I have to do my own thing—I have to be me.

RED AUERBACH
NBA Coach, General Manager and Owner
I have built up a reputation of saying what I believe. I'm not always right, but at least it's what I believe.

DUSTIN HOFFMAN
Actor
The people I feel closest to are people who don't compromise their basic nature and the way they feel.

JIMMY STEWART
Actor
You have to develop a style that suits you and pursue it, not just develop a bag of tricks. Always be yourself.

RON JAWORSKI
NFL Quarterback
I'm just emotional. Sometimes I even chase my receiver into the end zone. I'm just not very cool. When I make a big play, I get excited about it. I know Unitas and Hadl didn't do that sort of thing, but it just isn't in me to go "ho-hum, another big play." Maybe someday it will be, when I've won a lot of big games, but it isn't yet. I have to be me—not someone else.

HENRY WARD BEECHER
American Clergyman
Hold yourself responsible for a higher standard than anybody else expects of you. Never excuse yourself. Never pity yourself. Be a hard master to yourself—and be lenient to everybody else.

PETE DAWKINS
College Halfback and U.S. Army Colonel
To win by cheating, by an umpire error or by an unfair stroke of fate is not really to win at all. If athletic competition does teach, then what more valuable lesson is there to learn than that we have a responsibility to stand up for what is right?

JOHN MADDEN
NFL Coach and Sports Broadcaster
If there is a time when you're going to be angry, then you're going to be angry. And if you feel that way and let it go by, then you're being a phony. If I get angry, it's for a good reason, either for an action or as a reaction. The same applies when I'm happy.

GEORGE ALLEN
NFL Coach and Sports Broadcaster

You have to do what you believe and you have to be yourself. If you try to do anything else, it is not going to come over. Emotion is part of the game. Emotion is important in anything that you do. If you feel that you should do it, there is nothing wrong with it. The important thing to remember is to always be yourself.

FRANK ROBINSON
Major League Outfielder and Manager

One day during my first spring training as manager of the San Francisco Giants, a magazine reporter sat down beside me in the dugout and asked me who I admired most as a youngster, which ballplayer I tried hardest to emulate when I was starting out in baseball. "Frank Robinson," I replied without hesitation. "C'mon," he said with a chuckle, "who was it, really?" "Frank Robinson," I repeated.

The guy cocked his head to one side and stared at me with this blank expression. He knew I was serious, but he wasn't altogether sure what I meant.

"Look," I said, "the most important person any player should work to be as good as is himself. Your own excellence, success and greatest pride comes from only one person—you."

It's fine to look up to and learn from the best, not only in sports but in anything you're striving to achieve—in school, in a career or in your relationships with others. But whatever it is, your first responsibility is to be the best you can. There's nobody else like you, so why try to be like somebody else?

I've lived my life by this principle, and I've asked my players to do the same. Don't try to perform beyond your abilities—but never perform below them. You might be surprised to find out how much better you can be.

HENRI FREDERIC AMIEL
Swiss Essayist, Philosophical Critic and Poet

He who floats with the current, who does not guide himself according to higher principles, who has no ideal, no real standards—such a man is a mere article of the world's furniture—a thing moved, instead of a living and moving being—an echo, not a voice.

DENIS POTVIN
NHL Defenseman

Throughout my professional and non-professional career, I've felt that setting simple priorities and living and working by them was the key to my success. Grasping one's capabilities allows you to work within your limits, and to achieve emotional, spiritual and physical excellence within your realm. No one needs to be like someone else.

COTTON FITZSIMMONS
NBA Coach

I have a basic philosophy that I've tried to follow during my coaching career. Whether you're winning or losing, it is important to always be yourself. You can't change because of the circumstances around you.

JOE PATERNO
College Football Coach and Athletic Director

I want to change things. And I'm going to do my best to speak up about the things I think are wrong, whether it's in the university, in football or in the country. The only way you can bring about a change is to do something about it.

STEVE BARTKOWSKI
NFL Quarterback

If you don't stand for something, you'll fall for anything.

HAVE THE COURAGE OF YOUR CONVICTIONS

ROLF BENIRSCHKE
NFL Kicker

It is often difficult, especially for young people facing tremendous peer pressures, to stand up for what they believe and perhaps go against the grain. However, to be successful in life, you must not succumb to these pressures, but instead have the courage it takes to stand by your convictions.

HAYWOOD SULLIVAN
Major League General Manager

In all your endeavors, both present and future, remember to have the courage of your convictions.

ART STILL
NFL Defensive End

I was involved in some pretty bad things, the kind of things you do to impress the other guys. It was a way of being accepted. I had to learn to be somebody strong. You have to be an individual and let people accept you for what you are.

JAMES A. GARFIELD
Twentieth President

The men who succeed best in public life are those who take the risk of standing by their own convictions.

BOBBY MURCER
Major League Outfielder

Take care of your total well-being and begin to do so early in life. It is so important to build a solid foundation for yourself when you are young so you may build upon it throughout your entire life.

Keep a firm hold over your own life at all times and learn not to follow negative influences. Be a leader over your own self! Have the courage of your own convictions. Otherwise, there is no way that you will ever be able to lead others.

ANDRE GIDE
Nobel Prize Winner/French Novelist

It is better to be hated for what you are than loved for what you are not.

MUHAMMAD ALI
Professional Boxer

I sought advice and cooperation from all those around me—but not permission.

JOE PATERNO
College Football Coach and Athletic Director

Sometimes you've got to do the things you feel. Otherwise, you do things in a tiny corner. If you worry about how it's going to go over with fans or alumni, you'll never do anything worthwhile.

HANK STRAM
NFL Coach and Sports Broadcaster

On Kansas City's 1969/70 Season: The important thing was to believe in something strongly enough to make it work. In other words, to have the courage of your convictions. I believed at the start of the season that we had our best team ever. We then went out and proved it.

EVELYN ASHFORD
Sprinter — Three Time Olympic Gold Medalist

Drugs. It's the thing to do right now. I've heard people say that's why I run so fast. "She must be on drugs, she must be on steroids." People really believe that in order to do well you have to be taking something. And I don't understand that. I really don't. Damn! It does make you mad. American women athletes are so psyched out about what the East Germans are doing, what the Russians are doing. You hear it all the time: "They're all on steroids, they're all on drugs." I think that's a lot of crap. That's just those people's excuse for not running well. It's a cop-out. You don't know what you can do, and with drugs you'll never find out. I believe in women. I believe in myself. I believe in my body. I believe I can run faster not using drugs than people can using drugs, because that's the way I was put here.

I don't want to be around people who even look at drugs. It's all up in your head. Whatever muscles I have are the product of my own hard work—nothing else.

JOHNNY BENCH
Major League Catcher and Sports Broadcaster

There are too many false things in the world, and I don't want to be a part of them. If you say what you think, you're called cocky or conceited. But if you have an objective in life, you shouldn't be afraid to stand up and say it. In the second grade, they asked us what we wanted to be. I said I wanted to be a ballplayer and they laughed. In the eighth grade, they asked the same question, and I said a ballplayer and they laughed a little more. By the eleventh grade, no one was laughing.

CLASS

What is class? Class is Bjorn, Jack, Chris, Sugar Ray and Doctor J. Of all the chapters we have written for The Edge, this is the most difficult. Not because we feel it's less important, but because it's an intangible quality easily recognized, although not easily defined.

Better than any words that could be written, these five athletes define what class is. Why? Because they have demonstrated class with their actions under pressure, in victory and in defeat, for many years.

There are two ways to do anything in life or in sports — with class, as these champions have shown, or without class. It doesn't cost any more or take any extra time or energy to have class. Having class doesn't make you any less a competitor or any less aggressive as an athlete. You don't lose your edge by having class. You gain the edge.

How does class give you an edge over your opponent? Simple. You'll have the poise that allows you to concentrate better, which helps you win more. You'll have the confidence that allows you to play up to your potential, which also helps you win more often. You'll also have an edge over your opponent, because he or she will waste energy wondering why you have so much class and they don't. They'll wish they had the class you already have. Finally, in a close contest, you'll have the crowd behind you, which could be the edge you need to win.

What exactly is class? It's one of those valuable, "intangible", personal traits that's in high demand because it's so rare. Most people, unfortunately, do not have it. Class is being a good person, showing good sportsmanship, always taking responsibility for the consequences of your actions and being considerate to others. You have class if you show pride, have humility, poise, and display self-confidence without being arrogant.

Class athletes handle victory and defeat in the same way — graciously, with their heads held high. They don't brag in victory, or make excuses in defeat. They accept the thrill of victory and the agony of defeat in stride. They always praise their opponent for a job well done, and they admit their mistakes.

We can always recognize a class wrestler by the way he warms up before a match. He walks out onto the mat in a certain confident manner. He has tunnel vision during the match. All his energies and powers of concentration are directed towards getting the job done — and nothing else. No energy is directed towards the crowd or the referee. A class wrestler does not embarrass his opponent by being a showboat. He has a job to do and he does it. He is completely prepared. His actions speak louder than his words. Even his body language, including facial expressions, seems to indicate he is rising above everyone else in the arena.

Class always shows, whether you win or you lose. People can tell instantly if you have class by watching you perform and interact with others. If you have class, you don't need much of anything else to be a winner. If you don't have it, whatever else you have won't make up the difference.

Fame, fortune, trophies and glory are all fine, but they alone won't give you class. Only you can give yourself class.

GALE SAYERS— A STORY ABOUT COURAGE, LOVE AND CLASS

In 1968, Gale Sayers suffered a knee injury. A tackler collided with Sayers' knee, and the Chicago Bears' star running back went down. Surgery followed, and then the long road to recovery. Many questioned whether Sayers would ever play again.

A little more than one year later, Sayers stood at the banquet of the New York Chapter of Professional Football Writers of America to accept the George S. Halas Award as the most courageous player in pro football in 1969.

It was a time when many would have indulged in the self-satisfaction of their comeback, but instead Sayers told the audience that night of another football player who faced a more difficult battle than overcoming a knee injury. He told the audience of Brian Piccolo.

Piccolo's fight wasn't with a football injury he received as a running back. Piccolo's fight was with cancer.

"It is something special to do a job that many people say can't be done," Sayers said that night in Chicago. **"Maybe that's how courage is spelled out, at least in my case."**

"My teammate, roommate and friend, Brian Piccolo, kept after me. Brian kept urging me on, sometimes kindly, sometimes unkindly, to fight my way back. Brian Piccolo has the sheer, solid, raw courage which entitles him to win over a sickness that makes my knee injury seem unimportant."

Sayers accepted the George S. Halas award, but he accepted it for Brian Piccolo.

"You flatter me by giving me this award, but I tell you here and now that I accept it for Brian Piccolo. Brian Piccolo is the man of courage who should receive the George S. Halas Award. It is mine tonight, it is Brian Piccolo's tomorrow."

"I love Brian Piccolo and I'd like all of you to love him, too," Sayers continued. **"Tonight when you get down on your knees, please ask God to love Brian Piccolo, too."**

One thousand wet eyes blinked. There was a standing ovation from a crowd of 500 which included 24 of the 26 head coaches in pro football. Sayers had always stood tall in the minds of the men in pro football. Yet, he managed to suddenly stand taller.

Sayers went on to become one of the greatest running backs in the history of the National Football League. Brian Piccolo died of cancer. Together, they found the height of human courage.

CLASS

JACK NICKLAUS
Professional Golfer

Class is being honest—both with others and with yourself. Class is treating others as you would like them to treat you.

ROGER STAUBACH
NFL Quarterback and Sports Broadcaster

Class is striving hard to be the best at what you do while taking the needs of others into consideration.

PAUL BROWN
NFL Coach, General Manager and Owner

Class always shows.

ARA PARSEGHIAN
College Football Coach and Sports Broadcaster

Class is a quality that others admire because its behavior can be counted on as natural, simplistic, consistent, humane, and of the highest standard in all human relationships; it stands the test of time.

JOHN NEWCOMBE
Professional Tennis Player and Sports Broadcaster

The best description of class I can give you is not an original but comes from a famous work by Kipling. As you enter the Centre Court at Wimbledon, as you look up, you see the words, "If you can meet with triumph and disaster and treat those two imposters just the same, if you can do that, you will have class".

JOHN WOODEN
College Basketball Coach

Class is an intangible quality which commands, rather than demands, the respect of others.

This is because those who have it are truly considerate of others, are courteous and polite without being subservient, are not disagreeable when they disagree, are good listeners, and are at peace with themselves because they do not knowingly do wrong.

In short, a person with class might well be defined as one who practices "The Golden Rule" in both his professional and personal life.

GARY PLAYER
Professional Golfer

Class is good manners, cleanliness (body and mind), consideration for others, humility, and good sense of timing.

DAN GABLE
Wrestler—Olympic Gold Medalist and College Wrestling Coach

There is no mat space for malcontents or dissenters. One must neither celebrate insanely when he wins nor sulk when he loses. He accepts victory professionally, humbly; he hates defeat, but makes no poor display of it.

BOBBY HULL
NHL Left Wing

People ask me if I get tired at being interviewed or interrupted on my days off. The answer is no. If people think enough of me to want to shake my hand or talk to me or interview me, then time must be made for it.

KATHY WHITWORTH
Professional Golfer

Class is honesty. Honesty with yourself makes you comfortable with yourself. Being honest with yourself also makes you understand that you're no better or no worse than anyone else.

DIGGER PHELPS
College Basketball Coach

My definition of class is to always come off with a big first impression by looking good, feeling comfortable, yet, caring for others. If you respect yourself, you will respect others. Just be yourself, but remember—when you are in the public eye, someone is always looking for a negative. To show class is to show confidence in the way you look, the way you dress, and the way you act.

JOE NAMATH
NFL Quarterback and Sports Broadcaster

I can't get big-headed about anything...I've had six of my passes intercepted in a half. In one half. You're trying to keep your confidence up and here comes six guys running your passes back at you. We get some nice things done out there, and it feels good to do it right, but there's not much chance to get an inflated opinion of yourself. You have to learn respect for the other guy because you may beat him on this play, but he's a pro, and he's going to turn around and beat you on the next one. You learn how to be a gracious winner and an understanding loser. I appreciate the game for what it's done for my head.

ARTHUR J. ROONEY
NFL Owner

Class is an intangible thing. Different people show it in different ways, but it does not take long to surface and it is easily recognizable.

KATHY WHITWORTH　　ARNOLD PALMER　　ROGER STAUBACH

TOM SEAVER　　CARL YASTRZEMSKI　　LARRY BIRD

2
SET GOALS

- Desire – Determination – Dedication
- Enthusiasm – Love Your Sport
- Commitment to Excellence
- Courage to Succeed

Commitment To Excellence

I owe almost everything to football, which I spent the greater part of my life in, and I have never lost my respect, my admiration nor my love for what I consider a great game. Each Sunday after the battle, one group savors victory, another group wallows in the bitterness of defeat. The many hurts seem a small price to pay for having won and there is no reason at all which is adequate for having lost.

For the winner there is 100 percent elation, 100 percent laughter, 100 percent fun and for the loser the only thing left is a 100 percent resolution and 100 percent determination. The game, I think, is a great deal like life. Every man makes his own personal commitment toward excellence and toward victory. Although you know ultimate victory can never be completely won, it must be pursued with all of one's might and each week there is a new encounter, each year a new challenge.

All of the rings and all of the money and all of the color and all of the display, they linger only in a memory. But the spirit, the will to win, the will to excel, these are the things that endure and these are the qualities, of course, that are so much more important than any of the events that occur.

I'd like to say that the quality of any man's life is a full measure of that man's personal commitment to excellence and to victory, regardless of what field he may be in.

VINCE LOMBARDI   NFL Coach

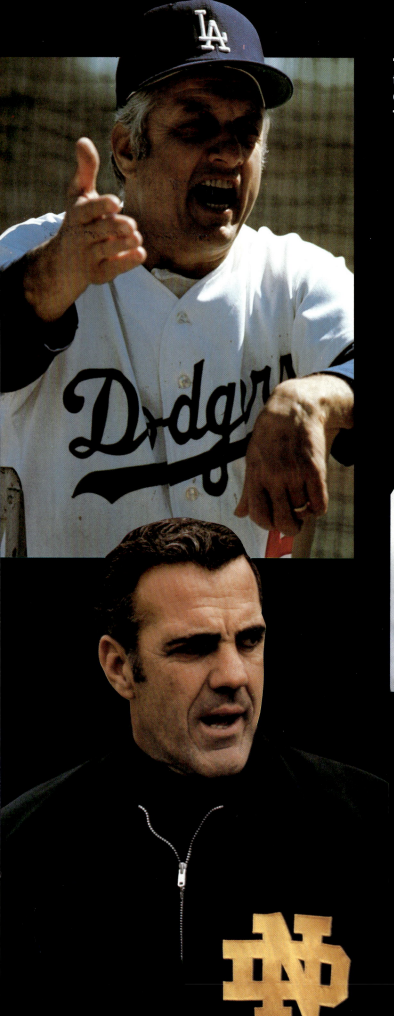

The difference between the possible and the impossible lies in the man's determination.
Tommy Lasorda, Major League Manager

I use the word hungry to describe what I mean when I talk about desire. Being hungry provides you with the physical and mental energies necessary for success. The sacrifices that are necessary become easier when one places a goal or objective at a high level.

Ara Parseghian,
College Football Coach and Sports Broadcaster

DESIRE — DETERMINATION — DEDICATION

To become a winning athlete, you must be hungry: hungry for success; hungry for victory; and hungry simply to become the best you can be. It always starts with a dream. Then, somehow, some way, you must be inspired to reach your goal or you'll never make it.

As you read this book, you'll see why desire is so important. The many stories you read about athletes overcoming serious physical disabilities shouldn't surprise you. It was because of their disabilities that these athletes developed such a fierce, burning desire to succeed. They had to prove to themselves they could do it — in spite of the odds.

The messages in this chapter show that sometimes desire is more important than talent, or even a healthy body. Desire is what motivated the boy with burned legs to set the world record in the mile run, and the young girl with polio to become an Olympic champion swimmer.

A parent or a coach can guide you by telling you what needs to be done and how often to do it. But you have to do the rest. Only your burning desire to succeed will enable you to push yourself when you're too tired to work out, and help you avoid the many outside distractions that frequently come your way. Every young wrestler I meet is asked the same question, "How good do you want to be?"

I'll never forget one of our wrestlers who came up to me at a wrestling banquet. He said, "Ferg, I just want to thank you for never yelling, 'You've got to want it,' while I was wrestling." In wrestling circles, this is the most frequently-used expression by coaches.

It's true that athletes must "want it" to win, but this desire must come from within, not from a coach. You either "want it", or you don't. There's no other choice. This wanting, this desire, must come to you long before you step out on the wrestling mat. That's why practice is so important. It builds the desire long before the match starts.

I knew one of my wrestlers wanted it "really bad," because I had seen him "pay the price" for four years. He never had to tell me — he showed me.

Once you have the desire, determination and dedication will help you reach your goals. It's very easy to get sidelined or distracted, so it's important to keep your mind focused on your goals and nothing else. The relentless quest, the thing that keeps you going day after day, is your determination. There are no shortcuts in the world of athletics. There are only goals to be set — and goals to be reached — competition to be faced and adversity to overcome. Only the truly dedicated athletes ever come close to attaining their goals. This is the true test of all great individuals who have the edge — they won't let anything interfere with their goals. That's why so few become champions.

Setting your goals lets you know where you're going and allows you to determine how far you've already come. The difference between where you are now and where your goal is, tells you how much further you have yet to go. A lack of opportunity is often nothing more than a lack of purpose or direction. That's why goals are so valuable. If you don't know where you're going, how are you going to know when you get there?

> What's wrong with dedication? It's the first demand I made on my kids when it came to the basic aspects of football. Today's players are more dedicated than they've ever been. They work like heck and they hit like heck.
>
> Woody Hayes, College Football Coach

GOALS

DON SUTTON
Major League Pitcher

Goals are essential! I really believe that without them we kind of flounder around like the cliche, "the ship without a rudder." We might go a long way, but we might end up going in circles too...This is why I believe goals are absolutely essential!

SUSAN POLIS SCHULTZ
American Poet

If you have a goal in life that takes a lot of energy, that requires a lot of work, that incurs a great deal of interest and that is a challenge to you, you will always look forward to waking up to see what the new day brings.

RAYMOND FLOYD
Professional Golfer

Set goals in life; set them high and persist until they are achieved. Once they are achieved, set bigger and better goals. You will soon find that your life will become happier and more purposeful by working toward positive goals.

DOCTOR J. A. HOLMES
American Clergyman

Never tell a young person that something cannot be done. God may have been waiting for centuries for somebody ignorant enough of the impossible to do that thing.

LOU BOUDREAU
Major League Shortstop and Manager

That night in Cleveland, when I played my first major league game, represented the attainment of a goal I had worked toward all my life. Some boys want to be policemen, others want to be cowboys, some want to be railroad engineers, some want to be airplane pilots, and I suppose today there are some who want to reach the moon. My goal was to be a ballplayer.

HERB ELLIOTT
Distance Runner—Olympic Gold Medalist

The resources of the human body and soul, physical, mental and spiritual, are enormous and beyond our present knowledge and expectations. We go part of the way to consciously tapping these resources by having goals that we want desperately—it is the only way we currently know how to use these hidden resources. Wanting desperately to achieve taps that hidden resource that everyone of us has.

MERLIN OLSEN
NFL Tackle, Sports Broadcaster and Actor

We need to know where we are going, and how we plan to get there. Our dreams and aspirations must be translated into real and tangible goals, with priorities and a time frame. All of this should be in writing, so that it can be reviewed, updated, and revised as necessary.

BASIL S. WALSH
American Businessman

An intelligent plan is the first step to success. The man who plans knows where he is going, knows what progress he is making and has a pretty good idea when he will arrive. Planning is the open road to your destination. If you don't know where you are going, how can you expect to get there?

KURT THOMAS
Gymnast — Olympic Gold Medalist

I feel that the most important step in any major accomplishment is setting a specific goal. This enables you to keep your mind focused on your goal and off the many obstacles that will arise while you're striving to do your best.

KEN SINGLETON
Major League Outfielder

If you want to hit .300, set your sights on .325. If you want to drive in 100 runs, go for 125. Then, if you fall a little short and hit .304 and drive in 100 runs, you won't be disappointed.

BENJAMIN DISRAELI
Prime Minister of England

I have brought myself by long meditation to the conviction that a human being with a settled goal must accomplish it, and that nothing can resist a will which will stake even existence upon its fulfillment.

CHARLES C. NOBLE
American Civil Engineer

You must have long-range goals to keep you from being frustrated by short-range failures.

THOMAS EDISON
American Inventor

Show me a thoroughly satisfied man and I will show you a failure.

ALBERTO SALAZAR
Distance Runner

Before I ever started running the marathon, my coach and I sat down and discussed some long-term goals that we wanted to achieve. One of them was that I would never lose a marathon during my entire career. There is no way I am going to allow anything to happen that might cause me to lose one.

BETH DANIEL
Professional Golfer

Set goals for yourself and work your hardest to achieve them. Some goals you will achieve and others you won't, but at least you will have the satisfaction of knowing where you were going.

TERRY DONAHUE
College Football Coach

Ever since I walked onto the UCLA campus to play football, my dream was to be head football coach at UCLA. I'd hate to leave this place, even for heaven.

STEVE GARVEY
Major League First Baseman

You have to set the goals that are almost out of reach. If you set a goal that is attainable without much work or thought, you are stuck with something below your true talent and potential.

DESIRE

BOB RICHARDS
Pole Vaulter—Two Time Olympic Gold Medalist
I have talked to people all over the world about what makes a champion and I've heard some of them say, "It's just sheer hard work. If a person's willing to work hard, that's all it takes." Others say, "No, it's great coaching. If you've got a good coach, a coach will pull you out, and you are bound to be good." Others say, "No, it's the opportunity. Give a man an opportunity and it will make him great. It's the circumstances that make men." Others say, "No, it's sheer God-given, naked, raw potential. If you've got the ability, that's all you need." Others say, "No, it's inspiration, it's encouragement, it's the pat on the back." I don't minimize any one of these things. You've got to have all of that. They are all important, but there's something far more fundamental. You show me a boy or a girl with a desire to win, and I'll show you a person who will work hard the thousands of hours it takes to win. Show me those who want to go to the top, and I'll show you people who will take coaching. They will welcome it. They will beg for it. They will use every God-given talent they have to its utmost. They will drink in inspiration. If they lack desire, they won't work. They won't take coaching.

CESAR CEDENO
Major League Outfielder
I hope I always stay hungry. If I get three hits, I want four; if I steal one base, I want two. Being hungry makes this game fun.

DAWN FRASER
Swimmer—Three Time Olympic Gold Medalist
I've always believed that the desire must come from within, not as a result of being driven by coaches or parents.

GALE SAYERS
NFL Halfback
I learned that if you want to make it bad enough, no matter how bad it is, you can make it.

MICHELANGELO
Italian Painter/Sculptor
I hope that I may always desire more than I can accomplish.

GEORGE BURNS, III
Professional Golfer
Although there are many thoughts I would like to share with today's young athletes, the main one is desire. Everything stems from this. If you have the desire to excel, the discipline required for the hours of practice and hard work will come more easily. There are no overnight successes. It takes time, work and patience.

CHARLES SAWYER
American Educator/Author
Of all the forces that make for a better world, none is so indispensable, none so powerful, as hope. Without hope men are only half alive. With hope they dream and think and work.

WALTER ALSTON
Major League Manager
Desire and determination must overcome disappointment.

L. G. ELLIOTT
American Author
The long span of the bridge of your life is supported by countless cables called habits, attitudes, and desires. What you do in life depends upon what you are and what you want. What you get from life depends upon how much you want it—how much you are willing to work and plan and cooperate and use your resources. The long span of the bridge of your life is supported by countless cables that you are spinning now, and that is why today is such an important day. Make the cables strong!

SAM SNEAD
Professional Golfer
To win, you have to have the talent and desire—but desire is first.

WOODROW WILSON
Twenty-Eighth President

We grow great by dreams. All big men are dreamers. They see things in the soft haze of a spring day or in the red fire of a long winter's evening. Some of us let these great dreams die, but others nourish and protect them, nurse them through bad days till they bring them to the sunshine and light which comes always to those who sincerely hope that their dreams will come true.

EMIL ZATOPEK
**Distance Runner—
Three Time Olympic Gold Medalist**

Anyone can get good results from a physically perfect individual who is forced into a scientific training regime. The beauty comes when someone who is imperfect but has great desire and as a result achieves great results.

THOMAS DREIER
American Author

Send the harmony of a great desire vibrating through every fiber of your being. Find a task that will call forth your faith, your courage, your perseverance, and your spirit of sacrifice. Keep your hands and your soul clean, and your conquering current will flow freely.

GERRY COONEY
Professional Boxer

I used to dream what it would be like to be heavyweight champion of the world, but I never let it interfere too much with my life. If you really want something bad enough, you can get it. I would like to go to my tenth year class reunion as the heavyweight champion of the world. When I was in high school, lots of people thought I was crazy, being a fighter. I just want to let them know I made it.

FREDERICK PHILIP GROVE
Canadian Author/Teacher

If the desire to get somewhere is strong enough in a person, his whole being, conscious and unconscious, is always at work, looking for and devising means to get to the goal.

BERNIE PARENT
NHL Goaltender

You never become successful by dreaming. You become successful by working to the best of your ability and having faith in yourself. To reach your goal, three main ingredients are necessary—self-discipline, determination and desire. There will always be dark days, but with this foundation you will be able to face the challenge.

JOE FRAZIER
Professional Boxer, Trainer and Manager

You can do anything you want to do if you really put your heart, soul and mind into it.

NEV CHANDLER
Sportscaster

An athlete with no ambition is an athlete in poor condition. That applies in both a mental and physical sense. There is no substitute for desire. It can make a mediocre athlete into a good one and a good athlete into a great one.

WILLIE SHOEMAKER
Professional Jockey

I've always believed that anybody with a little ability, a little guts and the desire to apply himself can make it. He can make anything he wants to make of himself.

EARVIN "MAGIC" JOHNSON
NBA Guard

Even when I went to the playground, I never picked the best players. I picked guys with less talent, but who were willing to work hard, who had the desire to be great.

LARRY BIRD
NBA Forward

When I was young, I never wanted to leave the court until I got things exactly correct. My dream was to become a pro.

SOMETIMES NOT TO BE HANDICAPPED IS TO BE HANDICAPPED

SHELLEY MANN—JUST ANOTHER VICTORY CEREMONY? NOT REALLY.

Shelley Mann, the American girl, stood to receive her gold medal at the Olympic Stadium. There was an American girl on her right and an American girl on her left. Tears were running down her cheeks as she stood there tall, straight and beautiful. Just another victory ceremony? Not really.

There was a time when Shelley Mann could scarcely move a muscle, much less stand. Stricken with polio at age five, Shelley began going to a swimming pool, not to become a champion swimmer, but just to get a little strength back into her feeble arms and legs. At first she was held up by the buoyancy of the water. She cried tears of joy the day she was able to lift an arm out of the water—a major triumph. Her first goal was to swim the width of the pool, then the pool's length. As she reached each goal, she set new ones. She swam two lengths, three lengths, four lengths…

Shelley Mann went on to become one of the greats among American female swimmers. She was the world record holder in all 100 and 200 meter butterfly events and won the 100 meter butterfly at the 1956 Melbourne Olympics.

The girl who at one time couldn't even hold her head up, the girl who had to fight just to lift an arm out of the water, was the same girl who won the Gold Medal in the most difficult butterfly stroke. Just another victory ceremony? Not really.

"I have to go all out in every practice. I can't stand the idea of loafing. It's the only way I can swim without consciously getting tired. I know that I'll be helped in whatever I do by what I've learned from swimming. There's no reason why I can't do what I want to do and also be good at it."

GLENN CUNNINGHAM—SPEND HIS LIFE IN A WHEEL CHAIR? NO CHANCE.

"Nothing can stop you from being a winner if you really give it all you've got."

After suffering severe burns on his legs at the age of five, Glenn Cunningham was given up by doctors as a hopeless cripple who would spend the rest of his life in a wheelchair. "He will never be able to walk again," they said, "no chance."

The doctors examined his legs, but they had no way of looking into Glenn Cunningham's heart. He wouldn't listen to the doctors and set out to walk again. Lying in bed with skinny, red legs covered with scar tissue, Glenn vowed, **"Next week, I'm going to get out of bed. I'm going to walk."** And he did just that.

His mother tells of how she used to push back the curtain and look out the window to watch Glenn as he would reach up and take hold of an old plow in the yard. With a hand on each handle, he began to make those gnarled and twisted legs begin to function. And with every step a step of pain, he came closer to walking. Soon he began to trot; before long he was running. When he started to run, he became even more determined.

"I always believed that I could walk again, and I did. Now I'm going to run faster than anybody has ever run." And did he ever.

He became a great miler who, in 1934, set the world's record of 4:06.8 and was honored as the outstanding athlete of the century at Madison Square Garden. With his desire, Glenn Cunningham wasn't going to spend his life in a wheelchair. No chance!

DETERMINATION

VINCENT G. MAROTTA
North American Systems Chairman

Determination is one of the most important prerequisites for virtually any endeavor one wishes to undertake. First, one must set a goal and truly believe in it. Then one must apply oneself to that end with all the honest determination that one possesses. Hard work (there is no easy way), total commitment, and patience in times of adversity will, in the long run, see one through. In short, set the goal, be determined to succeed with complete dedication toward that goal, and be totally honest with oneself. These are the specific precepts to success in any endeavor.

GERALD R. FORD
Thirty-Eighth President

I'm a determined person. And if I've got an objective, I'll make hours of sacrifice—whatever efforts are needed. Some people call it plodding. The word is somewhat downgraded, but I'd rather be a plodder and get some place than have charisma and not make it.

JACK LAMBERT
NFL Linebacker

Football is a professional game, you play it to win at all levels. There is no room for sentimentality. Either you play or you don't play. I was determined to play. I knew all along deep down inside that I could do it, that I was good even though nobody else much seemed to agree with me. My determination more than made up for any lack of speed, height, weight, or whatever else I wasn't supposed to have.

PAUL MEYER
Success Motivation Institute President

Crystallize your goals. Make a plan for achieving them and set yourself a deadline. Then, with supreme confidence, determination and disregard for obstacles and other people's criticisms, carry out your plan.

DAN DIERDORF
NFL Offensive Tackle and Sports Broadcaster

I think a lot of people get too concerned with their competition. They fall into the habit of worrying about everyone else. I don't pay attention to what others are doing. I feel strongly that if I have correct goals, and if I have the determination to keep pursuing them the best way I know how, everything else falls into line.

GARY PLAYER
Professional Golfer

To succeed in life one must have determination and must be prepared to suffer during the process. If one isn't prepared to suffer during adversities, I don't really see how he can be successful.

ROCKY BLEIER
NFL Halfback

I busted my rear end to get where I am and I don't want to throw it away. Given a chance, I'll take advantage of it. I've worked very hard, have been exceptionally determined. I want to stay.

C. LEEMAN BENNETT
NFL Coach

A winner is someone who sets his goals, commits himself to those goals, and then pursues his goals with all the ability that God has given him. This requires someone to believe in himself, make self-sacrifices, work hard and maintain the determination to perform to the best of his ability.

GARY CARTER
Major League Catcher

I was determined to get to the big leagues in three years. If it took hustle and putting-out more to get there, then that's what I was going to do.

DEDICATION

KEN NORTON
Professional Boxer

To succeed, you must be dedicated to whatever you hope to do, and you must set your mind to it completely. If you make up your mind to do something, you'll find that it can almost always be done. You must seek perfection, though you may never quite attain it. Do not delude yourself with short cuts. There are no short cuts in reaching the goals you set for yourself.

DOAK WALKER
NFL Halfback

No champion has ever achieved his goal without showing more dedication than the next person; making more sacrifices than the next person; working harder than the next person; training and conditioning himself more than the next person; studying harder than the next person; enjoying his final goal more than the next person.

DON SHULA
NFL Defensive Back and Coach

You set a goal to be the best and then you work hard every hour of every day, striving to reach that goal. If you allow yourself to settle for anything less than number one, you are cheating yourself.

JERRY COLEMAN
Major League Manager

Dedication and commitment are two priorities that are prized by all coaches and managers. When a young man brings these qualities to the playing fields, whether at the amateur or professional level, it can be a source for him to reach back to when stress factors begin to build.

Dedication and commitment, when exercised and developed at a young age, can command attitudes throughout a lifetime, not only in sport but in any given undertaking.

JOE DE LAMIELLEURE
NFL Offensive Guard

To be good at anything you do, you must be willing to work at achieving your goal. Your work toward a realistic goal cannot be a "sometime thing." You have to make it an "all the time thing." You have to dedicate yourself to your goal.

WILLIE MAYS
Major League Outfielder

In order to excel, you must be completely dedicated to your chosen sport. You must also be prepared to work hard and be willing to accept constructive criticism. Without a total 100 percent dedication, you won't be able to do this.

PAUL BROWN
NFL Coach, General Manager and Owner

The only thing that counts is your dedication to the game. You run on your own fuel; it comes from within you.

ROBERT A. LURIE
Major League President

I feel that one has to be completely dedicated, enthusiastic and knowledgeable about the task before him.

To be successful, one has to be unselfish about time put into a project and to know honestly that one has done one's absolute best. That is all that can be expected.

MARVIN HAGLER
Professional Boxer

It was tough. When people look at me today, they say, "Hey, you're a millionaire now, you've got it made." They didn't know me before I was a success and as a result they don't realize everything I got I worked for. I did my homework. I went home and practiced punches in the mirror...I dedicated myself to being the best.

EARL ANTHONY
Professional Bowler

To be successful in sports or in life, you must be completely dedicated to your goal or goals. You must be willing to sacrifice all other things to accomplish a level of superiority.

GIORGIO CHINAGLIA
Professional Soccer Player

You have to be hungry. You have to be dedicated 100 percent to play this game.

Fame and fortune haven't gone to my head. I just try to enjoy life, and have a little fun. As for basketball, I want to have fun. Jump up and down and scream. I love to play basketball.

Earvin "Magic" Johnson,
NBA Guard

ENTHUSIASM — LOVE YOUR SPORT

In Chapter 1, we discussed the importance of choosing the right sport. Another proven method of choosing the correct sport for you is to ask yourself, if you really love that sport passionately. If you don't have an intense, passionate love for a sport, there's no way you'll be able to work the long, hard hours it takes to become a winner. So choose a sport to please yourself, not someone else.

If you really love your sport, you'll be able to maintain your desire to excel. Don't fake enthusiasm. Some athletes do for a short time, but they can't keep it up. The practices become too long and too hard. When that happens, your lack of love for the sport will force you to leave.

To be happy in sports and in life, believe in yourself; and be a good person. If you don't believe in yourself, who will? A poor self-image is the biggest obstacle to success in life as well as sports. Find out why you have a poor self-image and do something about it. Nobody's going to do it for you; you have to do it yourself. Find out what you don't like about yourself and change it. Make lists of your strengths and weaknesses; seek advice.

Self-pity stinks. Don't dwell on the negative things in your life unless you can change them. If you can, do so. But if you can't, "don't let what you can't do interfere with what you can do," as a famous football coach says. The greatest victory you can ever achieve in life is the victory over yourself. We tend to be our own worst enemies at times. Understand what's best for you, and go after it. Know your strengths, and build upon them. The discipline and work habits you need to succeed can only come from within.

Many athletes start out with a love for their sport, but soon lose their enthusiasm when they don't achieve immediate success. It's important to obtain successes to maintain enthusiasm for your sport. Each victory brings renewed enthusiasm which makes you work even harder.

This cycle of "enthusiasm, hard work, success, more enthusiasm, more hard work and more success" builds champions. It's true that success breeds success.

But when you lose, your enthusiasm is gone. You work less because you feel "down." But now is when you really need enthusiasm the most to pick you back "up." For it's easy to maintain enthusiasm when you're winning; but it's crucial to maintain it when you lose. The solution is to get enthusiastic about something. It's virtually impossible to be unhappy when you're doing something you really love.

Surround yourself with people who love their jobs or their sport. You'll pick up on their enthusiasm, for it's very contagious. You can't be enthusiastic some of the time — you can't feel enthusiastic just on your good days. You've got to be enthusiastic all the time. That's what makes champions so different from other athletes. They don't dwell in self-pity, feeling sorry for themselves when things go badly. They're enthusiastic all the time.

In Chapter 4, we'll talk about how important it is to have a positive mental attitude and how it, too, can be contagious. So set the example for your teammates — be enthusiastic, be happy and have fun. You'll soon find out what the great champions know — there's nothing more powerful and more contagious than enthusiasm.

The most important thing is to love your sport. Never do it to please someone else—it has to be yours. That is all that will justify the hard work needed to achieve success. Compete against yourself, not others, for that is who is truly your best competition.

Peggy Fleming,
Figure Skater—Olympic Gold Medalist

You only lose energy when life becomes dull in your mind. You don't have to be tired and bored. Get interested in something. Get absolutely enthralled in something. Throw yourself into it with abandon.

Norman Vincent Peale,
Clergyman/American Writer

ENTHUSIASM—LOVE YOUR SPORT

DAN FOUTS
NFL Quarterback and Sports Broadcaster

I love football. I've been a quarterback since the seventh grade and I love it—the pressure, being able to lead guys and the pleasure of excellence.

AL OERTER
**Discus Thrower—
Four Time Olympic Gold Medalist**

In making my comeback, I'm not trying to prove anything to anyone. I'm doing it because I absolutely enjoy it.

JACK NICKLAUS
Professional Golfer

I'm a firm believer in the theory that people only do their best at things they truly enjoy. It is difficult to excel at something you don't enjoy.

DICK VERMEIL
NFL Coach and Sports Broadcaster

After I got my Masters, I still loved the game so much; I went into coaching so I could stay with it. My hobby is my work; I love it so much it's not work.

BO SCHEMBECHLER
College Football Coach and Athletic Director

Yeah, this is what it's all about for me. This is where the players eat their meals. It's not the coaching, not the winning. These kids, they're the ones who make it so special for me.

ENOS SLAUGHTER
Major League Outfielder

I gave 110 percent to baseball out of sheer love for the game. I asked no favors and gave none. I just concentrated on playing the game hard every day. I loved to play ball.

CLINT EASTWOOD
Actor and Mayor

I like people at their prime enthusiasm, when they're riding a crest. Promote a guy and he'll be dying to do good work for you.

BOB KNIGHT
**College Basketball Coach and
U.S. Olympic Basketball Coach**

I just love the game of basketball so much. The Game!! I don't need the 18,000 people screaming and all the peripheral things. To me, the most enjoyable part is the practice and preparation.

RON JAWORSKI
NFL Quarterback

I love to play football. I mean it when I say that I'd play for nothing. I could really see myself working all week in a factory and playing semi-pro ball on weekends. The game itself is fun and, hey, there's nothing like the feeling you have after a win.

MICKEY MANTLE
Major League Outfielder

To play ball was all I lived for. I used to like to play so much that I loved to take infield practice. Hitting—I could do that all day. I couldn't wait to go to the ballpark. I hated it when we got rained out.

HARRY TRUMAN
Thirty-Third President

The successful man has enthusiasm. Good work is never done in cold blood; heat is needed to forge anything. Every great achievement is the story of a flaming heart.

PAPYRUS
Old Egyptian Historical Papers

If you can't get enthusiastic about your work, it's time to get alarmed—something is wrong. Compete with yourself. Set your teeth and dive into the job of breaking your own record. No one keeps his enthusiasm automatically. Enthusiasm must be nourished with new actions, new aspirations, new efforts, new vision. It is one's own fault if his enthusiasm is gone; he has failed to feed it. If you want to turn hours into minutes, renew your enthusiasm.

PANCHO GONZALEZ
Professional Tennis Player

To me, there is a cycle in sports; "The more they enjoy it, the more they practice; the more they practice, the more they improve; therefore, they enjoy it more."

PHIL MAHRE
Skier — Olympic Gold Medalist

The day that I don't enjoy skiing is the day I'm going to quit.

TRACY CAULKINS
Swimmer — Three Time Olympic Gold Medalist

I know a lot of people think it's monotonous, down the black lines over and over, but it's not if you're enjoying what you're doing. I love to swim and I love to train.

KATHY WHITWORTH
Professional Golfer

Make sure that the career you choose is one you enjoy. If you don't enjoy what you are doing, it will be difficult to give the extra time, effort and devotion it takes to be a success. If it is a career that you find fun and enjoyable, then you will do whatever it takes. You will give freely of your time and effort and you will not feel that you are making sacrifices in order to be a success.

B. C. FORBES
American Publisher

First make sure that what you aspire to accomplish is worth accomplishing, and then throw your whole vitality into it. "What's worth doing is worth doing well." And to do anything well, whether it be typing a letter or drawing up an agreement involving millions, we must give not only our hands to the doing of it, but our brains, our enthusiasm, the best—all—that is in us. The task to which you dedicate yourself can never become a drudgery.

BABE RUTH
Major League Pitcher/Outfielder

The most important thing that a young athlete must do is to pick the right sport. Not one that they just like a little bit but one that they love. Because, if they don't really love their sport, they won't work as hard as they should. Me? I loved to hit.

JOSE CRUZ
Major League Outfielder

Nobody has ever written or said much about me, but I'm quiet and don't say much myself. I just love to play baseball. I play 12 months a year and never get tired. Is playing 250 games a year between two countries wearing? Not when you're doing something you love.

SAM GOLDWYN
American Motion Picture Producer

If a young man is going to get ahead, if he is going to reach the top, he must be all wrapped up in what he is doing. He has to give his job not only his talent, but every bit of his enthusiasm and devotion.

PAUL WESTPHAL
NBA Guard

Have fun doing whatever it is that you desire to accomplish. Learn it one step at a time, emphasizing the fundamentals, and do it because you love it, not because it's work.

JOE PATERNO
College Football Coach and Athletic Director

I still preach the same things I was preaching when I first became a head coach. I still feel that football is a game that has to be played with enthusiasm, that there has to be a certain recklessness involved, that the players have to take chances and that they can't be afraid to lose. They have to enjoy football, and that goes for the coaches, too.

WALTER COTTINGHAM
Canadian Businessman/Manufacturer

Merit begets confidence; confidence begets enthusiasm; enthusiasm conquers the world.

EDWARD B. BUTLER
American Scientist

Every man is enthusiastic at times. One man has enthusiasm for 30 minutes, another for 30 days, but it is the man who has it for 30 years who makes a success of his life.

TOM SEAVER
Major League Pitcher and Sports Broadcaster

Pitching is a physical art form. I know that it's going to be very difficult to find something that will supply me with as much fulfillment and satisfaction for another 25 years. Baseball's been the one thing I've loved since I was a little boy, and I haven't yet come close to finding anything as rewarding as pitching. Baseball is just so beautiful when it's played right.

GORDIE HOWE
NHL Right Wing

To me, hockey always was tremendous fun. That's what kept me going for so long. I simply love to play hockey.

DAWN FRASER
Swimmer—Three Time Olympic Gold Medalist

I probably have a different mental approach to swimming than most people. I actually enjoy training.

SIR WILLIAM OSLER
Canadian Physician/Writer

The very first step toward success in any occupation is to become genuinely interested in it.

MIKE REID
Professional Golfer

Love what you want to do. This is tough, but you must learn to love the practice, the sweat, the trials…in a word—everything. If you really want to succeed in this competitive world, you have to love a challenge. Learn to appreciate set-backs as necessary to growth, always believing in your heart that your hard work will be rewarded.

JACK DEMPSEY
Professional Boxer

I love to work. You've got to love what you do. It takes time, patience, long hours of work, trying to improve yourself every day.

GEORGE BRETT
Major League Third Baseman

I don't think I can play any other way but all out…I enjoy the game so much because I'm putting so much into it.

TED WILLIAMS
Major League Outfielder and Manager

It was always fun for me, I loved baseball so darn much. By the hours I practiced, you'd have to say I was working a lot of hours, but it was pretty near tireless fun for me. I'd rather swing a bat than do anything else in the world.

MARY DECKER
Distance Runner

I was born to be a runner. I simply love to train.

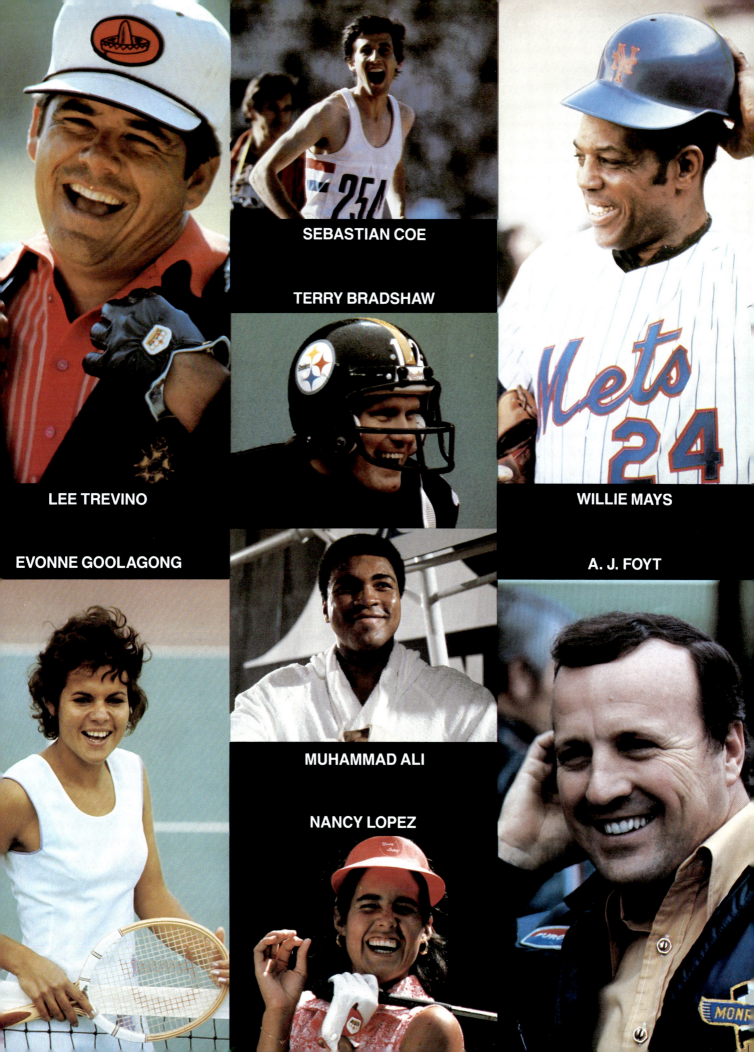

Some pitchers want to be known as the fastest thrower that ever lived. Some want to win 30 games in one season. Some want to pitch a no-hitter. All I want to do is the best I can, day after day. In other words, I want to prove I'm the best.

Tom Seaver, Major League Pitcher and Sports Broadcaster

COMMITMENT TO EXCELLENCE

How good do you want to be? If you answer, "Good enough to get by," then a commitment to excellence is not necessary. But if your honest answer is "the best," you must make a total commitment to excellence.

You don't have to tell anyone about your commitment — they'll know. How? By your actions. People will see your commitment in the time and energy you put into practicing and the intensity of your practice.

Never be ashamed to admit that you want to be the best. And never feel you have to explain your reasons. If you're committed to excellence, your answer will always be, "Why not be the best?" Don't be satisfied until you get what you want.

In my many years of coaching, I have seen a couple dozen young athletes make a sincere commitment to excellence. They had a burning desire to be great, not just "good." They craved coaching. They wanted to learn new moves every day. They worked harder than the other wrestlers during the season and they never stopped working in the off-season. They looked for tougher competition to improve their performance. They were very stubborn; they refused to settle for anything less than the best.

As a result, each one was a big winner. There was no luck or chance involved. These wrestlers worked so hard they always had an edge in their matches. They knew they would win — and they did.

Perfection is very elusive. Athletes know there are always ways to improve their performance. Many strive for perfection, but most fall short. You can only achieve perfection if you have a strong commitment to excellence. Ask any champion.

I often wonder if people can ever be at peace with themselves, or totally happy, unless they make such a commitment. How do they justify their lives? How do they go day after day without making an honest effort to be the best at what they do? It's up to you. If you really want something bad enough, don't let anything stand in your way. Don't settle for less than the best; that's how you become the best.

One thing I do want to make absolutely clear beyond any reasonable doubt is this: When you get involved in a project half-way and say, "Well, I just think I'll give it a good try and see if it works; that'll be good because if it doesn't work, I really haven't lost anything because I didn't put much into it." This is a sure way to lose.

The real reason most of us are afraid to make a total commitment to excellence is: Fear of failure. We say, "I don't want to try too hard to reach my goal, because if I do and don't reach my goal, it will hurt too much."

I'm going to tell you something, friends. If you start anything on this basis, you're not going to make it happen. When you get involved in something, man, you have to get after it. You have to go for it. No holding back. No half tries. Go for it with all your heart. Once you get it going, don't stop working. Maintain your steady workout schedule, and it will bring you more rewards than you possibly can imagine. Then, if you win, the harder you worked, the sweeter the victory. "Winning is living." "I love to win."

With my attitude and potential, I think I can possibly be the greatest ever to have played. I always set goals and push myself, and if I stay healthy, I feel I can do whatever I say I can do. I know I'm always going to push my God-given ability. In other words, I'm pursuing the ultimate.

Dave Parker, Major League Outfielder

My ambition is to be the best at what I do. That's all I'll ever really want. I decided that if I was going to be a designated hitter, I was going to be the best designated hitter in baseball.

Jim Rice, Major League Outfielder

COMMITMENT TO EXCELLENCE

VINCE LOMBARDI
NFL Coach and General Manager
A man can be as great as he wants to be. If you believe in yourself and have the courage, the determination, the dedication, the competitive drive and if you are willing to sacrifice the little things in life and pay the price for the things that are worthwhile, it can be done. Once a man has made a commitment to a way of life, he puts the greatest strength in the world behind him. It's something we call heart power. Once a man has made this commitment, nothing will stop him short of success.

JACK NICKLAUS
Professional Golfer
The one strongest, most important idea in my game of golf—my cornerstone—is that I want to be the best. I wouldn't accept anything less than that. My ability to concentrate and work toward that goal has been my greatest asset.

DICK BUTKUS
NFL Linebacker and Sports Broadcaster
My goal is to be recognized as the best. No doubt about it. When they say middle linebacker from now on, I want them to mean Butkus.

GEORGE FOSTER
Major League Outfielder
I've learned not to put limits on myself or to be satisfied. Some players hit 30 home runs, and they're happy. But I believe that you never really know what you can do. I have confidence that I can surpass myself each year.

STEVE BUSBY
Major League Pitcher
You can look back. But if you stand still and revel in the past, you won't have much of a present or a future. Right now, I wouldn't be satisfied if I were 15-0, because that would be in the past. I hope I'm never satisfied, because satisfied people are complacent. Maybe I'm searching for something I can't find. I always try to improve. I'm a perfectionist.

MUHAMMAD ALI
Professional Boxer
You could be the world's best garbage man, the world's best model; it don't matter what you do if you're the best.

ROGER BANNISTER
First Man to Run the Mile Under Four Minutes
The human spirit is indomitable. No one can say you must not run faster than this or jump higher than that. There will never be a time when the human spirit will not be able to better existing world marks. Man is capable of running a mile in three-and-a-half minutes.

WALTER MATTHAU
Actor
I don't want to stop growing in my work. I always want to stretch myself.

JOHN WOODEN
College Basketball Coach
Success is a peace of mind which is a direct result of self-satisfaction in knowing that you did your best to become the best you are capable of becoming.

DIGGER PHELPS
College Basketball Coach
Even if you're a philosopher sitting on a bench in Central Park and the pigeons are crapping on you, be the best bum there. If you don't try to be the best, people will walk all over you when you're trying to get that sales account or win that court case.

THOMAS HEARNS
Professional Boxer

I learned to fight. I worked and studied it. If I got beat up or did something sloppy in the gym, I'd go home and work on it until I got it right. Man, it was hard work but I didn't want to just be good. I wanted to be the best.

MARVIN HAGLER
Professional Boxer

People say, "You've reached your peak." There's no such thing for me. I feel as though I'm still learning. I'm getting better. I'm still young at heart. I've still got a long way to go. You never learn it all. There're many combinations just off a jab, off a right hand or off an uppercut. It's just learning how to put them together. It's an art. I'm a creator — an artist. I have nothing else. This is all I've got. I've got to be the best.

SUGAR RAY LEONARD
Professional Boxer and Sports Broadcaster

My ambition is not to be just a good fighter. I want to be great, something special.

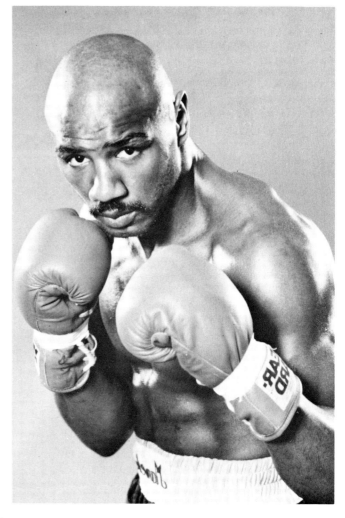

JOHN HAVLICEK
NBA Forward

What I've tried to do is reach the highest plateau of performance I can and then remain at that level consistently. Anytime you fall below it—well, you're just going to have to work a little harder the next few games to get back up there.

JOHN RALSTON
NFL Coach

The great ones set a standard for themselves to be the best at what they're doing. That's attitude. You never worry about outside pressure. The pressure of satisfying yourself by being number one is the only one that counts.

FORREST GREGG
NFL Offensive Tackle, Coach and College Football Coach

To be a winner, one must be totally committed to his sport. Total commitment means being willing to do whatever is necessary to become successful.

One must be willing to work hard, to push himself physically until it hurts. I believe that any player, who walks off the field after playing a full game, who is not physically spent has not worked to his physical potential.

To be a winner, one must be willing to make sacrifices. This means maintaining good training habits, getting the proper amount of rest, and eating a balanced diet.

If you want to be a winner, you will give up anything that does not help you become better at your sport.

All athletes are not endowed with the same physical abilities. One can, and many have before you, overcome a lack of ability with extra effort. These people are totally committed.

SAM RUTIGLIANO
NFL and College Football Coach

I believe I know what it takes to be a success in pro football. The structure in which I can accomplish all my goals is there with the Browns. I believe my character will serve me well. I just don't want to be a head coach. My aim is to be a great head coach.

ROCKY MARCIANO
Professional Boxer

There is no doubt that a man is a competitive animal and there is no place where this fact is more obvious than in the ring. There is no second place. Either you win or you lose. When they call you a champion, it is because you don't lose.

To win takes a complete commitment of mind and body. When you can't make that commitment, they don't call you champion anymore.

WILT CHAMBERLAIN
NBA Center

I never wanted to set records. The only thing I strived for was perfection.

LOU HOLTZ
College Football Coach

Actually, all I ever genuinely wanted was to be the best in my field.

LORD CHESTERFIELD
English Author/Statesman

Aim at perfection in everything, even though in most things it is unattainable. However, they who aim at it, and persevere, will come much nearer to it than those whose laziness and despondency make them give it up as unattainable.

TOM FLORES
NFL Quarterback, Coach and General Manager
A total commitment is paramount in reaching the ultimate in performance. You should always stand tall and proud when you have given your best. Success is measured in many ways. Winning isn't the only barometer of a person's achievements. There should always be personal goals intertwined with team goals. Don't ever stand still. Move forward and find better ways.

BOB RICHARDS
Pole Vaulter—Two Time Olympic Gold Medalist
Strive for perfection—never be content with mediocrity.

You don't win until you conquer the little flaws. You don't beat these great ones until your form is perfect. This is true in all of life. A flaw in a product can ruin a business. A personal failing, a little one, can ruin a person's life. Don't be content with mediocrity—strive to live up to the greatest within you.

WILLIE MAYS
Major League Outfielder
My idea was to do everything better than anybody else ever had. I concentrated on every aspect of the game.

LOU GEHRIG
Major League First Baseman
I worked real hard to learn to play first base. In the beginning, I used to make one terrible play a game. Then, I got so I'd make one a week, and finally, I'd pull a real bad one maybe once a month. At the end, I was trying to keep it down to one a season.

ALAN PAGE
NFL Defensive Tackle and Attorney
I grew up with the sense that if you're going to do something in life, do your best. When I was growing up, I didn't know what I wanted to be, what I would do, but I do remember being told, "If you're going to be a garbage man, be the best garbage man you can be." That stuck. If it's important to you and you want to be successful, there is only one person you can look at as being responsible for success or failure. That's you.

HALE IRWIN
Professional Golfer
I refuse to accept less than what I'm capable of achieving at any time. My goal every year is to play better than the year before.

MARY DECKER
Distance Runner
I know I'm nowhere near my potential. I'm looking forward to breaking the world record. All I care about is finding out what I can do, how fast I can go. Honestly, it's almost like the faster I go, the easier it becomes.

TOM LANDRY
NFL Defensive Back and Coach
As far back as I can remember, everything I did revolved around football. In a small Texas town, football is everything. We played in sandlots, everywhere. Accomplishing something in life to me meant being the greatest football player ever.

DAN HAMPTON
NFL Defensive Tackle/End

Don't be good, be great. Strive to be exceptional. Picture yourself making the great play. Picture yourself making the great tackle. Don't let anyone stop you.

JOE PATERNO
College Football Coach and Athletic Director

The important thing in life is to try to be your best. Be honest with yourself and make an honest commitment to yourself, your family, your friends, and your community. An honest commitment means 100 percent. It means self-discipline, it means loyalty, and it means being able to be counted on in the clutch.

MARIO ANDRETTI
Race Car Driver

Desire is the key to motivation, but it's the determination and commitment to an unrelenting pursuit of your goal—a commitment to excellence—that will enable you to attain the success you seek.

Even though circumstances may cause interruptions and delays, never lose sight of your goal. Instead, prepare yourself in every way you can by increasing your knowledge and adding to your experience, so that you can make the most of opportunity when it occurs.

CHARLEY TAYLOR
NFL Wide Receiver

Work hard and give it your best shot, never be a quitter. Each day do a little better than the day before, because no matter how good you are, you should always try to be better.

JOHNNY UNITAS
NFL Quarterback

In order to be successful at anything you choose to do, you must make a 100 percent commitment to what it is you're trying to do. If you put 50 percent of your ability into it, that is all that you will get out of it. You must discipline your body and your mind to work toward the goals you have set. Once you have made this decision, then the work begins.

BILL VIRDON
Major League Manager

I have always felt that young athletes have two large obligations. The first and most important is to themselves. They must make every effort to maximize their God-given talent and always be looking for ways to improve their skills.

The second obligation is to the fans and spectators that are always present when they are performing. They must convey to the fans that they have a great desire to succeed and are willing to put forth the effort expected to be the best possible athletes they can be.

VIRGINIA WADE
Professional Tennis Player and Sports Broadcaster

I always felt that I hadn't achieved what I wanted to achieve. I always felt that I could get better. That's the whole incentive. Even today, I still think I can get better. I'll never be satisified.

L. EDWIN SMART
Trans World Corporation Chairman

Success in any endeavor requires commitment and dedication. I am sure that everyone who has excelled in a particular athletic activity did so as a result of continued practice—which means a commitment. Even those blessed with unusual physical skills succeed only if they concentrate and have the self-discipline to force themselves to continue to improve.

STEVE STONE
Major League Pitcher and Sports Broadcaster

After a couple of frustrating years, I had to give up the idea that I was a mediocre pitcher. I realigned my thought processes and eliminated the negative. My number one goal has been to make myself the best pitcher I can be.

REGGIE JACKSON
Major League Outfielder and Sports Broadcaster

True success is one of our greatest needs.

Success is not something you stumble onto or come to by accident. It is something you must sincerely prepare for. Take a good look at successes and you'll see the same consistent qualities all of the time—qualities of one's character that make one strive for a goal with a standard of unmatched excellence.

JOE GREENE
NFL Defensive Tackle and Coach

What I'm waiting for is a game where I don't miss a tackle, where I and everyone around me do everything to the absolute letter of perfection. I do have that game in my repertoire and until that time, I will not be fulfilled.

TOM COUSINEAU
NFL Linebacker

A winner is never so satisfied with a victory that he fails to see where he could have succeeded by an even greater margin. A winner strives constantly to reach higher ground.

TONY LARUSSA
Major League Manager

Being involved in competition is a privilege and an opportunity. Seek to make the most of that opportunity by pushing yourself to the limit of your abilities. When it is over, you will have earned the respect of your opponents, your coaches and yourself.

EARL CAMPBELL
NFL Fullback

Every guy who lives on God's green earth who may be doing good is stupid if he thinks he can't do better. I want to be the best ever.

I don't think the mile has really been tapped yet. There's still time to come off. But you can only do it by being courageous and going fast at the start.

Sebastian Coe, Distance Runner —
Three Time Olympic Gold Medalist

COURAGE TO SUCCEED

If desire is your wishbone, then courage is your backbone. Your backbone gives you the gumption, the get-up-and-go, the guts to excel, the incentive to make any dream you dare to dream come true.

It's easy to be ordinary or mediocre, but it takes courage to excel, to be different from the crowd. That's why not many people can do it. The rewards are great, but so are the risks. It takes courage to sacrifice; to work long, hard hours when you could be relaxing; to work out when you're tired or sick; to focus on being the best you can be when there are so many distractions; to seek out tough competition when you know you'll probably get beaten. It's easy to be average, but it's hard to be the best.

It takes courage to stand by your convictions when all those around you have no convictions.

It takes courage to keep fighting when you're losing.

It takes courage to stick to your game plan and the unrelenting pursuit of your goal when you encounter obstacles.

It takes courage to push yourself to places that you have never been before physically and mentally, to test your limits, to break through barriers.

It takes courage to run a marathon, but then how would you ever know how far you could run if you never tried?

It takes courage to try to be the very best you can be when others around you settle for mediocrity.

I firmly believe we are put on earth to be tested — to be challenged with adversity and to see what we can accomplish. The successful person is the one who continually faces the problems and challenges that life brings — and overcomes them all, no matter what the obstacle is.

I also believe that most people have far more courage than they give themselves credit for. When tested, people find they have the courage to look deep into their souls; and do things they never thought possible. This amazes most people, who initially don't believe they have much courage. We all have it — we just don't realize it.

Most people are completely unaware that they possess this type of courage. Why? Because if they were aware of it, they'd have to test it — and that's risky. So most people play it safe and don't risk "Going for it." They're afraid of going into the unknown. There are no guarantees.

Unfortunately, people frequently tell you things can't be done before they tell you things can be done. They're what we call "SNIOPs" — people who are "Susceptible to the Negative Influences of Other People." It's easy to be negative because it's safe and deals with the known. It's hard to be positive because it means taking risks and deals with the unknown. It takes courage to succeed.

Sebastian Coe used the word "courage" to describe what it will take to run the super mile. He didn't say mental toughness — which is what you need at the end when your legs are dead and your lungs are bursting. Most good athletes can handle this; they can fight through the pain barrier. What Coe is saying is that you must be courageous — you must be brave enough to push yourself at the beginning when you're not hurting, knowing full well that by doing this, the more you'll hurt at the end. That is courage!

> I have no fear. I never have. I feel that if you're afraid to box someone, then you shouldn't be in the game.
> Tommy Hearns, Professional Boxer

> Being courageous requires no exceptional qualifications, no magic formula, no special combination of time, place and circumstance. It is an opportunity that sooner or later is presented to us all.
> John F. Kennedy, Thirty-Fifth President

COURAGE TO SUCCEED

LARRY CSONKA
NFL Fullback and Sports Broadcaster

Any time you try to win everything, you must be willing to lose everything.

JAMES HARVEY ROBINSON
American Historian

Greatness, in the last analysis, is largely bravery—courage in escaping from old ideas and old standards and respectable ways of doing things. This is one of the chief elements in what we vaguely call capacity. If you do not dare differ from your associates and teachers, you will never be great or your life sublime. You may be happier as a result, or you may be miserable. Each of us is great insofar as we perceive and act on the infinite possibilities which lie undiscovered and unrecognized about us.

BART STARR
NFL Quarterback and Coach

Anyone can support a team that's winning—it takes no courage. But to stand behind a team, to defend a team when it is down and really needs you, that takes a lot of courage.

DUFFY DAUGHERTY
College Football Coach

It is important to have a philosophy of life. I encouraged all of our young Spartans at Michigan State University to have the three-bones philosophy.

The first bone I wanted them is to have is a funny bone; to always have a sense of humor and to enjoy a good laugh each day, especially if it came at their own expense, and to take this responsibility seriously, but never take themselves too seriously.

The second bone I wanted them to have is a wishbone; to think big so their seeds will grow, to hitch their wagon to the proverbial star, and to have high goals and lofty ideals.

The third and probably the most important bone is a backbone. This gives you the gumption, the get up and go, the courage, the desire to excel, the motivation to make all of your dreams come true and to reach all your high goals and ambitions.

BERNARD EDMONDS
American Writer

To dream anything that you want to dream. That is the beauty of the human mind. To do anything that you want to do. That is the strength of the human will. To trust yourself to test your limits. That is the courage to succeed.

GEORGE BERNARD SHAW
Irish Dramatist

Some men see things as they are and say, "Why?" I dream things that never were and say, "Why not?"

ELEANOR ROOSEVELT
First Lady

I believe that anyone can conquer fear by doing the things he fears to do, provided he keeps doing them until he gets a record of successful experiences behind him.

CHET LEMON
Major League Outfielder

I got hit in the cheekbone in 1974 when I was playing at Birmingham. It was broken and I was out a couple weeks. But I couldn't worry about it once I started playing again. It was something I had to decide right then and there—either you dig in at the plate or you forget about it.

EUGENE V. DEBS
American Labor and Political Leader

Anybody can be nobody, but it takes a man to be somebody.

PETE CARRIL
College Basketball Coach

Whenever two teams or players of equal ability play, the one with the greater courage will win.

ANDRE GIDE
Nobel Prize Winner/French Novelist

Man cannot discover new oceans unless he has the courage to lose sight of the shore.

EUGENE F. WARE
American Lawyer/Poet

All glory comes from daring to begin.

HARRY TRUMAN
Thirty-Third President

To get profit without risk, experience without danger, and reward without work is as impossible as it is to live without being born.

GEORGE BERNARD SHAW
Irish Dramatist

The most sublime courage I have ever witnessed has been among that class too poor to know they possessed it, and too humble for the world to discover it.

JOHN L. LEWIS
United Mine Workers Union President

Courage is not how a man stands or falls, but how he gets back up again.

DALE CARNEGIE
American Author

Take a chance! All life is a chance. The man who goes farthest is generally the one who is willing to do and dare. The sure-thing boat never gets far from shore.

H. L. MENCKEN
American Critic

The one permanent emotion of the inferior man is fear—fear of the unknown, the complex, the inexplicable. What he wants beyond everything is safety.

RALPH W. SOCKMAN, D.D.
American Clergyman

The test of tolerance comes when we are in a majority; the test of courage comes when we are in a minority.

SAM RUTIGLIANO
NFL and College Football Coach

Success is never final. Failure is never fatal. It's courage that counts.

BOB RICHARDS
Pole Vaulter—Two Time Olympic Gold Medalist

Ingenuity, plus courage, plus work, equals miracles.

CONFUCIUS
Chinese Philosopher/Educator

To see what is right and not to do it is lack of courage.

JOE THEISMANN
NFL Quarterback and Sports Broadcaster

When I first came to the Redskins, I was trying to force George Allen to play me. I was trying to get him to say, "You're cocky, you're brash. I'm gonna put you out there so you'll fall flat on your face." That's all I wanted, a chance, even if it was to fall flat on my face.

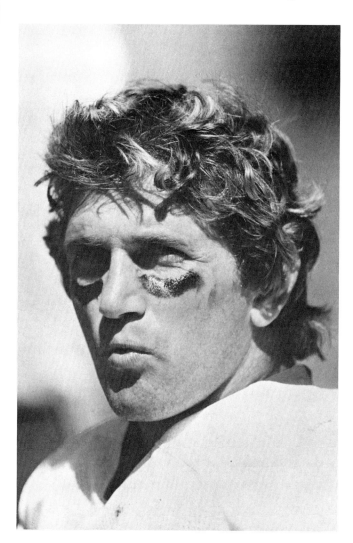

JACK DEMPSEY
Professional Boxer

The first thing one loses is the courage and ambition to fight. You lose that, you lose your speed, your timing—everything.

DONALD DOUGLAS
American Engineer/Author

It is a hard rule of life, and I believe a healthy one, that no great plan is ever carried out without meeting and overcoming endless obstacles that come up to try the skill of man's hand, the quality of his courage, and the endurance of his faith.

A. J. FOYT
Race Car Driver

You can't let it get you down, about guys always getting killed. You've got to carry on in racing. You can't be afraid.

SIR WINSTON CHURCHILL
Prime Minister of England

Courage is the first of human qualities because it is the quality which guarantees all the others.

RALPH WALDO EMERSON
American Writer/Poet

Whatever you do, you need courage. Whatever course you decide upon, there is always someone to tell you you are wrong. There are always difficulties arising which tempt you to believe that your critics are right. To map out a course of action and follow it to an end requires some of the same courage which a soldier needs. Peace has its victories, but it takes brave men to win them.

PAUL BEAR BRYANT
College Football Coach and Athletic Director

There's no substitute for guts.

MUHAMMAD ALI
Professional Boxer

He who is not courageous enough to take risks will accomplish nothing in life.

EDWARD LE BARON, JR.
NFL General Manager

The road to success becomes lonely because most are not willing to face and conquer the hardships that lurk on that road. The ability to take that extra step when you are tired and disillusioned is the quality that separates the winners from the also-rans. It's the courage to succeed.

JOHN F. KENNEDY
Thirty-Fifth President

The stories of past courage can define that ingredient—they can teach, they can offer hope, they can provide inspiration. But they cannot supply courage itself. For this each man must look into his own soul.

ANDREW JACKSON
Seventh President

One man with courage makes a majority.

R. R. M. CARPENTER, III
Major League President

At the professional level, we theoretically are dealing with the most gifted athletes in a particular sport. However, I have seen many professional baseball players with great physical ability fail to perform up to their capabilities. Most of the time, their failure, in spite of their physical talent, can be attributed to a lack of courage to become the best they possibly can.

MAXWELL MALTZ
American Writer/Surgeon

We must have courage to bet on our ideas, to take the calculated risk, and to act. Everyday living requires courage if life is to be effective and bring happiness.

JACKIE ROBINSON HAD A SPECIAL KIND OF COURAGE

"We are doing this because the American fans are just beginning to understand that a sport, to be a real sport, has got to be contested on the basis of the best man or team winning—and the best has got nothing to do with how much brown or red or yellow tint is in a man's skin."

During his baseball career, Jackie Robinson won many honors. He broke into the National League as the Rookie-of-the-Year, won the Most Valuable Player award and achieved a .311 lifetime batting average.

But none of those successes was greater than the courage he showed in breaking baseball's color line by becoming the first black to play in the major leagues.

Robinson made a deal with Branch Rickey, general manager of the Brooklyn Dodgers, when he was signed in 1945 that he would never fight, even if provoked. Rickey knew many prejudiced ballplayers would not make it easy for Robinson, and he wanted to make sure Robinson would be able to withstand the pressure.

"Mr. Rickey," Robinson asked, **"you want a coward on your ball team?"**

Rickey shook his head.

"I've got two cheeks; is that it?" Robinson asked.

Rickey nodded.

When he was verbally abused or when players slid into second base with their spikes high, Robinson kept his temper in check. He turned away, then got his revenge with a base hit or a diving catch. It is easy to fight back, but it takes real courage to turn the other cheek and show your class.

2-34

DAN GABLE HAD THE COURAGE TO SUCCEED

"When I lifted weights, I didn't lift just to maintain my muscle tone. I lifted to increase what I already had, to push to a new limit. Every time I worked, I was getting a little better. I kept moving that limit back and back. Every time I walked out of the gym, I was a little better than when I walked in."

During the summer before Dan Gable was a freshman at Iowa State, he worked out with Bob Buzzard. Buzzard had won two Big Eight wrestling titles. He recalls, "Dan was a tough kid. Some days I'd crunch him, some days I'd fool around and let him make some moves. But on this last day before I went back to Eastern Michigan University, I wanted to show him he had a ways to go, even though he had won three consecutive state high school championships."

After Buzzard finished with Gable that night, Dan fell to the mat crying tears of anger. Right then Gable recalls, "I vowed I wouldn't ever let anyone destroy me again. I was going to work at it every day, so hard that I would be the toughest guy in the world. By the end of practice, I wanted to be physically tired, to know that I'd been through a workout. If I wasn't tired, I must have cheated somehow, so I stayed a little longer."

To push one's body to the limit of endurance and beyond, to deny one's self normal pleasures while all around others are enjoying those pleasures, to persevere under grueling competition is, to me, a rare act of courage. Gable decided that he would never allow himself to get tired in a match again. Dan's strength and endurance allowed him to be on the offense all the time, always attacking, always pressing, never giving an opponent a chance to relax or counterattack.

After a college career in which Gable won two National titles and lost only one match, he found a new motivation—the Russians, the dominant force in wrestling. Before the Olympic games of 1972, Gable had defeated a dozen Russians in dual meets. At a banquet after one match, the Russians made a vow to Gable that they would find someone before the games in Munich who would beat him.

Between the banquet and the Olympics, Gable tore the cartilage in his left knee. The doctors recommended an operation, but Gable wouldn't hear of it—he just kept on practicing. The injury did, however, force Gable to alter his wrestling style.

"I changed my style of wrestling from simply offensive scoring to what I call defensive, offensive scoring. In this situation, I actually made myself a better wrestler because I learned a new way of scoring."

Once the games began, Gable encountered more adversity. He received a head-bump to the left eye in his first match and doctors sewed up the eye with seven stitches.

"The blood was obstructing my opponent's chances of wrestling, and consequently, the medical doctor almost disqualified me," he recalls. "I can remember thinking in my corner while the doctors were bandaging me up that nothing was going to stop me."

Neither the Russians nor any other country found a wrestler who could beat Dan Gable in the 1972 Olympics. He won the gold medal without giving up a point to any of six opponents. Dan Gable had a goal, and he would not allow anything or anyone to stop him.

3
PREPARATION

- Hard Work – Sacrifice
- Discipline – Organization – Consistency
- Change Your Weakness Into Your Power
- Practice it the Right Way

There is Greatness All Around You—Use It

There are many people who could be Olympic Champions, All-Americans who have never tried. I'd estimate five million people could have beaten me in the pole vault the years I won it, at least five million. Men that were stronger, bigger and faster than I was could have done it, but they never picked up a pole, never made the feeble effort to pick their legs off the ground trying to get over the bar.

Greatness is all around us! It's easy to be great because great people will help you. What is fantastic about all the conventions I go to is that the greatest in the business will come and share their ideas, their methods and their techniques with everyone else. I have seen the greatest salesmen open up and show young salesmen exactly how they did it. They don't hold back. I have also found it true in the world of sports.

I'll never forget the time I was trying to break Dutch Warmerdam's record. I was about a foot below his record, so I called him on the phone. I said "Dutch, can you help me? I've seemed to level off; I can't get any higher." He said, "Sure, Bob, come on up to visit me and I'll give you all I got." I spent three days with the master, the greatest pole vaulter in the world. For three days, Dutch gave me everything that he'd seen. There were things that I was doing wrong and he corrected them. To make a long story short, I went up eight inches. That great guy gave me the best that he had. I've found that sports champions and heroes willingly do this just to help you become great.

John Wooden has a philosophy that every day he is supposed to help someone who can never reciprocate; that's his obligation.

When in college working on his Masters' Thesis on scouting and defensive football, George Allen wrote up a 30 page survey and sent it out to the great coaches in the country. Eighty-five percent answered it completely.

Great people will share, and that is what made George Allen one of the greatest football coaches in the world. Great people will tell you their secrets. Look for them, call them on the phone or buy their books. Go where they are, get around them, talk to them. It is easy to be great when you get around great people.

BOB RICHARDS   Pole Vaulter — Two Time Olympic Gold Medalist

HARD WORK — SACRIFICE

You start with a dream. But without hard work, you may end up with nothing but the dream. Hold onto your dreams. They're very important. The ideal situation, however, is to go out and make those dreams come true. Only you can do this; nobody else can do it for you. If you're willing to work hard and make the necessary sacrifices, you can do it.

Unfortunately, there are no easy ways to become the best in a sport. If there were, everybody would do it. You can read books, get advice and watch the pros, but you must practice hard if you want to gain the edge on the rest of the field. Practice until you think you've done your best; then practice even more. Never be ashamed of having a goal, practicing hard or making sacrifices. They're important parts in realizing your dream.

Look at the record. The premier athletes are the hardest workers. Jack Nicklaus, Arnold Palmer, Curtis Strange, Pat Bradley and Nancy Lopez in golf; Ivan Lendl, Mats Wilander, Steffi Graf, Martina Navratilova and Chris Evert in tennis; Don Mattingly and Wade Boggs in baseball; Michael Jordan and Larry Bird in basketball. They're all constantly working to improve themselves, to stay ahead of the other players, to keep their edge.

The last professional baseball strike lasted one month. Some players sat around and got fat. Not Mr. Hustle — Pete Rose. At age 40, he was able to step right back in when the strike ended. He not only broke the National League all-time hit record, but he also slugged nine hits to be named Player of the Week the first week back. Do you think he spent his time off at the beach or in the batting cage?

At first, you may get by on your natural athletic ability; but this can only carry you so far. The top player on a high school team was not always the best player in junior high. The player who has worked the hardest is usually the one who becomes the best.

Hard work's constant companion is sacrifice. To get the edge, you have to be willing to pay the price for success. This means practicing according to a schedule, and not when you feel like it or when it's convenient. If you're serious about reaching your goal, you must be willing to practice when you'd rather be doing something else.

Even though you may love your sport, you may not love to practice. Everyone likes to win, but how many want to prepare to win?

When you sacrifice, the rewards will be sweeter when you reach your goal. The effort and time you put into reaching your goal will have paid off. Without sacrifice, it's easier to accept defeat because you haven't worked hard enough to expect to win. You don't really deserve to win and you know it.

The great athletes are the hardest losers. Why? They have worked harder than the others and they have more to lose. You know if you're prepared when it's time to perform. If you are, you feel good about yourself and you enter the arena with confidence. But if you cheat on your workouts, you only hurt yourself by creating self-doubt or guilt feelings that affect your performance. It's not the apple in the throat that causes problems, it's the doubt in the brain.

Use practice time to build your confidence. Make the sacrifice. Work hard. Do what it takes in practice to be a winner.

A lot of pros practice on the quiet and then say they don't practice. That's like a man bragging that he doesn't go to the office. I'm proud to say that I've been a hard practicer.

Gary Player, Professional Golfer

Even if I'm taking some time off, I'm out there beating golf balls. You've got to hit the ball in this game until your hands bleed.

Lee Trevino, Professional Golfer

HARD WORK—SACRIFICE

DAN GABLE
Wrestler—Olympic Gold Medalist and College Wrestling Coach

You can't ever work too much because there's no such thing as being in too good condition. You can't ever lift too many weights because you can't ever get too strong. You can't ever wrestle too much because you can always do better.

ROGER STAUBACH
NFL Quarterback and Sports Broadcaster

Nothing good comes in life or athletics unless a lot of hard work has preceded the effort. Only temporary success is achieved by taking short cuts.

Set a goal and go after that goal with integrity, self-confidence and a lot of hard work.

THOMAS EDISON
American Inventor

Genius is one percent inspiration and 99 percent perspiration. I never did anything worth doing by accident, nor did any of my inventions come by accident; they came by work.

GERALD R. FORD
Thirty-Eighth President

There is no substitute for hard work. There will be disappointments, but "the harder you work, the luckier you will get." Never be satisfied with less than your very best effort. If you strive for the top and miss, you'll still "beat the pack".

THOMAS EDISON
American Inventor

I am wondering what would have happened to me if some fluent talker had converted me to the theory of the eight-hour day and convinced me that it was not fair to my fellow workers to put forth my best efforts in my work. I am glad that the eight-hour day had not been invented when I was a young man. If my life had been made up of eight-hour days, I don't believe I could have accomplished a great deal. This country would not amount to as much as it does if the young men of 50 years ago had been afraid that they might earn more than they were paid for.

TOM OSBORNE
College Football Coach

Our approach for getting ready for a football game is a seven day process. All that fired-up emotion is good, but if a team lines up in a formation that we're not prepared for, then all that emotion doesn't do us much good. We believe a highly motivated team is a team that is basically very soundly prepared.

DICK VAN ARSDALE
NBA Forward

I discovered throughout my athletic career that there were no short cuts to success. Kids should realize that one doesn't get to the top by luck, but through hard work. Pros make any sport look easy because they have mastered the fundamentals of their particular game.

PAUL NEWMAN
Actor and Race Car Driver

It's always been 10 percent talent and 90 percent hard work.

WALTER O'MALLEY
Major League Owner

We're good because we work harder than anybody else.

DICK VERMEIL
NFL Coach and Sports Broadcaster

If you don't invest very much, then defeat doesn't hurt very much and winning is not very exciting.

WAYNE GRETZKY
NHL Center

I'm gifted, but I've worked for everything I've gotten. Gordie Howe and Bobby Orr worked hard too. Like them, I didn't say, "I'm gifted. I don't have to work anymore."

FRED LYNN
Major League Outfielder

The secret to being a great defensive player, outside of natural ability, is to work at it as hard as you work at your hitting. Not too many players do.

I used to go to Fenway Park early so I could work on my defense, having balls hit off the wall so I could learn to play them the right way.

JOHN L. GRIFFITH
American Author/Military Major

I do not want anybody to convince my son that someone will guarantee him a living. I want him rather to realize that there is plenty of opportunity in this country for him to achieve success, but whether he wins or loses depends entirely on his own character, perseverance, thrift, intelligence and capacity for hard work.

PELE
Professional Soccer Player

Everything is practice. I made a lot of goals with the head. I knew it was very hard to score with the head in Europe, but I made many goals because I practiced that shot.

ELROY HIRSCH
NFL Halfback and College Athletic Director

There is no substitute for hard work. When someone windsprints 50 yards, he should sprint 60. If somebody runs the sprints 10 times, he should run them 12 and so on down the line. Hard work will pay off in every way. We must always try to better ourselves and hard work is the only way to do it.

BUM PHILLIPS
NFL Coach

I'd rather have preparation than motivation. Everyone likes to play and no one likes to practice.

TUG MC GRAW
Major League Relief Pitcher

I have found throughout my career that preparation for the job at hand is the most important factor. On and off the field, mental and physical readiness are absolute necessities.

FRANCIS QUARLES
English Metaphysical Poet

I see no virtue where I smell no sweat.

TONY DORSETT
NFL Halfback

The reason a guy like myself has achieved some success in life is that I've worked very, very hard to do so.

JIM MC KAY
Sports Broadcaster

I believe there is a price tag on everything worthwhile, but it is seldom a monetary one. The price is more often one of dedication, deprivation, extra effort, loneliness. Each person decides whether he or she wants to pay the price. If you do, you achieve beyond other people.

WALTER PAYTON
NFL Running Back

I found this sandbank by the Pearl River near my hometown, Columbia, Mississippi. I laid out a course of 65 yards or so. Sixty-five yards on sand is like 120 on turf, but running on sand helps you make your cuts at full speed...I try to pick the heat of the day to run in, but sometimes that sand'll get so hot you can't stand in one place. It'll blister your feet...You get to the point where you have to keep pushing yourself. You stop, throw up, and push yourself again. There's no one else around to feel sorry for you.

GEORGE BRETT
Major League Third Baseman

When fans watch me hit, they think the game must have been easy for me. But it wasn't. I worked very hard to get where I am. For four years, I came to the parks early and worked with our batting coach, Charley Lau. There were a lot of things I could've done, and probably would have rather done, but I knew that if I was going to become successful in baseball, I had to do it; I had to work on it.

NANCY LOPEZ
Professional Golfer

When I had to give up swimming because it wasn't good for my golfing muscles, I began to think of what else I would have to sacrifice if I wanted to keep playing golf. In the years between 10 and 13, I gave up many things just so I could play golf.

ARTHUR J. ROONEY
NFL Owner

To become a top athlete, you must be willing to sacrifice and you must be determined to give long hours to practice. Practice helps to make perfection. The very best athletes among the Pittsburgh Steelers work the year around. If you want to be the best—number one—you have to work every bit as hard during the off season as you do during the season.

VINCE LOMBARDI
NFL Coach and General Manager

The dictionary is the only place success comes before work. Hard work is the price we must all pay for success. I think we can accomplish almost anything if we are willing to pay the price. The price of success is hard work, dedication to the job at hand, and the determination that whether we win or lose, we have applied the best of ourselves to the task at hand.

MERLIN OLSEN
NFL Tackle, Sports Broadcaster and Actor

Long hours of practice and repetition may be required to hone skills and develop knowledge and technique that will allow for successful performance. One of life's most painful moments comes when we must admit that we didn't do our homework, that we are not prepared.

MICHELANGELO
Italian Painter/Sculptor

If people knew how hard I have had to work to gain my mastery, it wouldn't seem wonderful at all.

DOUGLAS MAC ARTHUR
U. S. Military General

Preparedness is the key to success and victory.

MARK LIEBERMAN
Wrestler—National Champion

You have to be willing to pay the price. People don't play wrestling like they play tennis or golf. It's hard work and hardly any fun, but it can also be intensely satisfying.

PAUL BROWN
NFL Coach, General Manager and Owner

Leave as little to chance as possible. Preparation is the key to success.

JOSEPH ADDISON
English Essayist

I never knew an early-rising, hard-working, prudent man, careful of his earnings and strictly honest, who complained of hard luck. A good character, good habits and hard work are impregnable to the assaults of all ill-luck that fools ever dreamed.

MIKE PRUITT
NFL Fullback

In order to succeed greatly, you have to sacrifice greatly. Nobody ever said it would be easy.

FRANCO HARRIS
NFL Fullback

I work hard in practice. I do a lot of running. I do the things that help me as a running back. I want practice to get me in shape, maintain my endurance. I'm getting myself ready to play.

BUCKY DENT
Major League Shortstop and Manager

I knew that if I worked hard enough and sacrificed enough, I would make it to the big leagues.

WOODY HAYES
College Football Coach

They may beat us by outcoaching me. But I resolved a long time ago that nobody would ever beat me by outworking me.

MUHAMMAD ALI
Professional Boxer

Before I get in the ring, I'd have already won or lost it out on the road. The real part is won or lost somewhere far away from witnesses—behind the lines, in the gym and out there on the road long before I dance under those lights.

BILL RUSSELL
NBA Center, Coach and Sports Broadcaster

Defense is a science, not a helter-skelter thing you just luck into. Every move has six or seven years of work behind it.

ANDREW CARNEGIE
American Iron and Steel Manufacturer

The average person puts only 25 percent of his energy and ability into his work. The world takes off its hat to those who put in more than 50 percent of their capacity, and stands on its head for those few and far between souls who devote 100 percent.

SAMMY BAUGH
NFL Quarterback and Punter

When I was a boy in Streetwater, I used to practice more kicking than I did throwing. In the summertime, I used to go up on the football field by myself and kick for hours. I'd kick at those sidelines and then run down and get the ball and kick it back...I got where I could kick the ball out of bounds inside the five or the 10 yard line pretty good.

HENRY CLAY
American Statesman

The time will come when winter will ask what you were doing all summer.

VASILI ALEXEYEV
**Weight Lifter—
Three Time Olympic Gold Medalist**

The difference between my methods and others is great. The difference is that I train more often and lift more weights than others. I have become a great champion because of my love of hard work and my great striving to reach the target of victory.

JIM CRAIG
NHL Goaltender—Olympic Gold Medalist

Yeah, I worked hard for it. You get what you deserve.

FRANK ROBINSON
Major League Outfielder and Manager

Whether you're trying to excel in athletics or any other field, always practice. Look, listen, learn—and practice, practice, practice. There is no substitute for work, no short cuts to the top.

BRUCE JENNER
Decathlon—Olympic Gold Medalist
I learned that the only way you are going to get anywhere in life is to work hard at it. Whether you're a musician, a writer, an athlete or a businessman, there is no getting around it. If you do, you'll win—if you don't, you won't.

NADIA COMANECI
Gymnast—Five Time Olympic Gold Medalist
If I work on a certain move constantly, then, finally, it doesn't seem so risky to me. The idea is that the move stays dangerous and it looks dangerous to my foes, but it is not to me. Hard work has made it easy. That is my secret. That is why I win.

BILL RUSSELL
NBA Center, Coach and Sports Broadcaster
I hope that I epitomize the American Dream. For I came against long odds, from the ghetto to the very top of my profession. I was not immediately good at basketball. It did not come easy. It came as a result of a lot of hard work and self-sacrifice. The rewards—were they worth it? One thousand times over.

DON SHULA
NFL Defensive Back and Coach

Our theme has been that hard work equals success. We haven't done it with magic or with better plays or anything like that.

IGNACE PADEREWSKI
Polish Pianist

If I do not practice one day, I know it. If I do not practice the next, the orchestra knows it. If I do not practice the third day, the whole world knows it.

WALT MICHAELS
NFL Linebacker and Coach

Begin at an early age to dedicate yourself fully to the career you have chosen, and be ready at all times for your maximum effort. Since the age of 13, I have not known what the average person might call a relaxing summer, but I certainly enjoyed every one of them. Age 13 began a career in football that progressed from high school to college to the present time in professional football as head coach of the New York Jets. Summer trips to the beach or to the mountains were for exercise, conditioning training and thoughts of good things to come in September when the football season began. I feel very strongly that the work throughout these summers has been the backbone for the success that I have enjoyed throughout the years.

WILL ROGERS
Actor/Lecturer/Humorist

Even if you're on the right track, you'll get run over if you just sit there.

ROGER MARIS
Major League Outfielder

You hit home runs not by chance, but by preparation.

LOU HOLTZ
College Football Coach

I work from dawn to exhaustion. If there's not a crisis, I'll create one.

JOHNNY UNITAS
NFL Quarterback

Specialists can never practice their specialties too much. The danger is in not practicing enough. Make that mistake, and soon you may not be in the specialist business anymore.

J. KINDLEBERGER
American Manufacturer

The only worthwhile things that have come to use in this life have come through work that was always hard, and often bitter. We believe that this has always been true of mankind and that it will always be true. We believe not in how little work, but how much; not in how few hours, but how many.

PAT MC INALLY
NFL Wide Receiver and Punter

I was always just another athlete kicking a football. Then during the spring of 1981, I worked with my father back home in California. We kicked 96 balls a day—every day. The daily practice paid off. Now hopefully, I come close to being a punter.

HERBERT V. PROCHNOW
American Government Banking Official

The trouble with opportunity is that it always comes disguised as hard work.

SIR THOMAS BUXTON
English Philanthropist/Prison Reformer

Laziness grows on people; it begins in cobwebs and ends in iron chains. The more one has to do the more he is able to accomplish.

PARNELLI JONES
Race Car Driver

The greatest gift of life is being an American. Where else but in America can a person rise from a humble environment to whatever level one wishes to attain? However, a level cannot be attained unless specific goals are established; established goals can only be reached through hard work. Hard work results in success and this makes the end worth the means.

STEVE LARGENT
NFL Wide Receiver

I stay after practice to catch passes. I look at myself as encouragement to the common man who doesn't have great speed. I work hard. If you work hard too, you can make it.

CRIS COLLINSWORTH
NFL Wide Receiver

I see myself as someone who has to grit my teeth and scratch for everything I do. I want to be the best and the best I see nowadays are guys like Swann, Jefferson, Moore and Chandler. I want to be as good as them. It won't come easy. I'm going to have to work hard at it. But I'm willing to pay the price.

It has always been my thought that the most important single ingredient to success in athletics or life is discipline. I have many times felt that this word is the most ill-defined in all of our language. My definition of the word is as follows: 1. Do what has to be done; 2. When it has to be done; 3. As well as it can be done; and 4. Do it that way all the time.

Bob Knight, College Basketball Coach and U.S. Olympic Basketball Coach

I believe in discipline. You can forgive incompetence. You can forgive lack of ability. But one thing you cannot ever forgive is lack of discipline.

Forrest Gregg, NFL Offensive Tackle, Coach and College Football Coach

DISCIPLINE ORGANIZATION — CONSISTENCY

Every winning team or performer has a game plan. Sit down and set your goals. Figure out a training schedule that will help you reach those goals. Organize a consistent practice schedule.

Have the discipline to follow it. Be consistent in your workouts. Have a no-nonsense attitude at practice; work hard and you'll improve every day. Treat practice as if it were the real thing. Come early and stay late. Do it for yourself, not for your coaches or your teammates. Improving yourself is the best way to help your team and build your confidence.

During the off-season, prepare a daily workout schedule. If you're consistent, you'll work out every day, rain or shine. To get the edge, you have to train month after month. To reach your goal, keep the "big picture" constantly in your mind for the long term. Too many athletes start out strong for about a month, but lose interest after the initial excitement wears off. You can't win that way.

How many people do you know who were going to dedicate themselves to a sport but never made it? They lifted weights enthusiastically for the first month, but then missed just one workout? Missing the first workout is like telling a lie — the next one comes easier.

Several health and fitness clubs nationwide make a living from the many people who talk about being in shape, but are inconsistent in their workouts. These health clubs sell lifetime memberships to people they know will work out enthusiastically for a month, then quit, never to come again. The clubs know most Americans take better care of their cars, homes and yards than their bodies. What would happen if everyone who bought a membership showed up at the club's front door at the same time?

You don't have to spend every minute of every day working toward your goal. You would flunk out of school, alienate your family and have no friends. That's why you need a workout schedule. It's your game plan.

Your workout schedule must be followed every month, every week, every day to be effective. This is where your self-discipline comes in. This schedule should be part of your daily routine. It should be organized to include time for your family, school work and your friends, as well as your workout. If you want a two-hour workout every day, make sure you put in two hard, intense, concentrated hours. To get the edge, follow your game plan intensely.

When you're finished with your workout, check off that day. Relax, work on your studies, go to a concert or see your friends. You'll not only have a great time, but you'll also feel good about yourself. And there's nothing better than that. After all, you only have one body — so take good care of it.

To get the edge in your field, you need "Tunnel Vision." Set your sights on a goal; keep your eyes on this goal until you reach it. To avoid the many other good and fun things that can easily distract you from reaching your goal, put on your blinders. Avoid the many distractions and temptations currently available. Tunnel Vision is your discipline.

Please notice we used the word "other" to describe fun things which could distract you. Why? Because when you love your sport and have a goal, what could be more fun than working towards that goal? Not much.

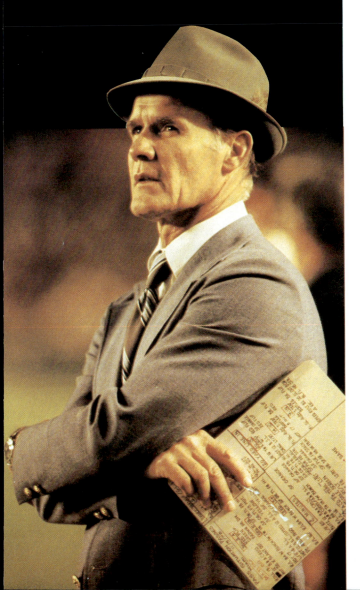

Setting a goal is not the main thing. It is deciding how you will go about achieving it and staying with that plan. The key is discipline. Without it, there is no morale.

Tom Landry, NFL Defensive Back and Coach

DISCIPLINE

EDWIN MOSES
Hurdler — Two Time Olympic Gold Medalist

Why do I dominate the 400 meter hurdles? That's easy. Training. Just expertise. I know what I'm doing. I concentrate on this as much as I would engineering or physics or whatever I'd be doing. The discipline I had from engineering and physics got me through school and really stayed with me.

VINCE LOMBARDI
NFL Coach and General Manager
discipline is a part of the will. A disciplined person is one who follows the will of the one who gives the orders. You teach discipline by doing it over and over, by repetition and rote, especially in a game like football where you have very little time to decide what you are going to do. So what you do is react almost instinctively, naturally. You have done it so many times, over and over and over again.

STAN MUSIAL
Major League Outfielder
I learned the meaning of discipline early. I wanted to be a big league ballplayer from the time I was eight years old. The point was to practice all the time, whether it be baseball or softball. I couldn't play enough to suit me.

PETE CARRIL
College Basketball Coach
If my players work hard every day, then they won't have to worry about game plans, or where they play, or whom they play, or about rankings and so on. They have their daily behavior—their discipline—to fall back on.

GEORGE FOSTER
Major League Outfielder
There are four parts of self that lead to success. The first part is discipline, the second is concentration, the third is patience, and fourth is faith.

BOB RICHARDS
Pole Vaulter—Two Time Olympic Gold Medalist
One of the great lessons I've learned in athletics is that you've got to discipline your life. No matter how good you may be, you've got to be willing to cut out of your life those things that keep you from going to the top.

Is not that a great principle for all of living? The people who will really accomplish great things in life are those who are willing to discipline their lives, who maintain their health, their vitality, their efficiency through this process of rigorous disciplining of what they take into their bodies and what they do in life. It's a very important thing in terms of championship living.

H. P. LIDDON
English Pulpit Orator
What we do upon some great occasion will probably depend on what we already are; and what we are will be the result of previous years of self-discipline.

NORM VAN BROCKLIN
NFL Quarterback and Coach
If you don't discipline them, they won't know you love them. There's no love on third down and one. You need discipline then.

SAM HUFF
NFL Linebacker
Discipline is the whole key to being successful. We all get 24 hours a day. It's the only fair thing; it's the only thing that's equal. It's up to us as to what we do with those 24 hours.

BYRON NELSON
Professional Golfer

The only way one can become proficient at anything is self-discipline and dedication. The people who succeed are the ones that really do not let personal feelings get in their way from giving their all in whatever they choose to do. The superstar golfers are people who are willing to do and give a little bit more than the others who do not succeed. When I was growing up and learning to play golf and during my career, I wouldn't even drink a cup of coffee for fear that it might affect my nerve control to some degree.

MIKE NORRIS
Major League Pitcher

When I was spending four seasons shuffling between the A's and the minors, I just over-indulged in everything. I figured life was one big party and I'd never have to get serious about anything. I drank too much and thought seriously too little. I didn't even have money left to pay my rent. That was the low point—the turning point—I knew I had to get more responsible, more disciplined. I figured I'd give baseball one more good shot.

TRACY AUSTIN
Professional Tennis Player

I rely on two important qualities to win—discipline and concentration. I carry self-discipline from my personal life onto the practice court and on to the center court. Then I concentrate totally on playing my game and on winning.

TOMMY JOHN
Major League Pitcher

Being a baseball player demands a tremendous amount of work, dedication, discipline, and, of course, talent. The area that demands the most from us is discipline. This discipline has three forms: physical, mental and spiritual.

PHYSICAL DISCIPLINE requires us to develop our bodies to the fullest extent without abusing them with drugs, drinking, or any other body-destroying agents. We should eat properly to give our bodies a chance to use the talents God has given to us.

MENTAL DISCIPLINE is the second aspect which demands our attention. To be mentally tough, we should study hard, try to retain what we have studied, and do our best in school. We owe this effort in schoolwork to the ones we love—our parents, our pastors, our priests, and our God.

SPIRITUAL DISCIPLINE is what we need when we are in church. If our minds are distracted while we are listening to God's Word, we must learn to be tough. The Bible is our rule book of life, and it helps us live full lives as God would want us to. Yet to do so, we must obey the rules. We have to be spiritually disciplined.

JERRY WEST
NBA Guard, Coach, and General Manager

You can't get much done in life if you only work on the days when you feel good.

LEE TREVINO
Professional Golfer

I believe the one idea, factor, strength, skill, force, experience, or motivation that has helped me most in achieving success has been my use or exertion of self-discipline. Believe me, without self-discipline, it is hard to get yourself up at 6:00 A.M., practice many long, hard hours, go to work until 11:00 or 12:00 at night, and still find time for your family, and do this for an extensive period of time. One of my reasons or motivations for maintaining such a schedule was my long range goal that was, and still is, to become the best golfer in the world.

ROCKY BLEIER
NFL Halfback

"How can I tell you the agony and tedium of that routine? The physical pain of those mornings—the creaking of my joints and the dull ache of my legs—was matched only by mental anguish of knowing what lay in wait. Something in my head said, 'Go back to sleep. Who's going to know if you miss this one lousy workout?'"

Describing his off-season self-disciplined routine of getting up at 6:00 A. M. to run, spending 8:00 A.M.— 1:00 P.M. in the office, lifting in the afternoons, returning to the office after dinner for a few hours and then heading back to the track for a few sprints.

ORGANIZATION

MERLIN OLSEN
NFL Tackle, Sports Broadcaster and Actor

I do not believe that there is any secret or single formula for success, but there are common threads of thought and action that characterize the successful people that I have been fortunate enough to know and observe. I do know, from my own experience, that our chance of succeeding is much greater when we organize and take charge of our lives. When we are willing to make decisions, we aggressively pursue those things in life that are important to us.

RICHARD CECIL
English Clergyman

The shortest way to do many things is to do only one thing at a time.

DICK VERMEIL
NFL Coach and Sports Broadcaster

I'm a detail man to the point where I am called a workaholic because I put so much time into detailing everything and making sure everything is organized in preparation.

CHUCK NOLL
NFL Linebacker and Coach

You don't win with computers or trick plays. You do it with good people and an efficient, organized operation. And right there you have a formula for success, be it in business, industry or sports.

JOHN WOODEN
College Basketball Coach

Without organization and leadership toward a realistic goal, there is no chance of realizing more than a small percentage of your potential.

CHUCK KNOX
NFL Coach

Always have a plan and believe in it. I tell my coaches not to compromise. Nothing good happens by accident—it happens because of good organization. There must be a plan for everything and the plan will prevent you from overlooking little things. By having that plan, you'll be secure and self-doubts will never become a factor.

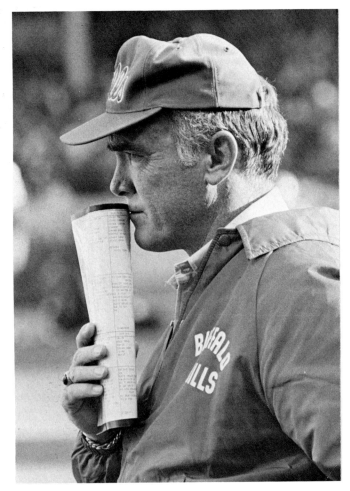

CONSISTENCY

HANK AARON
Major League Outfielder

Consistency is what counts; you have to be able to do things over and over again.

BILL RODGERS
Distance Runner

To repeat successes of the past, you follow your old program. Don't get fancy; just be consistent.

JOE TORRE
Major League Catcher and Manager

Whatever your job is, consistency is the hallmark. It's much more important than doing something spectacular just once. Do your job consistently and you will be considered good.

BUD WILKINSON
NFL and College Football Coach

Remember, "Rome was not built in a day." Instant success is never possible. Competence results only from sustained, consistent, self-disciplined effort over an extended period of time.

JANET LYNN SALOMON
Figure Skater

Some basic principles that I've found important to find fulfillment in whatever you do are: Love God, yourself and others, in that order. Set your priorities and work toward them with consistency, faith and self-discipline.

HENRY L. DOHERTY
American Industrialist

Plenty of men can do good work for a spurt and with immediate promotion in mind, but for promotion you want a man in whom good work has become a habit.

STEVE GARVEY
Major League First Baseman

The way I play baseball is an expression of my being, my personality—the consistency, the durability, the dependability, the control, the concentration, the release of emotion at the proper time.

BEN OGILVIE
Major League Outfielder

I'm seeking consistency. Three home runs in a game is nice, but I would prefer to spread them out. I'm trying to eliminate the slumping periods. Those aren't good for me or the team. I get concerned when I'm not doing anything. Not worried but concerned. I like to be consistent.

CHANGE YOUR WEAKNESSES INTO YOUR POWER

> My father taught me that the only way you can make good at anything is to practice and then practice some more. It's easy to practice something you're already good at and that's what most people do. What's tough is to go out and work hard on things you don't do very well. If you have trouble going to your right after ground balls, have your friends hit you balls to your right.
>
> Pete Rose, Major League First Baseman and Manager

If you're content with the best you have done as an athlete, you'll never be the best you can be. If you really want to get better, you'll go out of your way to change your weaknesses into your strengths. It's not easy, but it's an exciting challenge that will make you grow as an athlete and as a person.

First, determine what your weaknesses are. Strong competition will bring that out. Analyze where you need improvement. Then, turn that weakness into your strength.

The best athletes work hard to overcome their weaknesses. It's fun, and easy, to practice your strengths because those are what you do best. However, the only way to get better is to work long and hard on your weaknesses in order to turn them into strengths. It all boils down to how good you really want to be.

When you make a mistake, you can do one of two things. You can ignore it — deny it and convince yourself it wasn't a mistake. This way, you'll keep making the same mistake over and over. Or, you can admit your mistakes, learn from them and have the courage to test yourself again in competition. This way is more risky, but also more rewarding.

Admitting you have a weakness and not working on it is just as unproductive as hiding your mistakes. You won't improve either way. You'll continue to work on what you like to do, which is what you're the best at. The result is your strengths will get stronger, while your weaknesses will get weaker. You'll never reach your full potential this way.

You may be able to get by in the short run on your raw talent or ability; but in the long run, you have to improve your weaknesses if you expect to win. Take tennis, for example. You may be able to slide by sometimes by hitting your forehand, when you should be hitting your backhand. But when it's set point and your opponent hits a shot deep to your backhand, what are you going to do?

I'll tell you what you're going to do — you're going to lose.

When the game is on the line, there's no substitute for skill. When your skill is perfected, you'll have no weaknesses. You won't be vulnerable; you'll be in control and ready to counter anything your opponent might throw at you.

Don't misunderstand us. We're not saying you should work on your weaknesses until they no longer restrict you. We're saying you should work on them until they're the strongest part of your game. So they become your strengths.

Take a great running back with concrete hands. He works hard to get the softest hands in the league. Now he's the best receiver and still a great runner. What do you have? An all-pro, a future Hall of Famer. Why? Because he expanded his opportunities and didn't settle for less than he could be.

This holds true for athletes in all sports: The pitcher who can't field; the golfer who drives shots 250 yards down the middle, but can't putt; the basketball player who goes to the boards like Doctor J, but can't make a foul shot; the tennis player who has great ground strokes, but is afraid of coming to the net; and the wrestler who is great when he's on top, but is hopeless when he needs to escape.

To get the competitive edge over your opponents, make the weakest part of your game the strongest.

> My father saw me kicking with my right foot as a boy and he was the one who taught me to kick with my left foot too, so I could kick from any position in any direction, very quick! To kick with great power depends on leg muscles, but you must also practice how to use that power best with the nicest placement of the foot on the ball. The impact position is most important. I believed in this and I began to kick against the wall, to practice with both legs, kicking and rebounding hour after hour. Right foot, left foot, until I got the same power in both legs.
>
> Pele, Professional Soccer Player

CHANGE YOUR WEAKNESS INTO YOUR POWER

FRED LYNN
Major League Outfielder
I've always been told that I have this great potential—I just wasn't living up to it. I had to find out what I could do, playing injury-free and strong for an entire season. It took me a while to realize what a physical grind a major league season is. After that, I assessed my career and saw two problems: injuries and running out of gas in the dog days of August. I figured a Nautilus program could help me with both. I realized that the unlimited potential people were always telling me about was just that—potential. It was up to me to transform that potential into accomplishment.

ROBERT LOUIS STEVENSON
Scottish Novelist, Essayist and Poet
You cannot run away from a weakness, You must sometimes fight it out or perish; and if that be so, why not now, and where you stand?

BILLY CUNNINGHAM
NBA Forward, Coach and Sports Broadcaster
To have a championship team, you have to handle every phase of this game. You cannot excel in one area and ignore others. You have to be consistent in offense and defense. You have to find out what your weakest area is and work on it.

TOM SEAVER
Major League Pitcher and Sports Broadcaster
All my career, I've been able to deal with pitching problems because I know how to go about it. First, I have to be aware of the problem. Then, I have to define what it is, and finally, I solve it.

AL ROSEN
Major League Third Baseman, General Manager and President
The most complete athletes are those who strive to overcome their weaknesses by hard work and persistence. Practicing on one's strengths is more enjoyable and obviously much easier, but to work long and hard on one's weaknesses, while it may be the more difficult path to follow, has certain assurances of success.

BUM PHILLIPS
NFL Coach
You work to strengthen your weakest link, not to worry about the strongest one.

HUGH GREEN
NFL Linebacker
When I was in college, we all knew that for Pitt to win a national championship, everyone on our team had to do something he ordinarily didn't do. In other words, work on their particular weakness. For me, that was lifting weights to build up my strength.

BOB COUSY
NBA Guard
I dribbled by the hour with my left hand when I was young. I didn't have full control, but I got so I could move the ball back and forth from one hand to the other without breaking the cadence of my dribble. I wasn't dribbling behind my back or setting up any trick stuff, but I was laying the groundwork for it.

DUANE KUIPER
Major League Second Baseman
As an athlete, ask yourself what you can do and then ask yourself what you can't do. It is very important to an athlete that he or she evaluates himself. It's very easy to work on the things that come natural. In fact, it's human nature. On the other hand, it's very difficult to work on things that do not come easy. As an example - for Duane Kuiper, fielding ground balls is second nature; it's easy; it's fun. But on the other side of the coin, sacrifice bunting does not come easy at times; consequently, it is not fun to do. You as an athlete have to force yourself, whether it's fun or not, to work on the things that do not come natural. This is a must if you want to become a real winner.

JOE CRIBBS
NFL Halfback
Not breaking a long run was more a mental thing than an actual weakness. Now when we're out in practice, I'm trying to run the ball 40 or 50 yards. Before, I didn't do that. In practice, I'd run the ball 10 or 15 yards and come back. Your body gets used to going only 20 yards. After you pass those 20 yards, it takes a little out of you. So I'm pushing myself a little harder now to try to break some. That kind of thing is going to come. It's just a matter of time.

ROBERT RIGER
American Author/Artist
My philosophy as a creative artist is to work hardest on your weakest talent. When it becomes your strongest, stay with it and support it with a wise choice of what you do best.

JACK NICKLAUS
Professional Golfer

I always achieve my most productive practice after an actual round. Then, the mistakes are fresh in my mind, and I can go to the practice tee and work specifically on those mistakes.

DOROTHY HAMILL
Figure Skater—Olympic Gold Medalist

Every time you go out on the ice, there are slight flaws. You can always think of something you should have done better. These are the things you must work on.

JERRY REUSS
Major League Pitcher

I believe in working on my weaknesses. When I first came up, I couldn't hit at all. I never expect to be a great hitter because pitching is my job, but I feel I now can help myself. I think I've reached the point where the manager in certain instances will allow me to bat instead of using a pinch hitter.

RED AUERBACH
NBA Coach, General Manager and Owner

When I coached, win or lose, I'd calm down after the game and unwind. Before too long, I was scheming for the next game, remembering the mistakes and going to work on them to do my best to see that they didn't happen again. This is the only way a team improves—by working on their mistakes, correcting their weaknesses.

M. WINETTE
American Psychologist

Personal deficiencies might be termed negative qualities and include unreliability, failure to cooperate, laziness, untidiness, trouble making, interference and dishonesty.

Positive qualities would include willingness, cheerfulness, courtesy, honesty, neatness, reliability and temperance.

Many fail in their work because they are unable to overcome one personal deficiency. Check up on yourself. Don't be afraid to put yourself under a microscope.

Eliminate your negative qualities. Develop your positive ones. You can't win with the check mark in the wrong place.

BOB RICHARDS
Pole Vaulter—Two Time Olympic Gold Medalist

You've got to analyze yourself, recognize your weaknesses, and work on them. This is one of the hardest things for a person to do. It is very easy for us to take a negative attitude toward our weaknesses, justifying them by saying that, after all, we were born with this particular weakness or we have acquired it, and actually there is nothing we can do about it. Or, we can defend a weakness, and in the process of this defense, we may start to build our lives around it, making the weakness the center of our lives instead of conquering the thing and overcoming it.

BABE RUTH
Major League Pitcher/Outfielder

A part of control is learning to correct your weaknesses. The person doesn't live who was born with everything. Sometimes he has one weak point; generally he has several. The first thing is to know your faults and then take on a systematic plan of correcting them. You know the old saying about a chain being only as strong as its weakest link. The same can be said in the chain of skills a man forges.

HANK AARON
Major League Outfielder

I did a lot of thinking about hitting. I kept it up in my head. I studied the pitchers all the time, and when I found one giving me trouble, I studied him extra hard. I wanted to know why he was getting me out and what I could do about it. Don Drysdale of the Dodgers used to get me out with a change-of-pace pitch. In fact, all the Dodgers used to kill me with that pitch. So, after my first year, when I got home to Mobile, I got my brother Tommy to throw change-ups to me all the time. After that, they didn't throw me that pitch very often.

ROCKY MARCIANO TURNED HIS WEAKNESS INTO HIS POWER

Rocky Marciano didn't just walk into the ring and become a champion boxer. In his early days as a fighter, he lacked finesse, poise and also had one glaring weakness—he could barely hold his arms up. They were big arms, short and powerful. The tragedy was that after a couple of rounds in the ring his arms would get heavy and would begin to descend slowly to his sides, and then, of course, he would take a terrific beating from his sparring partners.

With that obvious weakness, few gave Marciano a chance to become a champion. But Marciano was aware of his weakness, and he changed it into his strength.

Rocky, undaunted, developed an ingenious method of striving to overcome his weakness. He would submerge himself in the local swimming pool and flail his arms as hard as he could against the water. He would swing them against the buoyancy of the water for hours, forcing the arm muscles to develop against abnormal difficulties.

"In order to develop strength in my arms, I practiced throwing punches under water in the YMCA pool. Art Bergman, a fireman I knew who was a terrific puncher, gave me the biggest, heaviest bag I ever saw. It weighed 180 pounds. The normal bag weighs 40 or 50 pounds. I had trouble with my hands before. Art told me to punch his bag with my bare fists, and that's the way I hardened them up."

When Marciano retired, he was undefeated. He won all 49 of his professional fights, 45 by knockouts. He hadn't walked into the ring a champion, but there was no question that Marciano was a champion, one of the greatest in boxing history, when he walked out of the ring for the last time. Why? Because he worked on a weakness, and made out of that weakness a strength that carried him to boxing's greatest glory. This can happen when a person meets a weakness head-on, when he does something about it.

"I was willing to make sacrifices. Even while traveling, when there were no facilities, I would spend hours in my hotel room working on my strength. I wanted more than anything else to be a fighter. Then I wanted to be a good one, and after that a great champion."

Uncorrected errors will multiply. Someone once asked me if there wasn't benefit in overlooking one small flaw. "What is a small flaw?", I asked him.

Don Shula, NFL Defensive Back, Coach

I tell the kids that it's as though we're putting on a play. I'm the director. I'm going to pick the script, and I'm going to give them their roles. They're the actors. Their job is to learn those roles—that's what practice is about. When we go out on the court, that's our stage. Out there they're supposed to perform as we practiced. I don't want anybody making up new lines, putting on their own act.

John Thompson, College Basketball Coach

PRACTICE IT THE RIGHT WAY

Practice does not make perfect; practice makes permanent. Perfect practice makes perfect.

Just putting in your practice time won't do, especially if it's the wrong way. Your hard work, sacrifice, discipline, organization and consistency won't mean a thing if you're practicing wrong. You'll get better, but you'll never reach your full potential or beat the outstanding athletes. Why? To beat them, you have to increase the quality of your practice time, not the quantity. How? Determine who's the BEST professional athlete in your sport. Read their books, watch them on TV and go see them in person.

This process of copying the best athletes works for individual sports like golf, tennis, track, swimming and wrestling as well as for team sports like baseball, football, basketball, hockey and soccer. Observe them; study them; analyze them. But most importantly, learn from them. Find out why they're consistent winners over and over again. Then go out and do the same.

For example, we saw wrestler Gene Mills of Syracuse University win two NCAA championships and set an all-time collegiate pinning record in the process. We wanted to learn how he did it, so our wrestling team invited him to the school for a clinic. We learned, studied and practiced his spiral pinning combination. As a result, the very next season, our team broke the all-time national high school team pinning record of 239 with 333 pins. Gene Mills gave us the edge; we had a move others didn't.

Once you see how a particular move or technique is done, practice it the right way. Over and over. Again and again. Remember how you saw the champions do it; check yourself repeatedly. Force yourself to do it the right way. Don't expect immediate results; you may even get worse for a while. That's OK. The improvement will come. Be patient and keep with it.

The great athletes do this many times during a season. They break down the game to the fundamentals. And it works — it brings out the best in them. We see this every year when our alumni return to St. Ed's after spending some time in college. They tell us the big difference between high school and college wrestling practices is that the colleges practice "smarter," waste less time and get right after it. They're not necessarily harder practices, but smarter ones.

Concentrate during practice. At a driving range, many golfers hit ball after ball the wrong way. They're wasting their time because they're not thinking or trying to correct their mistakes.

I have never seen a wrestler hit sloppy moves in practice, then go out in a match and do it the right way. Every wrestler has his own personality, style and favorite moves. We encourage this. But in wrestling, like all other sports, there are a few basics that simply must be done the "right way." We call these the "unforgivables." They must be done in practice perfectly, so that your muscles will automatically go only one way. This way, in a match, it'll be impossible for you to hit the move the "wrong way."

Practice time is very valuable. Don't waste it doing fancy shots or moves you'll never use in a game. Treat practice as rehearsal time before you go "live" on stage to perform. This builds confidence. When it's game time, you'll automatically produce without even thinking about it. You'll have the edge knowing you can do it right.

Practice does not make the athlete. It is the quality and intensity of practice that makes the athlete, not just repeated practicing.
Ray Meyer, College Basketball Coach

PRACTICE IT THE RIGHT WAY

JACK NICKLAUS
Professional Golfer

No matter how motivated you already are as a golfer, or want to become, it isn't going to move you one step forward if you can't hit a golf ball halfway decently. Neither are all the other big words like dedication and determination and confidence and concentration and commitment and so on.

So how do you become a better shot-maker? Obviously, through practice. But there's really an awful lot more to learning to hit good golf shots than belting out a few million balls.

The first thing you need is a crystal clear understanding of what you are fundamentally trying to achieve when you swing a golf club. Practice alone won't do it—you must practice it the right way.

PAUL BROWN
NFL Coach, General Manager and Owner

People think there are great mysteries connected with this game, but there are not. It's just teaching fundamentals, teaching players how to do things the right way.

REGGIE JACKSON
Major League Outfielder and Sports Broadcaster

Winning is the science of preparation and preparation can be defined in three words. "Leave nothing undone." No detail is too small. No task is too large. Most of the time, the difference between winning and losing, success and failure, can be the smallest detail or as they say in baseball, just a matter of inches.

JOHN WOODEN
College Basketball Coach

Don't mistake activity for achievement—practice it the right way.

BENJAMIN FRANKLIN
American Inventor

Being ignorant is not so much a shame as being unwilling to learn to do things the right way.

JOE PATERNO
College Football Coach and Athletic Director

I have a very strong feeling that if you practice well, you will win. A team just can't remain the same week after week; otherwise, you go backwards on Saturdays. You just have to practice better and better each week—and by better I mean more intense.

JOHANN CHRISTOPH VON SCHILLER
German Poet/Dramatist

Only those who have the patience to do simple things perfectly will acquire the skill to do difficult things easily.

ALBERTO SALAZAR
Distance Runner

I've never run a bad race when my training has gone well. If I train well, I'll run well.

TRACY CAULKINS
Swimmer — Three Time Olympic Gold Medalist

You just can't work out. You have to concentrate on what you're doing in workouts. There's a satisfaction when you have a hard set, a rugged workout, and you feel it, and you take it, and go beyond it. Don't you feel really good after something like that?

GERRY COONEY
Professional Boxer

When the bell rings, I've got to be in shape. If I just go in there and parry and parry with my sparring partner, how am I going to get in condition?

IVAN LENDL
Professional Tennis Player

I only play well when I'm prepared. If I don't practice the way I should, then I won't play the way that I know I can.

CHUCK KNOX
NFL Coach

Repeated actions are stored as habits. If the repeated actions aren't fundamentally sound, then what comes out in a game can't be sound. What comes out will be bad habits.

TOM HEINSOHN
NBA Forward, Coach, and Sports Broadcaster

Fundamental skills must be thoughtfully developed to maximize natural athletic talents. In short, you must become a master of technique and then be able to use it in an imaginative way. You must be able to do things the right way.

NORMAN VINCENT PEALE
Clergyman/American Writer

Nobody ever mastered any skill except through intensive, persistent and intelligent practice. Practice it the right way.

LOU HOLTZ
College Football Coach

We're gonna get in two good hours of practice even if it takes six hours.

CHARLEY BOSWELL
Professional Blind Golfer

I remember an experience I had while playing football at the University of Alabama. One day during spring practice, we were working on our offense and one play in particular. We weren't doing too well with this play and Coach Frank Thomas said to me, "Run it again, Charley." We did run it again. In fact, we ran it 11 times before we got it right. I was dog-tired by then, but not too tired to get Coach Thomas' message. Run it till you get it right, not just in football, but in life. Do whatever is necessary in order to succeed in life. If there is a moral to this story, and I think there is, it is to work hard and give 100 percent effort in everything you do—do it right or don't do it.

BILL SHARMAN
NBA Guard, Coach and General Manager

It's a game of habit, of repetition. You can't play one way in practice and another way in a game. It's a reflex. The game is so quick you don't have time to think.

GERRY FAUST
College Football Coach

We'll play like we practice. If we practice poorly, we'll play poorly.

PETE ROSE
Major League First Baseman and Manager

Practice the game the way you're going to play the game. Practice hard and play hard. Run hard, and above all else, hustle every moment you're on the field whether you're practicing or playing in a game.

EDWARD C. SIMMONS
American Painter

The difference between failure and success is doing a thing nearly right and doing it exactly right.

BUM PHILLIPS
NFL Coach

If we have been practicing terrible, then we'll play terrible. We always go out and play like we practice.

JOE NAMATH
NFL Quarterback and Sports Broadcaster

Every year, I go back to the basics about throwing the ball and work the whole throwing motion up from the bottom. I practice it the way it should be done.

ANDY VARIPAPA
Professional Bowler

All forms of athletics require highly skillful endeavors. To accomplish such skills, only concentrated practice helps toward perfection. Practice without concentration or without knowledge of what you're doing is worthless.

CHUCK KNOX
NFL Coach

Practice without improvement is meaningless.

ROD CAREW
Major League First Baseman

You've got to control your swing. And you got to take extra batting practice with that in mind. You got to use batting practice for certain situations—hitting to the opposite field, hitting behind the runner. You just can't stand up at the plate and swing away. You have to be always working on something specific. Make the most out of your practice.

CHARLIE WATERS
NFL Defensive Back

It's not how hard you tackle, but how efficiently you tackle. Learn to tackle the right way.

LEARN FROM OTHERS

JULIUS ERVING
NBA Forward

I watch players, all players. I watch them on television, at college games, in the playground. You can learn from anybody. Even now, I'll be watching a game somewhere and I'll see somebody do something that'll remind me of something I've forgotten—some little move. Maybe I'll practice it a little and I've got it back. And when the right situation comes along against some player, I've got a little extra edge that I didn't have before.

ROBERT HENRI
American Painter, Art Teacher

Many receive a criticism and think it is fine; think they got their money's worth; think well of the teacher for it, and then go on with their work just the same as before. That is the reason much of the wisdom of Plato is still locked up in the pages of Plato.

SYRUS
Latin Mimi Writer

Many receive advice, only the wise profit by it.

JOHN HANNAH
NFL Offensive Guard

I got films of some of the other offensive linemen and tried to study them. I tried to copy Kuechenberg because I thought my style would be suited to his. I also tried to copy Randy Rasmussen of the Jets because we were built similarly, the same wide base.

DON SHULA
NFL Defensive Back, Coach

If I see something that can be successful and even if it's not my style, I'll investigate it a little further. If it looks worthwhile, I might incorporate it. I'm not so hard-headed as to ignore something just because it might be a little different than what I'm doing.

THACKERAY
English Novelist

Might I give counsel to any man, I would say to him, try to frequent the company of your betters. In books and in life, that is the most wholesome society; learn to admire rightly; the great pleasure of life is that. Note what great men admire.

LYMAN BRYSON
American Educator

Education is anything that we do for the purpose of taking advantage of the experience of someone else.

JACK NICKLAUS
Professional Golfer

You learn by watching the best golfers. We all continue to learn. If we didn't continue to learn, we would be in trouble. I've learned an awful lot from playing with great golfers, with the exposure to them and with talking with them.

TED WILLIAMS

TONY DORSETT

ROGER STAUBACH **BART STARR**

4
PREGAME

- **Faith**
- **Positive Mental Attitude**
- **Confidence**
- **Inner Arrogance**
- **Have Fun**

Whether You Think You Can Or You Can't You're Probably Right

If you think you are beaten, you are;
If you think that you dare not, you don't;
If you'd like to win, but you think you can't,
It's almost certain you won't.

If you think you'll lose, you've lost;
For out in the world you'll find
Success begins with a fellow's will.
It's all in the state of mind.

If you think you are outclassed, you are;
You've got to think high to rise;
You've got to be sure of yourself before
You can ever win a prize.

Life's battles don't always go
To the stronger or faster man;
But sooner or later the man who wins
Is the man who thinks he can.

A plaque has hung in my office for many years carrying the above selection of free verse. I am not aware of its origin, but consider it a pertinent guideline for one to pursue in life and toward specific goals as well. It has always provided an energizing thrust to my career in golf.

ARNOLD PALMER   Professional Golfer

There is nothing in this world that can't be accomplished through hard work and with the help of God. Don't be afraid to talk to God; after all, He is our Father.

Johnny Unitas, NFL Quarterback

What you are is God's gift to you and what you do with what you are is your gift to God.

George Foster, Major League Outfielder

> I'd hate to say my faith's a rock, but it's true. It is my strength; it gives me inner peace. Without my faith, I'd be in real bad shape. Faith gives a man hope and hope is what life is all about.
>
> **Tom Landry, NFL Defensive Back and Coach**

FAITH

Whether you think you can or you can't, you're probably right. That, simply put, is what faith is all about.

The Bible emphasizes that a person can make something of himself or herself through beliefs, faith in God, faith in others, faith in one's self and faith in life. When you affirm big, believe big and pray big; big things happen to you.

Tom Landry is a reflection of his faith. He was the "rock" of the Dallas Cowboys football team. And he made very big things happen there for many years. Like Coach Landry, I believe my faith is my rock, my strength, my inner peace. It has allowed me to enjoy whatever successes I've had. Without it, I couldn't have made things happen. On the surface, many people think I've never had a problem in the world, that I've never been depressed or worried. I've had some very tough times, but I had too much pride and faith to let it show.

I believe that no matter how dark things look, everything happens for a reason. God is either challenging me or testing me. I motivate myself to work every fiber of every muscle in my body, including my brain, to find an answer to that challenge. The result? It's worked every time. How can you lose with faith as your rock — as your foundation? All you have to do is believe, work like you have never worked before, and never, never, never quit.

Faith acts as a safety valve to release the pressure that you put on yourself to perform at your best. It helps you put every athletic contest into proper perspective. It lets you see that there are many ways to become a winner. First, become a winner in life. Then, it's easier to become a winner on the playing field.

In my lifetime, I've gone through a lot of good times and some not-so-good times. When I look back at these experiences, I realize that I felt more alive during the frustration periods and disappointments. I had to do some serious soul searching by means of a good "gut check" to see what I was made of. It was during these times that I relied on my faith the most. It was the foundation from which I could go forth. It was, and still is, a tremendous help to me to know that no matter how bad things get, I'm not alone.

One final point. Don't ever think you're too important, too cool or too tough to talk to God. I do it all the time. I thank Him for the challenges and tests He has given me. Or, when the going gets real tough, I say something like, "Okay, I understand what you're doing; you're testing me. Couldn't you test someone else for a couple of days until I figure a way out of the mess I'm in now?"

On the other hand, when things are going smoothly and I'm a bit bored, I say, "What's wrong, don't you trust me anymore? I never let you down before, did I? Give me some more challenges. Lay them on me." I sincerely believe that the more problems or challenges a person faces, the more alive he or she is. Challenges build character.

But faith alone is not enough. Just thinking like a winner doesn't automatically make you one. If this was the simple formula to success, there would be no losers. The key to success is to blend positive thinking with hard work and perseverance. If you can do this, you'll be a winner. Our team motto is: "You can beat anyone if you work harder than he does." It works for us; it can work for you.

FAITH

TOMMY LASORDA
Major League Manager

Always remember these words: "Because God delays does not mean that God denies."

FLOYD PATTERSON
Professional Boxer

A dream is a seed which with hard work and discipline will grow; faith in God, which in turn will give you faith in yourself, will bear fruit.

DICK VAN ARSDALE
NBA Forward

Overall, a sound spiritual view of life and the placement of athletics in its proper place and perspective is more important than anything else.

GERRY FAUST
College Football Coach

It takes a special dedication to be an athlete. It is very similar to being a Christian and having faith in your God. Everyone has the opportunity to believe in God, but some do not work at it. Your faith is given to you by God, but it is up to you to nurture it and to make it stronger. The most important thing you have in your life is your faith, and it will help you through many trials and tribulations.

J. F. CLARKE
American Unitarian Clergyman

All the strength and force of man comes from his faith in things unseen. He who believes is strong; he who doubts is weak. Strong convictions precede great actions.

NORMAN VINCENT PEALE
Clergyman/American Writer

The greatest secret for eliminating the inferiority complex, which is another term for deep and profound self-doubt, is to fill your mind to overflowing with faith. Develop a tremendous faith in God and that will give you a humble yet soundly realistic faith in yourself.

JOE NAMATH
NFL Quarterback and Sports Broadcaster

I prepared myself beforehand until I knew that I could do what I had to do. Then I had faith.

CYRUS H. K. CURTIS
American Publisher

If you believe in the Lord, He will do half the work—but the last half. He helps those who help themselves.

GEORGE FOSTER
Major League Outfielder

The key to life is twofold. One needs to believe in his heart and confess with his mouth. Along those same lines, one needs to have balance in life. He should strive to be strong spiritually, physically and mentally. Also, remember that success is finding a need and filling it. It is not what one accomplishes that makes him grow, but the hurdles or obstacles he has to overcome. So believe in yourself, be disciplined, strive for that balance, and keep the faith.

JACOBI
German Philosopher/Writer

Every great example takes hold of us with the authority of a miracle, and says to us, "If ye had but faith, ye, also, could do the same things."

THOMAS J. WATSON
American Industrialist

The greatest asset of a man, a business or a nation is faith.

The men who built this country and those who made it prosper during its darkest days were men whose faith in its future was unshakable.

ROY CAMPANELLA
Major League Catcher

Without faith, you don't have much chance. I pray every day now, as I have every day of my life. I used to say a prayer before each game just before the National Anthem. I didn't pray for victory. The good Lord's not out there to win a ball game for you. You shouldn't ask him for that kind of help. I prayed that I would stay healthy and not get hurt. I don't think the Lord has turned His back on me.

RON TURCOTTE
Professional Jockey

You have to have faith in God and faith in yourself if you want others to have faith in you.

BUCKY DENT
Major League Shortstop and Manager

You must have a dream about your future. Remember that if you allow God to be a partner in your life, He will help you with all your dreams. But remember, the Lord expects your cooperation. You must be willing to give of yourself totally, that is, spiritually, mentally, emotionally, and physically. Have courage and put your faith in Christ, for He will help you fulfill your dreams.

STAN SMITH
Professional Tennis Player and Sports Broadcaster

If we prepare thoughtfully, work hard, have faith in God's plan for us and are honest with ourselves, we can most closely reach the perfection of our talents. By doing this, we can live in peace with ourselves and our accomplishments.

MIKE BOSSY
NHL Right Wing

Scoring goals is just something I've always been able to do—a talent from God.

RON GUIDRY
Major League Pitcher

I pray often and I know God hears all my prayers. He may not answer them in the way I desire, but He knows what is best for me. I say a prayer before each game that I pitch. It is not a prayer for victory; it is a prayer of gratitude for my health and a plea for God's continued blessings. There are so many more important things in life than winning baseball games. When I win a game, I know it is God's grace. When I lose, I know there are many people with more serious problems.

REVEREND JOHN F. MURPHY
Superintendent of Education
Diocese of Cleveland

Motivation in any competitive sports' program is linked with the ability of the individual to come into an inner contact with personal goals, objectives, feelings and attitudes. This coming into contact is achieved through setting aside some time each day for personal reflection or what is often called "prayer." In prayer, the athlete reviews the goal that has been set and reviews the objectives or steps that will help to achieve that goal.

MIKE SCHMIDT
Major League Third Baseman

I think the most rewarding thing a person can have happen to him is to find out what God's purpose is for him and go ahead and do it well. To come to know what the Lord's purpose is for you in life, and then do it well, to give it all you have is rewarding. Baseball is what God gave me—it's my purpose in life.

BOB RICHARDS
Pole Vaulter—Two Time Olympic Gold Medalist

One reason why I think a great deal of Jesus is because He never pointed out the weaknesses of people, never dwelt on their failures and their shortcomings. He always thought of the dream that God had for their lives. Never emphasizing their failures, He simply said, "Go and sin no more. Be what God intends you to be."

BROOKS ROBINSON
Major League Third Baseman

As a youngster I had several idols. One was Doak Walker, former three-time All-American from SMU and Detroit Lion All-Pro. I was fortunate enough to hear Doak Walker speak one night and someone asked him what was the most important thing in becoming a success in life. His reply was a very simple one, but one I have applied to my life ever since that day. He said the most important thing in becoming a success was the three P's—practice, perseverance, and **PRAYER**. You have to practice to do anything well. Nothing comes free. You have to pay the price to get to the top in anything you attempt. Perseverance is being able to bounce back from the many roadblocks that one finds along life's way. And prayer, the most important of all, is the art of honestly asking God to help you in everything you undertake in life.

RICHARD PRYOR
Actor

When there was nothing left but the raw nerves, I didn't call my mother or the bank or any producer. I called God.

KYLE ROTE, JR.
Professional Soccer Player

Doing anything well doesn't just lead to success—it is success. Real success in life begins with acceptance—acceptance of God's belief in you as a unique and special person.

STEVE BARTKOWSKI
NFL Quarterback

Being benched in 1978 was the lowest I've been in my life, but it was the best thing that ever happened to me. My priorities were all wrong. Football was the most important thing in my world. It was my god and I was losing the ability to handle it. Those boos totally overturned me as a person. I had to do a lot of thinking, but finally I gave everything to God. He's given it back to me tenfold.

Faith

We're a rugged breed, us quads. If we weren't, we wouldn't be around today. Yes, we're a rugged breed; in many ways, we've been blessed with a savvy and spirit that isn't given to everybody.

And let me say that this refusal of total or full acceptance of one's disability all hooks up with one thing—faith, an almost divine faith.

Down in the reception room of the Institute of Physical Medicine and Rehabilitation, over on the East River at 400 East 34th Street in New York City, there is a bronze plaque that's riveted to the wall. During the months of coming back to the Institute for treatment—two and three times a week—I rolled through that reception room many times, coming and going. But I never quite made the time to pull over to one side and read the words on that plaque that were written, it's said, by an unknown Confederate Soldier. Then one afternoon, I did. I read it, and then I read it again. When I finished it the second time I was near to bursting—not in despair, but with an inner glow that had me straining to grip the arms of my wheelchair. I'd like to share it with you.

ROY CAMPANELLA   Major League Catcher

A Creed For Those Who Have Suffered

I asked God for strength, that I might achieve.
   I was made weak, that I might learn humbly to obey…

I asked for health, that I might do greater things.
   I was given infirmity, that I might do better things…

I asked for riches, that I might be happy.
   I was given poverty, that I might be wise…

I asked for power, that I might have the praise of men.
   I was given weakness, that I might feel the need of God…

I asked for all things, that I might enjoy life.
   I was given life, that I might enjoy all things…

I got nothing I asked for—but everything I had hoped for.

Almost despite myself, my unspoken prayers were answered.

   I am, among men, most richly blessed!

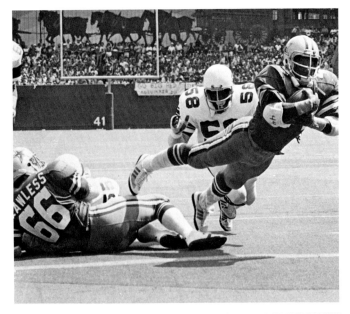
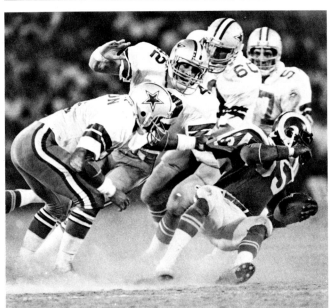

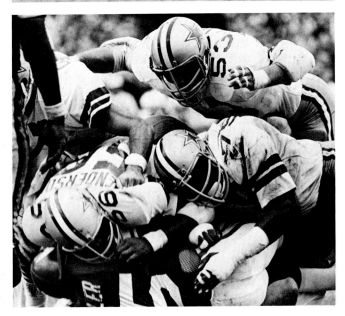

Trying To Win Is Everything

You have read where coaches have been quoted as saying, "Winning isn't everything; it's the only thing." I don't believe that this is true. I do believe that trying to win is everything. I've seen many outstanding winners in professional football that never played in a Super Bowl or won their Conference. One of our favorite slogans is "A winner never stops trying."

We recognize that God has given us the talent to become an athlete, even though some have more talent than others. I've discovered that it isn't how much talent you have that makes you successful; it is the ability to use all the talent you have—it is the ability to reach your full potential.

Winning then becomes a "state of mind". Most of the athletes who fail to become winners are those athletes whose fears and anxieties prevent them from reaching their potential. I overcame my fears and anxieties by a commitment to something far greater than winning a football game—a commitment to Jesus Christ.

Apostle Paul explained my discovery in I Corinthians 9:24-27 better than I can:

> "In a race, everyone runs, but only one person gets first prize. So run your race to win. To win the contest, you must deny yourselves many things that would keep you from doing your best. An athlete goes to all this trouble just to win a ribbon or a silver cup, but we do it for a heavenly reward that never disappears. So I run straight to the goal with purpose in every step. I fight to win. I'm not just shadow-boxing or playing around. Like an athlete, I punish my body, treating it roughly, training it to do what it should, not what it wants to. Otherwise, I fear that after enlisting others for the race, I myself might be declared unfit and ordered to stand aside."

TOM LANDRY   **NFL Defensive Back and Coach**

I believe everything begins with a positive idea. Positive thinking is the key to success in business, education, pro football, anything that you mention. The mind is our most powerful muscle. If you think you're tired, you'll feel tired. I go out there thinking I'm going to complete every pass.

Ron Jaworski, NFL Quarterback

My biggest problem was my mental attitude. I was just 17 when I won the overall men's world title and that just didn't seem right. It had to be a fluke. The guys I beat had all been beating me. They were all 25 years old and had been training all their lives. It wasn't until then that I knew that training the way I did would pay off. That I could really expect to get something in return for it. That now I could expect to win.

Eric Heiden,
Speed Skater—Five Time Olympic Gold Medalist

> I'm convinced that mental attitude has a lot to do with winning. Once I proved to myself that I could win, it was only victories that counted for me.
>
> Ingemar Stenmark,
> Skier — Two Time Olympic Gold Medalist

POSITIVE MENTAL ATTITUDE

A positive mental attitude (PMA) means developing a positive outlook in life that lets you do anything you want to do in any part of your life, at any time. You create an image of yourself as a winning athlete; then you go out and win. To do this, you must:

1. Acquire the skills required by your sport.
2. Improve these skills with hours of "perfect" practice.
3. Get yourself into peak physical condition.
4. Achieve some level of success which will motivate you to work even harder.

This cycle of success includes learning, working hard and succeeding. It then repeats itself. Once you enjoy the level of success you've achieved, you'll learn more, work more and succeed even more. This pattern continues until you've reached your full potential as an athlete.

To win, you must act as if it's impossible to fail. Decide that records exist only to be broken. Your will to win overcomes all obstacles that get in your way. You expect to win. It's as simple as that.

It comes down to this. If you expect the best, you'll get it. If you expect the worst, you'll get it. Your mental attitude determines your outcome. That's what separates winners from losers — in life and in sports. Champions always say that if you expect to lose, you already have.

There are two ways to look at things that happen to you — the positive way and the negative way. Losers and negative people discount good things that happen by calling them "lucky." Winners — positive people — refuse to perceive defeats or problems as bad. They're seen as temporary setbacks to learn from and improve.

Don't be susceptible to the negative influence of other people. During your entire life, you'll have someone telling you what you can't do. It's very easy to be negative; it's much harder to be positive. Don't let yourself be dragged down by other people's negative thoughts, words and actions. Negative attitudes are contagious, but so are positive ones. Show how positive you are by performing. Have a positive attitude — look for the best in other people and in every situation. Let others catch your enthusiastic attitude.

You make or break yourself by how you think. Success or failure depends on how you think about yourself. Positive thinkers get positive results; they believe in themselves. This self-confidence affects their careers, personal relations and even their health. They reach their career goals, get along with other people and are rarely sick.

Also, positive thinkers are drawn to, and attract, other positive people. They send out and receive positive impulses and thoughts from each other. They energize everything around them.

Negative thinkers are a dangerous group. They believe that everything and everybody is bad. They draw negative people to them; they react negatively to other people; and they always expect the worst to happen. And since they only look at one side of every situation — the worst does happen.

Get the edge over your competitors and start developing a positive mental attitude.

POSITIVE MENTAL ATTITUDE

DAN FOUTS
NFL Quarterback and Sports Broadcaster

It's hard to separate the mental and the physical. So much of what you do physically happens because you've thought about it and mentally prepared for it.

THOMAS A. BUCKNER
American Writer

I am glad I am an optimist. The pessimist is half-licked before he starts. The optimist has won half the battle, the most important half that applies to himself, when he begins his approach to a subject with the proper mental attitude. The optimist may not understand, or if he understands, he may not agree with prevailing ideas; but he believes, yes, knows, that in the long run and in due course there will prevail whatever is right and best.

DENNIS LEONARD
Major League Pitcher

I have a positive approach. Instead of thinking about how the guy at the plate hit me last time, I remember how I got him out.

JACKIE STEWART
Race Car Driver and Sports Broadcaster

I never look at racing from the darker side, always the brighter side. I don't get my kicks from flirting with death. I flirt with life. It's not that I enjoy the risks, the dangers and the challenges of a race. I enjoy the life it gives me. When I finish a race, the sky looks bluer, the grass looks greener, the air feels fresher. It's so much better to be alive.

BRUCE JENNER
Decathlon—Olympic Gold Medalist

The decathlon was a constant challenge for me. I always wanted to do better. I had a very positive mental attitude. If I ran 100 meters in 11.2, I felt sure I could do it in 11.1. If I broad jumped 21 feet, I was positive I could do 22.

THOMAS JEFFERSON
Third President

Nothing can stop the man with the right mental attitude from achieving his goal; nothing on earth can help the man with the wrong mental attitude.

LOUISE W. EGGLESTON
American Writer

Anyone who looks for the good can always find much for which to be grateful, or he can dwell on the present evil and wreck his composure…There is always an answer for every problem.

WOODY HAYES
College Football Coach

We control by attitudes—positive mental attitudes—not by rules.

ABRAHAM LINCOLN
Sixteenth President

Most people are about as happy as they make up their minds to be.

GERRY FAUST
College Football Coach

Have you ever had a day when you get up in the morning and something goes wrong and you say, "Jimminy, it's going to be one of those days?" I bet you do that a lot; I've done it. But you know what I say now? "Well, it started out bad, but it's still going to be a great day." And you'd be amazed how it turns a bad day into a good day.

DARWIN P. KINGSLEY
American Insurance Executive

You all have powers you never dreamed of. You can do things you never thought you could do. There are no limitations in what you can do except the limitations in your own mind as to what you cannot do. Don't think you cannot. Think you can.

WADE SCHALLES
Wrestler — National Champion and College Wrestling Coach

Winners expect to win before the contest starts; losers don't. Any individual becomes what he or she thinks about most. If you want to be a champion, then that thought must dominate your life. But most important, winners dwell on the rewards of winning; losers dwell on the penalties of failure.

NORMAN VINCENT PEALE
Clergyman/American Writer

If you or I or anybody thinks constantly of the forces that seem to be against us, we will build them up into a power far beyond that which is justified. But if, on the contrary, you mentally visualize and affirm and re-affirm your assets and keep your thoughts on them, emphasizing them to the fullest extent, you will rise out of any difficulty regardless of what it may be.

CHARLES SIMMONS
American Manufacturer

Our attitudes control our lives. Attitudes are a secret power working 24 hours a day, for good or bad. It is of paramount importance that we know how to harness and control this great force.

STEVE CARLTON
Major League Pitcher

Man is the only one who puts limitations on himself. There are really no limits. A lot of professional athletes play beneath their ability. They may believe they are giving 100 percent, but they aren't because they are not thinking at their peak. You can create an atmosphere about yourself, positive or negative.

STEVE STONE
Major League Pitcher and Sports Broadcaster

There are two halves to the mind—conscious and subconscious. The subconscious doesn't have the power of rationality, so it can work for you or against you. If you keep telling yourself that you can't do something, you won't do it. When you haven't had success, you have to reprogram your subconscious. It's like wiping a blackboard clean and starting over. The spring before I won the Cy Young Award, I had to sit down and convince myself that I was better than a .500 pitcher.

GENE MILLS
Wrestler—World Champion

The first thing you've got to do is believe. You know, if you believe you can do it, you can. Like when I saw Yugi Takada in the 1979 World Championships. I just didn't think there was anyone in the world who could go with him. That was in August of '79. In December I had to wrestle him in Japan. I said, "wait a minute," I'm going to give this man the best match of his life. And I really believed I could beat him. I thought I'd rip that guy apart. I just went out there and gave him everything I possibly could and it was 19-15. Even though I lost, nobody ever scored that much on him. I gave him the best match he'd ever had in his life. He came up to me after the match and said, "you-too much, too much," and then he retired. I don't know, I just think you have to believe in yourself and give it everything you possibly have. If you do, you can be happy with yourself. If you had a little more left, you should kick yourself in the butt.

FRANCO HARRIS
NFL Fullback

How you look at a situation is very important, for how you think about a problem may defeat you before you ever do anything about it. When you get discouraged or depressed, try changing your attitude from negative to positive and see how life can change for you. Remember, your attitude toward a situation can help you change it—you create the very atmosphere for defeat or victory.

HARRY CARSON
NFL Linebacker

Teams just beat themselves. They psyche themselves out. They don't think they can win, so they don't. They get beat by doubt.

J. H. BRENNAN
American Businessman/Executive

Almost everybody walks around with a vast burden of imaginary limitations inside his head. While the burden remains, personal success is as difficult to achieve as the conquest of Everest is with a sack of rocks tied to your back.

ARNOLD BENNETT
English Novelist and Playwright

Worry is evidence of an ill-controlled brain; it is merely a stupid waste of time in unpleasantness. If men and women practiced mental calisthenics as they do physical calisthenics, they would purge their brains of this foolishness.

RANDY WHITE
NFL Defensive Tackle

I'm kind of in my own world out there. I do something called psychocybernetics 15 minutes a day visualizing positive things, like sacking quarterbacks. By Sunday I'm in a shell. I don't know names and faces, just the guy I have to beat.

HARRY TRUMAN
Thirty-Third President

A pessimist is one who makes difficulties of his opportunities; an optimist is one who makes opportunities of his difficulties.

JOE PATERNO
College Football Coach and Athletic Director

You've got to believe deep inside yourself that you're destined to do great things.

JOE FRAZIER
Professional Boxer, Trainer and Manager

There's one thing I don't ever think about—losing. A fighter who thinks about losing is a born loser. Instead, I think about how I'm going to win, how I can do it the quickest way.

SUGAR RAY ROBINSON
Professional Boxer

I've always believed that you can think positive just as well as you can think negative.

BART STARR
NFL Quarterback and Coach

If there was just one word I could use to describe a successful person, that one word would be attitude.

JOHN RALSTON
NFL Coach

Success comes in cans, not in cannots.

JIMMY "THE GREEK" SNYDER
Sports Broadcaster

If you could only tell the mental attitude of a team before a game. That's the whole thing—attitude—which team wants to win more.

HAROLD SHERMAN
American Banker

If you are anticipating the worst while hoping for the best, you will get the worst. The things that happen to you are in direct accordance with the things wherein you place your faith. Believe you are licked—and you are.

BRUCE JENNER
Decathlon—Olympic Gold Medalist

Around Bruce Jenner you don't ever talk about losing and you never talk about the possibility of defeat. Talk about winning and believe it will happen.

JACK MC KINNEY—POSITIVE THINKING GOT HIM THROUGH A VERY ROUGH TIME

Jack McKinney nearly lost his life in a bicycling accident in November, 1979. His head and face were so severely smashed that the people who found him thought that he was dead. The accident did cause him to lose his job as coach of the Los Angeles Lakers, although he didn't know it at the time.

While McKinney was hospitalized, the Lakers put assistant coach Paul Westhead in charge of the team. Westhead led the Lakers to the NBA title and owner Jerry Buss decided Westhead would remain as head coach.

When McKinney found out that he wouldn't get his job back, he went into a deep state of depression. Then, Indiana Pacer owner Sam Nassi called McKinney and offered him the head coaching job with the Pacers.

He took over the Indiana team on June 2, 1980. In that season, McKinney led the Pacers to their first spot in the playoffs. He was named NBA Coach of the Year that season.

McKinney's special message about overcoming adversity is:

"That which has carried me through a very trying period of my life is the psychological factor of always thinking positively and looking forward to the best thing happening to me all the time. It seems to me that if you think negatively, you can condition yourself to expect negations, and usually end up with that. And I think back to one saying which I constantly shoot forth with when my team is laying down a little or feeling sorry for themselves. At this time, I give out one of my real winners. 'You want to lose, go ahead and lose; anyone can lose. Tough guys find out some way of winning the game. So get tough.'"

"No matter what happens, you can't expend energy worrying about what people think. I have to face things head-on. To overcome any adversity, all you need is time—just make sure that all your steps are forward."

When I perform now, I'm not really afraid because I know what I'm doing. You have to have the trick down or don't use it. To hit your routine the best you can possibly hit it, that's just a super feeling.

**Kurt Thomas, Gymnast —
Olympic Gold Medalist**

Nothing can shake my self-confidence. When you reach a certain level, you never experience the slightest anxiety. There's never the slightest apprehension.

**Jean-Claude Killy, Skier —
Three Time Olympic Gold Medalist**

Sometimes when I start a play, I never know if I will be able to do what I would like. But I always go ahead and try. I have confidence in my ability as a basketball player. I guess deep down inside I know it will work.

Julius Erving, NBA Forward

CONFIDENCE

Confidence enables you to perform to the best of your abilities. It also gives you the freedom to perform without the fear of failure holding you back.

Confidence is a combination of mental and physical skills gained from hours of practicing "the right way." You must develop the mental confidence which allows you to push yourself physically. Together, mental and physical confidence give you the edge. It's impossible to "think like a winner," unless you can prove to yourself that you have the capability to be a winner. That's why preparation and practice are so important. You can't just wake up one day and think you're good — you have to become good.

A coach can't tell a player to have confidence — although many do. Others criticize their players for lacking confidence. What they should do is point out that if a player hasn't prepared to win, then he or she hasn't worked hard enough. It's not a lack of confidence as much as it is a lack of preparation.

As a coach, I'll take a well-prepared wrestler over a highly-confident one any day. When an athlete has totally committed himself to hard work, sacrifice and practice, it's easy to get him fired up. He's earned the right to be fired up; he knows he's ready. All you have to do is remind him of the price he has paid. He's ready to receive his just rewards.

The greatest pep talk in the history of locker-room coaching won't help an athlete who has cheated on his or her preparation. Athletes are either ready or they're not. If they're not, it's because they haven't worked hard enough — that is, they haven't prepared. Get yourself ready to pay the price and earn the right to have confidence.

Be honest. Don't fool yourself. Learn a sport the correct way from the beginning. For instance, learn how to swing a golf club the right way. Hit a thousand balls a day. Get yourself in prime physical condition. Play some good rounds of golf. Only then will you have earned the right of self-confidence.

I love to get people to believe in themselves. That's very important because 95% of the people don't believe in themselves as they should. Most people feel they don't have as much talent, ability, intelligence or looks as other people. I tell them to answer only one simple question: "Am I doing the very best I possibly can; and am I doing it every day?"

If I tell our wrestlers they're terrible and they stink — guess what? They'll go to great extremes to prove me right. The most important thing I can do as a coach is to get people to believe in themselves; and to care about each other. At St. Edward High School, we say that when you bring a group of people together, it's a start. When you get them to stay together, it's progress. And when you get them to work together, it's success.

How do you get a group of people to work together? Get them to like one another, believe in one another and not feel insecure. When you don't feel insecure, it's easy to look for the good qualities in other people. If you don't believe in yourself, you're constantly looking for the negative things in other people.

CONFIDENCE

YOGI BERRA
Major League Catcher and Manager
I never blame myself when I'm not hitting; I just blame the bat and if it keeps up, I change bats. I know that sounds silly, but it keeps me from getting down in the dumps when I'm in a slump. It keeps my confidence up.

WOODY HAYES
College Football Coach
It's never an upset if the so-called underdog has all along considered itself the better team.

TOM LANDRY
NFL Defensive Back and Coach
I don't believe in team motivation. I believe in getting a team prepared so that it knows it will have the necessary confidence when it steps on the field and be prepared to play a good game.

JOHNNY UNITAS
NFL Quarterback
There is a difference between conceit and confidence. A quarterback has to have confidence. Conceit is bragging about yourself. Confidence means you believe you can get the job done. I have always believed that I could get the job done.

VINCE LOMBARDI
NFL Coach and General Manager
Confidence comes from planning and practicing well. You get ready during the week and the confidence will be there on Sunday. This confidence is a difficult thing to explain. But you do get it and the team gets it if you have prepared properly.

VELI SAARINEN
Skier—Olympic Gold Medalist
I'll win because I have been training for this minute all my life. All my life.

ROGER STAUBACH
NFL Quarterback and Sports Broadcaster
Confidence comes from hours and days and weeks and years of constant work and dedication. When I'm in the last two minutes of a December playoff game, I'm drawing confidence from wind sprints I did the previous March. It's just a circle: work and confidence, then more work and more confidence.

CHUCK KNOX
NFL Coach
One of the most important qualities for any young athlete is the ability to believe in oneself. If you have confidence in yourself, in your teammates and in your coach, you will succeed.

JOHN HAVLICEK
NBA Forward
Confidence comes from preparation and the only way to be fully prepared is to practice something until you have it down so well you're pretty sure it will work.

DICK VAN ARSDALE
NBA Forward
I'm a firm believer in quiet confidence. By that I mean knowing inwardly that you are good, and not exhibiting a boastful attitude outwardly. If an athlete doesn't believe in himself, no one else will.

CHUCK NOLL
NFL Linebacker and Coach
As you gain experience, you mature as an individual, and along with that comes the confidence that you have the ability to solve problems.

ROGER STAUBACH
NFL Quarterback and Sports Broadcaster
Every time I stepped on the field, I believed my team was going to walk off the winner, somehow, someway.

ARTHUR ASHE, JR.
Professional Tennis Player and Sports Broadcaster
One important key to success is self-confidence. An important key to self-confidence is preparation. Complete mental and physical preparation has to do with sacrifice and self-discipline. And that comes from within. Start by setting modest goals which are meaningful, but attainable. For example, every Sunday night write down four things that you want to accomplish for the following week, and then make sure that seven days later when you make up your next list, all four items have been crossed off. These small but meaningful completed tasks should generate much self-confidence as time goes by.

ROLLIE FINGERS
Major League Relief Pitcher
A big part of relief pitching is confidence. If you don't have it, you're not going to get many people out. Whenever we're in a jam, I always hope the call is for me when the telephone rings in the bullpen.

GARY PLAYER
Professional Golfer

On his 1974 Masters Golf Championship: I knew I was going to win on the first tee. It's the best golf I've ever played in a major championship, all the way.

When I work for something, I expect it to happen. No one works as hard at golf as I do. No athlete has ever traveled so much as I have. I say all this only to try to make everybody understand what it means to me to win. There's no way to properly describe the gratification from working so hard, and then being rewarded for it.

JOHN MC ENROE
Professional Tennis Player

I'm confident on the court. I like the way I play. I don't have any particular weaknesses. I have an all-round game. I think it's the mark of a great player to be confident in tough situations.

GEORGE BLANDA
NFL Quarterback/Kicker

I never think that I'll miss a kick. When they call on me, I'll be ready and when they set the ball down, I'll put it through.

Y. A. TITTLE
NFL Quarterback

You have to have a past history of some success to give yourself status and self-confidence. You have to accomplish something before you can believe in yourself.

MARTINA NAVRATILOVA
Professional Tennis Player

You have to want to win and expect that you are going to win. Top players have that edge. Even if they're down a few games, they know they're going to toughen up and come up with what it takes to win.

LARRY CSONKA
NFL Fullback and Sports Broadcaster

Inside, a good running back feels like he's somebody who can't be caught, who's always got the edge. He's the gambler who's always got the odds going for him. He's got tremendous confidence. One way or another, he knows he's going to get the touchdown or the first down. You've got to feel that you can do it. If you have the feeling that you're going to be stopped, you will be.

ERIC HEIDEN
**Speed Skater—
Five Time Olympic Gold Medalist**

Sometimes when I'm racing and I'm really stroking strong, I can feel the ice breaking away beneath me. It is a wonderful feeling because it means that I have reached the limit, the ice can't hold me back anymore. Confidence was the most important quality for me to develop before I could even think about running the big races.

TOM LANDRY
NFL Defensive Back and Coach

The basic problem that you face is developing a losing pattern. The most difficult thing in coaching is to overcome the feeling that you're going to lose. If you are prepared, then you will be confident and you will do the job. It's as simple as that.

TOMMY HEARNS
Professional Boxer

What my mother didn't realize, what nobody felt but me, was that I always knew I would make it to the top. I knew it.

HUBERT GREEN
Professional Golfer

Winning breeds confidence and confidence breeds winning.

JIM PLUNKETT
NFL Quarterback

In 1980, I played in Oakland a lot like I played in New England, but I was more mature and knew more about what I was doing. I still scrambled, threw on the run and played with reckless abandon, but this time I had no doubt in my mind that when we stepped on the field that we were going to win. The whole difference was a positive mental attitude. I had confidence.

JOE MONTANA
NFL Quarterback

Confidence is a very fragile thing. Just because you have it in college doesn't mean you're gonna have it in the pros. A lot of young quarterbacks get eaten up in the NFL because their confidence is shattered.

DAVE KINGMAN
Major League Outfielder

I've improved some aspects of my game, some of the negatives. The big thing is that I've learned to relax and be confident. Anyone performs better when he's relaxed. If you're relaxed, you're more patient, more selective. It's all in the head. Hitting is so much mental, so much confidence.

DALE MURPHY
Major League Outfielder

Confidence, I guess, is the name of the game. Last year, I didn't really do anything, and it's hard to stay confident when you're not doing anything. I never had doubts about my ability to play the game. I was just not happy, just disappointed, about the season I had. If you are out there doubting yourself, you won't be successful.

ROBIN YOUNT
Major League Shortstop

I had to learn to play in the major leagues. People said I had great potential, but they didn't understand that I needed time to learn to play the game after only a half-season in the minors. For me, it was a matter of confidence in myself. I'd get into bad streaks, and it would get to me, which made it worse. Now, I've learned to handle it better. I have more confidence in my ability to play major league baseball.

CAL RIPKEN, JR.
Major League Third Baseman

I started to use an uppercut swing because home runs were expected of me. Then, every day I didn't get a hit, my confidence sank lower and lower. It was starting to get to me. I was trying so many different stances, taking everybody's advice and getting confused. I had to realize that I had to go back to what I did to get here. Now, I'm driving the ball and my bat is quicker. I have my confidence back.

I'll tell you with my lead that I'm going to steal second base. You know I'm going to, but there's nothing you can do to stop it.

Lou Brock, Major League Outfielder

I am the greatest. I said that even before I knew I was. Don't tell me I can't do something. Don't tell me it's impossible. Don't tell me I'm not the greatest. I'm the double greatest.

Muhammad Ali, Professional Boxer

INNER ARROGANCE

All true champions have inner arrogance. It's that confident feeling they have that says, "I have the edge over you," or, "You don't have a chance against me." It's the same feeling that Lou Brock had standing squarely on the bag after stealing yet another base — as if it was his alone. It's the same feeling Muhammad Ali had as he prepared to prove once again that he was "the greatest."

This confident attitude of "I can't lose" is a powerful psychological tool great athletes use in gaining the edge over their opponents. They know there's plenty of time to be reserved and humble — but the period spent getting ready to perform is not one of them.

Before a game, you should remind yourself of the many long hours of work you've put into your sport, the sacrifices you've made, the skills you've learned and the many successes you've enjoyed. You know you're good. Soon you'll be on center stage again to prove it. It's a feeling of confidence only champions have the right to experience.

When you're flying, don't fly too high. Always play within yourself. Inner arrogance allows you to perform up to the level of your capabilities, not beyond. Only additional practice will take you beyond.

Play the percentages. Take calculated risks, but don't take unnecessary chances. When you gamble foolishly, you give up your edge. Be fundamental, not flashy. Don't forget the basics. If you become complacent, your skill will carry you for only so long; then you'll fail.

Some of the biggest thrills in my life have come from the athletes that I have coached. Just watching their demeanor on the mat was stimulating. So was their poise, presence, how they warmed up; the way they walked out onto the mat and shook hands with their opponents. Everything about them screamed, "I am the greatest!" They were truly great. They knew it. Their opponents knew it. They had inner arrogance.

The best example of inner arrogance I remember was a young man who was a three-year starter for us. In three years, he placed third, second and then first in the state, finishing high school with 123 wins and only three losses — 88 of those wins coming on falls.

What made that record exceptional was that he wasn't particularly strong or powerful. Actually, he had only average strength. What he did have, though, was above-average confidence. He honestly thought that everyone he wrestled was inferior, and that he was far superior. He made me laugh when he talked about his strength and made a muscle with his skinny arm. Then, I'd stop laughing as he walked onto the mat and put another wrestler on his back. He was a perfect example of inner arrogance.

There's no way to properly describe the gratification an athlete receives from working hard and being rewarded for those hours of work. There's also no way to describe the feeling you get when, after hundreds of hours of work, you realize that you have finally corrected your weaknesses and that you are good — very good. Not perfect, but on top of your game and better than your competition.

My advice to you is simple. Keep practicing. Become good. Become great. Then become the best. Use inner arrogance to your advantage. It will make you a winner!

INNER ARROGANCE

SUGAR RAY LEONARD
Professional Boxer and Sports Broadcaster

Everybody knows I don't have a knockout punch. I just keep coming on strong. Put King Kong in front of me and I'll still keep coming until I knock him out.

RON GUIDRY
Major League Pitcher

When I'm strong and throwing hard, the hitters aren't going to hit me much. I don't care if they bring a telephone pole up there.

GEORGE GERVIN
NBA Guard

I know that I can score if I have the ball in my hands. I know I can take whatever shot I want to and do it from any position and from any angle. Whether anybody believes it or not, I probably took 1,000 shots a day when I was a kid.

GEORGE BRETT
Major League Third Baseman

I feel I can hit a fastball as well as anyone. The harder they throw it, the better I like it.

LESTER HAYES
NFL Defensive Back

It's baffling, but I hit a streak where I felt that I had such a positive, driving force at work that I simply couldn't be beaten on a pass. Call it confidence or call it what you like, but it was a feeling of being in complete control.

LOU BOUDREAU
Major League Shortstop and Manager

I put a chip on my shoulder and spit on my hands and got ready to argue with the whole American League. (When many experts were forecasting the Indians for a third-place league finish in 1948. Led by Boudreau, they went on to win the pennant.)

PETE ROSE
Major League First Baseman and Manager

When people ask me, "Who was the toughest pitcher you ever faced?", I have to say that there has never been a pitcher who over-impressed me. That's not meant to be a bragging statement. It's just that I get up for good pitchers. Truthfully, I never faced a pitcher that I didn't think I could get a hit from.

JOE GARAGIOLA
Major League Catcher and Sports Broadcaster

Inner Arrogance. You're good; you know it, but you don't wear it on your sleeve. You don't have to tell anyone you've got it; they know it. You start to tell them and it usually ends up lip service.

Don't tell me you can hit…hit.
Don't tell me you can pitch…pitch.
Don't tell me you can sell…sell.

ROGER HORNSBY
Major League Infielder

When I was in the batter's box, I felt sorry for the pitcher.

WARREN SPAHN
Major League Pitcher and Coach

I was surprised when anyone got a hit because only I knew where I was going to pitch the ball and how fast it was going to go.

BOBBY LAYNE
NFL Quarterback

I've never lost a game in my life. Once in a while, time ran out on me.

RON JAWORSKI
NFL Quarterback

Some people think I'm cocky. I'm not that at all. I just feel that if they ask me to throw 100 passes, I can complete 100.

MUHAMMAD ALI
Professional Boxer

It's hard to be humble when you're as great as I am.

STEVE CAUTHEN
Professional Jockey

Sure my record is amazing, but it's not luck. I never stop to think of how lucky I am because luck has nothing to do with it.

WILLIE MAYS
Major League Outfielder

When I was going good, there was nothing they could do except walk me.

JOE MORGAN
Major League Second Baseman and Sports Broadcaster

To be a star and to stay a star, I think you've got to have a certain air of arrogance about you, a cockiness, a swagger on the field that says, "I can do this and you can't stop me". I know that I play baseball with this air of arrogance, but I think it's lacking in a lot of guys who have the potential to be stars.

TIM RAINES
Major League Outfielder

My fast start in the big leagues wasn't surprising. I knew I could hit major league pitching, and if I got on base, I knew I could steal bases.

JERRY WEST
NBA Guard, Coach and General Manager

I don't believe I can miss a shot out there. I think I can score every time I get the ball.

LESTER HAYES
NFL Defensive Back

The thing is to put yourself on a plateau where you say you can't be beat. It's imperative that you have a degree of cockiness. There's no mere mortal I fear. I am auspiciously euphoric.

CECIL COOPER
Major League Outfielder

I feel that nobody can get me out. No negative thinking. I'm the master of the plate.

BABE RUTH
Major League Pitcher/Outfielder

Do I deserve to make more money than President Hoover? Why not? I had a better year than he did.

JACK KRAMER
Professional Tennis Player

When a guy ran up a lead on me, I was surprised. I thought that he was either playing over his head or he was lucky.

DAN FOUTS
NFL Quarterback and Sports Broadcaster

My career has shown me that in order to win you must expect to win. It's the confidence factor. In fact, you might even call it an arrogance factor.

BOB GIBSON
Major League Pitcher

I guess I was never much in awe of anybody. I think you have to have that attitude if you're going to go far in this game. People have always said that I was too confident, but I think you'll find that most guys who can play are pretty cocky. I've always been that way. I always thought I was good enough to play with anyone.

DAVE PARKER
Major League Outfielder

I'm the leading talent in baseball today. I'm going to get 3,000 hits. I'm going to win the Triple Crown. I'm probably going to bat .400 one year. It may sound unreal, but I think in terms of dreams that are dreamed to be lived.

BILL HARTACK
Professional Jockey

If I was an owner or trainer, you know who I'd want riding my horse? Me. I want me because I want my jockey to come back mad when he loses.

BRIAN GOODELL
Swimmer—Two Time Olympic Gold Medalist

There are a lot of good swimmers in any race, but when I'm feeling good, no one can beat me.

INGEMAR STENMARK
Skier — Two Time Olympic Gold Medalist

I'm on top—I set the pace—the other guys have to beat me.

HARVEY MARTIN
NFL Defensive End

When I get this feeling, I just know no one's going to stop me. I just know…Everything becomes clear. I know no one is going to stop me.

JULIUS ERVING
NBA Forward

I've got enough confidence in myself to believe that when I'm healthy and hitting my shots, no one can beat me. Great athletes have to think like that.

CHRIS EVERT
Professional Tennis Player

Every time—all the time,— I'm a perfectionist. I feel I should never lose.

There is nothing like a soccer game. A full stadium, thousands of banners, the ball shining white ahead, a sure kick, goal. I love it!

Pele, Professional Soccer Player

They clutch and grab, and some teams play dirty, but it's the challenge that keeps you going. I love playing the game. It's no different than little kids who go out and play for the fun of it. We're just big kids playing a game. I love playing and I enjoy the thrill of the competing.

Wayne Gretzky, NHL Center

It's great to win, but it's also great fun just to be in the thick of any truly well and hard-fought contest against opponents you respect, whatever the outcome.

Jack Nicklaus, Professional Golfer

HAVE FUN

Faith, confidence and inner arrogance are prerequisites for success, but there is one more important feeling you should develop before an athletic contest. Decide that you're going to have fun.

Isn't that why you're involved in the sport in the first place? Are you enjoying yourself? Pressure is self-inflicted. The only pressure you have is the pressure you put on yourself. Stop worrying so much about winning and losing. If you're prepared, you shouldn't have to worry — you'll win.

The next time you're getting ready to play a game, ask yourself why you're playing. A game is not supposed to be work or something you have to do. It's not something you should be doing to impress your friends or your parents. Do it for fun. Do it because you want to do it. Do it to enjoy yourself. Practice is the hard part; it's rehearsal before you go "on stage." The game itself should be fun. If it isn't, you should be doing something else.

Give yourself a pre-game pep talk: "What are you worried about? You're good or you wouldn't be in the lineup. You've worked hard, sacrificed. You love challenges, you love competition, so quit worrying about winning or losing. Just try your best. And go out and have fun." If you find that you're having trouble having fun, it's probably because you're not doing very well. It's pretty difficult to have a good time when you're getting your brains beat out. So instead of pretending you enjoy losing, go back to the basics. Find out what you're doing wrong and go to work on it. The better prepared you are, the more confident you'll be, and the more fun you'll have.

It all goes back to character and honest self-evaluation. Don't kid yourself into thinking you love a sport if you don't. If you don't love it, find another sport. If you do love your sport, enjoy it and have fun. If you can be honest with yourself, you'll have gained another valuable edge.

For example, our wrestling teams must love to play the sport as much as we love to coach it. Our wrestling teams won ten consecutive Ohio AAA State Wrestling Championships as well as six National Championships. The first state championship was great fun. So were the second, third, fourth and fifth. That's when the pressure started to mount. It wasn't put on us by others; we did it to ourselves. We didn't want to break our winning streak. We worked hard. We were dedicated to keep on winning. And we did.

Somehow, without even realizing it, we weren't having as much fun in the later years as we had in the "building years." We were wrestling more "not to lose" than "to win." With this kind of negative thinking, we did lose. We started playing it safe instead of taking the risks that made us champions. Our winning streak of ten years was over. Sad? Yes. End of the world? No way.

As we write this updated version of "The Edge", our wrestlers have started a new streak — a new decade of dominance. As we said earlier, we see losses as temporary setbacks. This is not a problem, but a new challenge. We're more dedicated than ever. And we're more motivated. We've won back what we truly believe is ours: the Ohio AAA State Wrestling Championship and the National Title. And know what? We're going to have fun starting a new winning streak!

HAVE FUN

JOHNNY MILLER
Professional Golfer

When I am playing good and driving straight, I can't wait until the next tournament. It's gratifying to know you can do what you have to do in order to win. And it's a lot easier to do well when you're enjoying it, when you're having fun.

WALTER ALSTON
Major League Manager

I've always believed that baseball is still a game. You ought to enjoy it, get some fun out of playing, yet give it everything you have.

BUM PHILLIPS
NFL Coach

You must win, but you also must have fun or what's the use? Football is but a small part of all of our lives.

JOE NAMATH
NFL Quarterback and Sports Broadcaster

When you have confidence, you can have a lot of fun and when you have fun, you can do amazing things.

DAVE LOGAN
NFL Wide Receiver

I play football because I love the game, I love the competition and I love to win. I make up my mind at the beginning of every game that I'm going to block the pressures out of my mind. I'm going to go out there and have some fun.

DOAK WALKER
NFL Halfback

Playing the great game of football, or any sport, has always been a thrill to me in my life and still continues to be. But, I have to go back and give the credit to my dad who taught me in my early years that football is a great game as long as it is fun. When the game ceases to be fun, you should get out and retire.

JOE PATERNO
College Football Coach and Athletic Director

You should be playing football for the sheer enjoyment you get out of it—not because you have to win or you're afraid to lose.

JOHN JEFFERSON
NFL Wide Receiver

We put in some long hours, but game days are still fun. After the long week of hard work, that's when you test your skills. You're on center stage. And when things work out, it's still a real thrill.

TERRY BRADSHAW
NFL Quarterback and Sports Broadcaster

I made up my mind that I was gonna have some fun in this Super Bowl. I was gonna play my game, win or lose. I didn't give a hoot. I was going to do it my way and the one thing I didn't want to do was change what got me here.

KELLEN WINSLOW
NFL Tight End
One of my most satisfying feelings is to have the ball and suddenly be in the open. Then it's like pinball, bouncing along from one man to another. I love it.

JACK LAMBERT
NFL Linebacker
The cold wind will be blowing off the lake. It'll be nasty, intense...and I'll love it.

WILLIE STARGELL
Major League First Baseman and Coach
Whenever people talk about baseball, they don't say, "work ball;" they say, "play ball." It should be fun.

ROD CAREW
Major League First Baseman
I'd like to win another batting championship before I hang up my spikes. However, right now, I just want to go out there and have some fun, let baseball be the little boy's game it's supposed to be. I enjoy playing. I get the feeling that no one can do the things I can, that I can get a hit anytime I want. It's a good feeling. It's fun.

JIM VALVANO
College Basketball Coach

When I played sports, my parents never once said to me, 'Did you win?' They'd say, 'Did you have fun?' Winning the game was important, but not nearly as important as giving yourself a chance to win — playing as hard as you could and enjoying yourself. The joy of sport. That's what it is all about.

GRANT FUHR
NHL Goaltender

I live life to the fullest. I have fun. I wouldn't give up these days for anything. And you know why? I learn. You live. You learn. You have fun.

BRIAN BOITANO
Figure Skater — Olympic Gold Medalist

I wasn't thinking gold or anything. I was doing what I came to do, which was to have fun.

NICK FALDO
Professional Golfer

When I was starting off in golf, I would play every day from morning to night. I loved the routine, even had the same lunch every day. I'd get frustrated or tired but never bored. I was my own boss and I controlled the routine. My love of golf — not natural talent — has made me a great player.

JOE GIBBS
NFL Coach

People who enjoy what they are doing invariably do it well.

ANDRE AGASSI
Professional Tennis Player

Sometimes I find myself getting a little too serious. When I'm having fun it breaks the tension and I play much better.

RON HARPER
NBA Guard

I love to get into an open-court situation. I can maneuver myself to get layups, shots or draw fouls. When I get in the open-court I try to do something creative to get the crowd going nuts. When I can get the crowd to ooh or aah, that makes the game fun.

MARK MCGUIRE
Major League First Baseman

Life is really just a bunch of adjustments, isn't it? I think I've come to terms with things. I'm realistic. I don't know that I'll ever hit 49 home runs again. If I do, great. If not, that's OK, too. All I want to do is perform well. To tell you the truth, I just love the game of baseball. That's all there is to it.

JACKIE JOYNER KERSEE
Pentathlon, Long-Jumper — Two Time Olympic Gold Medalist

The medals don't mean anything and the glory doesn't last. It's all about your happiness. The rewards are going to come, but my happiness is just loving the sport and having fun performing.

MIKE SINGLETARY
NFL Linebacker

Do you know what my favorite part of the game is? The opportunity to play. It's as simple as that. God, I love that opportunity.

DOUG JONES
Major League Pitcher

When I was playing little league baseball I never actually had dreams or aspirations of playing in the major leagues. The one and only reason I ever played baseball at any level, including the majors, was my love of the game. I have always loved to play ball.

WILLIE MAYS
Major League Outfielder

All I ever wanted to do in life was play baseball — forever.

MICHAEL JORDAN
NBA Guard

I first realized how much I loved the game of basketball, when I began to look forward to practices. I mean, I enjoy the practices as much as the games.

Money is nothing to me. The bottom line is that I'm playing. I have a 'love-of-the-game' clause in my contract, which allows me to play basketball any time I want during the off-season.

DALEY THOMPSON
Decathlete — Two Time Olympic Gold Medalist

The medals aren't the important thing. The glory is nice but it doesn't last. It's all about performing well and feeling deeply about it.

BRAD DAUGHERTY
NBA Center

There are so many great players today in the NBA. When I go out onto the court I say to myself, 'Man, this is going to be a lot of fun playing against these guys.' The better the opponent the bigger the challenge and the more fun you'll have.

MATT BIONDI
Swimmer — Five Time Olympic Gold Medalist

I couldn't believe it during my final race — the 400 Medley Relay. We wanted to break the World Record, so the pressure was on. Then when our backstroker was in the water, one of our teammates started telling us jokes. I was next up and I was laughing on the starting block. I swam the most relaxed race in my life and, coincidentally, my best.

DARRYL STRAWBERRY
Major League Outfielder

The only pressure a person has to deal with is the pressure he puts on himself. I know what I can do. I'm healthy, playing well, and most importantly, having fun.

CURTIS STRANGE
Professional Golfer

This is the greatest thing I've ever done. This is the greatest feeling I've ever had. What does this mean to me? It means what every little boy dreams about, when he's playing golf late in the afternoon by himself with four balls. One of them's Snead, one of them's Hogan, one of them's Nicklaus — the fourth in my case was Curtis Strange.

It means all my dreams came true. All those imaginary golf tournaments I played when I was young were a blast. I had fun and I always won. Today was no different. I had fun and I won.

RAY MEYER
College Basketball Coach

'Guys, we're going to have a good time. I'm not going to make any changes with one exception: We're going to win the rest of the games and we're going to have fun doing it. You guys can do it.'

ANTHONY CARTER
NFL Wide Receiver

The art of catching a pass boils down to picking the ball up early. I seem to pick up the ball, see how fast it's coming, where it's going and how I can reach it before the defensive back can stop me. I enjoy all my catches not just the long gainers because it tells me that I was able to beat the defender. The one-on-one confrontations are what makes the game fun.

BERNIE KOSAR
NFL Quarterback

Although competition is important, you must put it in perspective. If it's overemphasized, you lose a sense of what you're doing. You'll stop having fun.

ALBERTO TOMBA
Skier — Two Time Olympic Gold Medalist

I don't want to become too serious. I'm considered the clown of the team, because I cannot be serious for two minutes. I'm afraid if I become more serious I will stop winning.

LARRY NANCE
NBA Forward

I don't like to think about injuries. I am just happy to be out there. I realize that I have been blessed with athletic ability so I just try to enjoy myself every game because after all, basketball is still just a game.

AL UNSER, JR.
Race Car Driver

It all comes down to winning the 'family war'. That's the process by which an Unser is kept on his toes. Sure we're competitive, but at the same time we're enjoying this. We both love to race. Yes, we both want to win, but more importantly, we love what we're doing.

WILL CLARK
Major League First Baseman

I've always known that baseball was a game and games were meant to be fun. Some people lable me as being lucky and arrogant, but what I am is emotional and confident. I'm enjoying myself out there all the time.

ROGER KINGDOM
Hurdler — Two Time Olympic Gold Medalist
If a man can work his own hours and make a living out of doing something he loves to do, don't you think he would go out and be the best he could be at it?

JOE MONTANA
NFL Quarterback
My first game after back surgery, I realized that this was the biggest challenge I'd ever faced. But as soon as I got out on the field, I remembered that it was just a game, and I was going to enjoy myself.

DR. A. BARTLETT GIAMATTI
Yale University President and Major League Baseball Commissioner
The end of every baseball season you count on it, rely on it to buffer the passage of time, to keep the memory of sunshine and high skies alive, and then just when the days are all twilight, when you need it most, it stops. Summer is gone.

It breaks your heart. It is designed to break your heart.

MARIO LEMIEUX
NHL Center
I approach hockey like a kid plays a game. I'm much more interested in playing than all the contract talk. That's the flip side of athletes that people rarely see.

DAN MARINO
NFL Quarterback
I enjoy the thrill of competition and the excitement of throwing the game-winning touchdown pass. That's what makes this game so much fun. If you're not having fun, then you're playing the wrong game.

WADE BOGGS
Major League Third Baseman
The art of hitting has become a habit for me. However, this is one habit I love. The more I work at it, the better I feel. I can't imagine getting up in the morning and not going to the park and hitting.

GREG BARTON
Kayaker — Two Time Olympic Gold Medalist
The payoff for all the preparation is personal satisfaction, seeing if I can be the best. Beyond that, I just like the feeling of being in a boat and feeling it accelerate through the water. I really enjoy what I do.

KIRBY PUCKETT
Major League Outfielder
I'm thankful for the ability God has given me. Without Him I certainly wouldn't be where I am today.

People say I'm charismatic. Maybe it's because I love this game and I don't mind showing it. Playing ball is all I ever wanted to do.

JOE CARTER
Major League Outfielder
Having fun is the name of the game. We all go out there and play as hard as we can to try to win. But the main reason we play is to have fun. Never do anything you don't enjoy. I've always said that when I stop having fun, I'll leave the game.

GREG SWINDELL
Major League Pitcher
There's no way I can describe the feeling I have when I'm on the mound. Every time I stand on the mound I feel like I'm on cloud nine and I'm loving it.

BOB GOLIC
NFL Defensive Nose Tackle

Playing football has always been a game to me. Games are supposed to be fun. Being able to play in my hometown was a great thrill. I am proud of the city I grew up in so on Sunday I wasn't just playing for the Cleveland Browns Football Team but also for the City of Cleveland.

I developed a certain comraderie with the fans of Cleveland because they looked at me as one of them. I think they could tell I really was enjoying myself out there. The day I stop having fun playing this game is the day I'll retire.

MARK PRICE
NBA Guard

Due to my size limitation coming into the NBA, people tried to test me right away. But once they saw I wasn't going to be tentative or intimidated, most of that stuff stopped. Now it's fun to go out there against the league's best, knowing that you have earned their respect through hard work and dedication.

JANET EVANS
Swimmer — Three Time Olympic Gold Medalist

My philosophy is that you only live once. I tell myself to enjoy my swimming, to have fun with interviews and to get the most out of being young.

On the starting blocks before my first Olympic race, I was smiling because I was having fun. That's what it is all about — to have fun.

CORY SNYDER
Major League Outfielder

Playing baseball was meant to be fun. The pitcher is trying to either blow the fastball by you, or to fool you with his other pitches. It is a great confrontation between two people.

LARRY BROWN
NBA and College Basketball Coach

The sport we play and coach has been fun for a very long time — it's one of the reasons we continue doing it. The key is to attempt to not tie 'fun' to winning and losing; we already know which is more enjoyable. The true fun comes from the competitive pursuit of victory through practice and games. It is that time in any contest when decisions and actions flow unencumbered by mechanics or deep thoughts. The work we all put in at practice allows that to happen. But only when we're having 'fun.'

JOSE CANSECO
Major League Outfielder

I don't think my attitude has changed since high school. I'm really just an easygoing guy with a good sense of humor. I try to have a lot of fun and let things fall where they may.

JIM RODGERS
NBA Coach

Don't ever allow the pressure of competition to be greater than the pleasure of competition.

SEAN ELLIOTT
NBA Forward

One thing I learned at the Olympic Trials was that you can't afford to be too timid. You have to let yourself go and enjoy the game — not to get caught up in the heat of the battle. I didn't know that then, but believe me, I learned from the experience that if I'm going to do anything, I had better relax and have fun doing it.

MATS WILANDER
Professional Tennis Player

My coaches told me I had potential, but they never pushed me. They told me to enjoy playing. If somebody had pushed me, I wouldn't have played. It would have been too serious for me.

Tennis is entertainment. I would be lying if I said I didn't enjoy myself out there.

STEFFI GRAF
Professional Tennis Player

I had an incredible year last year and I've started awfully well this year, but I'm not going to get myself in trouble and say it's going to happen again.

I like the feeling of being No. 1. I don't think about it from the point of view that the only way to go is down. I am enjoying playing tennis and just want to keep playing well.

As long as I can focus on enjoying what I'm doing, having fun, I know I'll play well.

CHRIS JACKSON
College Guard

All the comparisons to Pete Maravich are flattering, but I don't think about them much. I know I have God-given ability, and if I play within myself I'll be much better off. The combination of my ability and love of the game will enable me to play basketball for a long time.

DON MATTINGLY
Major League First Baseman

People say that I'm the most competitive person they have ever seen. But it's my passion for the game that makes me this way. I believe that playing every game at breakneck speed is fun.

STACEY KING
NBA Forward

I'm a guy who has always had everything going for me. But I'm also a regular guy who doesn't go around driving a sports car or spending lots of money. I don't want to be put on a pedestal. I'm just a guy who has fun. I get all of my satisfaction on the court.

TROY AIKMAN
NFL Quarterback

I want to play football. Most people assume you change with success. Not me. I believe you have to remember where you started to completely understand what you have accomplished. It's important to keep all things in life in perspective. Football is a game. Playing games is fun. I never want to lose sight of that.

EMERSON FITTIPALDI
Race Car Driver

The Indy 500 is the biggest race in the world. But I've been here for years and never won and still enjoyed myself. The competition here alone makes it worth it.

FLORENCE GRIFFITH JOYNER
Sprinter — Three Time Olympic Gold Medalist

Most competitors are so focused they don't want to take the time to say hello, but I'm always chatting. It relaxes me. When I run relaxed, I have fun, and no one can beat me.

JOE DUMARS
NBA Guard

Sometimes everything falls into place and it's an incredible feeling. We have several players who can carry the team for part of a game. The amazing thing is that we are able to recognize this. And I'll tell you something, we all get the same satisfaction out of it. We're all having fun. Working together is fun. Winning is fun. Heck, just playing is fun.

TONY MANDARICH
NFL Offensive Tackle

The satisfaction I get when successfully making a play is immense. Knocking a defender down is a thrilling play for an offensive lineman. Most people think that a lineman's job is unrewarding. They couldn't be more wrong. Until you experience it, you can't begin to understand what I mean.

BO JACKSON
NFL Running Back and Major League Outfielder

Standing in the on deck circle prior to my first at-bat of the All-Star game, I was pretty nervous. But, once I got to the plate everything was alright, because I feel at home in the batter's box. I've always played baseball because I love the game. So regardless of whether I hit a 440 foot home run or strike out, the game will always be fun. All I want is to be able to get in some quality cuts every at-bat.

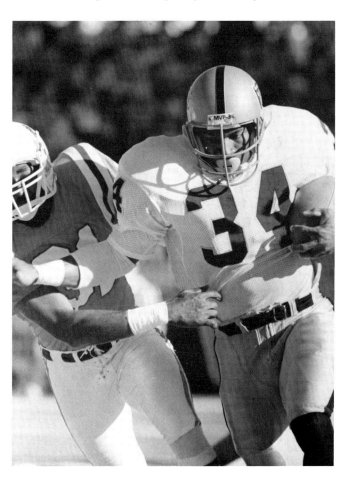

ERIC DICKERSON
NFL Running Back

Running is so natural to me. The feeling of the wind hitting me in the face is incredible. I know that if I can keep that feeling inside me, football will always be fun.

5
THE GAME

- Don't Apologize for Trying to Win
- Don't Be Afraid to Fail
- Leadership – Teamwork
- Concentration – Poise
- Go For It
- Extra Effort
- Welcome Competition – Challenge Yourself

Paradoxical Commandments of Leadership

1. People are illogical, unreasonable, and self-centered.
   Love them anyway.

2. If you do good, people will accuse you of selfish ulterior motives.
   Do good anyway.

3. If you are successful, you win false friends and true enemies.
   Succeed anyway.

4. The good you do today will be forgotten tomorrow.
   Do good anyway.

5. Honesty and frankness make you vulnerable.
   Be honest and frank anyway.

6. The biggest men with the biggest ideas can be shot down by the smallest men with the smallest minds.
   Think big anyway.

7. People favor underdogs but follow only top dogs.
   Fight for a few underdogs anyway.

8. What you spend years building may be destroyed overnight.
   Build anyway.

9. People really need help, but may attack you if you do help them.
   Help them anyway.

10. Give the world the best you have and you'll get kicked in the teeth.
    Give the world the best you have anyway.

I love to sweat, work and practice...then win. But to sweat, work and practice...then lose. I can't see that at all!
Lee Kemp, Wrestler—
Three Time World Champion

I love to win. Love it. Football is just too hard and too tough if you're not successful. This isn't recreation, and the sport isn't for everybody. I just don't want to expend all this time and effort and come up short.
Bo Schembechler, College Football Coach and Athletic Director

There's a winner in every game or it's not a game. Even debating teams in high school try to win. When they start putting the loser on top of the winner, losing is what I'll strive for.

Earl Weaver, Major League Manager

DON'T APOLOGIZE FOR TRYING TO WIN

Don't ever apologize for winning. Think about it this way. You've paid the price. You've worked long and hard; you've sacrificed. Why should you let the other person win? That isn't very smart; or very healthy. Win.

Don't be afraid to be a winner. Win with class, win with character. You deserve to win. You can fight like the devil to win and still have class. In fact, the harder you fight to win, the more people will respect you. Look at the photo of Y. A. Tittle on page 5-5. This was taken seconds after a tough loss when his touchdown pass fell incomplete in the end zone. No one ever fought harder to win. No one was ever more respected for trying to win.

Get used to competition because you'll be competing all your life, and not just in sports. In school, you compete for grades. In business, you'll compete to make a sale.

Don't let people convince you that winning is not that important. They'll tell you winning in sports is not important. What they fail to tell you is that since they can't win, they don't want you to win either.

Mentally, we all need our share of victories; otherwise, we won't be on the team for very long. If your goal is to get into graduate school, you had better plan on getting your share of A's. If you want to keep your job, you better make some sales. Nice tries and great efforts only count in horseshoes; they don't buy many groceries in the real world.

Winning is so important because each success helps maintain your enthusiasm. Without enthusiasm, you'll never become a winner. How long will you remain excited about your sport if you go out and get beat each week? Not long. Without enthusiasm, you're not likely to be motivated enough to work as hard as you should. Result? You're likely to develop a habit of losing, which is a very tough habit to break.

A winning habit helps you in many ways. It builds character, gives you the edge as a result of long hours of practice and brings you to a mental and physical peak. So when you step onto the field, the court or the mat, you'll soon find out who the winner is — you or your opponent.

Don't say you're not in a sport to win. No apologies are needed. Somebody is going to win — either you or your opponent. You make that decision.

This last point is an important one. Our wrestling team ran off a string of ten consecutive Ohio AAA State Championships. Winning became automatic. We expected to win and we did. It was very difficult to imagine not winning. Losing was something that happened to other teams, not us. Then it happened. We lost. Our streak was over. Finished. What we had worked ten years to build was no longer there. We were no longer the best high school wrestling team in the country. We weren't even the best team in Ohio. We not only lost the State and National titles, we also lost something more important — our identity.

Someone once said, "It doesn't matter if you win or lose until you lose!" Now we know how true that really is. After ten straight championships, we knew winning was very important to us. It didn't make any sense to work, sacrifice, sweat and then lose.

Now we have OUR TROPHIES back, and we're starting a new streak. No apologies needed; we want to win, we expect to win and we will win.

DON'T APOLOGIZE FOR TRYING TO WIN

BOB GIBSON
Major League Pitcher

It was all right playing a few basketball games with the Harlem Globetrotters, but I hated that clowning around. I wanted to play all the time. I mean, I wanted to play to win.

BILL HARTACK
Professional Jockey

I don't want to abuse anybody, but I want to win. And I want to win more than I want to worry about whether I'm abusing somebody or not.

CHRIS EVERT
Professional Tennis Player

The difference is almost all mental. The top players just hate to lose. I think that's the difference. A champion hates to lose even more than she loves to win.

DAVE WINFIELD
Major League Outfielder

To me, close is for losers. I play ball to win.

GEORGE ALLEN
NFL Coach and Sports Commentator

Winning is living. Every time you win, you're reborn. When you lose, you die a little.

PAUL BEAR BRYANT
College Football Coach and Athletic Director

Winning isn't everything, but it beats anything that comes in second.

BILL SHARMAN
NBA Guard, Coach and General Manager

I take the game very seriously. That's why I demand so much of my players. You have to win—everything, all the time. What is sleeping and eating compared to winning?

TONY DORSETT
NFL Halfback

I'm not accustomed to being second, third or fourth. I like to win.

JACK DEMPSEY
Professional Boxer

I had speed, a punch, and courage—either win or die.

AL UNSER
Race Car Driver

Whatever you are, be the best. Don't be satisfied with second; nobody ever remembers who finishes second.

DARRELL ROYAL
College Football Coach

The only way I know how to keep football fun is to win. That's the only answer. There is no laughter in losing.

LOU HOLTZ
College Football Coach

A team wins with the elimination of mistakes and with people who want to win and can't stand losing.

TY COBB
Major League Outfielder

I had to be first all the time—first in everything. All I ever thought about was winning.

TED SIMMONS
Major League Catcher

Everybody strives to win, but it's 10,000 times easier to lose. To win, you have to bust your tail. Losing drives me crazy. I don't beat my wife when we lose, but I'm a different person when the team's not doing well.

ARNOLD PALMER
Professional Golfer

I play to win; everybody knows I play to win. No way can I pretend that losing is a joke.

LARRY CSONKA
NFL Fullback and Sports Broadcaster

Just thinking about losing is enough incentive for me to win.

DR. A. BARTLETT GIAMATTI
Yale University President and Major League Baseball Commissioner

Winning in sports has a joy and a discrete purity to it that cannot be replaced by anything else. It is something powerful, indeed beautiful, something as necessary to the strong spirit as striving is necessary to the healthy character.

JOHN NEWCOMBE
Professional Tennis Player and Sports Broadcaster

It's not that I'm unsympathetic, but let's face it, I want to win too.

DAN FOUTS
NFL Quarterback and Sports Broadcaster

The bottom line for me is, and always has been, winning. Everything else goes hand in hand.

JOE LOUIS
Professional Boxer

The guys I fought wanted to beat me up as bad as they could, so I couldn't feel sorry when I beat them. I never apologized for winning.

JOE GARAGIOLA
Major League Catcher and Sports Broadcaster

Nobody likes to lose—just stay away from those who don't mind losing.

ROCKY MARCIANO
Professional Boxer

You're thinking only of ending it as quickly as possible. You find yourself wishing he'd go down, save himself more pain. People say, "Do you enjoy hurting the other fellow?" Of course not. But it's another man against me. I have to get cruel at fight time. When he is on the verge, I have to get meaner. After a couple of rounds, you feel the guy is your enemy. You have to feel that way. Otherwise you can't beat him. And you have to beat him.

Y. A. TITTLE
NFL Quarterback

I'm not an easy loser, anytime. Let the good losers play for other teams. I like to win.

CHARLEY BOSWELL
Professional Blind Golfer

If it doesn't matter if you win or lose, but how you play the game, why do they keep score?

JACKIE ROBINSON
First Black Player in the Major Leagues

It kills me to lose. If I'm a troublemaker—and I don't think that my temper makes me one—then it's only because I can't stand losing. That's the way I am about winning. All I ever wanted to do was finish first.

CARIN CONE VANDERBUSH
Swimmer

We all want to win. I don't like to come in second to anyone.

J. R. RICHARD
Major League Pitcher

I'm in the game to be number one. I can't be satisfied with less. Being number one is fantastic; it's the greatest thing in the world. Not wanting to be number one is something I just can't understand.

DON SHULA
NFL Defensive Back and Coach

When I first came to Miami, getting in the playoffs was our first goal. And making it the first year might have been an achievement for most teams but for us it was a frustration because we didn't beat Oakland. But the players told me something about themselves because they were just as unhappy as I was. As soon as I knew that, I was sure that we would be back to win it all.

C. LEEMAN BENNETT
NFL Coach

Chuck Knox always said that "What you do speaks so loud there's no need to hear what you say." I fully agree with him and I have adopted his philosophy. All the talking in the world doesn't matter. It's the base that counts, the winning that counts.

IVAN LENDL
Professional Tennis Player

I hate to lose even if a tournament is small. I care about winning. Second place means nothing.

JOE PATERNO
College Football Coach and Athletic Director

In the beginning, I hoped that the day would come when our fans would not only want us to win but would expect us to win. Just being close was not good enough for us. We had to begin thinking about winning all the time. We had to begin beating the UCLA's. We had to expect to win.

INGEMAR STENMARK
Skier — Two Time Olympic Gold Medalist

I ski to win. When the day comes that I can't get myself into a fighting mood anymore, I won't be able to win and I'll stop racing.

BOBBY LAYNE
NFL Quarterback

You must want to be a winner and you must work hard enough to finish number one. Who cares about second place?

AL DAVIS
NFL Owner

I want to win. That's it, all of it.

JOHN MC ENROE
Professional Tennis Player

People always ask if I'm surprised when I win a tournament. Was Bjorn Borg surprised to win Wimbledon the first time? Was he surprised to win it five times? As the time for a big tournament comes closer, I can feel myself getting hot, getting better. I want to get better and better and because of that, I work harder and harder. So, no, I'm not surprised at all when I win a tournament. I don't want to be surprised. I want to win because I deserve to win.

SUGAR RAY LEONARD
Professional Boxer and Sports Broadcaster

I like to train. I enjoy challenges, but most of all I like winning.

VINCE LOMBARDI

FORREST GREGG

JOE MONTANA

TONY DORSETT

JOE GREENE

JOHN JEFFERSON

What It Takes To Be Number One

You've got to pay the price. Winning is not a sometime thing; it's an all-the-time thing. You don't win once in a while; you don't do things right once in a while; you do them right all the time. Winning is a habit. Unfortunately, so is losing.

There is no room for second place. There is only one place in my game and that is first place. I have finished second twice in my time at Green Bay and I don't ever want to finish second again. There is a second place bowl game, but it is a game for losers played by losers. It is and always has been an American zeal to be first in anything we do and to win and to win and to win.

Every time a football player goes out to ply his trade, he's got to play from the ground up—from the soles of his feet right up to his head. Every inch of him has to play. Some guys play with their heads. That's O. K. You've got to be smart to be number one in any business. But more important, you've got to play with your heart—with every fiber of your body. If you're lucky enough to find a guy with a lot of head and a lot of heart, he's never going to come off the field second.

Running a football team is no different from running any other kind of organization—an army, a political party, a business. The principles are the same. The object is to win—to beat the other guy. Maybe that sounds hard or cruel. I don't think it is.

It's a reality of life that men are competitive and the most competitive games draw the most competitive men. That's why they're there—to compete. They know the rules and the objectives when they get in the game. The objective is to win—fairly, squarely, decently, by the rules—but to win.

And in truth, I've never known a man worth his salt who in the long run, deep down in his heart, didn't appreciate the grind, the discipline. There is something in good men that really yearns for the discipline and the harsh reality of head-to-head combat.

I don't say these things because I believe in the brute nature of man or that men must be brutalized to be combative. I believe in God, and I believe in human decency. But I firmly believe that any man's finest hour—his greatest fulfillment to all he holds dear—is that moment when he has worked his heart out in a good cause and lies exhausted on the field of battle—victorious.

THERE IS NO ROOM FOR SECOND PLACE

THE OBJECTIVE IS TO WIN

FIRST PLACE IS OUR OBJECTIVE

VINCE LOMBARDI   NFL Coach

WOODY HAYES
College Football Coach
Without winners there wouldn't be any gosh darn civilization. We make no apologies for winning or for aiming our entire program toward that goal.

JOHN MADDEN
NFL Coach and Sports Broadcaster
The only yardstick for success our society has is being a champion. No one remembers anything else.

Winners vs Losers

When a winner makes a mistake, he says, "I was wrong;"
When a loser makes a mistake, he says, "It wasn't my fault."

A winner works harder than a loser and has more time;
A loser is always "too busy" to do what is necessary.

A winner goes through a problem;
A loser goes around it, and never gets past it.

A winner makes commitments;
A loser makes promises.

A winner says, "I'm good, but not as good as I ought to be;"
A loser says, "I'm not as bad as a lot of other people."

A winner listens;
A loser just waits until it's his turn to talk.

A winner respects those who are superior to him and tries to learn something from them;
A loser resents those who are superior to him and tries to find chinks in their armor.

A winner feels responsible for more than his job;
A loser says, "I only work here."

A winner says, "There ought to be a better way to do it;"
A loser says, "That's the way it's always been done here."

PAT WILLIAMS   NBA General Manager and Vice President

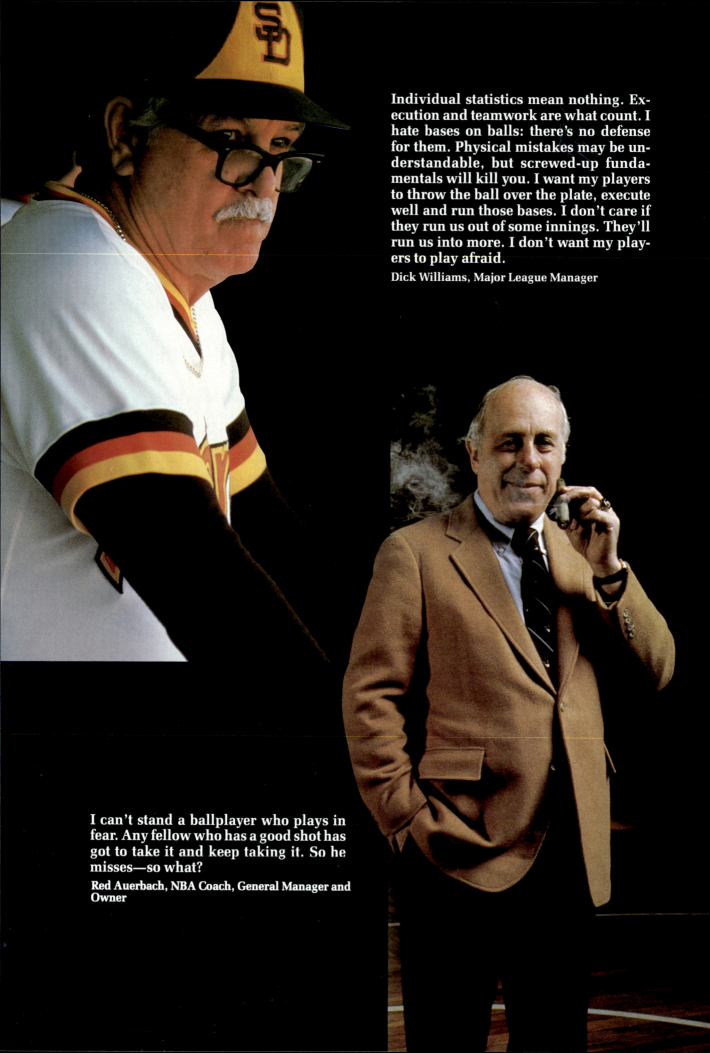

Individual statistics mean nothing. Execution and teamwork are what count. I hate bases on balls: there's no defense for them. Physical mistakes may be understandable, but screwed-up fundamentals will kill you. I want my players to throw the ball over the plate, execute well and run those bases. I don't care if they run us out of some innings. They'll run us into more. I don't want my players to play afraid.

Dick Williams, Major League Manager

I can't stand a ballplayer who plays in fear. Any fellow who has a good shot has got to take it and keep taking it. So he misses—so what?

Red Auerbach, NBA Coach, General Manager and Owner

DON'T BE AFRAID TO FAIL

Athletes, as with all people, fall into two motivational classes: Those who truly want success, and those who simply try to avoid failure. The success types are the highly competitive leader types. They perform better under pressure because they thrive on it. They know what they want and they go after it. The avoidance types don't want failure, and they don't know how to succeed. They have developed a habit of losing, which is a very hard habit to break.

A major difference between these two types is their effort to win. Success types know that they can control their effort. So they prepare fully and they expect to win.

Avoidance types don't focus on their personal effort. They are emotionally attached to results that they can't control; they get anxious and try too hard when it's time to perform. When they're challenged by someone equal or better than they are, they often panic and lose quickly. They may want to win, but they aren't prepared to win. And they usually don't.

If you want to win so badly that you can't stand losing, practice, work hard and sacrifice. And do it every day, not just the day before the game. As long as you're willing to "pay the price" for victory, you'll win. That means putting more time in than your opponent; working harder; being more intense; and working smarter.

Only when you do all this, will you have deserved the right to win; for you'll have earned it. When you reach this point, and the great feeling that comes with it, you'll never be afraid to fail again. Why should you? You'll be a success type who has paid the price for winning. Enjoy it.

A quick way to become a loser is to want to win so badly that you become afraid to lose. When this happens, you get very cautious and you fail to reach your full potential. You start to play it "safe": You hit your irons to avoid the traps instead of going for the flag; you throw the pass away from the defender, instead of to the receiver, to avoid being intercepted. You tense up, get anxious and lose.

No matter what the outcome, you'll never be a loser if you always look at an athletic contest as a valuable opportunity and learning experience. It's a chance for you to succeed, plus a way to discover weaknesses that need to be corrected. Winners seek the toughest competition to test their own limits and determine what areas need to be developed more. If you have prepared correctly, you should go into a game or match having every reason to expect you'll win. But if you don't, pick up the pieces and start again.

Winners are always remembered for their number of wins and for the records they set, not for the times they lose or for the frequency of their losses. Take Babe Ruth, for example. He's a legend today because he was baseball's Home Run King, but he was also baseball's Strikeout King. People remember his home runs, not his strikeouts.

Many great champions didn't win every tournament they entered: Steffi Graf and Ivan Lendl in tennis; Jack Nicklaus and Curtis Strange in golf. This didn't tarnish their reputations.

So don't waste your energy worrying about losing. Concentrate that energy toward your effort to win. Valor grows by daring, fear by holding back. Dare and you might; hold back and you never will. So dare to be great.

> Fear of failure can restrict a player; it can kill him as an individual. If one continually worries about failing, he'll get so tight that he will fail...We want to be properly prepared for anything in a game, but we don't want to worry about losing the game. If we lose it, we'll find out why. But one of the reasons shouldn't be that we were so tight that we were afraid at the outset.
>
> **Chuck Noll, NFL Linebacker and Coach**

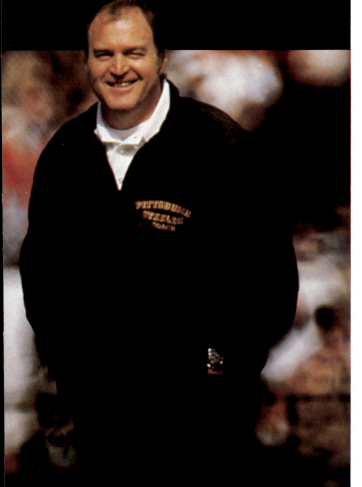

DON'T BE AFRAID TO FAIL

JOHN J. MC HALE
Major League President

Don't be afraid to fail. Give it everything you have, but don't be embarrassed or inhibited by what your parents, friends or family will think if you lose. If you aren't afraid and you give it your best, you will win more than you lose.

BILL FOSTER
College Basketball Coach

Negative thoughts are contagious and they get passed around like a disease. I try to inoculate myself from the fear of failure.

JOE PATERNO
College Football Coach and Athletic Director

We play with enthusiasm and recklessness. We aren't afraid to lose. If we win, great. But win or lose, it is the competition that gives us pleasure.

JIM RYUN
Distance Runner—Olympic Silver Medalist

If you are not afraid to go out and compete, then you will run your best race. But if you go out with a fear of something, even against yourself or against the clock, then you have lost the race before you start.

KEN VENTURI
Professional Golfer and Sports Broadcaster

It is not that you have to be better than anyone else, but you have to be better than you ever thought you could be. The disgrace is not in losing; it's in not trying. You should never be afraid to fail.

JOHN CHARLES SALAK
American Writer

Failures are divided into two classes—those who thought and never did, and those who did and never thought.

MERLIN OLSEN
NFL Tackle, Sports Broadcaster and Actor

Putting all of it together, making it happen, requires all of us to compete and to be able to accept a certain amount of risk—even the risk of failing. It's essential that we learn to critique and evaluate our own performances in competition by examining positive elements that we wish to sustain, and seeking ways to grow and improve as we learn from our mistakes.

MARY TYLER MOORE
Actress

Take chances, make mistakes. That's how you grow. Pain nourishes your courage. You have to fail in order to practice being brave.

GEORGE BROWN
Canadian Journalist

Many times, the best way to learn is through mistakes. A fear of making mistakes can bring individuals to a standstill, to a dead center. Fear is the wicked wand that transforms human beings into vegetables.

CHESTER BARNARD
American Utilities Executive

To try and fail is at least to learn. To fail to try is to suffer the inestimable loss of what might have been.

DANNY WHITE
NFL Quarterback

I feel it's easier to win if you aren't afraid to take a chance once in a while and if the other team knows you aren't afraid.

REGGIE JACKSON
Major League Outfielder and Sports Broadcaster

Fear of failure is a powerful obstacle to overcome. Sometimes we must realize that our best may just not be good enough.

JOE GARAGIOLA
Major League Catcher and Sports Broadcaster

Don't be afraid to fail. Experience is just mistakes you won't make anymore.

KEN DRYDEN
NHL Goaltender

To play well, you must be mentally aggressive. Instead of worrying about failing—about stopping the shooter and what he might do—my attitude is that he has to beat me.

MARIE BEYNON RAY
American Author/Editor

Indecision is fatal. It is better to make a wrong decision than to build up a habit of indecision. If you're wallowing in indecision, you certainly can't act—and action is the basis of success.

TOMMY HEARNS
Professional Boxer

You can't win 'em all. You have your good days and you have your bad days. Don't be afraid to lose.

JAMES F. BYRNES
U.S. Supreme Court Justice

Too many people are thinking of security instead of opportunity. They seem more afraid of life than death.

HORACE FLETCHER
American Businessman

Fear is an acid which is pumped into one's atmosphere. It causes mental, moral and spiritual asphyxiation, and sometimes death; death to energy and all growth.

JOE LOUIS
Professional Boxer

Oh, I thought about getting beat, especially when I was just starting out scared. After I won the title, I didn't worry about it no more. Oh, I knew that if I kept on fighting, some guy would come along and take the title away from me, but not this guy, not tonight.

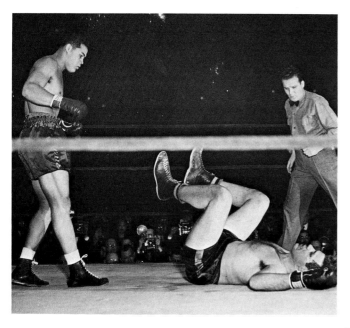

F. SCOTT FITZGERALD
American Novelist

I never blame failure—there are too many complicated situations in life—but I am absolutely merciless toward lack of effort.

JOE PATERNO
College Football Coach and Athletic Director

I tell our kids to never be afraid to lose. Think about winning. I don't ever want anybody playing for me who is afraid when he walks out on that football field that he's going to make a mistake that will cost us a football game. All I want them to do is pull up their pants, look the other guy in the eye and say, "Let's go. Let's find out which of us is the better man."

RONALD E. OSBORN
American Clergyman/Author

Undertake something that is difficult; it will do you good. Unless you try to do something beyond what you have already mastered, you will never grow.

THEODORE N. VAIL
American Telephone Pioneer

Real difficulties can be overcome, it is only the imaginary ones that are unconquerable.

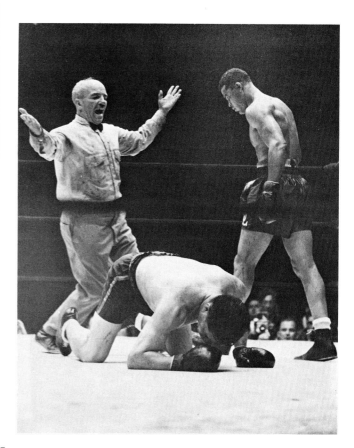

CORY SNYDER
Major League Outfielder

When you're in a slump, you start going up to the plate trying to hit a home run. You stop doing the little things and you start beating yourself. You start pressing instead of just letting things happen, relaxing and taking your good cuts. You let all the negatives come floating through your mind.

STEVE LARGENT
NFL Wide Receiver

You're never as good or as bad as they say you are. In the context of eternity, my football achievements mean very little. To a large extent, my job consists of running downfield, beating a guy, and catching a ball — no big deal. Nothing to worry about.

GREG LOUGANIS
Diver — Four Time Olympic Gold Medalist

Hitting my head on the board was difficult to overcome, because I had to go back up there right away. However, I never thought about giving up or messing up my next dive. I just envisioned myself hitting the dive perfectly.

GREG NORMAN
Professional Golfer

Every time you lose, you think that life's unfair. You think of the bad breaks. But when you're winning and playing well, you still get those bad breaks, only you overcome them. It just depends on how strong your mind is.

Unlike most players, I have no fear of golf, no worry in the back of my mind that the insidious game can take back what it has given me. I don't let anything bother me, because I know that if I work harder and harder, I'm going to win. I knew I was going to win a major title. I believe in myself to the nth degree, and if you feel like that, you won't have any problems.

RODGER CLEMENS
Major League Pitcher

If someone tells me that I can't do something, it becomes more of a challenge. In high school, I was always considered a good pitcher, but I was never considered the best. The thing was, though, I felt I was the best. When people who don't have any idea what they're talking about say something bad about me, tell me that I'll fail, it just adds fuel to my fire. Everybody wants to win, but it burns much deeper in me than it does in other people. That's my edge. It's always like, 'I'll show you.'

JOE GIBBS
NFL Coach

Failures are expected by losers, ignored by winners.

KIRK GIBSON
Major League Outfielder

When he got that second strike on me in the Series, the thought of striking out never crossed my mind.

I live for pressure moments. Regardless of what happens, I can't worry about not delivering. I know another opportunity will come along.

ROGER CRAIG
NFL Halfback

The transition from college to pro football could have been more difficult than it was. I accepted the challenge because I knew if I gave it my all, there was no way I could fail.

My pain tolerance is so high, I feel I can conquer anything. But in the end, I train not so much for football as for character — for myself and my life after I'm done playing. I want to be able to look into the mirror, and go on with the rest of my life knowing I gave everything I had.

No matter how bad you feel, you can never worry about not being successful. You just go out and do the job. As soon as you start looking too far ahead — worrying about winning or losing you're going to lose.

JERRY RICE
NFL Wide Receiver

I've matured. When I drop passes, I don't get down on myself the way I did when I was a rookie. On the short drops I used to tense up. I tried to do too much. I started to think too much. Instead of just doing what I had done in practice a thousand times (catch the ball), I worried about dropping the ball.

That's the absolute worst thing a receiver can do — worry about not catching the ball — or about getting hit. Now I do what I have worked so hard on being able to do. I catch the ball.

GREG SWINDELL
Major League Pitcher

All you can do is your best and hope that it's good enough. There isn't enough time to worry about losing. As a pitcher you don't have control of every aspect of the game. When I try to do too much myself, I start to overthrow the ball, trying to strike everyone out. I struggle because I rush myself and lose my concentration. I have to realize that there are eight other people who are out there trying to get the opponent out. I can't worry about giving up base hits. All I have to do is concentrate on the batter and give it my best shot.

LARRY BROWN
NBA and College Basketball Coach

Failure does not come from losing, but from not trying. The results of a contest are to some degree uncontrollable and all the preparation in the world may fall short. To mentally and physically 'lay it on the line' will always allow a greater chance for victory, and even if defeated the loss offers no shame, but rather more insight for future attempts.

MIKE TYSON
Professional Boxer

The worst thing that could happen to me is I could get knocked out. So what. I'm not going to die. A lot of worse things could happen to me.

I believe in taking chances. There's nothing I won't try. In my business, there is no room for fear.

ANDRE AGASSI
Professional Tennis Player

What I've learned from others is that it can mess you up if you worry about everybody, worry about winning, hoping to be the next great American player. What people want to think, what they want to hope is their business. I'm just going to play the way I want to play. I'm not going to be afraid to lose. If I start worrying about losing, I'll never win.

FLORENCE GRIFFITH JOYNER
Sprinter — Three Time Olympic Gold Medalist

You never fail until you stop trying.

BERNIE KOSAR
NFL Quarterback

Every defense, no matter how good, has to surrender something in order to guard against something else. That's how defenses operate. My job and the job of our coaching staff is to find out what they're giving away, in order to take what we want. That's how the game is played, and that's how games are won or lost. We concentrate on doing what we have to do to score. We never think about winning or losing — just about being able to do what we want to do. To get the job done.

DALEY THOMPSON
Decathlon — Two Time Olympic Gold Medalist

Even to lose, I think I'd still compete. No matter how it goes or how I go, I wouldn't change anything. It fulfills me to be able to compete. I never worry about winning or losing because when you compete, you are already a winner.

MARK PRICE
NBA Guard

I just said, 'The heck with it. If I tear it, I tear it. There's no tomorrow.' It was time for me to carry my end of the load on offense. If I had a chance, I'd unload. No time to worry about throwing up a brick.

LARRY NANCE
NBA Forward

Sometimes I need someone to tell me to quit hesitating with my shot. I don't realize it when I am passing up good open shots. But, after someone makes me aware of it, I tell myself to just take the shot and don't worry about the results.

CURTIS STRANGE
Professional Golfer

In the 1985 Masters, I was more worried about losing than winning and guess what — I lost. Now I just play the same and allow the rest of the players to worry about winning or losing. When I stopped worrying about winning and losing, I started to win.

I let my scoring and my clubs do my talking. In golf, the one thing you cannot control is your opponent's score. So I never worry about what I can't control — I just go for the flag.

JIM RODGERS
NBA Coach

If you never try you can never succeed. If you try and do the best you can, you will never fail.

JOE CARTER
Major League Outfielder

Show me someone who hasn't failed and I'll show you someone who has never done anything or even been outside the house. Failure is evident every day in our society. We all fail. In God's eyes we fail every day. You can never learn anything by always succeeding. You have to fail — you have to stumble, but the main thing is to get back up and keep striving to be that perfect person that God wants you to be.

BRAD DAUGHERTY
NBA Center

I never think about missing a free throw. All that goes through my mind when I'm at the free throw line is seeing the ball go through the bottom of the net. I'm going to make it. No doubt about it.

DEBI THOMAS
Figure Skater — Olympic Silver Medalist

If you trust your nerve as well as your skill, you're capable of a lot more than you can imagine. I never felt that if I didn't win the gold medal, I was nothing. I just had to give it my best shot.

BOB GRIES
Businessman, NFL Owner and Ultra Marathon Runner

To venture into the unknown, to search for your maximum potential, to achieve the impossible or highly improbable is life's greatest satisfaction. It takes intense preparation, total dedication and the risk of failure. If you have paid the price and give 100%, you're a winner.

GEORGE BELL
Major League Outfielder

If things don't go your way, what can you do? You cannot control the outcome. All you control is your effort. If you worry too much about the results, then your effort will suffer.

PIRMIN ZURBRIGGEN
Alpine Skier — Olympic Gold Medalist

No one expects me to be perfect. If I fail again, it will be no surprise, no problem.

JOHN SMITH
Wrestler, Olympic Gold Medalist

I never, never go into a wrestling match thinking I could get beat. The thought of losing never crosses my mind. There is no reason for me to get beat. I know that I have more ability than anyone I wrestle. When I lose it means I didn't wrestle to my full potential. The solution to everything is to work harder.

DOMINIQUE WILKINS
NBA Forward

No question, I definitely accepted the responsibility of being the team leader. The players know what I'm capable of. More importantly, they know I have a can't-fail attitude.

JOHN ELWAY
NFL Quarterback

When things go bad, it's easy to point fingers. People who attempt to switch the blame are afraid to fail. We've all been afraid to fail before a game, but it shouldn't stop a person from continuing, and from doing what you have to do to get the job done.

RICK MEARS
Race Car Driver

I go out on the track to do the best job I can do. If a record happens, then it's great. I got it. But I don't go into a race saying I want a record. I don't let things like that influence my job. If I work hard enough the rest will come. I try to keep everything on an even keel, as much as possible.

OREL HERSHISER
Major League Pitcher

This M.V.P. Award is very special to me, but not as important as the Dodgers' winning the Series.

I had a great run of scoreless innings, but I honestly wasn't trying to set any records. I had the same philosophy I always have when I pitch.

It doesn't do you any good to hang your head and get upset. If you get beat, you should learn something from it. If it was your best pitch, well, you gave it your best shot. If it wasn't, you shouldn't throw it again.

DOC EDWARDS
Major League Manager

Being afraid to fail keeps many athletes from being successful. When you're afraid to fail, it takes away your aggressiveness and keeps you from playing at a higher level. Why? Because you're afraid of looking bad.

CARL F. HUGHES
Businessman

Falling into the deepest valley is nothing to fear. It just means that you are in the perfect position to climb the world's highest mountain.

BONNIE BLAIR
Speedskater — Olympic Gold Medalist

On the ice I'm aggressive. To race is to go all out, every time, no matter what happens. I never worry about falling.

BO JACKSON
NFL Running Back and Major League Outfielder

Winning the Heisman was a dream come true for me. Our team had a great year. I enjoyed every minute of it. I never worried about the trophy. I just played every game as hard as I could.

Now people are telling me I can't play two sports professionally. I can take criticism. I know what my capabilities are and as long as I do my best, I'll never worry about not being successful. I'll just take it one day at a time. One season at a time. And play as hard as I can.

GREG LeMOND
**Professional Cyclist —
Two Time Tour De France Winner**

I was confident going into the final day of the Tour De France. Once I relieved myself of the pressure of wearing the "yellow" jersey, I knew the possibility of winning was there. But even more importantly, since I was no longer the leader, I didn't have to worry about losing. I was going to give it my all, and whether it would be good enough only time would tell.

DAVID ROBINSON
NBA Center

Basketball is just something else to do, another facet of life. I'm going to be a success at whatever I choose because of my preparation. By the time the game starts, the outcome is already decided. I never think about having a bad game because I have prepared.

RON HARPER
NBA Guard

I come out and play 'in-your-face' defense and take chances going for steals. Making a great defensive play gets me pumped up as much as a good slam-dunk. If someone burns me on defense, so be it. I'll try even harder the next time down the court. To play great defense you can't worry about getting beat.

DAN MARINO
NFL Quarterback

I feel it's important to bounce back after a bad performance. The sooner you get back out there, the better you feel inside. The only people who are failures are those who give up and don't continue fighting.
Look at it this way. How would we be able to judge success if we didn't experience failure? As a quarterback, you can't be apprehensive about throwing the bomb just because it might be intercepted. No matter what your occupation, you should never be afraid to fail.

JULIE KRONE
Professional Jockey

You can't tell someone to 'Go For It', to be whatever they want to be, and at the same time to be careful. If we all ride the safe road, who will we look up to?

ALBERTO TOMBA
Skier — Two Time Olympic Gold Medalist

I don't think about the competition. I only go as fast as I can. That's it. The results will come.
To be a good racer today, you must be brainless. By that I mean be able to turn off the brain. For that reason, I win a lot of races.

BOB TWAY
Professional Golfer

I've been on a roller coaster since I won the PGA championship in '86. When I'm playing well I have a lot of confidence. When I'm not, I have none. That's when I aim for the center of the green instead of the flag.

I know I can play well. I know I can win. I just have to stop seeing all the trouble in front of me (water, the beach, out of bounds). Concentrate on only the flag and give it a good rip.

STEFFI GRAF
Professional Tennis Player

I feel I need to accomplish all my goals early in life. I have learned from my father the guidelines to success. You can't measure success if you have never failed. My father has taught me that if you really do want to reach your goals, you can't spend any time worrying about whether you're going to win or lose. Focus only on getting better.

DWIGHT GOODEN
Major League Pitcher

Every time out I learn more and more about myself. People can give advice, but when you are out there on the mound, you're all alone — you against the batter. All you can do is bring your best to the ball park and not worry about the results.

DOUG JONES
Major League Pitcher

In baseball success is very elusive, considering that the greatest hitters of all times only got a hit 3 to 4 times out of every 10 at bats. That means that they actually failed 6 to 7 times out of 10. If any of the great hitters took time to think about how many times they failed, they never would have been successful.

BARRY SANDERS
NFL Half Back

I realize that it's a whole new game in the NFL. I'll have to improve in many aspects of my game. I know that as long as the effort is there, the results will be good. I didn't worry about failing in college, so I'm not going to waste time wondering and worrying about making it with the pros.

JANET EVANS
Swimmer — Three Time Olympic Gold Medalist

I never see myself as being small. Size doesn't matter as long as you can get to the end of the pool faster than everybody else. I don't worry about winning or losing — just getting to the end of the pool as fast as I can.

Coming down the stretch, I think about the same thing all the time. Put your head down and go as fast as you can — put winning or losing out of your mind — just concentrate on swimming as fast as you can.

MATT BIONDI
Swimmer — Five Time Olympic Gold Medalist

There is too much emphasis on success and failure, and too little on how a person grows as he works his way toward the Olympics. To me, it was the path getting there that counted, not the number of golds I won. My advice to young people is to relax, enjoy the journey, enjoy every moment and quit worrying about winning or losing.

I don't have to go up to the guys and tell them to hustle. They see the way I play. Leadership comes by example.

Willie Stargell, Major League First Baseman and Coach

I'm convinced that a team of good character—and by that I mean a bunch of guys who are morally sound and who really care about each other—will win the close games and come through in the clutch and perform well under adverse circumstances.

Terry Bradshaw, NFL Quarterback and Sports Broadcaster

> One man can be a crucial ingredient on a team, but one man cannot make a team.
>
> Kareem Abdul-Jabbar, NBA Center

LEADERSHIP — TEAMWORK

Leaders aren't always the loudest or the most popular. They don't have to be. Yet they're essential to a winning team. They're respected by their teammates who depend heavily upon them to win.

Leaders are molded from the highest character and are generally the hardest workers on the team. They're the first to come to practice and the last ones to leave. During practice, they lead by example with their mouths closed, concentrating hard. They understand the team's goals so they know what has to be done. They realize that practice is precious, preparation time for the real thing — the game.

At St. Edward, we've been blessed with a number of such leaders. They all loved to win and hated to lose. They were willing to pay the price to make themselves better athletes. Their won-loss records have been impressive, but their work ethic even more so. The important point here is that the work ethic and positive mental attitudes of these leaders were contagious. They were valuable because they made everyone feel that nobody could stop them from winning.

Teammates realize this and sense that leaders are people who know where they are going. It's natural that these people become leaders because they want to go where the team wants to go: To the winner's circle. The rest of the team will follow.

A leader is uniquely unselfish. He or she's often the most talented member of the team, but uses his or her talent for the benefit of the team, not just for himself or herself.

Such a person may not be the life of a party, but when the going gets tough at the end of the game, this is the one person above all the others you want on your team. Being a leader is a tough and demanding business, but the rewards are well worth it. Leaders have the respect and admiration of the entire team. That's better than being the most popular person or the team comedian — by a wide margin.

But a leader cannot do it alone. Basketball teams with one great scorer consistently lose to teams that know the value of teamwork.

The team player knows that the team comes first. It doesn't matter who gets the credit as long as the job gets done.

The team player is the one who makes it all go — the one who throws the key block, hits behind the runner or comes off the bench to pick up the team. He or she's the one who sleeps the best the night after each game, and proudly looks at himself or herself in the mirror the following morning saying, "I did all I could possibly do to help our team win."

One of my favorite wrestlers was a prime example of the ultimate team player. He was a young man who wasn't a state champion or a state finalist. In fact, he never even made our starting lineup. But he always wrestled hard in practice and helped prepare several of our state wrestling champions. How? He challenged them, pushed them to their limits, prodded them, encouraged them and respected them. They, in turn, returned that respect.

At our annual awards banquet, in a year when we had five state champions, he won our Most Valuable Wrestler award. And, he went to Miami University (Ohio) on a wrestling scholarship. That's leadership. That's teamwork.

LEADERSHIP

GARY CARTER
Major League Catcher

What you need is about seven or eight leaders. If I'm a leader, I want to be one of a bunch of them. Then I know we're going somewhere.

JOE NAMATH
NFL Quarterback and Sports Broadcaster

To be a leader, you have to make people want to follow you, and nobody wants to follow someone who doesn't know where he's going.

HARRY TRUMAN
Thirty-Third President

Leadership is the ability to get men to do what they don't want to do and like doing it.

JOHNNY BENCH
Major League Catcher and Sports Broadcaster

Within months they were saying I was a sure thing, a can't miss. I never shirked that kind of pressure; in fact, I realized that it was also a once-in-a-lifetime opportunity. Everyone said the team needed a leader. I was cocky enough—forget Babe Ruth, remember Johnny Bench. At the age of 19, I had to run the defense and handle pitchers who were around when I was still shagging Milnot cans. I hustled my butt to show them that I basically knew what I was doing. That was the only way I knew how to lead—to play out every play just as hard as I possibly could.

DWIGHT D. EISENHOWER
Thirty-Fourth President and U.S. General

A platoon leader doesn't get his platoon to go by getting up and shouting, "I am smarter, I am bigger, I am stronger, I am the leader." He gets men to go along with him because they want to do it for him and they believe in him.

SID LUCKMAN
NFL Quarterback

Today's high school students will be the leaders of tomorrow. To be a good leader, you must be honest, responsible and willing to put the best interests of everyone before personal gain.

JOE DI MAGGIO
Major League Outfielder

Motivation is something nobody else can give you. Others can help motivate you, but basically it must come from you and it must be a constant desire to do your very best at all times and under any circumstances. A person always doing his or her best becomes a natural leader, just by example. The youth of our nation is what will keep us strong and young athletes are the natural leaders of the future.

DAVE CONCEPCION
Major League Shortstop

When I first made it into the big leagues, I was very down—very homesick. I was lost and afraid. When I left the ball park, I was shaking. I asked myself 100 times why I come here. I no speak English, I have no friends. Things worked out good but I haven't forgot about other Latins. I go to the minor league complex and make sure the Latin players know what to do. I lead them by example. I yell, "Work, work, work. It is not easy. Don't think you are too good. Your talent is not enough, it's hard up here. You must work."

VINCE LOMBARDI
NFL Coach and General Manager

Contrary to the opinion of many people, leaders are not born. Leaders are made, and they are made by effort and hard work.

CARDINAL GIBBONS
American Cardinal

The higher men climb the longer their working day. And any young man with a streak of idleness in him may better make up his mind at the beginning that mediocrity will be his lot. Without immense, sustained effort he will not climb high. And even though fortune or chance were to lift him high, he would not stay there. For to keep at the top is harder almost than to get there. There are no office hours for leaders.

CHUCK NOLL
NFL Linebacker and Coach
You can't tell someone to go out and lead. You become a leader by doing. So if you want to be a leader, go do it.

EARL WEAVER
Major League Manager
Leadership can be defined in one word—honesty. You must be honest with the players and honest with yourself. Never be afraid to stick up for your players.

TOM LANDRY
NFL Defensive Back and Coach
Leadership is a matter of having people look at you and gain confidence by seeing how you react. If you're in control, they're in control.

TEAMWORK

BABE RUTH
Major League Pitcher/Outfielder

The way a team plays as a whole determines its success. You may have the greatest bunch of individual stars in the world, but if they don't play together, the club won't be worth a dime.

JIM PALMER
Major League Pitcher and Sports Broadcaster

You can't win if nobody catches the ball in the outfield. You're only as good as the team you have behind you.

KAREEM ABDUL-JABBAR
NBA Center

I don't get a big charge out of being the leading scorer. The object of competing is winning. I just try to do what has to be done for us to win. That might be anything at any time—defense, rebounding, passing. I get satisfaction out of being a team player.

JACK HAM
NFL Linebacker and Sports Broadcaster

This is going to sound corny, but I really want to contribute my one-forty-fifth that goes into helping the team win a championship. I remember one year when I made All-Pro and our team didn't do very well—the All-Pro thing didn't have much meaning. You can talk to your mother and your wife and kids about being All-Pro, but that's about it.

CHARLEY TAYLOR
NFL Wide Receiver

You can't do it alone. Be a team player, not an individualist, and respect your teammates. Anything you do, you'll have to do as a team. Many records have been made, but only because of the help of one's teammates.

FRANKLIN D. ROOSEVELT
Thirty-Second President

People acting together as a group can accomplish things which no individual acting alone could ever hope to bring about.

Y. A. TITTLE
NFL Quarterback

My job is to try to direct the team over the goal line in some way. It doesn't make a heck of a lot of difference whether it's 100 yards passing and 300 yards running or 300 passing and 100 running.

JOHN WOODEN
College Basketball Coach

The main ingredient of stardom is the rest of the team.

TOBY HARRAH
Major League Third Baseman

Talk about batting averages, batting titles and hitting .300 means nothing to me. I don't even know what my batting average is. It took me a long time to break myself of the habit of checking my average on the scoreboard before every at-bat.

Baseball is a team game. What really counts is the standings—wins and losses. Besides, statistics don't measure the full worth of a player. They don't show when he advances a runner, or when he drives in a player from third with less than two outs.

JACK WHITAKER
Sports Broadcaster

The sports world is a classic example of the game of life. Much can be accomplished when nobody becomes too concerned with who gets the credit. Great plays are made possible by unselfish and disciplined individuals who are more concerned with end results than with personal ones.

ROBIN YOUNT
Major League Shortstop

It feels great to get this type of praise, but I enjoy the wins more because that's what it's all about. We're out to prove we can beat anybody and prove we're the best in baseball. My goal never has been to break records. My goal, my only goal, is to help our team win a World Series.

VINCE LOMBARDI
NFL Coach and General Manager

Individual commitment to a group effort—that is what makes a team work, a company work, a society work, a civilization work.

KNUTE ROCKNE
College Football Coach

The secret of winning football games is working more as a team, less as individuals. I play not my 11 best, but my best 11.

WALTER ALSTON
Major League Manager

Baseball's a team game. It's not just the nine guys on the field but all 25 of them. No one man or two men can do it all.

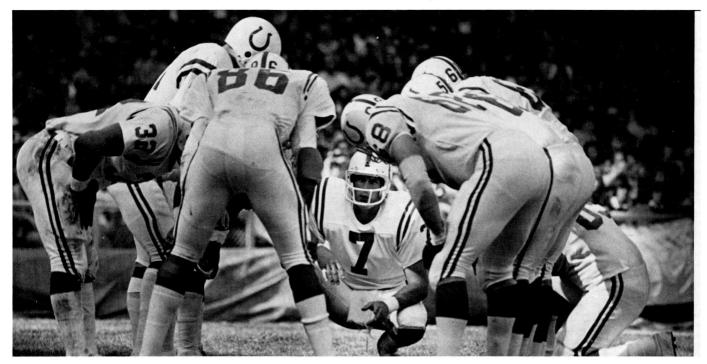

BERT JONES
NFL Quarterback

Teamwork is absolutely essential to winning football games. Football is not a one-man game, but a team undertaking, a team endeavor. Each man must be willing to sacrifice personal ambition for the good of the team.

KEN ANDERSON
NFL Quarterback

I feel I've had a consistent career, but I could only be as good as the team. Contrary to what some people think, I didn't just get good again in 1981. It was no comeback. The team just got better.

MIKE ERUZIONE
Amateur Center — Olympic Gold Medalist

We all came together six months before the 1980 Winter Olympics with different styles of hockey and different ethnic beliefs...but we made ourselves a team. Individually, we could not have done it.

WAYNE GRETZKY
NHL Center

One guy can't win the Stanley Cup or the Boston Bruins would have won it seven straight years with Bobby Orr. The better the team plays, the better you play.

JIM CLARK
Race Car Driver

Preparation is a combination of a lot of effort by a great many people. The engine manufacturers and our own mechanics, who strip the cars from the last race, test everything to make sure that we're setting up as good of a car as we can for the next race. I get a lot of the glory, but it is not a one-man effort. It is all these people working together very enthusiastically to make certain I've got the best car possible.

B. C. FORBES
American Publisher

Large-scale success today is spelled "Teamwork." The successful teamworker doesn't wear a chip on his shoulder, doesn't look for slights, isn't constantly on the alert lest his "dignity" be insulted. He puts the good of the house—the company or team—first. And if the whole prospers, he, as an active, effective, progressive part of it, will prosper with it.

VINCE LOMBARDI
NFL Coach and General Manager

Teamwork is what the Green Bay Packers were all about. They didn't do it for individual glory. They did it because they loved one another.

LARRY GURA
Major League Pitcher

As far as I'm concerned, you shouldn't keep individual stats. Baseball is a team game. The only thing that counts is how many games the team has won.

PETE CARRIL
College Basketball Coach

In a team sport like basketball, every time you help somebody else, you help yourself.

RUDYARD KIPLING
English Poet/Novelist

Now this is the law of the jungle—
As old and as true as the sky;
And the wolf that keep it may prosper,
But the wolf that shall break it must die.
As the creeper that girdles the tree trunk,
The law runneth forward and back—
And the strength of the pack is the wolf
And the strength of the wolf is the pack.

BLANTON COLLIER
NFL Coach

It's amazing how much can be accomplished if no one cares who gets the credit.

FRANK GIFFORD
NFL Halfback/End and Sports Broadcaster

I was a better football player because the team was better—the same is true today with Don and Howie.

KEITH HERNANDEZ
Major League First Baseman

The only statistics I pay close attention to are the number of runs scored and the number of RBI's because those are the production categories. They are the only ones that help the team win ball games.

GREG PRUITT
NFL Halfback

One man can't do it alone. Football is a team sport. A running back is only as good as his offensive line.

TONY DORSETT
NFL Halfback

The fact that I'm getting my yards and the fullback's getting his means only one thing—the offensive line is doing its job.

ARCHIE GRIFFIN
NFL Halfback

I got a good hand-off, had some great blocking and I kept seeing daylight so I just ran, that's all. There wasn't anything fancy about it. The hole was there. The blocking was good. I was just one of 11 guys doing their job.

ROY CAMPANELLA
Major League Catcher

I am proud of all my trophies, but truthfully when I was playing, I never thought of records. I just tried to do all I possibly could to help the team win.

BILL FOSTER
College Basketball Coach

There is no letter I in the word teamwork.

FRAN TARKENTON
NFL Quarterback and Sports Broadcaster

Quarterbacks don't win or lose football games. Teams do.

SIDNEY POWELL
American Clergyman/Author

Try to forget yourself in the service of others. For when we think too much of ourselves and our own interests, we easily become despondent. But when we work for others, our efforts return to bless us.

PHIL ESPOSITO
NHL Center and General Manager

In the game of hockey, it takes six to tango. You gotta stand up for your teammates.

TOM LANDRY
NFL Defensive Back and Coach

There's a misconception about teamwork. Teamwork is the ability to have different thoughts about things; it's the ability to argue and stand up and say loud and strong what you feel. But in the end, it's also the ability to adjust to what is best for the team.

BOB BERRY
NHL Coach

My coaching philosophy won't fill a book. Stated very simply, it's to be prepared for anything. There has to be discipline and strong defense. What I mean by strong defense is not only having good defensemen. It means all six men playing good defense at the same time. We are a group...a team.

DIGGER PHELPS
College Basketball Coach

A few mistakes don't worry me; what worries me is when you make the mistakes and then forget your role on the team and start to worry about your ego.

JOHN MADDEN
NFL Coach and Sports Broadcaster

There is one key point about picking the so-called "great athlete." It doesn't mean a thing if he doesn't perform with the team in mind.

RED HOLZMAN
NBA Coach

Work as hard as you possibly can within the team structure.

JIM ZORN
NFL Quarterback

I'm only a reflection of what our team is.

JULIUS ERVING
NBA Forward

When people tell me fans are cheated because they came to see me do this or that, I tell them that supposedly they are coming to see the team win. The role of a player should be results first, effects second. I don't go in to dunk the ball or dribble behind my back for the effect of doing it. Those were skills that were developed in the course of trying to reach my potential as a player. My methods have created a reputation for myself because it has a certain effect on people watching the game. If they like it and dig it—hey, that's cool. But if they don't like me shooting a lay-up instead of dunking the ball, they'll have to realize that I'm out there to help the team win.

ALAN ALDA
Actor, Producer and Director

On the set, I like for everyone to eat together, share food and stories, and kid and joke because some of that comes over into the working day. The comfort you establish among each other shows on the screen.

JACK PARDEE
NFL Linebacker, Coach

The finest compliment that anyone can pay to a person is to say that he is a complete team player. To deserve this tribute, your every thought, action, and deed should be one that you are doing for the team.

TOMMY LASORDA
Major League Manager

If you take 25 players, seven coaches, a manager and the front-office staff and put them all on one end of a rope pulling together, they will win. They can't be stopped.

PAUL BROWN
NFL Coach, General Manager and Owner
Don't be afraid to remind any players who are out of line or not in the spirit of your training rules that they owe it to the school to straighten themselves out. You win when everyone works together as a team—never let one or two players pull your whole team down.

STAN ALBECK
NBA and College Basketball Coach
As a player, remember that the bench is not a prison but an extension of the first group. Concentrate on the quality of your play when you do get into the game. If you play 20 minutes, play the best 20 you can possibly play.

RICK BARRY
NBA Forward and Sports Broadcaster

I was taught to play the game from a total team concept—to be able to do everything reasonably well and some things extraordinarily well. If I'm not shooting well, I'll try to be an asset in other ways—like defense, passing, rebounding and hustle.

PATRICK EWING
NBA Center

I figured everybody we played was intimidated. I'm satisfied with the way I played, but I don't evaluate my performances. I worried about the team and about what I could contribute defensively. I don't need to score. As long as we won, I didn't care how many points I scored.

EARL RED BLAIK
TALKS ABOUT LEADERSHIP

Good fellows are a dime a dozen, but an aggressive leader is priceless. The 1955 season was most trying for me as we had a lean squad and no quarterback. A coach has never known trouble, unless he too has the senseless temerity to change an All American End into a "T" quarterback in one season. There was hardly an officer or cadet at West Point who didn't believe this switch was a colossal error. Even my friends of the press called the move 'Blaik's Folly.'

Sunday afternoon after the Michigan defeat, the Superintendent, my former football teammate, came to my office and inquired as to whether I was aware of the local sentiment about Holleder, our quarterback. I told him that the team was aware, but he would still be our quarterback.

A few minutes after the Superintendent left, Holleder came to see me. As he entered the office, I got up, placed my hand on his shoulder and said, "Holly, you played a good game yesterday and I am proud of you. You're making fine progress as our quarterback." With moisture in his eyes, Holly replied, **"I know what the cadets are saying. I have heard the officers talk, and I came fully prepared to get my old number back, but I want you to know that I prayed all the way here that you would not give up on me."** Now it is many weeks later. It is the night before the Navy game. As usual, I took the squad for a bedtime walk on the golf course, which ended with a few words about the big game. I recall saying: "Three times this season, I took the long walk across muddy fields to congratulate first Benny Oosterbaan, then Ben Schwartzwalder, and then Jordon Oliver. It has been a trying season and I am a bit weary from those walks. Tomorrow before 100,000 spectators and fifty million television viewers, I want you men to know it would be the longest walk of my coaching career if I have to cross the field to congratulate the Navy coach."

There was silence for a moment—then a voice spoke out with resolution. It was Holleder. **"Colonel, you're not taking that walk tomorrow."** The Cadets won an upset victory over the Navy. The press stated it was Holly's vindication. It wasn't—it wasn't at all. It was an unforgettable demonstration that an aggressive leader is priceless.

My concentration level blocks out everything. Concentration is why some athletes are better than others. You develop that concentration in training. You can't be lackadaisical in training and concentrate in a meet.

**Edwin Moses, Hurdler —
Two Time Olympic Gold Medalist**

When I play, I'm boiling inside. I just try not to show it because it's a lack of composure, and if you give in to your emotions after one loss, you're liable to have three or four in a row.

Chris Evert, Professional Tennis Player

CONCENTRATION — POISE

It's easy to have poise and concentration when everything is going well. Great athletes are the ones who maintain their poise and concentration when they're staring defeat in the face.

A sure way to be defeated is to lose your composure. By doing so, you give the mental edge to your opponent. For example, if you think the referee or umpire is against you, you start battling him rather than your opponent. That's a surefire way to lose your concentration, and probably the game or match.

The solution to gaining control of your game is to think only about the next play or point, not the last one. Concentrate hard on what you can do now to win. All your worrying and complaining is not going to change what just happened. You can only change what will happen next. Focus on that.

If you commit an error in the field, think about how you will field the next ball hit to you.

If you make a turnover, think about how you're going to help your team get the ball back.

If you drop a pass, think about watching the ball sink into your hands the next time it comes your way. Or about making a great block to help one of your teammates score a touchdown.

Don't look back. Don't brood. Don't complain. Don't worry or wonder how you got yourself into the alligator swamp. Keep your cool and concentrate only on how you're going to get out of that swamp. Focus your concentration on what you can do next time and forget the past — it doesn't exist anymore.

Concentration in many sports may be something as simple as keeping your eye on the ball, or simply re-creating what you have prepared in practice. If you are totally concentrating on what you're doing, you'll have total control of yourself. This will give you the edge. You'll be oblivious to the crowd and the noise, as well as the pressure to win. The champion is the one who is able to reach peak performance and win in stressful situations.

There's a famous saying in sports that, "It's not over until it's over." This means don't give up when things are going badly, because the momentum may shift back to you again. Don't lose your temper or your cool. If you do, you lose your edge and you punish yourself for another's shortcoming. If you maintain your composure, anything can happen. The game or match can be turned around by a single event. Concentrate and keep your poise.

I've coached a lot of wrestling matches over the years, but there's one particular one I've never forgotten. One of our wrestlers was in a big match. For five minutes and 50 seconds of a six-minute match, he was soundly beaten. He was losing 5-0 to a better wrestler. I stood up and was getting ready to give him a hug for good effort when he scored six points in the last ten seconds.

He kept his poise. He kept his concentration. He was undoubtedly the only person in the entire gymnasium who felt that he still had a chance to win. Even I, his own coach, had given up on him. But because he kept his cool, he walked off the mat a winner. His opponent was clearly the better wrestler — or was he?

You can't let yourself look at the mountain below. It might soften you with its beauty. Instead, you must think only of the course and the darkness of the challenge.

Franz Klammer, Skier—Olympic Gold Medalist

CONCENTRATION

CHRIS EVERT
Professional Tennis Player

I won't even call a friend the day of a match. I'm scared of disrupting my concentration. I don't allow any competition with tennis.

TOM SEAVER
Major League Pitcher and Sports Broadcaster

You can never let up and that applies more to concentrating than the actual throwing of the ball. You must have the ability to block everything out. Forget that the second baseman just muffed a double-play ball or that the umpire is missing a lot of calls or that your wife just charged $700 at Bloomingdale's.

TOM LANDRY
NFL Defensive Back and Coach

Concentration is when you're completely unaware of the crowd, the field, the score. The real secret to success as an athlete is control of yourself and concentration. Those are what make the difference once you get techniques down and training wrapped up. It comes down to the ability to control yourself in stress situations.

DICK WEBER
Professional Bowler

It's hard to socialize out on the lanes and bowl well. I have to think about each execution.

TONY ESPOSITO
NHL Goalie and General Manager

What I tried to do was concentrate. It's all concentration. On the morning of a game we'd have a meeting. Then I'd go back home if it was a home game or back to my hotel if it was a road game and spend time getting mentally prepared. I'd like to get to the rink fairly early and think about the game—what I'd have to do once the game started—how I would stay alert—how I would be ready. Even though I'd been playing a while, I'd still concentrate as hard as I always did.

DONNA CAPONI
Professional Golfer

In golf, you can never think too far ahead—not even to the next hole. It is very important to work on the shot you are on, not "I can birdie the 15th hole" when you are still trying to par the fifth. Patty Berg told me once, "Never think behind you or too far in front. Never think of the bad hole that you just had; just concentrate on the hole you are playing!"

MERLIN OLSEN
NFL Tackle, Sports Broadcaster and Actor

If you take it easy for 10 minutes, it takes a long time to get it back. Like everything else, concentration is a habit.

REGGIE JACKSON
Major League Outfielder and Sports Broadcaster

Hitting is concentration. Free your mind of everything. Study the flight of the baseball from the pitcher.

REGGIE SMITH
Major League Outfielder

Too much conversation. Too much talk. That's one of the big problems for some teams. You've got to concentrate on what you're supposed to be doing, and that's playing ball. Less talk and more action.

TERRY BRADSHAW
NFL Quarterback and Sports Broadcaster

Total concentration has been the key to the success of the Pittsburgh Steelers. During the regular season, there were teams we didn't concentrate on enough, but in the playoffs, our concentration was total.

LAMARR HOYT
Major League Pitcher

The one thing I needed to improve on was my concentration. I had to learn patience, to always take what the batter gave me. For example, if the batter is up there with a wide-open stance, throw to the outside corner. I had to concentrate on those little, but important, things.

MICHAEL FRIEDSAM
American Businessman/Military Colonel

Concentrate on finding your goal, then concentrate on reaching it.

WILLIAM MATTHEWS
American Author

One well-cultivated talent, deepened and enlarged, is worth 100 shallow faculties. The first law of success in this day, when so many things are clamoring for attention, is concentration—to bend all the energies to one, and to go directly to that point, looking neither to the right nor to the left.

JOHN JEFFERSON
NFL Wide Receiver

Catching the football is all mental. You can put all the stickum on your hands you want, but what it really comes down to is pure concentration.

BOB GRIESE
NFL Quarterback and Sports Broadcaster

In a game, I always had total concentration. I thought of myself as looking down on a situation from above, like a chess player. I could see moves coming and I was ready to make them. When you have total grasp and knowledge of what's going on, you can effectively maneuver people around, manipulate your offense to take advantage of what the defense is showing.

DALE BROWN
College Basketball Coach

Motivation and hard work are not enough; concentration is imperative. Concentration is the supreme art, because no art can be achieved without it. While with it, anything can be achieved. The masters all have the ability to discipline themselves to eliminate everything except what they are trying to accomplish.

ANDREW CARNEGIE
American Iron and Steel Manufacturer

Concentration is my motto—first honesty, then industry, then concentration.

CHRIS EVERT
Professional Tennis Player

Ninety percent of my game is mental. It's my concentration that has gotten me this far.

DANNY WHITE
NFL Quarterback

The way I look at football is, if you're going to beat me, you've got to beat everything I've got, everything I can do to you. You will have my total, complete concentration.

FRANK GIFFORD
NFL Halfback/End and Sports Broadcaster

Most people think football is strictly a muscle game. In the pros, though, every club is loaded with so much power that sheer strength is cancelled out. You've got to outsmart the other team to win and that takes enormous concentration on details.

BRIAN SIPE
NFL Quarterback

What I try to achieve during the season is a relaxed state of concentration. I simply try to cleanse my mind of the pressures that people are trying to heap on me.

TOMMY HEARNS
Professional Boxer

When I'm getting ready for a fight, I like to concentrate on what I have to do, and talking about it beforehand won't get the job done.

ROGER BANNISTER
First Man to Run the Mile Under Four Minutes

Without the concentration of the mind and the will, the performance would not result.

ALAN ALDA
Actor, Producer and Director

When I'm trying to solve a problem or learn something, I do tend to get obsessed with it. But I find I can only accomplish what I want to accomplish by a process of total absorption.

BEN HOGAN
Professional Golfer

I had to learn to concentrate, to ignore the gallery and the other golfers—and shut my mind against everything but my own game.

JIM BROWN
NFL Fullback and Actor

The nine years I was in pro ball, I never quit trying to make my mind an encyclopedia of every possible detail—about my teammates, about players on other teams, about the plays we used and about both our and other teams' collective and individual tendencies. Every play I ran, I had already run 1,000 times in my mind. You get a jump on the game when you visualize beforehand not only the regular plays you run, but also the 101 other things that might happen unexpectedly. So, when you're in the actual game, whatever happens, you've already seen it in your mind and plotted your countermoves—instantly and instinctively.

GRAIG NETTLES
Major League Third Baseman

A lot of people ask me if I work on my diving. That's something you can't work on. It has to be instinctive to do it because the first time you practice it you'll probably fracture your shoulder. When I dive for a ball, very rarely do I feel myself hit the ground because there are so many things going through my mind. The key to fielding is total concentration.

JACK NICKLAUS
Professional Golfer

Concentration is a fine antidote to anxiety. I have always felt that the sheer intensity Ben Hogan applied to the shotmaking specifics was one of his greatest assets. It left no room in his mind for negative thoughts. The busier you can keep yourself with the particulars of shot assessment and execution, the less chance your mind has to dwell on the emotional "if" and "but" factors that breed anxiety.

POISE

JEAN-CLAUDE KILLY
Skier—Three Time Olympic Gold Medalist

People ask me what makes a great skier. It takes the gift; but besides the gift it takes that availability of mind which permits total control of all the elements that lead to victory—total composure.

RAY NITSCHKE
NFL Linebacker

Most of the clubs we played against gave it their all in the first half, and when they found out they couldn't dominate us at their peak, they usually had a tremendous psychological letdown in the second half. They lost their poise and character. We played the same all the way through the game, so it's not that we played harder in the second half, but that the other clubs gave up.

BRYANT GUMBEL
Sports Broadcaster and Talk Show Host

My ability is to digest a lot of information, which I dispense calmly and articulately while everyone around me is going bananas.

HERB BROOKS
U.S. Olympic Hockey Team and NHL Coach

During the last 10 minutes of the game against Russia in the 1980 Winter Olympics, we started to panic. We started reverting to an individualistic type of play. We started to withdraw. I told them to play with poise and patience and to stay with what got them there.

LARRY BOWA
Major League Shortstop and Manager

Being cool and relaxed is a big part of it. Even if you've just made three errors in a row or are in a batting slump, you have to keep your composure.

NORM SONJU
NBA General Manager and Vice President

How a person responds to life situations is absolutely critical! In fact, how a person responds is oftentimes even more important than the situation itself!

MIKE SCHMIDT
Major League Third Baseman

I want to always convey to my teammates and to the opposition that I am in control of myself. I don't want anyone to think that I am intimidated by anything going on out on the field.

BJORN BORG
Professional Tennis Player

Changing sides and continuing after being outclassed is always terribly uncomfortable, but the most important thing in such circumstances is to keep a cool head. Play with ice in your stomach and do not show by the slightest flicker of an eyelid that your opponent is making an impression on you.

BOBBY HULL
NHL Left Wing

Always keep your composure. It's silly to get penalties. You can't score from the penalty box and to win, you have to score.

F. EDISON WHITE
American Businessman

Poise is a big factor in a man's success. If I were a young man just starting out, I would talk things over with myself as a friend. I would set out to develop poise—for it can be developed. A man should learn to stand, what to do with his hands, what to do with his feet, look his man straight in the eye, dress well and look well and know he looks well.

E. W. HOSE
American Author/Journalist

When I am angry with myself, I criticize others.

JOHN WOODEN
College Basketball Coach

Poise and confidence will come from condition, skill and team spirit. To have poise and be truly confident, you must be in condition, know you are fundamentally sound, and possess the proper team attitude.

JULIUS BOROS
Professional Golfer

Poise. Concentration. No indecision. No wasted motion. No strong-arm tactics. Only an easy, fluid motion. That's the secret of my game.

TOM WEISKOPF
Professional Golfer and Golf Analyst

I try not to let anything interfere with my game plan. I know I need patience and I'm determined to maintain a good attitude. After all, that's the sign of a pro—keeping your cool. Look at those pro quarterbacks. They don't get flustered when they're behind with two minutes to go. They just keep their poise and let things happen.

BRIAN SIPE
NFL Quarterback

I learned a long time ago that one way to maximize potential for performance is to be calm in my mind.

PAUL BROWN
NFL Coach, General Manager and Owner

Maintain your composure. The worst thing you can do to an opponent is to beat him.

JOE TORRE
Major League Catcher and Manager

Stick to your strength. Don't panic. Don't improvise. Be yourself. Wait for the moment, the right pitch. Wait. Be patient.

JIMMY "THE GREEK" SNYDER
Sports Broadcaster

Don't steam. Don't be angry. Don't lose your head. It's the best part of your body.

BENJAMIN FRANKLIN
American Inventor

Anger is never without a reason, but seldom with a good one.

TERRY BRADSHAW
NFL Quarterback and Sports Broadcaster

Quite often, the mark of an experienced quarterback, one who has poise, is the amount of time he holds on to the ball before releasing it. The quarterback who can be patient enough for lanes to open and receivers to clear will be more successful. I played a long time before I had poise and I suffered for it, and so did my team. Now I think I have poise. I'm not saying I have an oversupply of it, but I've learned patience back there.

BJORN BORG LEARNED TO KEEP HIS COOL

"**Personally, I draw a sharp line between stubborn play and hot-temperedness. A player who cannot control his temper on the court will never become a great player. Occasional outbursts of anger can perhaps happen to anyone, but otherwise I am convinced that everyone gains from limiting such outbursts.**"

Bjorn Borg has been a dominant figure in tennis since the early 1970's. Throughout that time, he has been consistently excellent. There have been very few off-days for Borg.

His personality has also been consistent on the court. Rarely does he question a call or show emotion. His game appears always under control.

But, there was a time, at the age of 12, when Borg was known as the "Bad Boy" of Swedish tennis. He would throw his racquet and would hit the ball at the fence over calls he questioned. Because of his actions he was suspended for six months by the Swedish Tennis Association.

That experience embarrassed Borg and made him examine his game. The result is obvious to anyone who has seen him play.

"**Now if my opponent cheats, or if I get a terrible call, I don't say a thing. Inside I may say it all. But if I objected out loud, I know I would get so flustered and turn red that I'm determined never to do it. I guess the memories of my humiliation have stuck with me so that I'll never again do anything crazy or unsportsmanlike in front of a lot of people.**"

KAREEM ABDUL-JABBAR
JULIUS ERVING

PAUL NEWMAN

JOHN STALLWORTH

JOHN MC ENROE

BEN HOGAN

LARRY BOWA

JOHNNY BENCH

JOE NAMATH

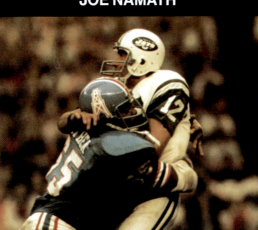

GO FOR IT

When you're properly prepared, both physically and mentally, you're ready to "Go For It" in the game. Game time is the time when all those long hours of practice pay off. Now's the time to let your instincts take over.

If you have confidence in your ability, you'll know every move instinctively. You'll have performed them many times successfully in practice. You won't have time to figure out the angles. You'll just know what you have to do. You can just feel it. It's been etched into your brain so many times, you'll respond automatically without thinking.

Tightrope walkers offer us some insight on this. They realize that the easiest way to fall off the tightrope is to think about what they're doing. Their solution is to not think about it, but just do it and keep on walking.

If basketball is your sport, go for the ball and don't be afraid to hit the floor. On offense, always look for open teammates, but if you have a sure shot, take it. Don't stop and think about it — just shoot.

Baseball players have many opportunities to "Go For It": Break up that double play; back up your teammates; go from first to third on a single; hit behind your teammate on first base; take a head-first slide; or make a diving catch.

Football players can also do a lot on instinct: Hit somebody; knock someone down; get your uniform dirty; make that great block; break your pattern and go for broke; sense where the ball will be thrown and go for the interception; sense where the next play will be run and make the tackle; make the big play and turn the game around. Remember, though, you're just one part of a team; don't forget to play your position. Your teammates are counting on you.

If you're a golfer, hit the ball instinctively. Don't think about your swing. Don't be too careful or too cute; hit the ball like you've hit it thousands of times before in practice.

When I first started coaching, I had an idea on how to produce winners. I had my mind set on having our wrestlers practice the moves our way. We would pick out certain high-percentage moves and practice them over and over. Our wrestlers learned the moves. In matches, we'd allow them to perform only this short check-list of high-percentage moves. It sounded good in theory and for some of our wrestlers, it worked. But for the most part, we were restricting our guys, for we didn't allow their individual talents to develop. In short, we made them robots.

So we changed. We realized that many (probably most) of our wrestlers had more ability, and were more talented, than our coaching staff had ever been when in school.

We still taught our wrestlers the high-percentage moves, but at the same time we allowed them to develop winning styles, based on instinct, of their own. We let them have fun and told them to "Go For It!". It worked tremendously.

Now the matches were no longer high-pressure events done "our way." They became "Show Time" performances based on gut instinct with each wrestler's unique talents and abilities dominating. The results were amazing. We became winners and morale was never higher. We've coached young men who have become better athletes and wrestlers than we ever dreamed possible, since we made the decision to "Go For It."

If you're a good, experienced player, you know what to do. If you're in trouble, you know how to change. One hundred percent of my game is instinct. I never stop and think I'm going to hit a ball crosscourt or down the line. I just do it.

Bjorn Borg, Professional Tennis Player

When a fighter is busy, I move and look for what's opening. It's sort of like surveying the land, looking for an area that's not protected. I'm waiting for a spot to open. If he gets careless, I move.

Sugar Ray Leonard, Professional Boxer and Sports Broadcaster

GO FOR IT

Believe In Yourself

and in your dream
Though impossible
things may seem.
Someday, somehow
you'll get through
to the goal you have in view
Mountains fall and seas divide
before the one who in their stride
takes a hard road
day by day
Believe in yourself
and in your plan
Say not I cannot but, I can.
The praises of life
we fail to win,
because we doubt
the power within.

Author Unknown

VINCE LOMBARDI
NFL Coach and General Manager
Fundamentals win it. Football is two things: It's blocking and tackling. I don't care anything about formations or new offenses or tricks on defense. If you block and tackle better than the team you're playing, you win.

FRANK ROBINSON
Major League Outfielder and Manager
I believe you should do everything to win, short of hurting someone deliberately. If you're going into second on a ground ball, you've got to break up the double play. If you just go in there with one of those easy slides because you and the shortstop are having dinner afterwards, you're letting your teammates down.

BENJAMIN DISRAELI
Prime Minister of England
Action may not always bring happiness; but there is no happiness without action.

DAVE COWENS
NBA Center and Coach
The times I go really hard after the ball are when I know we must have it. It's my job to get it then. I don't worry about injuries. I don't get hit because I'm doing the hitting. I just get the ball.

PELE
Professional Soccer Player
Playing offensively is the best defense. When you have the ball, only you can score.

JOE GREENE
NFL Defensive Tackle and Coach
When I get into a game, I haven't got time to think about what I ought to be doing. The game, that's it. I play football no-holds-barred. Any edge I can get, I'll take.

A. J. FOYT
Race Car Driver
You get out in front—you stay out in front.

MERLIN OLSEN
NFL Tackle, Sports Broadcaster and Actor
At the beginning of each new play, I thought of it as the most important play of the year. I went into it as if the game depended on it.

JOE PATERNO
College Football Coach and Athletic Director
Don't just stand back and play the way you're coached. A great player must rise to the occasion and turn the game around on his own.

BO SCHEMBECHLER
College Football Coach and Athletic Director
If I make a mistake, I'm going to make it aggressively and I'm going to make it quickly. I don't believe in sleeping on a decision.

PETE ROSE
Major League First Baseman and Manager

People say I don't have great tools. They say that I can't throw like Ellis Valentine or run like Tim Raines or hit with power like Mike Schmidt. Who can? I make up for it in other ways—by putting out a little bit more. That's my theory—to go through life hustling. In the big leagues, hustle usually means being in the right place at the right time. It means backing up a base. It means backing up your teammate. It means taking that head-first slide. It means doing everything you can do to win a baseball game.

JOE MORGAN
Major League Second Baseman and Sports Broadcaster

I've always been a lot pushier than other people. Joe Morgan has never waited for things to happen. No, sir. Joe Morgan has always made things happen.

KEN EASLEY
NFL Defensive Back

Something comes over me during the course of a game. On the field, I just like to go out and initiate contact. I play with relentless and reckless abandon. It's not that I hate the people I play against; I just like to see them go down.

INGEMAR STENMARK
Skier — Two Time Olympic Gold Medalist

To win, I have to get angry. My anger is directed at the course, at attacking it and beating it.

JACK DEMPSEY
Professional Boxer

I'd try to take 'em quick. You don't know what can happen in a fight. Move in and get 'em fast.

EDDIE ARCARO
Professional Jockey

You've got to be quick in judgment. You probably don't have but two seconds to make your decisions. Two seconds, two strides and you're committed.

TY COBB
Major League Outfielder

Don't let anyone tell you that I was a dirty player. When you're out on those base paths, you've got to protect yourself. The base paths belonged to me, the runner. The rules gave me the right. I always went into a bag full speed, feet first. I had sharp spikes on my shoes. If the baseman stood where he had no business to be and got hurt, that was his fault.

HARVEY MARTIN
NFL Defensive End

I'm boring to be around—the game is all I care about. I don't worry about bills or anything. I just want to win. When you play football, you have to give it your all. You've got to go for it. You can't get involved in other things.

JOE PATERNO
College Football Coach and Athletic Director

Don't stand around and wait for something to happen. Don't be afraid to take chances. Gamble. Be reckless. Make things happen! Force a fumble, get an interception, block a kick, create confusion in the other team. We want to make our opponent afraid to make a mistake. That's when they make 'em and we'll take advantage of it.

GREG LOUGANIS
Diver — Four Time Olympic Gold Medalist

You just follow your instincts. When you're in the air, you have something like a cat's sense. You're aware of where your body is going, and your peripheral vision tells you how high off the water you are so you can plan your dive and entry. If you are diving well, you have all the time in the world to attend to the details.

GALE SAYERS
NFL Halfback

I have no idea what I did. I heard people talk about dead leg, shake, change of pace and all that, but I did things without thinking about them.

LARRY BIRD
NBA Forward

I always know what's happening on the court. I see a situation occur and I respond.

CHARLES E. WILSON
General Motors President and Secretary of Defense

I have always liked bird dogs better than kennel-fed dogs myself—you know, one that will get out and hunt for food rather than sit on his fanny and yelp.

JERRY PATE
Professional Golfer

Every day is another new day of our lives. Think not of what you did yesterday, but what you can do for yourself today. Don't be known as one that could have or should have, but as one that did.

JOE DI MAGGIO
Major League Outfielder

If you keep thinking about what you want to do or what you hope will happen, you don't do it, and it won't happen. I have never seen it fail. Live in hope and die in despair.

RICKEY HENDERSON
Major League Outfielder

If my uniform doesn't get dirty, I haven't been doing anything in the baseball game.

JACK WHITAKER
Sports Broadcaster

"Go for broke" is usually associated with taking a risk, of gambling on the unpredictable situation, of shooting the works, even of putting one's own pride and reputation on the line. Consistent winners refuse to wait for breaks to happen. The unexpected is part of their game plan and they thrive on the element of surprise. They'll "go for broke" anytime, anywhere. Their performance implies that there is no tomorrow.

RENOLDO NEHEMIAH
Hurdler and NFL Receiver
I get myself out in front, which is where I want to be. I'm used to the loneliness out there.

STEVE OVETT
Distance Runner — Olympic Gold Medalist
My strategy is simple. I get out in front early—run as hard as I can—for as long as I can.

STANLEY FLOYD
Sprinter
I was in condition for a world record. Everything came together and I did it. Simple, natural, neat! And do I feel good? Oh yes!

DO YOUR BEST

BOB COUSY
NBA Guard

In whatever sport or field of endeavor you are interested, you should do whatever is necessary to compliment your God-given talent with proper mental preparation so as to do "the best you can." The criterion should be to fully exploit your potential rather than to win at any cost. What more could anyone ever ask of you than to be the best you possibly can?

JIM PALMER
Major League Pitcher and Sports Broadcaster

The most important thing about my pitching is that I'm satisfied, that I know I'm being the best pitcher I can be.

JOE FRAZIER
Professional Boxer, Trainer and Manager

If I lose, I'll walk away and never feel bad because I did all I could. There was nothing more to do.

GARY MADDOX
Major League Outfielder

Suppose I say I should be the All-Star center fielder and tomorrow I go into a slump. You can't get too ambitious. It only hurts you. You start worrying about your hitting streak or your batting average and you start pressing. Why put additional pressure on yourself? The only thing I can control is how much effort I put forth on the field. I try to play at 100 percent of my capacity every day, so whether I go 4-for-4 or 0-for-4, I can accept it because I gave my best.

BILL SHARMAN
NBA Guard, Coach and General Manager

While I was coaching, I believe the motivation talk I gave my players that achieved the best results was in reference to their present game-day effort.

I stressed the fact that today's performance could be the most important of their life. Yesterday's performance was already history and nothing could be done about it. Tomorrow really never comes, so today's performance is what really counts.

GEORGE BRETT
Major League Third Baseman

When I walk onto the field, I dedicate myself to giving 100 percent on every play. I owe it to myself, my family, my teammates and the fans. As long as I give this effort, I can never second-guess myself, but more importantly, I know I will be successful.

JIM MUELLER
Sportscaster

As the saying goes, "nothing in life worthwhile comes easy"—this is especially true in sports. Without dedication, perseverance, courage and pain, there are no winners. To me, a winner is an individual who sets out to accomplish something and in the end, win or lose, can say to himself I gave it my best.

B. C. FORBES
American Publisher

There is no fun equal to the satisfaction of doing one's best.

The things that are most worthwhile in life are really those within the reach of almost every normal human being who cares to seek them out.

HARRY CARSON
NFL Linebacker

I just believe that whatever it is you do, you should do the best you can. Put your all into it. If you don't utilize your talents, don't cultivate them, make them grow, then that's a shame. It's a sin, really.

STEVE CARLTON
Major League Pitcher

I look back to previous seasons but I don't compare. What I'll do is try and recapture the feeling of a certain pitch, my slider for example. But I don't pay attention to wins, dates, or those things. I go at each team, each hitter, individually. All I'm concerned with is doing my best.

GEORGE ALLEN
NFL Coach and Sports Broadcaster

Success is what you do with the ability that you have, how you use your talent. It doesn't necessarily mean any one thing. It could be any menial job. If you are the best or one of the best at that job, you have given everything of yourself and you know it. You have to live with yourself. That's success!

BILLY MARTIN
Major League Second Baseman and Manager

If you play for me, you play the game like you play life. You play it to be successful, you play it with dignity, you play it with pride, you play it aggressively, and you play it as well as you possibly can.

JOSEPH ROBBIE
NFL Owner

There is no substitute for effort. If someone with superior natural ability permits you to outwork him, you can defeat him. If you permit someone of lesser skill to excel you in effort, he will likely excel you in accomplishment. Always play up to your full potential in every endeavor. The greatest extravagance of all is to waste human potential.

PHIL MAHRE
Skier — Olympic Gold Medalist

So many things can be a factor—the snow, the weather, is it warm so that waxing is a factor? Will you fall? Will someone else just have an incredible run? All I can do is run my race, run it the best I can, and we'll see after everybody gets to the bottom.

BARBARA ANN COCHRAN
Skier—Olympic Gold Medalist

The secret to success is doing the best that you can do. Forget about whether you might win or lose. By working hard and practicing the skills that you need to perform, the results will take care of themselves. Being successful is doing your best.

H. W. DRESSER
American Publisher

Be true to the best you know. This is your high ideal. If you do your best, you cannot do more. Do your best every day and your life will gradually expand into satisfying fullness. Cultivate the habit of doing one thing at a time with quiet deliberateness. Always allow yourself a sufficient margin of time in which to do your work well. Frequently examine your working methods to discover and eliminate unnecessary tension. Aim at poise, repose, and self-control. The relaxed worker accomplishes most.

WILBERT MONTGOMERY
NFL Halfback

I don't like to rate myself. I've got a job to do. It's just like going to work every morning and I'm just trying to do the best I can at my job. I don't try to put myself on any scale with other running backs. I just do my job.

STEVE CAUTHEN
Professional Jockey

You always want to win, sure, but the important thing is to get the most out of your horse. If he runs the best he can, wherever he finishes, I feel good.

GEORGE ROGERS
NFL Halfback

I've learned that the important thing is to know that you've tried your very hardest, gave 100 percent on every play.

MARK SPITZ
Swimmer—Nine Time Olympic Gold Medalist

I'm trying to do the best I can. I'm not concerned about tomorrow, but with what goes on today.

TOM SEAVER
Major League Pitcher and Sports Broadcaster

As quickly as I can, I want to decide the best I have to work with. I start to break down the game: What's the easiest way to set up hitters with what I have tonight? That's what gives you so much satisfaction. It's one-on-one, but not the way people imagine it, me against the hitter. No, it's me against what I'm trying to accomplish with what I have to work with.

SPARKY ANDERSON
Major League Manager

Inner peace is not found in things like baseball and world championships. As long as I feel I've done the best job I possibly could, I'm satisfied.

BILL WALTON

WALTER PAYTON

TRACY AUSTIN

FERNANDO VALENZUELA

JOHNNY MILLER

NOLAN RYAN

FRAN TARKENTON

OSCAR ROBERTSON

EXTRA EFFORT

There's no doubt that Vince Lombardi was right when he said, "Fundamentals win it." But when both teams are fundamentally sound, something more is needed to win — extra effort. Once in a while, you have to reach deep down for that something extra. Some call it adrenalin, some call it second effort. Call it what you like, but be prepared to give it.

The great athletes rely on this extra effort because they want to win. Every time they step on the court or walk onto the field, they've made up their minds that they'll do whatever is needed. They'll make that extra effort.

A winner knows exactly what this extra effort is and when to use it. Athletes have lost big games or matches, not because of a lack of effort, but because of too great an effort. They tried too hard to win and became tense and anxious, instead of playing with a relaxed concentration.

Extra effort means different things in different sports. But a common trait is outstanding performance based on inner confidence and desire. In highly skilled sports like tennis, gymnastics and bowling, or when kicking a football, shooting a basketball and hitting a baseball, extra effort means having a deeper concentration and complete self-control. If you try too hard you'll lose your rhythm or tempo.

In more physical sports such as wrestling and boxing, or when blocking and tackling in football, running bases in baseball and rebounding in basketball, you don't have to worry quite so much about tempo. You can go a little berserk. Still, though, you must maintain your self-control.

Sometimes this extra effort comes down to conditioning. When two players or two teams are evenly matched, the one in the best condition will win. If your opponent runs 30 minutes after practice, run a hard 33 minutes. That extra effort can give you the edge to win.

This is one area that I feel very strongly about. This advice on extra effort could also be written under the chapter on "Conditioning", but since they're so closely related to winning performance, it also applies here.

Why? Because no matter how badly you want to win, no matter how much noise the crowd is making, no matter what your coach is telling you, your extra conditioning will make you a winner. An extra effort is impossible when you're tired. When your legs are gone, you're gone. When your arms are shot, you're shot.

The solution is to get your mind and your body working in sync. Your mind may be telling you to run faster or hit the ball harder, but if your body won't cooperate, you're in trouble. Your body will say, "Sorry, pal, it's all over. You should have wanted to win this badly a couple months ago, because if you had, you would have worked me (your buddy — your body) a little harder."

Your extra effort ties in directly with the other factors we've already discussed that will make you a winner: Desire, determination, dedication, sacrifice and conditioning. Champions know that you need every single one of these factors to succeed.

Think about it. If you're willing to pay the price to get your body in the right condition for that big game or match and if in addition, you reach back for that extra effort, you deserve to win. And you probably will.

You have to give 110 percent at anything you do. Because if you only give 100 percent, the guy you're playing against might be giving 100 percent and it's going to be a stand-off. If you give that extra 10 percent, you've got a chance to win.

Pete Rose, Major League First Baseman and Manager

I'll bet if you took all the players in this game and had a race, you'd find I have just a little more than average speed. But, I've led the league in triples three times and doubles once. Seven or eight of my triples last year were really just doubles. I stretched them. Baseball's no fun if you don't go out there and be, well, berserk.

George Brett, Major League Third Baseman

EXTRA EFFORT

DIGGER PHELPS
College Basketball Coach

I want our guys to develop a killer instinct so they can capitalize on the other team's mistakes. I want our guys to make that second effort.

FRAN TARKENTON
NFL Quarterback and Sports Broadcaster

None of us really pushes hard enough. People always talk about playing over your head when you are up against someone really good. Maybe you don't play over your head at all. Maybe it's just potential you never knew you had.

HERB BROOKS
U.S. Olympic Hockey Team and NHL Coach

You're not going to succeed by just doing what is required, it's going to be the little extra. Working five days a week, you're not going to get it done. I mean you'll have a nice job, be somewhat comfortable; but to get the real peace of mind, maybe you need to work that sixth day or even the seventh.

BOB KNIGHT
**College Basketball Coach and
U.S. Olympic Basketball Coach**

I very conscientiously try to look at what's right whenever I do anything. I don't care what you think or what somebody else thinks or how it is interpreted. I just do it. What I'm so very intent on is not winning. I'm intent on getting every player at Indiana to play up to his potential. I don't see anything wrong with trying to get kids to play not only as well as they can, but as hard as they can—to make that second effort.

PAUL BEAR BRYANT
College Football Coach and Athletic Director

You put out, boy, you suck up your gut, give it all you've got and you give me that second effort. You give me that much, boy...and I'll show you glory.

GENE MILLS
Wrestler—World Champion

This I say—be the best,
be yourself and not like the rest.
Work real hard to be real tough,
and remember that 100 percent is not good enough.
Set the impossible as being your goal,
then reach deep inside from within your soul.
All you've got is all you could ask,
to give your all to achieve this impossible task.

MERLIN OLSEN
NFL Tackle, Sports Broadcaster and Actor

You take the best team and the worst team, and line them up, and you would find very little physical difference. You would find an emotional difference. The winning team has a dedication...They will not accept defeat...They make the extra effort.

GEORGE GERVIN
NBA Guard

What I like most is going out and giving it all I have—giving that extra effort. A team in an ordinary frame of mind will do only ordinary things. In the proper emotional stage, a team will do extraordinary things. They will make the extra effort. To reach this stage, a team must have a motive that has an extraordinary appeal to them.

CHARLES KENDALL ADAMS
American Historian/Educator

No student ever attains very eminent success by simply doing what is required of him; it is the amount and excellence of what is over and above the required, that determines the greatness of ultimate distinction.

JANET GUTHRIE
Race Car Driver

Racing takes everything you've got—intellectually, emotionally, physically—and then you have to find about 10 percent more and use that too.

DAN HAMPTON
NFL Defensive Tackle/End

I have new goals each year. This year, I'm looking for any edge. I'm not going to get bigger or faster, so I have to study harder, prepare myself better, attune myself to go for a whole 60 minutes. I'm going into this season thinking it may be my last time on a field, thinking that I won't ever have another chance. Every time I go out, I'll be thinking that this is my last game, my last series, my last play.

TY COBB
Major League Outfielder

Live each day to the hilt. Play every game as hard as you can, as aggressively as you can. Make that second effort on every play. You can't worry about the next play or tomorrow because you don't know what tomorrow is going to bring.

HANK AARON
Major League Outfielder

I think the most important thing in life and in playing any sport is to try and do the very best that you possibly can at all times. Accept defeat only if you are able to come back and not make the same mistake. Always remember that no matter what you achieve in life, if you try a little harder, if you make that second effort, you can achieve much more.

BUCKY DENT
Major League Shortstop and Manager

They say that we're the greatest team money can buy, but you can't buy what's inside players. You can't buy their hearts. You can't buy the extra effort.

CHRISTIAN NESTELL BOVEE
American Author

Great designs are not accomplished without enthusiasm of some sort. Enthusiasm is the inspiration of the great. Without it no man is to be feared, and with it none despised.

JACK WHITAKER
Sports Broadcaster

When talents are equal, it's that extra effort that makes the difference in the close ones.

In almost every endeavor, success or failure depends on execution, precision, inches, seconds, unbelievable skill, unbelievable performances, unbelievable happenings. Next time you're put to the test, say to yourself, "I can make that extra effort. I can win the game of inches." Sometimes it only takes an inch more, but the results make all the difference in the world.

DON ZIMMER
Major League Manager

What you lack in talent can be made up with desire, hustle and giving 110 percent all the time.

BILL RODGERS
Distance Runner

It's what the race means to you that often affects how you run the race. How much extra effort you put into it may be the difference between winning and second place.

ELBERT HUBBARD
American Editor/Writer

People who never do any more than they are paid to do are never paid for any more than they do.

DAVE COWENS
NBA Center and Coach

I feel less talented than a lot of the guys I play against and I know that most of them are a lot taller. To be effective, I've got to use my speed all the time—I've got to out-hustle them.

MUHAMMAD ALI
Professional Boxer

Only a man who knows what it is like to be defeated can reach down to the bottom of his soul and come up with the extra ounce of power it takes to win when the match is even.

ROGER BANNISTER
First Man to Run the Mile Under Four Minutes

In the last 300 yards of my record run, my mind took over. It raced well ahead of my body and drew my body compelling forward. I felt that the moment of a lifetime had come. The world seemed to stand still. With 50 yards left, my body had long since exhausted all its energy, but it went on running just the same. The last few seconds seemed never-ending. I leaped at the tape like a man taking his last spring to save himself from the chasm that threatens to engulf him. It was only then that real pain overtook me.

The Winning Edge

The words "Winning Edge" represent a concept for achieving victory that I brought with me to Miami. They are linked together, much as a ring links man and woman together in marriage.

You set a goal to be the best and then you work every waking hour of each day trying to achieve that goal.

The ultimate goal is victory, and if you refuse to work as hard as you possibly can toward that aim, or if you do anything that keeps you from achieving that goal, you are just cheating yourself. I feel that way about athletics, but more importantly, I feel that way about life in general.

Extra study, extra determination, extra gassers and extra effort cover three areas that I feel are keys to success—mental, physical and emotional.

We want the Dolphins to be better prepared mentally than our opponents and realize the importance of not making mental errors in a game. A player can be the greatest physical specimen and execute flawlessly in practice, but if he can't carry out the detail of his assignment in a stress situation during a game on Sunday afternoon, he really isn't of significant value.

All things being equal, the team that has the best-conditioned athletes and the fastest ones will have the winning edge. I'm a stickler on condition.

I demand total involvement from our players. After God and family, the only other thing that's important is what the Dolphins do on game day.

What we want to dedicate ourselves to is establishing a standard of excellence in the future and we are always looking for "The Winning Edge."

DON SHULA   **NFL Defensive Back and Coach**

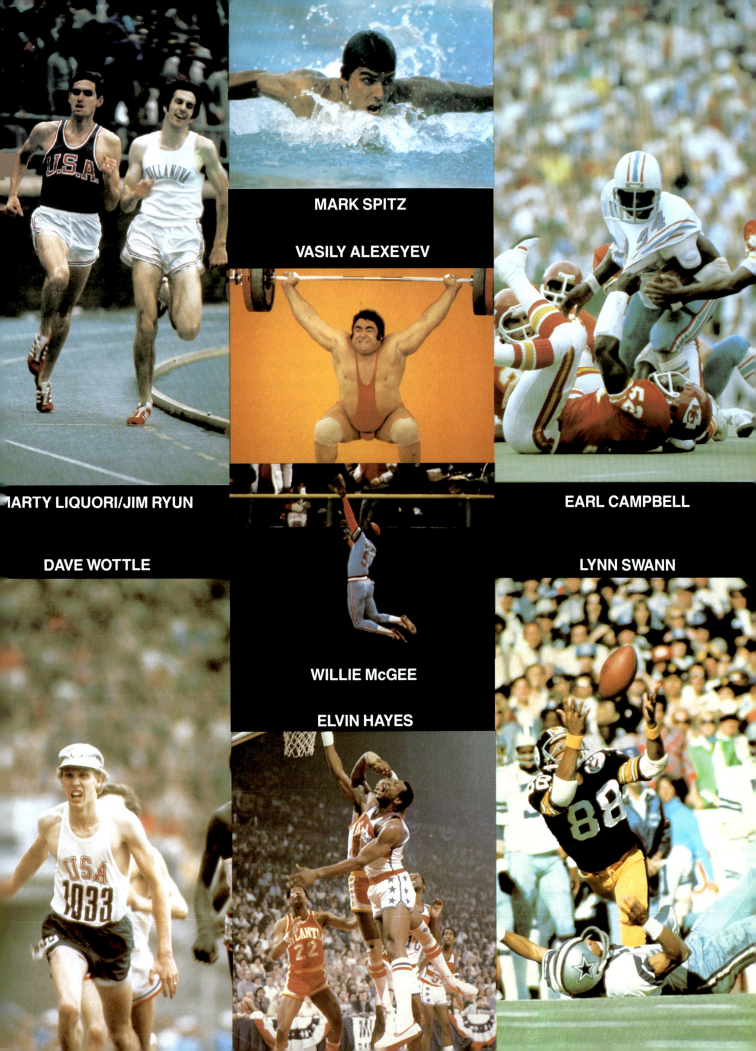

The tougher and closer the competition, the more I enjoy golf. Winning by easy margins may offer other kinds of satisfaction, but it's not nearly as enjoyable as battling it out shot by shot right down to the wire.

Jack Nicklaus, Professional Golfer

If you're a racing driver, you drive. It's the only way to keep sharp. You drive the big ones and the little ones. You drive and you compete. You can't get any better if you don't compete.

A. J. Foyt, Race Car Driver

> What I like most about the game is the competition, seeing how well I can do against other guys. Naturally, I don't like to lose, but if I feel I haven't done my best, winning isn't much fun either.
>
> Billy Sims, NFL Halfback

WELCOME COMPETITION — CHALLENGE YOURSELF

You should not only welcome stiff competition, you should actively seek it. You'll never realize your full athletic potential unless you're challenged. When you're challenged to the max, you dig deeper into your reservoir of athletic talent and stretch yourself further than you have ever gone before. This kind of competition constantly sets new performance standards to shoot for as your personal goal.

Most people don't compete hard enough or push themselves to their limits because they fear losing. They give up too easily. They level off and let their own performance standards dominate them, instead of seeking higher levels of competition. They never really find out how good they can be.

True champions constantly push themselves to see how far they can go. A world-class runner going for a world's record in the mile run needs a "rabbit", a stiff competitor, to set the pace, to push him or her to the limit.

We tell our wrestlers to work out with someone better than they are. Why? They'll find out why they're getting beaten. They use it as a learning experience to correct their mistakes until they can beat their opponent; then they find someone better. You'll never improve by always playing someone you can easily beat. You'll never be pushed to your limit. You'll only be as good as your competition.

The success pattern to gain the edge is: competition ...mistakes...corrections...improvement...success... tougher competition...more mistakes...more corrections ...more improvement...more success.

The main reason to go after tough competition is to test yourself. But there are other good reasons:

1. The better the competition, the better the performance.
2. The tougher the competition, the greater the incentive to practice.
3. The greater the competition, the more fun the contest.
4. The tougher the competition, the more motivated you'll be to excel.
5. The greater the competition, the more excited you'll be.
6. The better the competition, the stronger you'll become mentally.
7. The tougher the competition, the sweeter the victory.

Our wrestling team has always sought the best competition available. Recently, we have defeated state championship teams from Michigan, Pennsylvania, Rhode Island, West Virginia, Maryland, Nevada, Oklahoma, New York, New Jersey and Arizona. Playing this caliber of teams helps us tremendously — it forces us to play on a higher level.

You're only as good as your competition. If you want to be the best, you have to beat the best. So challenge them. If you aren't the best, find out how good the best is, for that's how good you'll have to become. We set up matches with other state champions well in advance. It motivated our team when needed the most — during the off-season.

The successful athlete is the one who performs best when the odds are slightly against him or her. Ambitious people derive little joy, if any, when their ability remains uncontested. The great athletes don't dwell upon their losses, but concentrate upon that part of their performance that limited their excellence. That's why they're true champions.

WELCOME COMPETITION—CHALLENGE YOURSELF

ERIC JOHNSTON
American Businessman/Government Official

Beaten paths are for beaten men.

TOM LANDRY
NFL Defensive Back and Coach

We like competition, we think it brings out the best in people.

W. D. TOLAND
American Author

Competition, as the "life" of trade, surely is a tremendous spur to progress. Is it not the pursued man or business that advances through persistent effort to keep ahead? The constant striving to maintain leadership ever involves new ways and means of accomplishing more efficiently and thus it is that the "pursued is the progressive man." Put your pursuers on the payroll.

JOHN MC ENROE
Professional Tennis Player

I'm gonna get stronger, hit a little harder, mix it up even better. I'm still rounding off my game, so I need to play a lot—compete more. This will give me more confidence too, so I can go into the big events mentally right.

DAVE WINFIELD
Major League Outfielder

A winner is one who is not afraid of the challenge, who rebounds from his setbacks, and who is flexible enough to make adjustments to succeed the next time.

CHRIS SCHENKEL
Sports Broadcaster

In 30 years of sports broadcasting, I've seen hundreds of winners and winning teams from Olympic Gold Medalists to professional and college champions. And every winner I've seen has been the master in a competitive situation, committed to beating the competition. Every winner was determined to succeed, to excel, and to enjoy every minute of glory.

They have all learned that winning is more fun than losing. Winning is the foundation of greatness—our investment in our future.

KEN DRYDEN
NHL Goaltender

I believe the main drive comes from the challenge. There's no way you can tell yourself you can do something until you dare to try.

BOB RICHARDS
Pole Vaulter—Two Time Olympic Gold Medalist

If you want to be the person you ought to be, you've got to welcome competition.

DON SHULA
NFL Defensive Back and Coach

How can you prove you're the best unless you have competition?

BOB KNIGHT
College Basketball Coach and U.S. Olympic Basketball Coach

I think there are three things that are really important in basketball. The first one is quickness. That is a natural thing to some extent, but kids can be made quicker through mental motivation. The second thing is concentration and anybody can concentrate harder than he normally does. So you can improve on both of these. And quickness and concentration lead to the third thing—competitiveness—you must love to compete.

PELE
Professional Soccer Player

The more difficult a victory, the greater the happiness in winning.

REGGIE JACKSON
Major League Outfielder and Sports Broadcaster

I love competition. It motivates me. It stimulates me, excites me.

JOE PATERNO
College Football Coach and Athletic Director
I want things to be difficult. It's more fun to win with handicaps. If you have the best players and no problems and you win, it's not very intriguing.

HUBERT H. HUMPHREY
U. S. Senator, Vice President
A smooth sea never made a skillful mariner.

BRUCE LIETZKE
Professional Golfer
I love competition so much that when I'm alone, I compete with myself. Shooting baskets or playing golf or whatever I do, I pretend that I'm someone else. I take my shots, then take the opposition's shots. I've always been that way. I play hard against myself.

TOM WATSON
Professional Golfer
Sometimes you have to lose major championships before you can win them. It's the price you pay for maturing. The more times you can put yourself in pressure situations—the more times you compete—the better off you are. It's a learning experience that's worth a fortune.

TERRY BRADSHAW
NFL Quarterback and Sports Broadcaster
When you've got something to prove, there's nothing greater than a challenge.

HALE IRWIN
Professional Golfer
I'm always looking for a competitive stimulus. I was paired with Lou Graham once and he was playing well, so I played harder to try to catch him. I've always been that way. When I was a little kid, I would pretend I had a shot to win the Masters, which was something to make me try my best.

DON SCHOLLANDER
Swimmer—Five Time Olympic Gold Medalist
I enjoy doing things that people don't think I can do. I like proving them wrong. I like the individual challenge.

TOMMY HEARNS
Professional Boxer
I like to win—period. I like the sport; I like the artistry of boxing. I like the challenge. I like the competition. I like it when they say that I can't beat a fellow, and then when I beat him, I look forward to the excuses they make. If it's only money, why is Pete Rose still playing? Why is Tony Dorsett still playing? It's the competition—they love the competition and so do I.

ROGER MARIS
Major League Outfielder

When you've got good, strong competition, you drive harder.

JEAN-CLAUDE KILLY
Skier—Three Time Olympic Gold Medalist

I will always be someone who wants to do it better than others. I love competition.

MOLIERE
French Author/Playwright

The greater the obstacle, the more glory in overcoming it.

BRIAN GOODELL
Swimmer—Two Time Olympic Gold Medalist

I don't like to see my records broken. But I'm glad when someone comes close. I need the challenge of having someone I have to beat.

BEN HOGAN
Professional Golfer

I am often asked if I'm not a bit envious of these young golfers making all the money today. A man must wind up with self-satisfaction. It's the game, the performance that counts. The big thing is the thrill of the competition. I would have played as hard for an orange as a big purse. I have no bitterness. I made out very well when I played and I don't envy the present crop.

VINCE LOMBARDI
NFL Coach and General Manager

The important thought is that the Packers thrived on tough competition. We welcomed it; the team had always welcomed it. The adrenalin flowed a little quicker when we were playing the tougher teams.

NANCY LOPEZ
Professional Golfer

I think that because golf was so demanding and because I had to work so hard to accomplish something, I really stayed with it. There has always been something new, demanding and testing every day I play. I love the challenge.

JOE DI MAGGIO
Major League Outfielder

What I would like best in all the world would to be 25 again; to be putting on those Yankee pinstripes and running out on the field to play ball. I'd give up all my trophies and records just to be able to compete again. The one thing that I both loved and now miss the most was the competition.

JOE CRIBBS
NFL Halfback

There are a lot of people who are cocky. To be honest, I feel deep down that I'm cocky, too. I'm not the kind of guy who is just going to go out and say, "Hey, I'm this and that," because that's just not me. But at the same time, if I see this other guy and he's super, I'm not going to say that he's the best. I'm going to say, "I'm going to be better than he is. I'm going to compete with him."

ART SCHLICHTER
NFL Quarterback

I play because I enjoy it. I enjoy the competition. It gets tougher the longer you play, but once you go so far into it, you don't want to quit. You want to compete more, to challenge yourself, to just show how good you really are.

TOM COUSINEAU
NFL Linebacker

It is inevitable that we all will endure setbacks—losses. If you have not lost, you have not played in enough games. Never be afraid to compete. Gain the strength and courage to try as hard as you possibly can, and play, play, play!

AL OERTER
**Discus Thrower—
Four Time Olympic Gold Medalist**

So what if I never win my fifth gold medal. It's only one end of the string. It's competing that matters. It's proving that there is a place for guys like me in sports. It's a personal challenge to extend myself.

DEAN SMITH
College Basketball Coach

You improve by playing the good teams. The effort is the big thing. If we play hard, the best I think we can, and still lose, then I have to be pleased regardless of the outcome.

THEODORE ROOSEVELT
Twenty-Sixth President

Far better it is to dare mighty things, to win glorious triumphs, even though checkered by failure, than to take rank with those poor spirits who neither enjoy much nor suffer much, because they live in the gray twilight that knows not victory nor defeat.

BRUCE JENNER
Decathlon—Olympic Gold Medalist

What does a fellow compete for anyway? A gold medal? Money? Glory? No, it's fulfillment. I've interviewed a lot of players going into the Super Bowl. They don't care about the $25,000 victory bonus. The money is nothing. They're athletes—they want to compete.

JACK NICKLAUS
Professional Golfer

I was competitive in everything I did—sports, schoolwork, everything. You have to be a competitor. You can't be soft. You have to want to be the best.

EDDIE ARCARO
Professional Jockey

Everyday riding gets to be a terrible bore. But you can't just ride the celebrities on Saturdays; you've got to ride every day. If you're not going to compete regularly, get out.

SIR EDMUND HILLARY
First Man to Climb Mount Everest

You don't have to be a fantastic hero to do certain things—to compete. You can be just an ordinary chap, sufficiently motivated to reach challenging goals. The intense effort, the giving of everything you've got is a very pleasant bonus.

GRETE WAITZ
Distance Runner

You can't be a better runner unless you are willing to run and be beat. You've got to look for tough competition. You've got to want to beat the best.

CHARLEY BOSWELL FOUND A NEW CHALLENGE

"Golf came to me when I desperately needed something to get me interested in living—I needed a challenge. But it was merely a means that allowed me to use abilities I had. The important thing for any disabled person is to identify those abilities and to find some way, as I found golf, to give a suddenly altered life new and solid meaning."

Charley Boswell came a stone's throw away from major league baseball. After proving himself as an outstanding centerfielder at the University of Alabama, Boswell was hopeful of being signed by the New York Yankees. He was expected by many to contend for Joe DiMaggio's spot in the lineup.

Then, Charley was drafted and thrown into World War II rather than Yankee Stadium. All thoughts of becoming a major leaguer ended when he was permanently blinded as he saved a soldier from a burning tank.

His sight taken away, Boswell felt he would never again compete in sport activities. But because of the persistence of a friend and an Army rehabilitation officer, Boswell tried golf, even though he had never played the sport in his life.

After hours of practice that enabled him to perfect his swing and establish a rhythm in his mind, Boswell was shooting in the 90's. He continued to improve and won seventeen U. S. tournaments for blind golfers and many other international championships.

More important, golf had given Boswell confidence in himself once again. He began his own insurance office and became a success.

In 1974, the Charley Boswell Celebrity Tournament was established to raise funds for the Eye Foundation Hospital in Birmingham, Alabama.

"What happened to me wasn't an unusual change in fortune. Tens of thousand of people lose their vision or the use of arms or legs in accidents—if not in wars—every year. Each of them must find some way to adjust to meet life's demands. Those demands don't make allowances for the plans that have to be set aside, the endless wondering about what might have been. Lives can be turned into new directions by new interests, as mine was through golf. Golf became my way back into the mainstream of life."

5-69

6
OVERTIME

- **Condition**
- **Thrive On Pressure**
- **Mental Toughness**
- **Don't Quit**
- **Pride**

Don't Quit

When things go wrong, as they sometimes will,
When the road you're trudging seems all uphill,
When the funds are low and the debts are high,
And you want to smile, but you have to sigh,
When care is pressing you down a bit—
Rest if you must, but don't you quit.

Life is queer with its twists and turns,
As every one of us sometimes learns,
And many a person turns about
When they might have won had they stuck it out.
Don't give up though the pace seems slow—
You may succeed with another blow.

Often the struggler has given up
When he might have captured the victor's cup;
And he learned too late when the night came down,
How close he was to the golden crown.

Success is failure turned inside out—
So stick to the fight when you're hardest hit,—
It's when things seem worst that you mustn't quit.

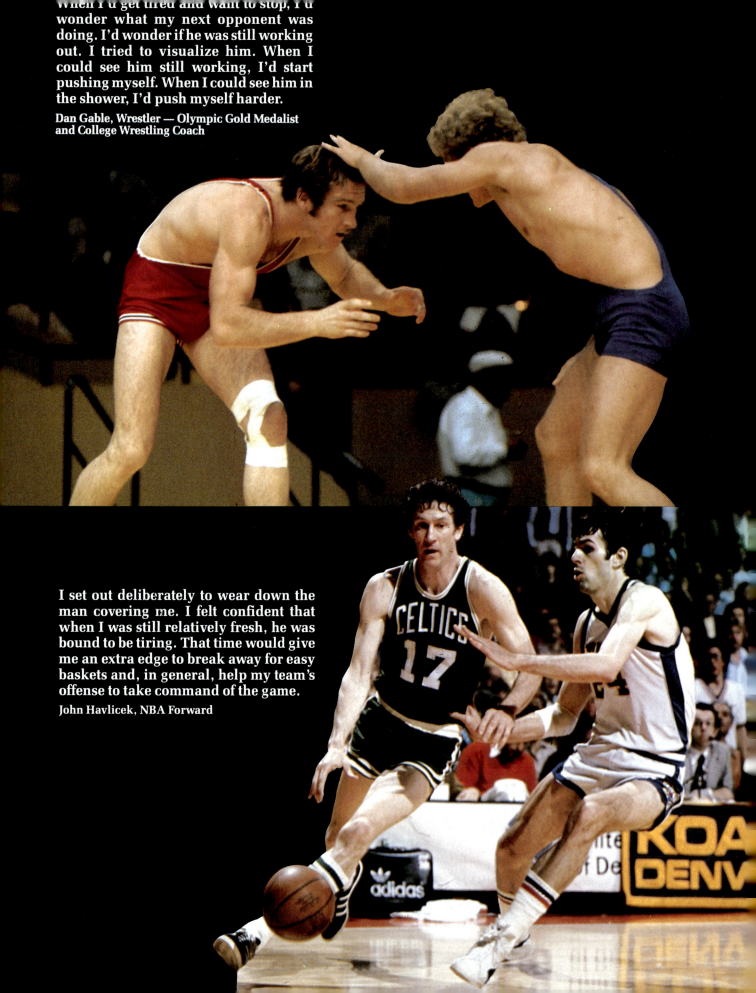

> When I'd get tired and want to stop, I'd wonder what my next opponent was doing. I'd wonder if he was still working out. I tried to visualize him. When I could see him still working, I'd start pushing myself. When I could see him in the shower, I'd push myself harder.
>
> Dan Gable, Wrestler — Olympic Gold Medalist and College Wrestling Coach

> I set out deliberately to wear down the man covering me. I felt confident that when I was still relatively fresh, he was bound to be tiring. That time would give me an extra edge to break away for easy baskets and, in general, help my team's offense to take command of the game.
>
> John Havlicek, NBA Forward

CONDITION

Fatigue makes cowards of us all. When you're tired, your problems seem bigger. Fatigue drains you of energy so you lose the edge over your opponent. Fatigue robs an athlete of his precious skills. Once your tempo, rhythm, coordination and split-second timing are gone, you've lost your edge. As a result, the long hours of practice you put in and the sacrifices you've made are wasted. You have a choice, however. You can conquer fatigue by becoming the best-conditioned athlete you can be.

John Havlicek was a perfect example of a superbly-conditioned athlete. He always excelled at the end of a basketball game. Havlicek worked so hard to get in shape that he was able to play full-court the entire 48 minutes of the game. Rarely was an opponent as well-conditioned as John. When his opponent slowed down due to fatigue, Havlicek gained the edge and made the big play.

It's the best-conditioned athlete, not the most talented, who generally wins when the going gets tough; when the last pressure points need to be scored; or when the really "big" point is needed to turn the game or match around. You can't always beat your opponent in talent, but you can when it comes to conditioning — because it's something you control.

When we have a big wrestling match coming up, we'll work on our techniques after our two and one-half hour long practice. The wrestlers and the coaches hate it. But we do it because it makes us winners. At the end of a match when you're fatigued, your skills must be their sharpest. You've found the edge in conditioning, when you can hit a move with the same intensity in the third period as in the first. It's as simple as that.

Many of today's athletes have the same sophisticated equipment and facilities to work out with. Modern training methods may be the great equalizer of athletes' abilities. If the talent becomes equal, where do you get the edge? The answer is simple — you get into better condition than the rest of the pack. The only way to do this is to work out on your own, to do something extra every day before and after practice.

In most cases, this will mean running, not for an extra five minutes, but for an extra 30 minutes. Push yourself. Don't jog for 30 minutes and expect to get the dedicated athlete of the year award. Run hard — hurt — for 30 minutes. Make that extra effort in practice as well as in the game. If you do, you'll find that when the going gets tough, you can handle it.

Dan Gable became America's greatest wrestler, not because he was the most talented, but because he was by far the best-conditioned. His message is one of my personal favorites. It says exactly what I mean by getting the edge on your opponent by being in better condition. "Work until you can picture your opponent in the shower — then work even harder."

There are few feelings worse than the frustration of reaching down deep for that something extra at the end of the hard race, a close game or a tough match — and finding it isn't there. That's why superbly-conditioned athletes win so frequently: They have the edge when they want it. And when they need it.

I go to the Bahamas every winter to get in shape for the season. I run 15 miles every day. Sure I get fed up sometimes and say, "What am I doing?" But if you want to score goals and play well, you can't just lie on the couch and say, "I'll work out tomorrow."

Giorgio Chinaglia, Professional Soccer Player

CONDITION

BILL SHARMAN
NBA Guard, Coach and General Manager

There are no big secrets. A player who is in the best shape possible is in a position to function and reach maximum efficiency.

FRANK KUSH
NFL Coach

Being in peak physical condition is just as important as throwing and kicking the ball. In fact, it's probably more important than some techniques. If you're not in shape, you can't respond physically or mentally.

LARRY GURA
Major League Pitcher

In my weight program, I try to improve my upper body strength and beef up my endurance. I want to be as strong at the end of a game as at the start.

MIKE PRUITT
NFL Fullback

Life is a game of survival of the fittest; the strong will survive. It's not how much talent you have, but how much of it you make use of and what kind of physical condition you are in.

JACK NICKLAUS
Professional Golfer

Perhaps no one realizes how important a good diet has been for me. I can't describe how important it is. You go along for years weighing too much. Then you change your diet, you start feeling good and you don't even mind looking in the mirror. Gradually, you rise to a different physical and mental level. It reflects on all your life, not just on your ability as an athlete.

GARY PLAYER
Professional Golfer

When I run, I feel better, eat better, rest better. My stamina is greater. I'm stronger and, as a consequence, I hit the ball farther. All these considerations make me a better player. But I think the single most important thing that running does for me—and can do for any reasonably healthy golfer—is sharpen my reflexes. For some reason, you never hear or read about reflexes in golf, but they're crucial. Golf is not a game for a sluggish person, and if you are just a little bit dull, you are apt to hit a fraction of an inch behind the ball. You may not miss making a good shot, but that little difference can add strokes to your score. Reflexes are very, very important in golf. Believe me.

VINCE LOMBARDI
NFL Coach and General Manager

I think good physical conditioning is essential to any occupation. A man who is physically fit performs better at any job. Fatigue makes cowards of us all.

DICK VERMEIL
NFL Coach and Sports Broadcaster

If anybody uses tired as an excuse for losing, then I'll find someone to play that position who isn't tired.

JOE FRAZIER
Professional Boxer, Trainer and Manager

You can map out a fight plan or a life plan, but when the action starts, it may not go the way you planned, and you're down to your reflexes—which means your training. That's where your roadwork shows. If you cheated on that in the dark of the morning, well, you're going to get found out now under the bright lights.

GEORGE ALLEN
NFL Coach and Sports Broadcaster

Good condition is vital to success. My teams were always in good physical condition. We never lost a game because somebody outconditioned us. We were strongest in the fourth quarter and this is when we won a lot of our games.

GENE UPSHAW
NFL Offensive Guard and NFLPA President

When a defensive lineman gets ready to play the Raiders, he doesn't have to wonder what we are going to do. We're coming after him. We just pound at him play after play—power stuff—and if we're close in the fourth quarter, it's all over, because the fourth quarter is the Raider quarter.

JULIUS ERVING
NBA Forward

You've got to "have it" at the end of the game—that's when it's the most important.

DAVE COWENS
NBA Center and Coach

Be hard—well conditioned
Be tough—mentally prepared and confident
Be yourself—know your strengths and weaknesses
Be patient—listen to criticism, understand the value of creating disciplines
Be fair—to yourself and others

JIM BROWN
NFL Fullback and Actor

I always made it a practice to use my head before my body. I looked upon playing football like a businessman might. The game was my business; my body and my mind were my assets and injuries were my liabilities. The first basic was to be in absolutely top-notch physical condition. I always tried to train harder than anyone else. I even developed my own set of calisthenics, things I could do in a hotel room if I had to.

WILT CHAMBERLAIN
NBA Center

I've prided myself on being in excellent condition—as good as any man in my profession. Now this doesn't come from sitting on your rear end. This comes from hard, hard work.

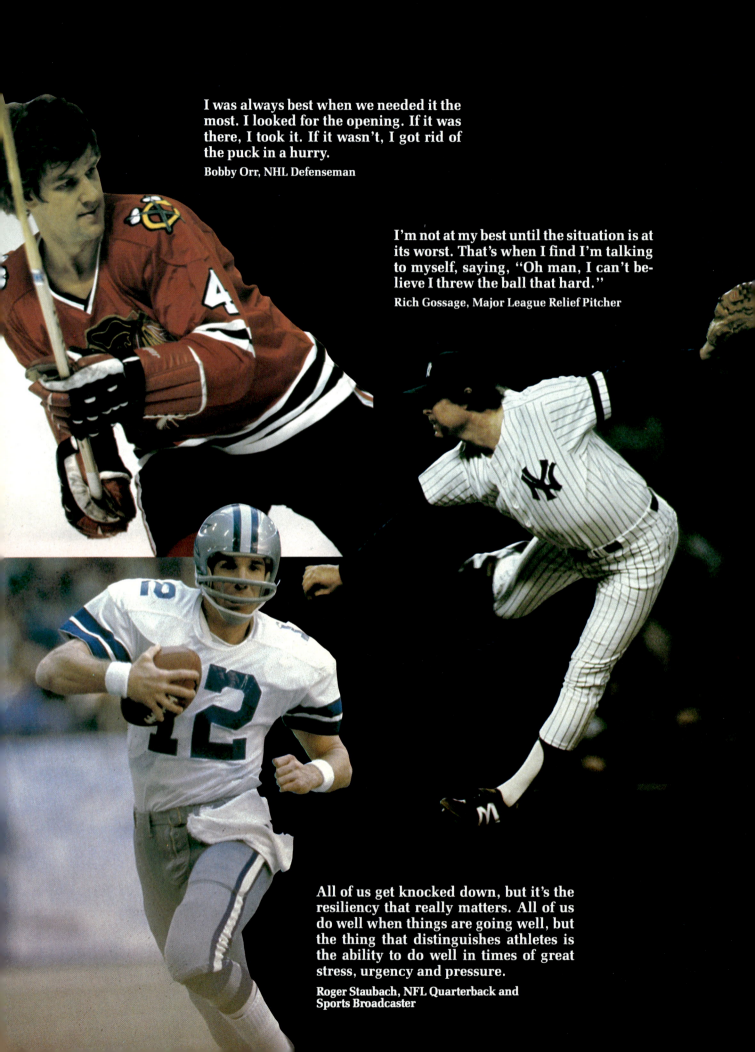

I was always best when we needed it the most. I looked for the opening. If it was there, I took it. If it wasn't, I got rid of the puck in a hurry.

Bobby Orr, NHL Defenseman

I'm not at my best until the situation is at its worst. That's when I find I'm talking to myself, saying, "Oh man, I can't believe I threw the ball that hard."

Rich Gossage, Major League Relief Pitcher

All of us get knocked down, but it's the resiliency that really matters. All of us do well when things are going well, but the thing that distinguishes athletes is the ability to do well in times of great stress, urgency and pressure.

Roger Staubach, NFL Quarterback and Sports Broadcaster

In the closing seconds of every game, I want the ball in my hands for that last shot—not in anybody else's, not in anybody else's hands in the world.
Larry Bird, NBA Forward

THRIVE ON PRESSURE

Pressure. The very word puts fear in the hearts of many athletes. It separates the men from the boys, and the women from the girls. To be a great champion, you have to learn to handle the stress of pressure. When the going gets tough and the pressure mounts, you'll be tested. Winners thrive on pressure; losers fear it.

If you've prepared mentally and physically, you won't have to worry about pressure. In fact, you'll go out of your way to put yourself into pressure situations. You'll thrive on a close game or a tight match.

Pressure can cripple you when you're not prepared. If you don't have faith in what you're doing and you fear the unexpected, you're not prepared. All pressure is self-inflicted; it comes from within. You control how you handle pressure, and it determines whether you're a winner or a loser.

Winners look forward to pressure. It brings out their best performance against top opponents. Losers cringe under pressure for they aren't prepared to do their best even when it counts. Our advice to you is to welcome pressure. Look at it as an opportunity to show what you're made of. If you welcome pressure, you'll be amazed at how successful you'll be. When the going gets tough, you'll have the edge because: (1) You'll know there's just as much pressure on your opponent, (2) you'll understand exactly how to handle it, and (3) chances are your opponent won't be able to do so.

Pressure comes from two things: Being unprepared; and playing "not to lose" instead of "playing to win." If you're unprepared, the simple fact is you'll lose. If you haven't practiced long, hard and correctly, there's no way you can win when the pressure is on. Desire won't do it; neither will wishful thinking. Only preparation will give you the edge.

Ben Hogan, one of the world's greatest golfers, believed preparation was a key to winning. On the way to winning the U. S. Open Golf Tournament, he hit an unbelievable shot. Afterwards a young reporter asked, "Mr. Hogan, what were you thinking back on the 16th hole when you hit that shot?" Hogan's reply was simple and right to the point. He said, "Son, I've hit that same shot a thousand times in practice."

If you play "not to lose" instead of "playing to win", you'll put unnecessary pressure on yourself. This negative thinking is more concerned with the end result than with the effort expended.

No matter how confident you are, sometimes you'll doubt your ability. Don't panic; it's natural and happens to all athletes. Even the great ones like Jack Nicklaus, Steffi Graf, Greg Louganis, Pele and Orel Hershiser have moments of fear. The secret to their success is that they can handle these moments. They know they can't avoid them, so they don't lose their cool. They handle it by slowing the pace down, going back to fundamentals and concentrating. These great athletes block everything else out of their minds, except doing what they have done so many times before in practice.

You can do the same thing. Stay cool. Slow it down. Return to the fundamentals. Get your confidence back. Get the edge back. Then face the pressure head-on. Chances are you'll be a winner. And next time you won't hide from pressure situations. You'll look for them.

THRIVE ON PRESSURE

NANCY LOPEZ
Professional Golfer

The pressure makes me more intent about each shot. Pressure on the last few holes makes me play better.

CHUCK NOLL
NFL Linebacker and Coach

Some place along your life, you are going to have to function in a pressure situation and if you can learn to do it in a game where the results are not life and death, you can come to a situation where it is life and death and be better able to cope.

LOU BROCK
Major League Outfielder

You have to decide what your purpose is in this game. You have to have that quest for the final moment of glory. You have to love the pressure situations.

SEBASTIAN COE
**Distance Runner —
Three Time Olympic Gold Medalist**

All pressure is self-inflicted. It's what you make of it— or how you let it rub off on you.

GERRY FAUST
College Football Coach

I think you put pressure on yourself. There are some outside pressures, but I think the most pressure is put on by yourself.

JACK NICKLAUS
Professional Golfer

Pressure creates tension, and when you're tense, you want to get your task over and done with as fast as possible. The more you hurry in golf, the worse you probably will play, which leads to even heavier pressure and greater tension. To avoid this vicious circle, I'll take a couple of deep breaths and quickly review why I'm doing what I'm doing. Basically, I'm doing it because, win or lose, I enjoy playing golf and competing. This usually eases any mental tension I'm feeling by re-establishing my perspectives on victory and defeat in relation to life in the whole.

TED WILLIAMS
Major League Outfielder and Manager

I always did my best when I realized the assignment was going to be difficult. From there, my attitude was better, more serious, and I got down to the job of preparing myself better than if I thought it was going to be easy. Nobody with any pride wants to do it second best, and I found out that with this type of mental preparation, the results were always better.

GEORGE ROGERS
NFL Halfback

There are guys on the team who have said in the huddle, "Don't call my play" or "Don't give me the ball." But that's exactly the time that I want it, when the tension and the pressure are the highest.

GEORGE BLANDA
NFL Quarterback/Kicker

The question people ask most is what I think about when I line up for a kick. They want to know if I feel the pressure, but I never think about that. Instead, I concentrate on looking at the spot where the ball will be put.

HALE IRWIN
Professional Golfer

I try to make pressure and tension work for me. I want the adrenalin to be flowing. I think sometimes we try so hard to be cool, calm and collected that we forget what we're doing. There's nothing wrong with being charged up if it's controlled.

MIKE SCHMIDT
Major League Third Baseman

No player ever played well when he tried too hard. The guys who always play well under pressure are the guys who block out the pressure.

PHIL ESPOSITO
NHL Center and General Manager
I love pressure situations. If you can't get up for the big games, then what's the use? I always told myself that when I couldn't get up for the games anymore, I'd get out.

BOB GIBSON
Major League Pitcher
You hear a lot of talk about the pressure of the game, but I think most of that comes from the media. Most guys don't let things worry them. Pressure comes when you're not doing well or when you're not prepared. When you're fully prepared, there should be no pressure.

RON JAWORSKI
NFL Quarterback
When I first came to the Eagles, I found a bunch of guys shell-shocked from losing. They had been through some lean years, they just didn't know how to handle the pressure. They were quiet, they kept to themselves. I said, "Hey, this has gotta change. Let's make pressure fun."

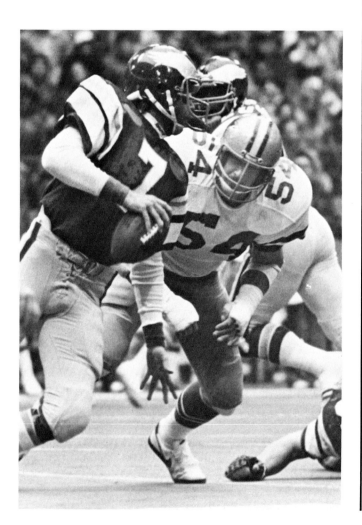

AL MC GUIRE
College Basketball Coach and Sports Broadcaster
I really think pressure is something you put on yourself and it's a sign of incompetency. If you don't have faith in what you are doing, it's probably because you are not properly prepared.

MARCUS ALLEN
College Tailback
I can't press—I can't get too tight—because then there's the danger that I'll try so hard to do well that I'll mess up.

JACK NICKLAUS
Professional Golfer
Many times when fear starts to hit me, my best chance of overcoming it lies in facing it squarely and examining it rationally. Here's what I say to myself. "OK, what are you frightened of? You've obviously played well or you wouldn't be here. You're still playing well overall. You're always telling yourself you get your biggest kicks out of the challenges of golf. Well, go ahead and enjoy yourself. Play each shot one at a time and meet the challenge."

FRANK ROBINSON
Major League Outfielder and Manager
The worst pressure can come from within yourself. I never allowed that pressure on myself as a ballplayer and I'm not going to do it as a manager. I'm just going to surround myself with a bunch of high quality players. Then go out and do the best job I possibly can.

BILLIE JEAN KING
Professional Tennis Player and Sports Broadcaster
Match point is a love-hate relationship. The torment of "Oh, God, what am I doing here?" and "This is it! This is what I've been working for." I know this is why I paid the price. This is what it's all about if you want to be a champion. The challenge of that moment. Match point!

ROLLIE FINGERS
Major League Relief Pitcher
I like pressure situations and I get pumped up when I'm involved in one. I really feel like a performer out there. You know people pay to come see you and you don't want to mess up.

DAN QUISENBERRY
Major League Relief Pitcher
I don't feel tense on the mound. I feel great. Pitching in tight situations is great for the mind and body. You void everything else out of your system when you're on the mound. It's refreshing. Relieving never makes me nervous because I try to envision it from about the fourth inning on. That's the most tense time for me. I have this terrible fear of failure. I try to think what can happen by the time I get into a game. Somewhere in that maze, I start to see how I'm gonna get them out and I begin to relax. I see myself throwing low sinkers, and then when I begin to warm up, it's almost therapeutic.

MIKE BOSSY
NHL Right Wing
Maybe one of the reasons I do score so much is because I put so much pressure on myself every game. I thrive on pressure.

GEORGE FOSTER
Major League Outfielder
I project my thoughts into the situation that I'm going to be in later so that I'm prepared. Then nothing surprises me because I've been there before in my mind. That's the only way to handle pressure.

DENNIS JOHNSON
NBA Guard
I'm probably the worst shooter of the five players on the court for the Suns. But when the game is coming down to the final seconds, I want the shot. It's not a point of accuracy; it's poise, confidence and loving the pressure.

AHMAD RASHAD
NFL Wide Receiver and Sports Broadcaster

We reached their 28 with 21 seconds left — maybe three plays to go. I felt terrific. I love it this way. I don't think I ever play better than when I feel really needed, when the pressure is on me and I've got a chance to do really great things.

MATT BAHR
NFL Kicker

Pressure is what you put on yourself. What's important is how you handle it. One thing you've got to do as a kicker is want to go in and kick. And if you miss, you have to want to go right back in there and kick again. You have to always look forward to the challenge. Once you become afraid of the situation, it's time to question whether you should be out there.

Mental toughness is many things. It is humility because it behooves all of us to remember that simplicity is the sign of greatness and meekness is the sign of true strength. Mental toughness is spartanism with the qualities of sacrifice, self-denial, dedication. It is fearlessness, and it is love.

Vince Lombardi, NFL Coach and General Manager

Although I didn't really feel tired or sore, I didn't feel smooth. I started to feel bad as we were still going up Heartbreak Hill, but I felt the worst when we started to come down with about five miles to go. I never considered dropping out because…well, I just never considered it. I wasn't concerned with what (Dick) Beardsley was trying to do. I was just concentrating on staying with him. I kept telling myself, "There's no way I'm going to lose this race."

Alberto Salazar, Distance Runner

MENTAL TOUGHNESS

Nobody ever said it would be easy.

Sometimes you have to perform at your best when you're feeling your worst. Handle it the way the champions do — block out the hurt, the pain and the sickness from your head. Concentrate instead on what you must do to win. Shape up. Get it together. And just do it. Excuses don't count. Anybody can make them up. Nobody cares if you're hurt, sick or tired. Either do it or don't. It's that simple.

There are times when you'd rather be elsewhere doing something more exciting. But we know that the winners in life face up to the challenge at hand, while the losers make up excuses to avoid them. You must win the mental battle, if you really want to be a winner.

You must remain confident, enthusiastic and positive. You must work even harder when you're sick, hurt, sad or troubled. That's mental toughness.

Life is easy when the going is good. Mental toughness comes into play when the going gets bad. Mental toughness is also the ability to keep working towards a long term goal, while going full throttle to win a short-term battle — even in the face of adversity.

I've never met Bobby Knight, the basketball coach at Indiana University, but I would love to. I like his story on mental toughness. One of his players came into his office and said, "Mr. Knight, I can't practice today, I'm sick." Bobby looked up from his papers, said "Get better!" and went back to work.

One of the oldest and most common locker-room signs is: "When the going gets tough, the tough get going." Believe it. That's what separates the winners from the losers.

During my 20 years of coaching, I've always placed a high priority on developing mental toughness in athletes. Each year, we put our wrestlers through a tough, pre-season conditioning program. We run four miles a day and build up to 15. We do this for two reasons: (1) For the cardiovascular conditioning, and (2) to let them know they can do it.

We want our wrestlers to know they can break through the pain barrier and do something they never dreamed possible. This confidence-building program develops mental toughness. Once they believe in themselves, they've gained an edge no one can take away from them.

Another highly successful way we gain mental toughness is through our annual "Red Flag" day. One day each year we hang a large red flag from the rafters. On this day, our wrestlers work for two and one-half solid hours: Wrestling, running, calisthenics. Again and again. Non-stop.

We hear comments like, "I never thought I could do it," or "That was the hardest thing I ever did." This day sticks in our wrestlers' minds for a long time. After they graduate, they call yearly to find out when the "Red Flag" is going to fly again.

You see, for us it's much more than just conditioning. It's showing a group of young men, that they can do something they never thought they could.

It's tradition. It's pride. It's mental toughness.

> If you let yourself limp, it gets to be a habit. If you don't limp, then you won't favor your leg. So I just told myself that no matter how much my ankle was killing me, I wouldn't give in, I wouldn't limp.
>
> Phil Mahre, Skier — Olympic Gold Medalist

MENTAL TOUGHNESS

BOB KNIGHT
College Basketball Coach and U.S. Olympic Basketball Coach

Mental toughness is to the physical as four is to one.

GEORGE STEINBRENNER
Major League Owner

I don't believe that the non-tough boss gets too far, especially with the competition all over the world today. I think mental toughness is the number one quality a business executive or a ballplayer needs.

JOHN HAVLICEK
NBA Forward

Over the years, I have pushed myself mentally and I have pushed myself physically. A lot of people say, "John Havlicek never gets tired." Well, I get tired. It's just a matter of pushing myself. I say to myself, "He's as tired as I am; who's going to win the mental battle?" It's just a matter of mental toughness.

STEVE PREFONTAINE
Distance Runner

A lot of people run a race to see who is fastest. I run to see who has the most guts, who can punish himself into an exhausting pace and then at the end, punish himself even more. Nobody is going to win a 5,000 meter race after running an easy two miles. Not with me. If I lose forcing the pace all the way, well, at least I can live with myself.

FRAN TARKENTON
NFL Quarterback and Sports Broadcaster

Tough. What do they mean by tough? You don't show the enemy when you're hurt. No matter how badly you may feel, you don't let those other guys know you're hurting. That's tough.

SHUN FUJIMOTO
Gymnast—Olympic Gold Medalist

Yes, the pain shot through me like a knife. It brought tears to my eyes. But now I have a gold medal, and the pain is gone. (After performing in the 1976 Montreal Olympics with a broken leg.)

GAYLORD PERRY
Major League Pitcher

You've got to have players who can still play well with minor injuries. It's part of your work. You need guys who will sacrifice—who are mentally tough. The only goals I set for myself are to be ready to pitch when the manager calls on me and to keep my team in the game. It's hard work. I grew up like that. You've gotta fight and work for it.

WILLIE SCHAEFFLER
U. S. Olympic Ski Team Coach

No matter how much you think you suffer, how much you think you sacrifice, there are thousands of others who have suffered more, given more.

JIM PLUNKETT
NFL Quarterback

Pain is a mental thing. You can always bounce back, but the hard part is the realization that the pain is not going to stop. You keep going and try your best to block it out of your head, but it's always going to be there.

FLOYD LITTLE
NFL Halfback

To keep going in this game, you've got to make a distinction between pain and injury. I wouldn't play more than one game a year—the first one—if I let pain keep me out. The trouble is that a lot of guys don't know the difference between hurting and being hurt.

JERRY KRAMER
NFL Offensive Guard

In 1968, I had my knee torn up in Detroit. I stretched some ligaments so badly that it looked like I was going to need an operation that same night and that I was going to have to retire from football right then. But I decided to wait a couple days and the knee started to heal. At least, I could limp. I didn't practice all week and I didn't expect to play, but when one of our guys got shaken up in the third quarter, I didn't want to be asked how I felt. I ran out on the field. I stayed out there for two plays—didn't do anything but survive—till the coaches pulled me off. Despite my injuries, I felt wonderful. We had shown the mark of champions; we had won the game we had to win.

ROGER BANNISTER
First Man to Run the Mile Under Four Minutes

The mental approach is one of the most important things in running. The man who can drive himself further once the effort gets painful is the man who will win. Most people train by racing. I tried to make each race an event in my life.

DAN FOUTS
NFL Quarterback and Sports Broadcaster

I don't think about the defensive men. That's not my job. I've got the ball back there in the pocket. I'm supposed to throw it straight. That's my job. It's a very personal thing. If I don't get the ball to the right guy, I'm failing—and I don't like to fail. Everybody else on my team is playing his heart out. I'm going to stand in there and make the play work and if I'm going to do that, I can't be afraid of getting hurt.

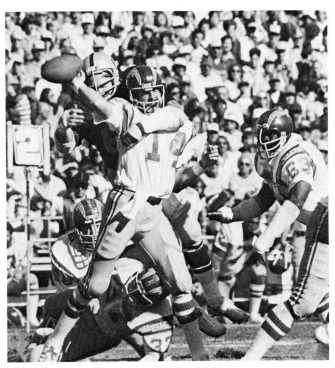

GRETE WAITZ
Distance Runner

It only looked easy. I was suffering. I felt a cramp coming in my left thigh with six miles to go. I just said, "Now forget about the time, just be first." It has to do with your will, and how much pain you put in your running. At 23 miles, I saw the time and I knew I had a chance to break the record.

ROBERTO CLEMENTE
Major League Outfielder

I don't know if I will ever play in another World Series. Thus, I must not think that my body hurts me all the time. I must play hard.

JOHN WOODEN
College Basketball Coach

I always stress condition with my basketball players. I don't mean physical condition only. You cannot attain and maintain physical condition unless you are morally and mentally conditioned.

KELLEN WINSLOW
NFL Tight End

I know what it is to play with pain and to play with injury. There's a big distinction. You play with pain—block it out of your head—but you don't play with an injury because you'd only be hurting yourself worse and would be out even longer. You have to have some smarts as well as some guts.

DICK BEARDSLEY
Distance Runner

Around 17 miles into the '82 Boston Marathon, I picked up the pace as part of my plan. I thought Alberto (Salazar) would try to run hard on the hills. I was a little hesitant about how I'd do on the uphills, but I really wanted to push the downhills because I feel that's the strongest part of my running. My plan was to get through the hills feeling good and then to cut loose coming off Heartbreak Hill. Basically, that's what I did. The crowd really helped. I couldn't even hear myself think; I couldn't feel myself hurt.

I knew Alberto was there with me, but I had a feeling he wasn't going to challenge me. I thought I was hurting him. I can't remember ever trying to break someone harder than I tried to break Alberto. I never looked back, but the way the sun was positioned, I could see the shadow of his head. A couple of times the shadow would loom up bigger and I'd figure he was getting ready to jump me, so—boom!—I'd take off because I wanted to get the first jump. The shadow never disappeared. I couldn't get rid of it—but I never quit trying.

TERRY BRADSHAW
NFL Quarterback and Sports Broadcaster

I caught an elbow in the back of my knee and my right hand was going numb from a blow I couldn't remember. I felt sort of, well, goofy, like I was on something. But by the time they punted, I was ready to get back on the field.

JOE DI MAGGIO
Major League Outfielder

You ought to run the hardest when you feel the worst. Never let the other guys know you're down.

DON SCHOLLANDER
Swimmer—Five Time Olympic Gold Medalist

You learn pain in practice and you will know it in every race. As you approach the limit of your endurance, it begins coming on gradually, hitting your stomach first. Then your arms grow heavy and your legs tighten—thighs first, then the knees. You sink lower in the water as though someone was pushing down on your back. You experience perception changes. The sounds of the pool blend together and become a crashing roar in your ears. The water takes on a pinkish tinge. Your stomach feels as though it's going to fall out—every kick hurts like heck—and suddenly you hear a shrill, internal scream...It is right here, at the pain barrier, that the great competitors are separated from the rest.

VINCE LOMBARDI
NFL Coach and General Manager

Mental toughness is essential to success. You've got to be mentally tough.

Mental toughness is many things and rather difficult to explain. It's qualities are sacrifice and self-denial. Also, most importantly, it is combined with a perfectly disciplined will that refuses to give in. It's a state of mind—you could call it character in action.

J. R. RICHARD
Major League Pitcher

Physical pain can't stop you if your mental outlook is strong enough.

JOHN MC ENROE
Professional Tennis Player

I was pleased with the 1980 Wimbledon because I pushed myself. At one point, I started getting a cramp in my foot. Then my knee hurt. But I pushed myself anyway. I felt that I did my best. It was like I was playing from within.

DEWEY SELMON
NFL Linebacker

Mental toughness is the strength to know yourself, to know your own truth, and to put that forth even when others tell you you're wrong. It's that consistency in yourself.

JOE NAMATH
NFL Quarterback and Sports Broadcaster

The first time you get knocked down, it's kind of a shock. But you get yourself back together and throw a few more, and then you get hit again. The second one is not as bad as the first. And by the time you've been knocked down 20 times and got up 20 times, what difference does the twenty-first make? Heck, they can have you then. You've got a job to do. It gets to where you almost don't know what's happening to you. I've had guys come up to me after the game and say, "Man, you took a couple of shots." I don't remember getting hit. By the time I'm climbing up from going down, I'm already thinking about the next play.

ERIC HEIDEN
Speed Skater— Five Time Olympic Gold Medalist

I like the 1,500 meter race the most, but I've got to prepare for the pain. The only way you can win it is by suffering a lot—by working through the pain.

LEE KEMP
Wrestler—Three Time World Champion

With me, it's all a state of mind! I feel a person's will is what's going to make the difference when things get tough. A person's will or mental toughness or mental commandment is what makes a true champion in anything, because it is this unique ability that allows a person to demand of himself anything and everything needed to get the job done!

I conditioned myself at an early age to mentally demand my body to do what was needed to win in wrestling. Whatever it took to win, I was prepared to put forth that effort. With this type of mental attitude about winning, I found myself working extremely hard and long at preparing for competitions. With all this time and work invested, it made winning a precious and valuable thing which, in effect, made me even mentally tougher.

JOHN S. ROOSMA
Military Colonel

One of man's finest qualities is described by the simple word "guts"—the ability to take it. If you have the discipline to stand fast when your body wants to run, if you can control your temper and remain cheerful in the face of monotony or disappointment, you have "guts" in the soldiering sense. This ability to take it must be trained—the training is hard, mental as well as physical. But once ingrained, you can face and flail the enemy as a soldier, and enjoy the challenges of life as a civilian.

WILLIS REED—SOMETIMES YOU HAVE TO PLAY WITH PAIN

"There comes a time, when the game or the season is on the line, when you have to block out pain and contribute whatever you can."

Willis Reed had been plagued with painful knee and hip injuries during the 1970 season in which he had led the New York Knicks into the NBA playoffs against the Los Angeles Lakers and Wilt Chamberlain. The injuries had caused him to miss the sixth game of the series, but no way was Reed going to sit on the bench when the buzzer rang to start the seventh and deciding game.

"For all my life, ever since I was 13 years old, that was where I wanted to be. I wanted to be playing for a championship team," Reed said then.

Before the game he said, **"Ain't no way they're going to play that last game without me. I've got to go out there. Now, I don't know if I can walk, but I've got to go."**

Reed was able to play only the first few minutes in that game, but he was around long enough to score two quick baskets. More important, his effort so inspired his teammates that they went on to an easy 113-99 win over the Lakers.

Later, he said, **"I was in pain, but I knew I had to go out and play a man so many inches taller than me and so much stronger than me, a man who had just had a 45-point game. And I knew I had to go out and play him on one leg. I couldn't run and I really couldn't jump and somehow I was going to have to compensate for all that. All the nice words and all the applause and all the feelings of the fans and all the words in the newspapers that I had a lot of courage to do what I did would not be any consolation to me if we lost."**

When the buzzer rang, you could count on Willis Reed.

LOU GEHRIG—MENTAL TOUGHNESS WAS HIS MIDDLE NAME

On any other team, Lou Gehrig would have been THE star. He is considered by most baseball experts to be the finest first baseman who ever played the game, yet his career was played in the shadow of Babe Ruth.

"The Babe is one fellow, and I'm another and I could never be exactly like him," Gehrig said. **"I don't try. I just go on as I am in my own right."**

His "own right" was an example in consistent excellence. The great pride that carried him beyond illness and injury allowed him to set one record in baseball which will probably never be broken—playing in 2,130 consecutive games.

It took a rare illness, amyotrophic lateral sclerosis (now known as Lou Gehrig's disease), to stop him in 1939. Yet, he never complained, and set an example even as he neared death.

On July 4, 1939, the Yankees honored Gehrig. On that day he said, **"Fans, for the past two weeks, you have been reading about a bad break I got. Yet today, I consider myself the luckiest man on the face of the earth."**

He closed his speech, saying, **"I might have had a tough break, but I have an awful lot to live for."**

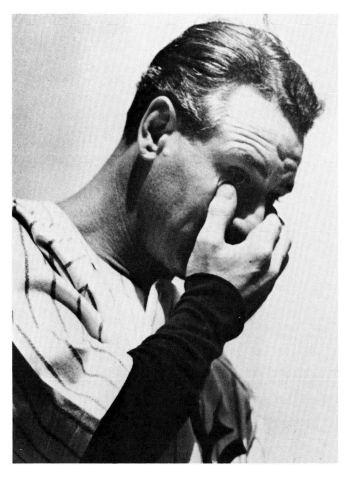

I've always made a total effort, even when the odds seemed entirely against me. I never quit trying; I never felt that I didn't have a chance to win.
Arnold Palmer, Professional Golfer

Never undress until you die.
Al McGuire,
College Basketball Coach and Sports Broadcaster

Never give in. Never, never, never, never! Never yield in any way great or small, except to convictions of honor and good sense. Never yield to force and the apparently overwhelming might of the enemy.
Sir Winston Churchill,
Prime Minister of England

DON'T QUIT

There's a famous saying, "It's not over 'til the fat lady sings." In other words — never, never quit. Momentum can change in a second. One big play can change the entire complexion of a game: a turnover in football; a three-point shot followed by a steal in basketball; a couple of walks, an error, then a shot over the left field fence in baseball. See what I mean?

When the going got tough and he found himself trailing by a shot or two late in the final round of a tournament, Arnold Palmer would hitch up his trousers and make a run at the leader. He'd pull out his 3-wood and go over the water even though the logical shot was to play it safe. Such charges were legendary. Palmer may have been down on the scoreboard but he was never out. That's why he has become one of golf's all-time greats.

Winston Churchill was not an athlete; he was the Prime Minister of England during World War II. His inspirational speeches became legend. He told the Allied forces to keep on fighting — under any circumstances. His speeches obviously worked.

As the head basketball coach at Marquette University, Al McGuire recruited athletes who grew up on the streets, guys who played basketball in school yards down on the corner. These were kids who knew what a hard time was and knew how to survive. McGuire's teams never quit or gave up. They played with heart and they were winners. When McGuire finally left college coaching, he did so with a tear in his eye — and a national championship.

No matter what happens in business, life or in sports, don't quit. Quitters are losers; they have the bad habit of giving up before it's over. Winners set goals and work hard; they don't let anything stop them from reaching their goal. The only true way to fail to reach your goal is to quit. It makes sense that the more time you spend in preparation, the more you'll want to win. Why? Because you have more of yourself involved in the process. When you develop the habit of winning, you'll do anything not to lose or quit.

Not quitting sounds easy but it isn't. If you aren't in condition or haven't sacrificed, it will be a lot easier to quit because you'll have little to lose. If you don't have lots of pride or take the time to develop it, it'll be easier for you to quit because you'll have little motivation to win.

Finally, one of my strongest beliefs that's repeated many times in this book is: The less time you spend on preparation, the less you'll have sacrificed or "paid the price"; and the less pride you'll have — making it easier to quit. Quitters are good losers because they have developed the habit.

It's logical that the more you commit yourself to what you're doing, the more you'll want to win. Likewise, the more you can't stand losing, the harder it will be to quit.

Winners have a strong mental attitude which refuses to let them give up. Some people call this heart. But there are times when you lose — even the great champions do on occasion. When you lose, lose with pride. And in style. Go down swinging. Take your best shot. And DON'T QUIT!

DON'T QUIT

BABE RUTH
Major League Pitcher/Outfielder

If Henry Ford hadn't kept going in the early days despite ridicule, we would never have seen the Ford car. It's been much the same with every great man you could name. He kept plugging when everybody said his chances of making first base were nil. You just can't beat the person who never gives up.

GEORGE WEINBERG
American Engineer

Don't give up whatever you're trying to do. Giving up reinforces a sense of incompetence; going on gives you a commitment to success.

SUGAR RAY LEONARD
Professional Boxer and Sports Broadcaster

When I knocked out Tommy Hearns, I had to dig down in my guts. I knew I was behind; I knew I had to keep the pressure on. I knew I wasn't going to quit. There wasn't anything I could do but find out what was inside of me.

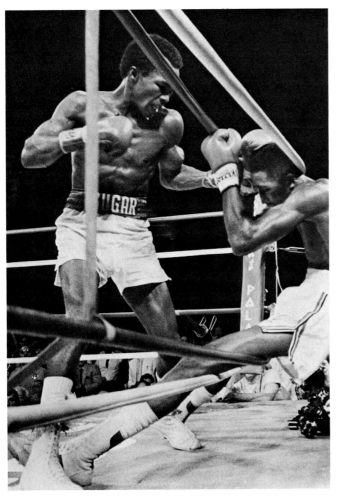

THOMAS EDISON
American Inventor

Our greatest weakness lies in giving up. The most certain way to succeed is to always try just one more time.

JAMES CORBETT
Professional Boxer

Fight one more round. When your feet are so tired that you have to shuffle back to the center of the ring, fight one more round. When your arms are so tired that you can hardly lift your hands to come on guard, fight one more round. When your nose is bleeding and your eyes are black and you are so tired that you wish your opponent would crack you in the jaw and put you to sleep, fight one more round. Remember that the man who always fights one more round is never whipped.

ELMER WHEELER
American Engineer

People seldom want to walk over you until you lie down.

JOHN WAYNE
Actor

True Grit is making a decision and standing by it, doing what must be done. No moral man can have peace of mind if he leaves undone what he knows he should have done.

SATCHEL PAIGE
First Black Pitcher in the Major Leagues

Don't look back. Someone might be gaining on you. When you look back, you know how long you've been going and that just might stop you from going any farther.

FRANK SHORTER
Distance Runner—Olympic Gold Medalist

I didn't want to quit and say for the rest of my life, "Well, maybe I could have been..."

H. E. JANSEN
American Writer

The man who wins may have been counted out several times, but he didn't hear the referee.

JOE BLACK
Major League Pitcher
Quitting is a cinch. You walk away. For the time being, you're the boss. You're free as a bird. When you're young, people excuse a lot of things. But when you get older, people stop feeling sorry for you and quitting isn't so popular.

JOHN W. GALBREATH
Major League Owner
It's a tireless effort, but that's how you succeed. You never quit; you keep on going day and night. You don't ever despair. If you do, you work on your despair.

JOE FRAZIER
Professional Boxer, Trainer and Manager
When you get tired of getting knocked down and want to pack it all up, don't. Just brush yourself off and keep on smokin', because the fight is not over until God rings the final bell.

FRANKLIN D. ROOSEVELT
Thirty-Second President
When you get to the end of your rope, tie a knot and hang on.

JOE FERGUSON
NFL Quarterback
A couple of times, I wanted to pack my bags and leave without telling anyone that I was going. But then my inner self said, "Don't quit". If you're a competitor, you don't want to quit.

MUHAMMAD ALI
Professional Boxer
I hated every minute of the training, but I said, "Don't quit. Suffer now and live the rest of your life as a champion."

WILLIE SCHAEFFLER
U. S. Olympic Ski Team Coach
I was repeatedly wounded during World War II on the Russian front over a period of 20 months. The physical training that my parents gave me and the beliefs that I experienced in childhood extended right through to the action in battle. I had only one thing to believe in—my own body—my own strength, and the conviction that I would make it, that I would hold together. There was no panic. I believed it. It came true. It was not so much a miracle to me, as a gift—a return for my original faith in fitness. It always helped me recuperate faster than the average person did. The will is so strong and the body is so prepared—that you can do it—you just don't quit.

TOMMY JOHN
Major League Pitcher
My Doctor told me that I would never pitch again, but I told him, "You're a great doctor and I believe in you. But you're wrong. I won't quit. I will come back. You did an excellent job inside my arm. Now it's up to me. I know how much pain my body can stand—and it's quite a bit. I know how hard I can work, and if it takes 18 hours a day, I'll do it. I will come back."

BO SCHEMBECHLER
College Football Coach and Athletic Director

I can certainly understand why the PAC-10 wants to continue its association with the Big 10. But I'm not going to quit. I'm going to keep coaching till I win the Big One—the Rose Bowl—if for no reason than to shut the writers up.

BUD GRANT
NFL Coach

We've had some bad breaks over the years, I suppose you could call them that. But we have always been ready. Always prepared, and we always will be. We have dedicated players—we'll be back. We want to win the big one—the Super Bowl—and we won't quit until we do.

BILL FITCH
NBA Coach and General Manager

When first starting the Cleveland Cavaliers franchise, we adopted the slogan "Never Surrender No Matter What the Odds." I've always felt that this was good advice to any athlete and the harder the athlete works, the more effort he puts toward his goal, the less likely it will be that he will surrender short of his goal.

With the 76ers ahead of us three games to one during the 1981 NBA Championship Playoffs, "Never Surrender No Matter What the Odds" paid off for the Boston Celtics with an eventual World Championship.

ABRAHAM LINCOLN DIDN'T QUIT

Abraham Lincoln could have quit many times—but he didn't and because he didn't quit, he became one of the greatest Presidents in the history of our country.

"The sense of obligation to continue is present in all of us. A duty to strive is the duty of us all. I felt a call to that duty."

Probably the greatest example of persistence is Abraham Lincoln. If you want to learn about somebody who didn't quit, look no further.

Born into poverty, Lincoln was faced with defeat throughout his life. He lost eight elections, twice failed in business and suffered a nervous breakdown.

But Lincoln was a champion and he never gave up. Here is a sketch of Lincoln's road to the White House:

- 1831—Failed in business.
- 1832—Defeated for Legislature.
- 1833—Second failure in business.
- 1836—Suffered nervous breakdown.
- 1838—Defeated for Speaker.
- 1840—Defeated for Elector.
- 1843—Defeated for Congress.
- 1848—Defeated for Congress.
- 1855—Defeated for Senate.
- 1856—Defeated for Vice President.
- 1858—Defeated for Senate.
- 1860—ELECTED PRESIDENT.

"The path was worn and slippery. My foot slipped from under me, knocking the other out of the way," Lincoln said, after losing a Senate race. **"But I recovered and said to myself, 'It's a slip and not a fall.'"**

ROCKY BLEIER REFUSED TO QUIT

The Pittsburgh Steelers took Bleier as their last pick of the 1968 draft in the 18th round. But Bleier was also drafted by the Army that year and sent to Vietnam. While he was there, he had the bottom of his right foot ripped open by a grenade, his right leg shredded by shrapnel and his left thigh hit by gunfire. He was listed as 40 percent disabled.

Still, Bleier wanted to play football. He would rise in the early hours of the morning and jog with the help of a special sole he designed for his shoe. And when Pittsburgh's training camp opened in 1970, Bleier was there, battling eight running backs for only five spots.

"I didn't want to face the truth," Bleier said. "I have a certain self-discipline, an ability to persuade myself that reality is not what it seems. During that training camp, I convinced myself that I actually had a chance to make the ballclub. I forced myself to ignore the fact that I still had a noticeable limp, especially late in the day when I was tired. Years later, in better times, players told me how they collectively shook their heads in 1970."

It became evident to those at the Steeler camp that Bleier wouldn't quit, despite the advice of coaches, trainers and doctors that he should give up football rather than take a chance of suffering permanent injury. Bleier almost made the team that year, but was the last player cut before the final roster was set.

He underwent another operation on his foot and was put on the Steeler's injured reserve list. He scouted for Pittsburgh and was reactivated for the team's final game. And he worked to get ready to take another shot at the NFL. **"I tried to rationalize the workout. Ten laps, two and a half miles. That's all I could do,"** Bleier remembered. **"My right toes ached; I still couldn't push off them. I was still running cockeyed on the heel and side of my foot. My toes had no strength, no endurance, no flexibility. I couldn't do any more."**

"Then I thought of the other running backs—Bankston, Pearson, Fuqua, plus the rookies who would be coming in. Ten laps would be nothing for them. Then I imagined myself...in super shape, running the football, breaking tackles, the crowd roaring. I got up and ran some more."

At the next training camp, Bleier ripped a hamstring muscle in the leg that had been shot in Vietnam. Again, he was advised to give up football. But by that time, the doctors undoubtedly knew what the answer would be. Bleier taped up his leg and returned to the field.

By 1972, Bleier was playing every game with the Steelers on their specialty teams. He was timed faster than he had been before he suffered his wounds.

In 1974, Bleier moved into the starting backfield. In 1976, he gained over one thousand yards. He became a key player in Pittsburgh's emergence as the dominant team of the 1970's.

Rocky Bleier became a great football player simply because he refused to quit.

I never stay away from workouts. I work hard. I've tried to take care of my body. I'll never look back and say that I could have done more. I've paid the price in practice, but I know I get the most out of my ability. Pride, intense pride, that's what it comes down to.

Carl Yastrzemski,
Major League Outfielder/First Baseman

Without being bashful, I thought I was the best baseball player I ever saw. Nobody in the world could do what I could do. If you play ball, you have to believe that you are the best. You have to have pride.

Willie Mays, Major League Outfielder

When I lose, it doesn't just go to my head. It goes to my heart, too. If you're at all in the match, if you love to play and win, it must go to your heart.

Ivan Lendl, Professional Tennis Player

PRIDE

Great athletes never, never quit! Why? In a word, Pride! They believe in themselves very strongly; and feel they're the best in their sport — bar none. Such feelings drive champions to perfection. They want to be No. 1 — pure and simple. It's their pride that makes them No. 1 and keeps them there.

Proud athletes have confidence in themselves. They aren't necessarily arrogant, but they can be. They've worked long and hard, made sacrifices and have paid the price of success. They've earned the right to be proud.

Losing is very difficult when you have pride. The more of it you have, the harder it is on you when you lose. Athletes are aware of this. That's why they hurt so much when they lose. Winning, on the other hand, increases your pride. And the prouder you are, the harder you'll work to deserve your sense of pride.

Pride is developed in an athlete. You won't gain it by a half-hearted performance. You have to give 100% all the time. When you do, your pride will increase dramatically. Why? Because the more intense your effort is, the more intense your pride will be. The more intense your pride is, the more you'll want to win.

So eliminate the negative elements in your life and stress the positive. A key way to do this is to set a realistic goal for yourself. Don't set vague goals. Instead, set specific goals like, "I want to be the best gymnast on the balance beam in the country within two years." Whatever your goal, strive to become the best person, best student or best athlete you can become.

Stress the positive aspects of your life and eliminate the negative elements. If you don't like what you're doing, don't do it anymore. If you don't feel you're working hard enough to be proud of yourself, work harder. It isn't that difficult. If you really don't like what you see in the mirror, change it. How? By taking responsibility for your own life. If you want to be successful, then think, act and look successful. Take risks and go beyond the ordinary. That's the only way to become a winner and have pride in yourself.

When two athletes have:

Equal natural ability,

Equal preparation,

Equal conditioning,

Equal concentration,

Equal reaction to pressure,

Who will have the edge? Who will win?

The answer is simple. The athlete who is at his best, who loves a hard battle and who refuses to lose.

The athlete with the most pride.

No matter what happens — never let them take away your pride.

I don't want to hear about number two. There's only one number one. It's not a matter of money—just pride—pure and simple. I want to be the best.

Jimmy Connors, Professional Tennis Player

PRIDE

JOHN MADDEN
NFL Coach and Sports Broadcaster

The first quality that makes an athlete a winner is simply pride. He has such a desire to excel he will take enormous pains. He will work out beyond what is demanded, build his body during the off-season, guard his weight and study the problems of his position. The second quality is toughness—doing what the job requires without worrying about the physical consequences. A wide receiver will make the catch, untroubled by the possibility of getting blindsided. A quarterback will hold the ball until the final instant, knowing the rusher will flatten him. The winning player has no fear in doing what must be done in order to be great.

SIR EDWARD BULWER
English Diplomat

Whatever you lend let it be your money, and not your name. Money you may get again, and, if not, you may contrive to do without it; name once lost you cannot get again, and, if you cannot contrive to do without it, you had better never have been born.

PETE ROSE
Major League First Baseman and Manager

The one thing I've got more than anything is pride. My pride keeps me going. That's why I work so hard. How do I test my pride?—By taking a hundred ground balls before every game—with early batting practice on the first day back from a trip or on Sunday mornings after a Saturday night game—by testing my reflexes by having a batting practice pitcher throw as hard as he can to me from 45 feet. I wouldn't care if I played in Philadelphia or Cincinnati or Albuquerque. I'd play the same way.

EDWIN MOSES
Hurdler — Two Time Olympic Gold Medalist

People tend to look at what I've done strictly as athletic ability. It's also said that the reason I don't get recognition is that I win so much. This doesn't make any sense; try paying somebody else to do it. That's the way I can put it bluntly. If it's so easy to do, give somebody any budget you care to imagine and most likely it'll be impossible to do what I've done. Just like if you give somebody ten million dollars to produce a Picasso, he won't be able to do it. There'll be one stroke on there that isn't right. I'm just doing my thing, something I created myself, and I'm very proud to be able to say that so far, nobody's been able to do anything about it.

JOE GREENE
NFL Defensive Tackle and Coach

Have respect for yourself. Love yourself and realize that whatever you attempt to achieve in life is a direct reflection of you. Be proud.

PARNELLI JONES
Race Car Driver

Many people in today's world have allowed pride in performance to fall by the wayside because exemplary performance requires hard work. Nothing happens unless you make it happen. Establishing goals and reaching the established goals requires perseverance and self-discipline. It is very easy to become discouraged and to decide there must be an easier way; however, always remember, "When the going gets tough—the tough get going—have pride in yourself and your performance".

JACK NICKLAUS
Professional Golfer

My urge for self-improvement has very little to do with winning, and nothing at all to do with making money or other materialistic factors. I've always believed that performance takes care of those things.

Anytime that there's a cooling off in this impulse to improve, one emotion above all others will get a good blaze going again. It's embarrassment. I am very easily embarrassed by myself. No single emotion is more responsible for whatever I've achieved.

HENRY L. DOHERTY
American Industrialist

A great business success was probably never attained by chasing the dollar, but is due to pride in one's work—the pride that makes business an art.

JACK LAMBERT
NFL Linebacker

Take pride in whatever it is you do—whether it be playing football, or playing the piano. Always give your best effort, for if you fail to do so, you cheat not only those around you, you cheat yourself. Strive to be the best. Although it's a goal that's not always obtainable, it's a great feeling of accomplishment for one to achieve goals that were once only imagined.

Take pride in yourself. Be your own person. Don't do things because everyone else does them. Don't be part of the crowd...dare to be different. Never be afraid to stand up for what you believe to be right...even if it means standing alone!

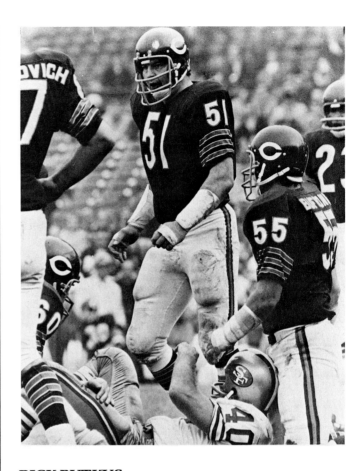

DICK BUTKUS
NFL Linebacker and Sports Broadcaster

Ever since I was in eighth grade, I've been nuts about this game. I love to hit and I love to win. It has to be that way. You can never let yourself be embarrassed. I always keep in mind that any game could be my last. You never know in this business. I wouldn't ever want my last game to be a stinker.

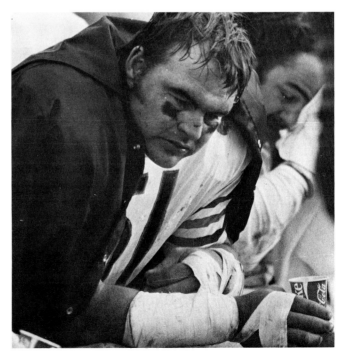

JOE PATERNO
College Football Coach and Athletic Director

When you lose, you get that sick feeling in your stomach. Then it turns to anger and the anger gets you to work harder and gets you to show some real pride. Darn it all, there's nothing in this world as bad as losing.

JOHN MADDEN
NFL Coach and Sports Broadcaster

There must be desire, intensity and a feeling of wanting to be the best on the part of the player. That comes from within him. You can't manufacture pride.

CHUCK KNOX
NFL Coach

Attack your responsibilities with energy and enthusiasm. Give a maximum effort at all times and never permit yourself to become discouraged. When the true test comes, reach down deep within yourself for that pride, that self-motivation, that great burning desire that will get the job done.

RON FAIRLY
Major League First Baseman

Certainly I feel the Dodgers made a mistake in trading me. I wouldn't be human if I didn't. But the only way I'm going to prove this point is with my bat and glove. I'm not motivated by vengeance. Call it pride, the same pride that made me want to win for the Dodgers.

JAMES LOFTON
NFL Wide Receiver

I like to play a major role in the offense. I personally want to catch the ball a lot. I don't want to catch just one for a touchdown. I have a lot of pride. I want to be good all the time.

BJORN BORG
Professional Tennis Player

My pride keeps me going for the big titles—I want to win as many as I can. When I retire and people look back at me, maybe they'll say that I was the best tennis player ever.

CHUCK KNOX
NFL Coach

Pride is not like a coat; it's not something that you lay down for two or three days and then decide when you get up some morning that you'll have pride that day and put it on. It must be there every day and it takes constant work to achieve it, to keep it.

ROCKY MARCIANO
Professional Boxer

What could be better than walking down any street in any city and knowing that you are the champion? It would hurt—it would hurt a lot—to find a guy who could lick me. It's everything. You lose the title and you lose people's respect and admiration and, of course, you lose some personal pride.

WILLIE STARGELL
Major League First Baseman and Coach

I know there were some people saying I was through, but nobody remembered to ask me about my feelings on the subject. People don't realize how much pride and deep feelings can be worth.

GALE SAYERS
NFL Halfback

If you don't have enough pride, you're going to get your butt beat every play.

SUGAR RAY ROBINSON
Professional Boxer

Once you've had acclaim as a world champion, once you move into that sphere, you never want to move out. I didn't fight for money. I fought for the pride of being champion.

YOGI BERRA
Major League Catcher and Manager

People seem to find it hard to believe that I'm a serious person. I have a lot of pride in what I do. It wasn't luck that I became a ballplayer. I never wanted to be anything else and I never considered anything else and I worked my tail off for it. To say that I don't have any worries or nerves is the opposite of the truth.

CARL YASTRZEMSKI
Major League Outfielder/First Baseman

The competition drives me. I like facing the pitcher, one on one. Once you get into the batter's box, pride takes over. Nobody can help but you.

DAN GABLE
Wrestler — Olympic Gold Medalist and College Wrestling Coach

More enduring than any other sport, wrestling teaches self-control and pride. Some have wrestled without great skill; none have wrestled without pride.

TED WILLIAMS WAS A VERY PROUD MAN

Ted Williams was a great baseball player, probably the best pure hitter who ever played the game. He became that by hours of practice and study of his swing.

Ted Williams was also a proud man. He was the last man to hit over .400. He could just have easily batted below the coveted mark. When his manager suggested he sit out the last game of the season to preserve his batting average, he elected to take his chances and play. He was too proud not to play.

"I'm going to play. I don't want to slip into the .400 circle through the back door. I don't care to be known as a .400 hitter with a lousy average of .39955. If I'm going to be a .400 hitter, I want to have more than my toenails on the line."

Williams' tremendous pride is what enabled him to make two of the most memorable comebacks in baseball.

After his hero's duty in the Korean War, he played the last 37 games of the 1953 season and, in 91 times at the plate, connected 37 times including 13 home runs. And, after a two-and-a-half-month absence to heal a broken shoulder, he jumped into a double-header and had eight hits out of nine times at bat, two of them homers.

Williams' inner drive left him no energy to court the adulation of fans or even to observe the common decencies. After his rookie year, when he was last known to tip his hat to the cheering grandstands, Williams became notorious—and fascinating—for his refusal to acknowledge applause. It was, he announced, the fickleness of fans, as ready to boo as to cheer, which decided him. The people in Boston learned to love this proud man.

In time, "Tempestuous Ted" became "Our Teddy" and the most admired sports figure in Boston. When, in 1960, Williams hit his last homer, number 521 and the longest of his career, the stands at Fenway exploded with pride and affection. He left the field without tipping his hat—his own man to the last.

"All I want out of life is that when I walk down the street, folks will say, 'There goes the greatest hitter who ever lived.'"

SATCHEL PAIGE— PRIDE KEPT HIM GOING

"Never look back, someone may be gaining on you."

Baseball discovered the Fountain of Youth when it discovered Satchel Paige. Paige had pitched for more than 20 years in the Negro Leagues before he got his shot in the majors. When the Cleveland Indians signed him, he was 42. At least that was his reported age, for nobody ever quite found out exactly how old Paige really was.

There are some who say Satchel was the greatest pitcher who ever lived. Legend says he pitched more than a hundred no-hitters and won over two thousand games. Yet because he was black, Paige never got his chance in the majors until late in his career.

He did get the chance to face major league competition in exhibitions, once beating Dizzy Dean (1-0) in a 13-inning game. Mostly, though, he barnstormed throughout the country, going from team to team, pitching nearly every day.

"I promised myself I'd keep throwing until somebody figured they needed me bad in the majors," Paige said. **"Before that arm of mine gave out, I was going to taste that major league living."**

When he finally made the major league, fans in Cleveland gave him a 10 minute standing ovation.

He went on to pitch for the St. Louis Browns and was selected by Casey Stengel to pitch in the 1952 All-Star Game. He got his taste of major league living long after he deserved it. Satchel Paige may not have always had professional baseball, but he did always have his pride.

"When they treat you bad," he said, **"you just got to take care of your pride, no matter what."**

7
POST GAME

- Are You Strong Enough to Handle Success?
- Are You Strong Enough to Handle Critics?
- Are You Strong Enough to Handle Adversity?
- Accept Responsibility – Don't Make Excuses
- Perseverance – Persistence

Are You Strong Enough To Handle Critics?

It is not the critic who counts, not the man who points out how the strong man stumbles or where the doer of deeds could have done them better. The credit belongs to the man who is actually in the arena, whose face is marred by dust and sweat and blood, who strives valiantly, who errs and comes short again and again because there is no effort without error and shortcomings, who knows the great devotion, who spends himself in a worthy cause, who at the best knows in the end the high achievement of triumph and who at worst, if he fails while daring greatly, knows his place shall never be with those timid and cold souls who know neither victory nor defeat.

THEODORE ROOSEVELT   Twenty-Sixth President

The above is one of the most impressive and impacting philosophies I have ever heard. It was a thought expressed by one of the greatest competitors of our time, Theodore Roosevelt, our twenty-sixth President. It embodies my basic feelings as to what success is really all about. The same philosophy applies to just about every phase of one's life. The common thread of thought for people in our sports world is to always try, try, and try again…to know in your heart that you did your best. Then, if victory does come, you will know that you made a very special contribution.

TEXAS E. SCHRAMM   NFL President

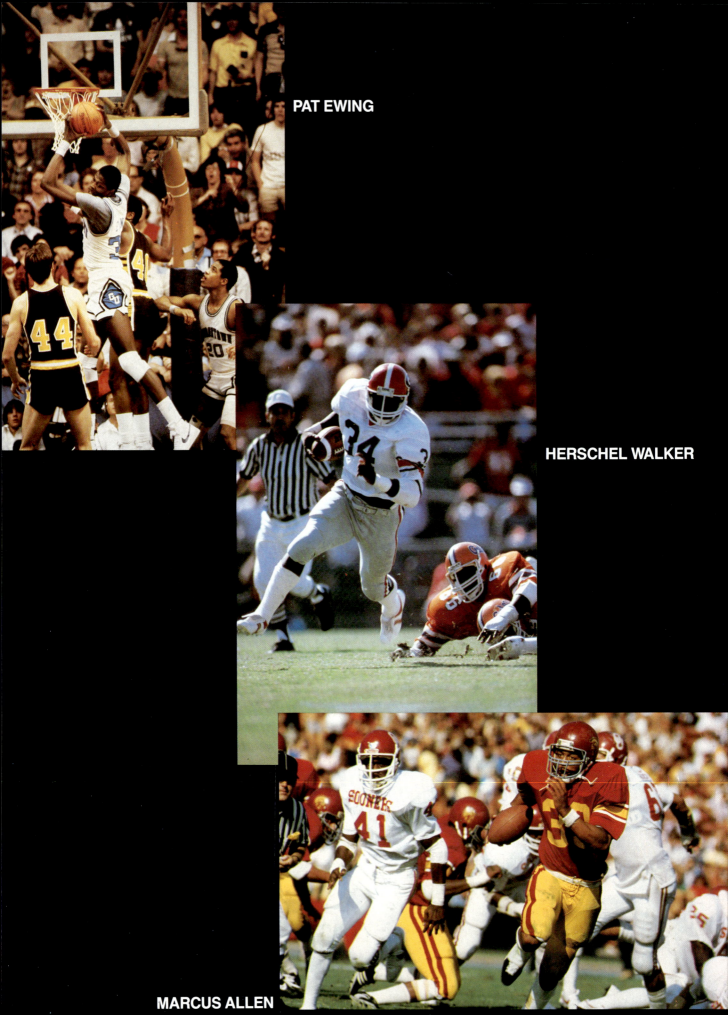
PAT EWING

HERSCHEL WALKER

MARCUS ALLEN

RALPH SAMPSON

ARE YOU STRONG ENOUGH TO HANDLE SUCCESS?

While success is something that every athlete wants, it creates an entirely new set of pressures and problems. Not every athlete who achieves success handles it well.

When you are No. 1, everybody takes his best shot at you. Every night, every game, there'll be someone trying to dethrone the No. 1 player in the world. Or there will be a team trying to make its entire season by beating the champion. The key to remaining a champion is how well you handle the pressure and constant challenges.

Former UCLA basketball coach John Wooden once said it was more difficult to stay on top, than it was to win the first of his team's ten NCAA titles.

When Virginia's Ralph Sampson entered college, he probably felt more pressure than any other college basketball player in history. He was expected to help a team, which had previously enjoyed only limited success, win the national championship. Sampson was expected to do whatever was needed to make his team win. He handled the pressure well, however. He was selected NCAA Player of the Year as a sophomore and his team won.

Like Sampson, Patrick Ewing of Georgetown was viewed as a dynasty-builder when he entered college. He had to deal with enormous pressure from fans, alumni and the media because of their great expectations. How did he do? He led Georgetown to a national title his junior year and to the championship game three out of the four years he played. Obviously, he was strong enough to handle success.

All athletes who step into the spotlight and stand above their teammates face similar situations. For most running backs in football, a 100-yard gain in any game is outstanding. But for Georgia's Herschel Walker and Southern Cal's Marcus Allen, a 100-yard game was expected. Such players have established a new set of standards for future champions.

When victory is achieved, the feeling can be overwhelming. It's important to keep your common sense and be gracious. Silence is often the best tactic after a win. If you're part of a team and you must talk, praise your opponents and your teammates. Never brag about yourself. Stand for something greater than just yourself.

Why do so many athletes feel the need to tell everyone what happened? How they won? How well they performed? If you win and you're good, people will see it. They will know without being told. Your job is to perform — not report.

Self-praise is for losers. When you win, say nothing; when you lose, say less.

The most important thing to do after winning is to get back to work. Winning can have a negative influence, if you become too satisfied or complacent with your performance. Even in victory, be critical and look for mistakes you might have made. Why? To avoid them next time. Never be completely satisfied; keep searching for ways to improve.

The key to repeatedly winning championships is to immediately analyze every facet of your game. You'll stand a much better chance of repeating as champs. If you don't search for mistakes or seek to be even better next time, back-to-back championships will be impossible.

ARE YOU STRONG ENOUGH TO HANDLE SUCCESS?

JOHN MADDEN
NFL Coach and Sports Broadcaster

My biggest guard is against becoming too satisfied when we win. There are many times when you've got to put the joy of winning behind you and look ahead to what really is uncertainty.

BUM PHILLIPS
NFL Coach

Lots of people know how to be successful, but very few people know how to handle success!

KEN VENTURI
Professional Golfer and Sports Broadcaster

You are never better than anyone else until you do something to prove it, and, when you are really good, you never need to tell anyone. They will tell you.

DEAN SMITH
College Basketball Coach

The road is better than the ending, the hoping is better than the realization. I may wake up in three weeks and see the mail I have to answer and ask if it's been worthwhile.

ROBERT MONTGOMERY
American Writer/Poet

If you achieve success, you will get applause, and if you get applause, you will hear it. My advice to you concerning applause is this: enjoy it, but never quite believe it.

ALAN GREGG
Rockefeller Foundation Educator

The human race has had long experience and a fine tradition in surviving adversity. But we now face a task for which we have little experience—the task of surviving prosperity.

BOB KNIGHT
**College Basketball Coach and
U.S. Olympic Basketball Coach**

You can't become too satisfied with success. Let's say that we had a good year and went 25 and three. The only thing I'd be concerned with is why we lost those three games. Was there one consistent thing? If there was, let's do something about it!

SEBASTIAN COE
**Distance Runner —
Three Time Olympic Gold Medalist**

Holding the mile record doesn't make it any easier to run a mile in the future.

MICHAEL BURKE
NBC President

Even if you're one of the stars on the team and have tasted success, you still have a lot to learn. Listen to your coaches and give it your best shot every day. If you don't, if you loaf or coast on your reputation, you are cheating only yourself.

STEVE BARTKOWSKI
NFL Quarterback

When everything's going well, it's only natural that you just ride the crest and don't worry about anything. The Lord tried to get through to me by saying that I'd better get off my butt.

OSCAR WILDE
Irish Poet/Playwright

There is always something about your success that displeases even your best friends.

EDWIN MOSES
Hurdler — Two Time Olympic Gold Medalist

You have to work harder to maintain being number one. There's more pressure on me than on the average guy who goes out there with nothing to lose. More people are looking at me. When I run, people stop and tune in on the race. This doesn't happen to a lot of runners.

DON SHULA
NFL Defensive Back and Coach

Success isn't final. Past performance is forgotten in every new competition. It is harder to stay on top than it is to get there.

NANCY LOPEZ
Professional Golfer

Just because I shot a 66 one day and won a tournament doesn't mean anything. There are no guarantees that I'll do it the next day.

DON SCHOLLANDER
Swimmer—Five Time Olympic Gold Medalist

Once you get on top, there is terrific pressure to stay there. At the peak of my career, I was swimming not as much to win as not to lose. A real champion must learn to handle success, which in some ways is even more difficult than dealing with defeat.

JACK NICKLAUS
Professional Golfer

Complacency is a continuous struggle that we all have to fight. I constantly have to work on getting tougher on myself. You must have the edge in tournament play. You must hold the edge, and the only way to hold it is to work on it.

CHRIS EVERT
Professional Tennis Player

Before, winning was a habit, a routine. Now it's a choice. I think more now; I question more. Thinking can be bad for your tennis. In the past, I relied on instinct. I could win ruthlessly without full awareness of what I was doing. It's harder now that I'm on top, but a lot more rewarding.

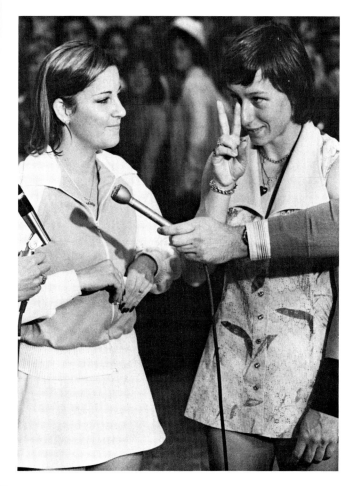

HUMILITY

RED GRANGE
NFL Halfback

All I would remember about a long run were the key blocks rather than what I did. I've never had the idea that anybody, just because they do certain things, should be any better than anyone else.

WILLIAM SHAKESPEARE
English Dramatist/Playwright/Poet

Everyone I meet is in some way my superior.

JOE MONTANA
NFL Quarterback

Me, a Notre Dame legend? I can't picture my name up there with Rockne, Leahy, Gipp…guys like that. Heck, they practically built Notre Dame. I can't believe legends do the things I do. I mean, every afternoon I go to the barn—I have two Arabian horses—and shovel it out. Do legends do that? I go to the store, buy milk, and forget the bread. I try to hammer a nail, I hit my thumb. Do legends do that?

GEORGE GERVIN
NBA Guard

I try not to listen to the stuff that inflates people. A guy in the limelight can lose control if he does.

SPENCER HAYWOOD
NBA Forward

I'm called a superstar. Heck, the real superstar is a man or woman who is raising six kids on $150 a week and teaching them good values.

BENJAMIN FRANKLIN
American Inventor

If thou hast wit and learning, add to it wisdom and modesty. Words may show a man's wit, but actions will show his meaning. Speak little; do much. Well done is better than well said.

JACK LAMBERT
NFL Linebacker

Always take the time to show compassion for those less fortunate, and there are many. Take the time to help a young child cross the street, or to carry a bag of groceries for an elderly lady. And every now and then, look up into that big, beautiful, blue sky and admit that there are things in this world more wondrous than yourself.

STAN MIKITA
NHL Center

Always give a total effort. Pride in oneself and one's ability comes through knowledge and hard work. Self-discipline is the key to harnessing the energy and dedication necessary to succeed.

When you think that you have mastered it all, humble yourself with the thought that learning is a lifetime process. The margin between a winner and a champion is only a little extra work.

KNUTE ROCKNE
College Football Coach

Egotism is the anesthetic that deadens the pain of stupidity.

MIKE BOSSY
NHL Right Wing

They say that I've got the fastest hands in hockey, but you'd never know that from the way that I play Space Invaders.

WOODROW WILSON
Twenty-Eighth President

A fault which humbles a man is of more use to him than a good action which puffs him up.

CHARLES B. ROGERS
American Merchant

A man need not extol his virtues, nor comment on his failings. His friends know the former, and his enemies will search out the latter.

ADAM W. BURNETT, D.D.
American Educator

Lack of proper humility, which is the fundamental aspect of Christianity, is the reason many men fail to display the courage and foresight that comes through complete faith in God.

JOE DI MAGGIO
Major League Outfielder

I feel I've been unusually privileged to play all my major league baseball for the New York Yankees. I'm just a ballplayer with only one ambition, to give all I've got to help my club win. I've never played any other way. I just want to thank the good Lord for making me a Yankee. But as great as it has been being a Yankee, it has been even a greater privilege to play baseball at all. It has added much to my life. What I will remember most in the days to come will be the great loyalty of the fans. They have been very good to me.

LAO-TZU
Chinese Philosopher

I have three precious things which I hold fast and prize. The first is gentleness; the second is frugality; the third is humility, which keeps me from putting myself before others. Be gentle and you can be bold; be frugal and you can be liberal; avoid putting yourself before others and you can become a leader among men.

ST. BERNARD
Italian Bishop

It is no great thing to be humble when you are brought low; but to be humble when you are praised is a great and rare achievement.

BENJAMIN FRANKLIN
American Inventor

A man wrapped up in himself makes a very small bundle.

BOB COUSY
NBA Guard

There are some people who think that they're more important than anyone else just because they have some God-given talent—maybe they're athletes, maybe artists, maybe stage or screen people, maybe writers. But no matter how big a person is, no matter how many championships his team has won, there's never an excuse for his having a big head.

TREAT WINNING AND LOSING THE SAME

TOM HEINSOHN
NBA Forward, Coach, and Sports Broadcaster

I have found through 22 years of professional basketball experience that winning requires the proper blending of thinking, doing, and emotional commitment. Perhaps the hardest thing to acquire is the ability to focus the emotions properly when needed. Victory breeds oversatisfaction and defeat gives birth to despair. Neither is desirable.

JOE PATERNO
College Football Coach and Athletic Director

Success is never final; failure is never fatal.

SAM RUTIGLIANO
NFL and College Football Coach

The key to success and happiness is to find a middle level. The one problem with football is that there is no middle point—football's all highs or lows. That brings things out in people that normally wouldn't surface. A lot of good men become Jekyll and Hydes and everyone they touch suffers.

LARRY CSONKA
NFL Fullback and Sports Broadcaster

I sincerely hope that if a team plays well and loses that it will not be held against them. America loves professional football because the country loves action. I hope that somebody in this country will recognize the fact that not everyone can be the champion. There has to be a place for sportsmanship that is appreciated when it doesn't result in total victory.

CHUCK KNOX
NFL Coach

Winning and losing are both very temporary things. Having done one or the other, you move ahead. Gloating over a victory or sulking over a loss is a good way to stand still…or worse.

BJORN BORG
Professional Tennis Player

I think that I get over my losses pretty quickly. I also don't gloat over my victories. Both are part of the same family of emotions. Once a match is over, it's over. I don't carry either the pain or the glory with me for very long.

DEAN SMITH
College Basketball Coach

I don't feel the great ecstasy or the emptiness whether we've won or lost. If we lost, I'd have another shot; I'd feel for those kids who wouldn't have another chance. Just because they won, I won't like them any more than last year's team.

AL MC GUIRE
College Basketball Coach and Sports Broadcaster

Coaching really taught me to live for the moment and enjoy each particular time. It has taught me to feel a loss and enjoy a win, but then always go back out the gate again the next day.

Are You Strong Enough To Handle Success?

Unfortunately, the road to anywhere is filled with many pitfalls, and it takes a man of determination and character not to fall into them. As I have said many times, whenever you get your head above the average, someone will be there to take a poke at you. That is to be expected in any phase of life. However, as I have also said many times before, if you see a man on top of a mountain, he didn't just light there! Chances are he had to climb through many difficulties with a great expenditure of energy in order to get there, and the same is true of a man in any profession, be he a great attorney, a great minister, a great man of medicine or a great businessman. I am certain he worked with a definite plan, and an aim and purpose in life and, will be envied by those less successful. I have always thought that the following little verse contained a good philosophy for every coach:

> By your own soul learn to live,
> And if men thwart you, take no heed,
> If men hate you, have no care;
> Sing your song, dream your dream,
>   hope your hope and pray your prayer.

I am sure that if a coach will follow this philosophy of life, he will be successful. To sit by and worry about criticism, which too often comes from the misinformed or from those incapable of passing judgment on an individual or a problem, is a waste of time.

ADOLPH RUPP   College Basketball Coach

I didn't pay attention to the things people said about me. I didn't want to know what they were saying, because I figured I was the only one who knew the truth.

Moses Malone, NBA Center

Coming to a contender like Milwaukee was all I was interested in. I wanted to play in another World Series. I know they're looking at somebody who is 34. I was told I was washed up my last year in Oakland, and San Diego kept waiting for me to run out of gas. All I can say to my critics is this is the best year of my career. I should have been doing this when I was 25. Maybe I get better with age. Maybe I'll be better next year.

Rollie Fingers, Major League Relief Pitcher

You can turn the negative around and use it as a motivating force in your life. One of my biggest desires has always been to prove certain people wrong—to prove to them I can do it despite what they think or say.

Tony Dorsett, NFL Halfback

ARE YOU STRONG ENOUGH TO HANDLE CRITICS?

Criticism can be easily avoided by saying nothing, doing nothing and being nothing. Mediocre people play it safe and avoid criticism at all costs. Champions, however, risk criticism every time they perform. The more you do in life, the more you accomplish, the more you risk being criticized.

If you're successful, people will be jealous of and criticize you. Don't let that distract you from reaching your goal. It's easy to criticize other people, but it's hard to duplicate their efforts. Critics aren't the leaders or the doers in life. The leaders and doers are too busy with their own accomplishments to criticize.

Pride is very important. It builds a foundation of courage that allows you to take risks to be better than the rest. The road to the top is not easy, but if you have pride in yourself, you'll make it. When you reach your goal — be proud. You paid the price to get there. You deserved to win. Because you're more disciplined, worked harder and sacrificed more than the others. Hold your head high.

There's an interesting connection in sports between being a consistent winner and an increase in criticism. It's happened to the New York Yankees in baseball, the Dallas Cowboys in football and the Boston Celtics in basketball. When a team wins consistently year after year, they become a powerful dynasty. People hate them for winning.

The same thing happened to our wrestling team. The more we won, the louder the critics got. We kept on winning. For ten consecutive years we won the State Wrestling Championships in Ohio. The critics grew louder with each championship. Then it happened. In 1988, we lost our first dual meet in seven years. It was our first tournament loss in 11 years! The critics had nothing to talk about.

The critics never bothered us, though, because we knew how hard we had worked and the sacrifices we had made. That's the key. The more we won, the bigger competitive edge we gained. While the other teams were busy criticizing us, we were busy working harder than ever toward another state title. We were directed in a positive manner toward our goal, while they were being diverted negatively against us, instead of toward their goal.

One of our co-captains summed it all up at the end of that season. He said, "You know what really stinks, Ferg? People will probably start liking us since we lost." We had become used to the critics; they were our constant companions. When they were gone, we missed them. Our co-captain and I vowed to work harder than ever to give the critics something to talk about the next year. We worked — we won — and yes the critics came out of the woodwork.

There will always be a critic. Picture him as overweight, chewing on a cigar, drinking a beer, sitting in front of the TV screaming at the quarterback for not spotting the receiver 60 yards downfield. He has all the answers once the play is over. The question is not who called the quarterback a bum, but who called the bum a critic?

The next time you're criticized, picture the fat man with his beer. Smile and say to yourself, "Buddy, come on down here where the action is. You have no idea what's going on; you can't do any better." The more confidence you have, the less you'll be bothered by critics. You won't even listen to them any more.

ARE YOU STRONG ENOUGH TO HANDLE CRITICS?

IOWA UNIVERSITY WRESTLING TEAM
Nine NCAA Championships in a Row

> He worked by day
>   And toiled by night.
> He gave up play
>   And some delight.
> Dry books he read,
>   New things to learn
> And forged ahead,
>   Success to earn.
> He plodded on with
>   Faith and pluck;
> And when he won,
>   Men called it luck.

GEORGE BLANDA
NFL Quarterback/Kicker

I would never give my critics the satisfaction of seeing me get sloppy.

BRIAN SIPE
NFL Quarterback

The criticism about my size and my arm doesn't bother me because I know I can compensate inside myself for any physical shortcomings I might have. When the going gets tough, I know I can gut it out.

PHIL ESPOSITO
NHL Center and General Manager

You can't compare (Bobby) Orr and me or (Bobby) Hull and me. They bring people to their feet. They are spectacular players. I know that my role is to score goals, to pick up loose pucks and put them behind the goaltender anyway I can. So that's what I try to do—and people still call me a garbage collector. That's life, I'm afraid, so I'll just ignore those people and keep putting the puck in the net.

EVONNE GOOLAGONG
Professional Tennis Player

When everybody said that I'd never be any good again, it just made me push on.

ABRAHAM LINCOLN
Sixteenth President

Truth is generally the best vindication against slander.

CHUCK NOLL
NFL Linebacker and Coach

It's what you do on the field that counts, not what you say. You can win the battle of the press, please all your critics and still lose the game.

OSCAR WILDE
Irish Poet/Playwright
The critic is one who knows the price of everything and the value of nothing.

FRANK GIFFORD
NFL Halfback/End and Sports Broadcaster
The two most valuable areas of my life, football and broadcasting, would perhaps never have been had I listened to the advice of well-meaning friends and associates. "I was too slow, not big enough", etc. were the comments about my football, while the comments about my initial efforts in broadcasting are too embarrassing to reveal. Belief in oneself is one of the most important bricks in building any successful venture. Lack of it almost assures failure.

JIM BIBBY
Major League Pitcher
I've always had confidence in my ability, no matter what other people might have thought. I just never listened to them. When I'm in a good groove, things fall into place. I set the hitters up, and I throw the ball where I want it. It's a good feeling and no matter what people say, I'm in charge.

RED AUERBACH
NBA Coach, General Manager and Owner
A boo is a boo. Generally, you don't take the time to figure out what kind of boo it is, whether it's a good-natured boo, for instance. It's a boo and the heck with it.

JERRY SHERK
NFL Defensive Tackle
Don't believe those "who know" when they say that you can't. The occupations that are rewarding are full of people that have been told many times that they can't make it.

CALVIN R. GRIFFITH
Major League President
Don't be hurt, be not surprised, if what you do is criticized. There's always one or more who can find fault with anything you plan. Mistakes are made, we can't deny, but only made by those who try.

RON CEY
Major League Third Baseman
So many people told me that I couldn't make it. Now that I have, that's extra icing on the cake. They can't see inside of you. That's why I'm critical of people who pass judgment without knowing someone.

MARVIN POWELL
NFL Offensive Tackle

I used to dare to believe that I could be all these things I read about. I think the difference between me and my contemporaries was that I believed that I could, and deep down, they didn't. I was so serious about it that I would break down in tears. My motivation was the people telling me that I couldn't.

JOE PATERNO
College Football Coach and Athletic Director

I never look upon a critic's letter as vicious. After all, vicious is only vicious to the guy who reads the letter. If he's sensitive, the letter can be vicious. Personally, I could care less about the critic's comments.

MIKE SCHMIDT
Major League Third Baseman

You can never block out a hostile crowd—you just have to develop a way of dealing with it. Now, I just think they're booing some guy who plays third base for the Phillies.

BUD GRANT
NFL Coach

When making decisions, there are three things you have to watch out for. The first is that you can never be afraid of what the critics will think or say. The second is not to make decisions too soon. If you make them before you have to, you'll have a hard time changing your decision should new information become available to you. The third is that when your decision is to make a rule, you had better be prepared to enforce it. If you are not, then don't make the rule.

DICK BUTKUS
NFL Linebacker and Sports Broadcaster

It makes me sad sometimes. Some people think that I have to get down on all fours to eat my couple of pounds of raw meat every day. Nobody thinks I can talk, much less write my name. When I cut a record of Shakespeare quotes—a parody—the record company said it was too good. What the heck is this society doing to people? I did what it told me I could do. I didn't have any identity crises. In the fifth grade, I knew what I was going to be—a professional football player. I worked hard at becoming one, just like society says you should. It said you had to be fierce. I was fierce. Be tough. I was tough. I knew my trade. When I got to the Bears, I made it and I made it beyond the Bears. I made it to All-Pro. And then what happened? They called me an animal.

ELBERT HUBBARD
American Editor/Writer

The world is moving so fast these days that the man who says it can't be done is generally interrupted by someone doing it.

ED HOWE
American Editor/Writer

If you succeed in life, you must do it in spite of the efforts of others to pull you down. There is nothing in the idea that people are willing to help those who help themselves. People are willing to help a man who can't help himself, but as soon as a man is able to help himself, and does it, they join in making his life as uncomfortable as possible.

LEWIS SIMMS
American Newspaper Executive

He who would acquire fame must not show himself afraid of censure. The dread of censure is the death of genius.

DALE CARNEGIE
American Author

Any fool can criticize, condemn, and complain—and most fools do.

TOBY HARRAH
Major League Third Baseman

You can't worry about what the fans or media say about you. So many players are made by the media. They push themselves in that area. I don't have the personality to do that and I don't need to do it. I can't control what people write or say about me. But the other players, they are the ones that count, they are the ones you can't fool.

JIM PLUNKETT
NFL Quarterback

Critics never bother me. When you play well, you get more attention. When you play poorly, you get attention too. I knew perfectly well why people weren't coming around before and why they started coming around in 1980.

When things were coming together for me during the 1980 season, I never read the newspapers too much to see what they said about us. I tried to keep up on other teams, but as far as we were concerned—as far as I myself was concerned—I basically wasn't that interested in what the reporters had to say.

WALTER BAGEHOT
English Economist/Essayist

The greatest pleasure in life is doing what people say that you cannot do.

ARTHUR GUITERMAN
American Poet

The stones that critics hurl with harsh intent a man may use to build a monument.

You know you will have players who will always be there when the team is winning. But when things aren't going well, they aren't around. They can't seem to handle adversity very well.

Tony Esposito, NHL Goalie and General Manager

If it weren't for the dark days, we wouldn't know what it is to walk in the light.

Earl Campbell, NFL Fullback

Sure you feel better and you sleep better when you win, but there's nothing you can do about a game once it is over. You can't change it. You can replay it as many times as you want, but the score is always the same. All you can do is learn from it and look ahead to tomorrow.

Walter Alston, Major League Manager

ARE YOU STRONG ENOUGH TO HANDLE ADVERSITY?

All athletes face adversity. Great hockey goaltenders like Tony Esposito have nights when almost everything gets past them. Great running backs like Earl Campbell have trouble holding onto the ball in some games. Even successful baseball managers like Walter Alston of the Dodgers have nights when they make wrong decisions.

Adversity builds character. It forces you to analyze yourself to see what went wrong and to correct your mistakes so you can improve. I've seen very little character in athletes who have never faced adversity.

When you lose or are faced with a problem, you have two options: (1), you can quit and walk away; or (2), you can stay and meet the challenge head on. When you face adversity, you must face the situation immediately. Don't put it off, hoping the problem will go away. Grab your problems by the throat and shake them until you find the solution.

Champions do this all the time. Timing is the important thing here. By analyzing yourself immediately, you'll discover your weaknesses and quickly work to improve them. How you handle your losses determines whether you're a winner or a loser. Losers won't admit their mistakes. Their solution is to feel sorry for themselves.

Winners are seldom discouraged. They have weak moments, as we all do, but they come roaring back. Winners treat adversity as a challenge or a test, not as a threat. Competition is a learning opportunity, regardless of outcome. Adversity makes winners work harder and accomplish even more.

You read in the papers about coaches quitting because they get burned out. This happens to coaches, lawyers, doctors, salespeople, students and teachers. There's nothing wrong with getting down-hearted or discouraged. That's natural and very human. But it's wrong to stay down — that's for losers. People are always asking me if I'm burned out. I tell them I get down and out and discouraged plenty of times. But, I don't let it control me. I acknowledge the disappointment, analyze the problem, learn from the situation, and then get on with the business of winning.

For example, last year we lost a wrestling match. It was our first loss in seven years! People asked me how I felt after that loss. I told them I slept like a baby — "I woke up every two hours and cried." I had that sick feeling deep down inside. It's a normal human feeling. As they say, "Nothing's as good as it seems; and nothing's as bad as it seems; and where you are now is somewhere in between."

That's why it's so important to put your victories and defeats in proper perspective. It's easy to get down on yourself. We all get down, but the winners refuse to stay down. Use adversity as a measuring stick for your success. Success can be measured by the obstacles you overcome. Every time adversity comes your way, face it directly and turn it into something good. You can never replay yesterday's loss. Once it's over, it's over. But learn from it.

Someone once called this "making lemonade out of lemons." It all comes right back to a positive mental attitude. You need this outlook when things are going well in addition to when adversity comes your way. A positive mental attitude turns every bad situation into a good one.

ARE YOU STRONG ENOUGH TO HANDLE ADVERSITY?

STEVE LARGENT
NFL Wide Receiver
FAILURE:
In our society, the saying, "Winning isn't everything; it's the only thing" seems to apply. All the books and seminars available that teach us how to succeed are too numerous to count. What happens now—heaven forbid—should we fail? I believe how a person deals with personal failure determines, to a large degree, how successful that person will be. Everyone fails at one time or another, so it's essential to know how to respond to failure. Here's a pneumonic device that I feel teaches how we can properly cope with failure.

- F—Forget about your failures. Don't dwell on past mistakes.
- A—Anticipate failure. Realize that we all make mistakes.
- I—Have intensity in everything you do. Never be a failure for lack of effort.
- L—Learn from your mistakes. Don't repeat previous errors.
- U—Understand why you failed. Diagnose your mistakes so as not to repeat them.
- R—Respond; don't react to errors. Responding corrects mistakes; reacting magnifies them.
- E—Elevate your self-concept. It's O.K. to fail, everyone does. Now, how are you going to deal with failure?

MICKEY RIVERS
Major League Outfielder
There isn't any sense in worrying about things that you have no control over. If you have no control over them, you can't change them anyway. The mistakes, the ups and downs—that's life.

BOB RICHARDS
Pole Vaulter—Two Time Olympic Gold Medalist
It may sound strange, but many champions are made champions by setbacks. They are champions because they've been hurt. Their experience moved them, and pulled out this fighting spirit, making them what they are. Sometimes in life, God gives us a difficulty in order to bring out the fighting spirit. Everything that happens to you can happen for good if you have this spirit. The essential thing in life is not in the conquering, but in the fight.

ALEXANDER GRAHAM BELL
American Inventor/Scientist
When one door closes, another opens. But we often look so long and so regretfully upon the closed door that we do not see the one which has opened for us.

AL ROSEN
Major League Third Baseman, General Manager and President
The path to success is a most difficult one. To constantly walk in the middle of the road does not necessarily insure one's safety or success. Enduring hardships makes one stronger mentally and morally.

GORDON GRAHAM
Scottish Author
There are two kinds of discontent in the world: the discontent that works, and the discontent that wrings its hands. The first gets what it wants, and the second loses what it has. There's no cure for the first but success; and there's no cure at all for the second.

J. J. PROCTOR
British Author
The child's philosophy is a true one. He does not despise the bubble because it burst; he immediately sets to work to blow another one.

TEXAS E. SCHRAMM
NFL President
Never let yesterday take up too much of today.

LYMAN FERTIG
American Writer
If I could have one hope for our young people as they go out into the world, it would be this: I hope they fail. I hope they fail at something that is important to them, for failure, like nothing else, is able to stimulate the right kind of person to that extra action that always makes all the difference.

TOM COUSINEAU
NFL Linebacker
A winner does not become despondent over a loss, nor does he believe that winning is an outcome reserved for a select few. Rather, he gives his opponent the credit due him, picks himself up, and gets ready to go again.

CESAR CEDENO
Major League Outfielder
I want to win and I want to play my best every day. I don't panic. Some guys put their head down when things go bad. But the worse things get, the harder I play.

DIGGER PHELPS
College Basketball Coach

Whether it's playing or coaching, socially or professionally, there have to be some tough days to make you a better person.

MONTE CLARK
NFL Offensive Tackle and Coach

I made up my mind before I became a head coach that I wouldn't become a crybaby or a complainer. I would take the personnel they gave me to work with and I would take the hard knocks as they came along. It would just be a way to speed up my learning process. But I would neither cry nor complain.

TERRY DONAHUE
College Football Coach

Adversity is a reality of life. You are never really sure when it will come or how long it will stay, but the way each human being handles the situation in his life is a direct reflection of the character he possesses. The real test of a person doesn't come when everything is going well. The real test of a person comes after adversity has struck and he overcomes and conquers it.

B. F. SKINNER
American Writer/Psychologist

A failure is not always a mistake; it may simply be the best one can do under the circumstances. The real mistake is to stop trying.

JACK YOUNGBLOOD
NFL Defensive End

You learn that whatever you are doing in life, obstacles don't matter very much. Pain or other circumstances can be there, but if you want to do a job bad enough, you'll find a way to get it done. I honestly believe that if a man has talent and he learns how to control his intelligence and direct the talent, the sky is the limit.

BILLY MARTIN
Major League Second Baseman and Manager

When you're a winner, you come back no matter what happened the day before.

DAN FOUTS
NFL Quarterback and Sports Broadcaster

The key is to concentrate your way through the bad times. I really believe that you can have some of your best games that way. You play better because you have to concentrate harder when you're facing some adversity.

JOHN WOODEN
College Basketball Coach

Things turn out best for those who make the best of the way things turn out.

THOMAS CARLYLE
Scottish Historian/Social Critic

Of all our troubles, great and small, the greatest are those that don't happen at all.

TOM OSBORNE
College Football Coach

I feel that when you do lose a ball game, you shouldn't dwell on the loss and the negative aspects of the game. Very quickly, you must turn it into something positive.

EDDIE MURRAY
Major League First Baseman

In anything you do in life you have to expect some failure. Baseball is no different. I'm going to have 0-for-4, 0-for-5 games. You can't avoid them. But the thing I try to avoid is letting them stay with me. When it's over, it's over. I don't carry one game over to the next, no matter if I hit three homers or strike out three times.

JERRY COLANGELO
NBA General Manager

The only road to success is a road full of potholes and adversity, but through this adversity comes opportunity.

THOMAS JEFFERSON
Third President

Successful men usually snatch success from seeming failure. If they know that there is such a word as defeat, they will not admit it. They may be whipped, but they are not aware of it.

MALTBIE BABCOCK
American Presbyterian Clergyman

Pay as little attention to discouragement as possible. Plough ahead as a steamer does, rough or smooth, rain or shine. To carry your cargo and make your port is the point.

HENRY FORD
Founder of Ford Motor Company/Inventor

Failure is only the opportunity to begin again, more intelligently.

STEVE CARLTON
Major League Pitcher

You can't let yourself get on that emotional roller coaster ride over wins and losses. That's why you have to keep an even level of intensity. There are so many deviations in this game. So often you just have to isolate yourself from everything else to try and keep up with your goals.

TUG MC GRAW
Major League Relief Pitcher

Always accept that if you're willing to enjoy winning, you must bear the burden of occasional losses as well.

PETE ROSE
Major League First Baseman and Manager

Once you accept defeat, it becomes easy to lose. If defeat comes, face it and take it, but don't accept it.

BRYANT GUMBEL
Sports Broadcaster and Talk Show Host

I've always found that the greatest obstacle to success is one's ability to depress himself. It's easy and it's natural. You see the disorder in the world, take note of the long road ahead, calculate its difficulty and figure there's no way you'll ever hook up with success.

My formula to combat that is quite simple. You start by knowing yourself and by giving yourself credit for the real abilities you have. The people who are what you'd like to be are not, in most cases, innately superior. Having properly evaluated yourself, you begin your road up exactly as you climb stairs—one at a time. Don't look at the top of the stairs and moan how far up it is! Just know it's there and start climbing. With each step, you'll find your self-esteem growing and your pace quickening. Soon, that top of the stairs will appear to be reaching for you as quickly as you're reaching for it.

Through it all, remember—nothing is given away! What you get, you earn with diligence and intelligence. It's amazing how lucky you get after working on something long after others have given up. Success—it's easier than you think!

LOU BROCK
Major League Outfielder

A champion doesn't give up, he gets up when adversity hits. The donkeys stay down; the thoroughbreds respond to pressure in a positive way.

GEORGE ALLEN
NFL Coach and Sports Broadcaster

Turn your losses into a plus. I think if you approach it right, you can turn every setback you have into an advantage.

DON SHULA
NFL Defensive Back and Coach

Everything in life can't always be flowery. You have to be strong enough to take the attacks, to roll with the punches. Facing adversity and overcoming it is part of being a champion

JOHN F. KENNEDY
Thirty-Fifth President

Only in winter can you tell which trees are truly green. Only when the winds of adversity blow can you tell whether an individual or a country has courage and steadfastness.

GERRY FAUST
College Football Coach

It hurts me to lose. I don't want to lose that competitive edge, but you can't brood about each loss for a year. Brooding for about 12 hours is long enough. Then you've got to get back to work.

AL GEIBERGER
Professional Golfer

Problems usually aren't as complicated as we make them. Adversity can be good for you. It can make you get off your fanny and get to work. A problem is an educational opportunity in disguise if you look at it constructively. There are a lot of potential lessons in any difficulty. I don't feel that I ever reach bottom when I get down. I get down so far and then it's like an extra motor fires up and I fight back.

FRANCOIS DE LA ROCHEFOUCAULD
French Moralist/Writer

A clever man reaps some benefit from the worst catastrophe, and a fool can turn even good luck to his disadvantage.

ARTHUR COLTON
American Author

Times of general calamity and confusion have ever been productive of the greatest minds. The purest ore is produced from the hottest furnace, and the brightest thunderbolt is elicited from the darkest storm.

BEN CRENSHAW
Professional Golfer

Be strong, mentally more than physically, and always prepare yourself for certain pitfalls along the way. Everyone, regardless of how talented he or she is, goes through some rough times. If they have a genuine love for the endeavor that they choose, they will most certainly work harder and analyze their mistakes and bounce back quicker. Patience and hard, hard work will win out in the end.

NOLAN RYAN
Major League Pitcher

You've got to realize that in any competition there is always a winner and loser. When it turns out that you're the loser on a given day, you can be a graceful loser, but it doesn't mean that you're a loser in the sense that you're willing to accept losses readily. Concede that on that day you weren't the best and that you were beaten in competition. But that should make you more dedicated and hard-working. It's wrong to accept defeat as a loser. Be graceful about losing, but don't accept it.

TONY DORSETT
NFL Halfback

The thing that turned it all around for me was one of our NFL championship games. I didn't get a lot of yards and we lost to Philadelphia. I know I didn't lose the game alone, but something came together then that made me want to reach out more. I'd always worked hard before but then I wasn't. I decided I would run and lift weights and do whatever it took. If I failed, I wanted it to be all of me. If I ran only two times a game, I'd be the best 'two carry a game runner' that I could be.

MARCUS AURELIUS
Roman Emperor

As for me, let what will come. I can receive no damage from it unless I think it a calamity; and it is in my power to think it none if I so decide.

JOE PATERNO
College Football Coach and Athletic Director

It is always good to know what it is to lose. I guess it means that we've got to get back to work.

JACK DEMPSEY
Professional Boxer

Motivation. Pretty fancy name for a necessity of life. It was motivation that put food on our plates, thoughts in our heads, and blankets on our bodies when it was pretty damn cold at night. Motivation taught us all about life—sometimes good, sometimes not so good. As my Pa used to say, "If you can't go over an obstacle, go around it. If that don't work, go through it…and make sure you don't trip, boy." I guess that's motivation for you. Sometimes, my motivation didn't feel so good, so I just fed it some courage and hope. It worked as long as I supported it.

J. R. ROGERS
American Sculptor

The successful man lengthens his stride when he discovers that the signpost has deceived him; the failure looks for a place to sit down.

ABRAHAM LINCOLN
Sixteenth President

I am not concerned that you have fallen; I am concerned that you arise.

RICKEY HENDERSON
Major League Outfielder

Stealing is a contest between you and the pitcher and the catcher. You're racing two guys. If a pitcher picks me off, I'll write myself a little note. He got me that time, fine. Next time though, I'll make an adjustment and I'll get him.

JOHN RALSTON
NFL Coach

We strive to eliminate all the negatives. To do so, we add the lessons we've learned from our disappointments. Adversity taught us some fantastic lessons that we should use to our own advantage whenever we get into tight spots in the future.

DAVE LOGAN
NFL Wide Receiver

Take each day one day at a time. Don't ever let things over which you have no control bother you. When things don't go exactly right every day, count all the good things you have—your life, your health and your family.

REGGIE JACKSON
Major League Outfielder and Sports Broadcaster

I feel that the most important requirement in success is learning to overcome failure. You must learn to tolerate it, but never accept it.

CHUCK NOLL
NFL Linebacker and Coach

If you're losing, you try to find out what really is causing it. You want to make the effort to find out, but at the same time, you don't want to panic.

ISIAH THOMAS
NBA Guard

I enjoy winning, but there are benefits in losing, too. Before you can be a winner, you have to learn to lose.

EPICTETUS
Greek Philosopher

On the occasion of every accident that befalls you, remember to turn to yourself and inquire what power you have for turning it to use.

JAMES SHARP
Scottish Clergyman

It is not every calamity that is a curse, and early adversity is often a blessing. Surmounted difficulties not only teach, but hearten us in our future struggles.

NORMAN VINCENT PEALE
Clergyman/American Writer

Stand up to your obstacles and do something about them. You will find that they haven't half the strength you think they have.

TOM LANDRY
NFL Defensive Back and Coach

Something constructive comes from every defeat. One football game, after all, is quite a small fragment of one's total life.

DOCTOR SAMMY LEE
Diver—Two Time Olympic Gold Medalist

When your workouts and your game plan don't lead to victory, remember that you can be disgusted, but you should never be discouraged with yourself. After years of competing and coaching, I know that every defeat is a lesson for eventual victory.

WENDELL PHILLIPS
American Orator/Reformer

What is defeat? Nothing but education; nothing but the first step to something better.

PHIL NIEKRO
Major League Pitcher

I realize that success is having the courage to meet failure without being defeated. I also recognize that although I cannot always control what happens to me, I can control how I respond to my wins and losses.

WOODY HAYES
College Football Coach

You learn when you get knocked down to get back up and go again. The tough will make it. People are getting tougher… You have to work for everything that's worthwhile.

PAUL BROWN
NFL Coach, General Manager and Owner

There is nothing wrong with losing unless you learn to like it. When you lose, you must learn what caused you to lose and how to overcome it.

BILL WALSH
NFL Coach, President and Sports Broadcaster

Adversity can be a great motivator. Football, as anything else, is always a series of problems. Your success will depend on how well you are prepared and how well you handle those problems as they come along.

ROLF BENIRSCHKE FOUGHT BACK FROM ADVERSITY

"It sounds like a cliché, I know. But when you've been very ill, the good things look different. I love the beautiful sunshine we have here in San Diego. I love laughing and being around people. And yes, I love kicking footballs again."

In November of 1978, Rolf Benirschke, kicker for the San Diego Chargers, was diagnosed as having Crohn's Disease—an incurable illness.

Suffering pain and experiencing weight loss, Benirschke spent his weekdays in the hospital and his Sundays playing football.

"I kept on playing because athletes are supposed to play with pain. In spite of my weakened condition, I managed to make it through the first four games of the 1979 season," he said.

Then he was hospitalized and he underwent two major operations.

Benirschke spent one month in the hospital and then he came home weighing only 125 pounds. On November 18th, the Chargers named Benirschke an honorary captain for the Pittsburgh Steelers game.

"That was the beginning," he remembers. **"I decided I was going to come back in 1980...I began with little steps, unimaginably slow, by walking on the beach."**

He soon took bigger steps, ran and lifted weights. At training camp, Benirschke weighed over 180 pounds. He was ready for the 1980 season.

"I remember the first game I played last season," he said. **"I thought back to all those moments when I was watching the games from the hospital bed. When I got back out there on the field again, I thought to myself, 'Amazing. Here I am again.'"**

In 1980, Benirschke was second in the NFL in scoring with 118 points. He made 24 of 36 field goal attempts; 1981 was an even better year as he hit on 19 of 26 field goals and helped get his San Diego Chargers into the American Conference Championship game.

FLOYD LAYNE—ALL HE EVER WANTED WAS A SECOND CHANCE

"Floyd was a tremendous influence in my life. He was responsible for keeping me off the streets. He told me I had the ability to finish high school and college. He made me pursue a career in basketball. There isn't enough I can say about what he did for me."

That statement comes from NBA standout Nate Archibald, speaking about Floyd Layne, a man who was thrown out of City College of New York (CCNY) for taking money from gamblers to help fix a basketball game.

Layne was a star on the CCNY teams of 1949/50 and 1950/51. He led his team to victories over many top-ranked teams in the country and in 1951, CCNY won both the NIT and NCAA Championships.

But then it was discovered that Floyd had been involved with gamblers and rigging games. He tried to break into the NBA, but was shut out because of a ban on any players who had been involved in fixing games.

Layne was frustrated, but determined to remain involved in basketball. He returned to the black inner city of New York and worked at a recreation center. He worked with many problem children, some already involved with drugs, others with criminal records.

It was a rough area Layne worked in, but he went right into the heart of it. He went into homes, jails and walked the streets in search of kids who needed help. He told them to work on their grades, stay in school and avoid the wrong people.

Layne tried to find a coaching job, but countless applications were returned. Finally, twenty-five years after he was thrown out of CCNY, that same school hired Floyd Layne to coach its basketball team.

"I've traveled a wide circle to get back home. I've never asked for any sympathy or handouts; all I want is a chance," Layne said. **"I made a mistake and I paid a heavy price for it. But that mistake put my feet on the ground. It taught me about adversity. It led me to dedicate myself to kids so that they wouldn't make the same kind of error and pay the same price."**

> If you could have won, you should have.
> Chuck Knox, NFL Coach

> The superior man blames himself. The inferior man blames others.
> Don Shula, NFL Defensive Back and Coach

> A man can make mistakes, but he isn't a failure until he starts blaming someone else.
> Sam Rutigliano, NFL and College Football Coach

> Don't tell me how rocky the sea is. Just bring the darn ship in.
> Lou Holtz, College Football Coach

ACCEPT RESPONSIBILITY — DON'T MAKE EXCUSES

Accept responsibility for yourself. If you're wrong, admit it, take the blame and get on with it. Don't dwell on the past. You can only change the present. Be responsible for others with whom you're involved, such as teammates. Do your best to help them reach their goals.

Don't waste your time or energy worrying about how tough the challenge is going to be. Focus instead on your preparation and practice. Nobody cares about how rough you're going to have it. It's bad enough to make excuses after a game, but it's even worse to do so before the game starts. Why? You'll hurt your poise and your concentration, two important factors you'll need once the game starts. Don't let anything interfere with getting the job done, especially your own insecurities. Too often, we're our own worst enemies.

Don't be afraid of making mistakes; we all do. The difference between a wise person and a fool is that the fool makes the same mistake twice. Likewise, you aren't a failure until you start blaming someone else for your mistakes. Take responsibility. You own your mistakes.

There are two things losers do when they make mistakes: (1), they refuse to admit it was their fault; or (2), they admit that it was their fault and dwell on it. Winners take the blame for what went wrong. People respect that. They set an example for others to follow. And once they've admitted it was their fault, they drop it. They immediately go to work to prevent similar mistakes.

The best wrestlers I've ever coached were the ones who simply could not live with losing. When they lost, they always said the same thing, "I got killed" — even if it was only by one point. But they didn't sulk, brood or hide from anyone. They were good and they knew it. They came to practice a little earlier, stayed a little later and worked harder. They were determined not to lose again.

Finally, we come to the referees, the umpires and the officials. Over the season, you get your share of good calls. When the calls go your way, you don't give them back, do you? So why complain when a few calls go the other way? It's your fault if the score is so close that a referee's decision can cost you the game. Don't blame them for the loss.

The minute you start to complain and argue over a call, you lose your poise and concentration. Without these, you don't have a chance to win. When a call goes against you, there's only one thing to do — bear down and concentrate even harder on the next play. Block everything completely from your mind except what you have to do next. That's exactly what tennis champion Mats Wilander does so well. He never lets a bad call bother him. He just focuses on the next rally. Curtis Strange, Greg Norman, Jack Nicklaus, Arnold Palmer — all the great golfers have the same attitude; "I hit it there so I guess I'll hit it out of there." That's the key for you: When you lose your poise and/or concentration, go back to the fundamentals.

It's your game to win or lose. You alone are responsible. So accept responsibility for your actions as true champions do — and don't make excuses.

ACCEPT RESPONSIBILITY—DON'T MAKE EXCUSES

MAX O'RELL
American Businessman

Luck means the hardships and privations which you have not hesitated to endure, the long nights you have devoted to work. Luck means the appointments you have never failed to keep; the trains you have never failed to catch.

RUDYARD KIPLING
English Poet/Novelist

We have forty million reasons for failure, but not a single excuse.

TOM LANDRY
NFL Defensive Back and Coach

We don't make excuses. If we'd been playing football as we should have, we wouldn't be in a position where a call settles a game.

RON JAWORSKI
NFL Quarterback

When we lose, I hope we're a mature enough team to be able to look at ourselves and realize we didn't play well. We won't try to blame everyone else. We'll take the attitude that this was just one of those days where nothing seemed to go right.

BILLY MARTIN
Major League Second Baseman and Manager

When you make a mistake, admit it. Say, "It was my fault." Don't alibi.

AL MC GUIRE
College Basketball Coach and Sports Broadcaster

I believe in a business boarding up early. If you make a mistake, you put the boards in the window of the store and say, "Hey, I made a mistake." Let me take two shots in the arm and a punch in the nose and let me get on to the next thing. I don't believe in worrying over failures. I worry about successes. This is opposite from most people. Most people zero in on their failures. I try to keep all my attention on a pyramid type of philosophy rather than the averaging-down philosophy.

PAUL BEAR BRYANT
College Football Coach and Athletic Director

When you make a mistake, there are only three things you should ever do about it: (1) admit it; (2) learn from it, and (3) don't repeat it.

REGGIE JACKSON
Major League Outfielder and Sports Broadcaster

I knew the Brewers were too good of a team to be embarrassed like they were in the first two games of the 1982 playoffs. No sense in rehashing, though. They beat us fair and square. We have no excuses.

BILL HARTACK
Professional Jockey

I never make excuses. You either ride a horse good or you ride him bad.

LOU HOLTZ
College Football Coach

The guy who usually tells you about the football taking crazy bounces is the guy who dropped it.

STEVE SLOAN
College Football Coach

If you make a mistake, admit it. It's sort of like being an alcoholic. If you're an alcoholic, you're never going to be cured until you say, "I'm an alcoholic."

Same way if you make a mistake. If you have too much pride to say that you are wrong, then you won't ever grow as a person.

Whenever one of our guys gets into a little trouble, the first thing we do is get him to admit, "Yeah, it was my fault." Once they admit that, they can go about correcting the mistake, and they're a better person for it. But if they can't admit it, they're never going to grow properly as a person. Each time you admit you're wrong, you're a deeper person, and a better person.

JERRY SHERK
NFL Defensive Tackle
Don't blame others for your losses. Recognize your mistakes from seconds before, but don't linger on them. Use them only to improve your performance in the present moment. If you grieve the mistakes you made a second ago, you are in the process of losing.

BJORN BORG
Professional Tennis Player
Overall, I think officials are pretty good. I get angry over bad calls, but over a long match, they even out. I don't make excuses.

GORDIE HOWE
NHL Right Wing
My philosophy is to never start talking about if or but, or the past, because 90% of what follows will be negative.

CHUCK NOLL
NFL Linebacker and Coach
We tell our players that if they are going to point a finger, to point it at the mirror. The attitude has to be, "If we are not winning, it is my fault."

ERIC HEIDEN
Speed Skater—
Five Time Olympic Gold Medalist
Skating is a clean sport. There is no one else to blame, no one to rely on. You just have a pair of skates.

JOE FERGUSON
NFL Quarterback
Anyone who doesn't admit that he makes mistakes is crazy.

CONFUCIUS
Chinese Philosopher/Educator
A man who has committed a mistake and doesn't correct it is committing another mistake.

S. SMILES
American Writer
It will generally be found that men who are constantly lamenting their ill luck are only reaping the consequences of their own neglect, mismanagement, and improvidence, or want of application.

CHRIS EVERT
Professional Tennis Player
I've always felt that a champion shouldn't let things like questionable linecalls bother her.

JOHN MADDEN
NFL Coach and Sports Broadcaster
If you make a mistake, admit it quickly and emphatically, and don't dwell on it.

JEAN-CLAUDE KILLY
Skier—Three Time Olympic Gold Medalist
There can be no excuses. You can't say that you didn't like the snow or that you didn't feel in top form.

JOE GREENE
NFL Defensive Tackle and Coach
You have to be critical of yourself, not super critical, but you have to call the play as it is. Then you can grow from there. If you make excuses for yourself, you're telling yourself everything is all right. You're going nowhere. You can't ever let yourself be satisfied.

TOMMY JOHN
Major League Pitcher
I was never taught to hit the next guy after I gave up a home run. When you become that mean, you lose perspective of what you're trying to do. If a guy hits a ball off me, it's because it was my fault. I made a mistake.

STAN MUSIAL
Major League Outfielder

When a pitcher's throwing a spitball, don't worry, don't complain—just hit the dry side like I do.

DIGGER PHELPS
College Basketball Coach

Don't be looking around for any excuses tonight or someone else to blame. If something goes wrong, look inside yourself and say, "It's my fault."

JOHN MADDEN
NFL Coach and Sports Broadcaster

Once something is done, there are two things you have to do. One, you must evaluate what happened and two, you must work towards it not happening again.

STAN DZIEDZIC
U. S. National Wrestling Coach

If should be eliminated from a wrestler's vocabulary. I hear so many athletes lamenting their lack of success by its use: "If I had more strength; if I had better technique; if I had a better coach; if I had more experience."

The success that U. S. wrestlers have achieved to date has been achieved because these individuals accepted responsibility, dedicated themselves to excellence and utilized whatever physical characteristics with which they were endowed.

For future Gold Medalists, there is no other course except to take the responsibility of one's own destiny.

WALTER ALSTON
Major League Manager

Learn to work harder when things go wrong. Don't alibi.

DON SHULA
NFL Defensive Back and Coach

When you lose, you simply look a person in the eye and say, "Yes, we did blow it, but there is nothing we can do about it now except work toward getting another opportunity."

AL MC GUIRE
College Basketball Coach and Sports Broadcaster

We don't go for the injury bit or the sick bit. We win or we lose, that's all.

NIKKI GIOVANNI
American Poet

Mistakes are a fact of life. It is the response to the error that counts.

EARL WILSON
American Columnist/Radio Commentator

Success is simply a matter of luck. Ask any failure.

JOHN H. PATTERSON
American Manufacturer

Only fools and dead men don't change their minds. Fools won't. Dead men can't.

JOE GREENE
NFL Defensive Tackle and Coach

Every play, you are the one that has to wear the hat. You have to make it happen. You have to take responsibility for yourself, and you have to take responsibility for your team.

GEORGE W. CARVER
American Scientist/Educator/Author

Ninety-nine percent of the failures come from people who practice the habit of making excuses.

DICK VERMEIL
NFL Coach and Sports Broadcaster

Sometimes, you just get into a street fight out there. When you lose, it's not always an indication that some Eagle messed up.

JOE PATERNO
College Football Coach and Athletic Director

Don't get me wrong. I don't like to lose. I think I take a loss as hard as any coach and a lot harder than I hope my players take it. If we lose, it's my fault. That's my responsibility as the head coach. I don't brood over a game, but I do second-guess myself, analyzing where I made my mistakes. After all, I have more control of the game than the players. I have to prepare them. I have to design the game plan. I run the game from the sidelines. Sure, the players on the field do or don't make the big play, but it's my job to give them the tools to win.

HERSHEL WALKER
NFL Running Back

I love one-on-one sports. If anything goes wrong, it's your fault, nobody else's.

KEN DRYDEN
NHL Goaltender

I can't rationalize that my mistakes were the last ones in the series of other people's mistakes. A goal is my responsibility, pure and simple.

JOHNNY MILLER
Professional Golfer

The harder you work, the luckier you get. If you hit erratic shots, you get erratic breaks. If you hit perfect shots, you don't have to worry about breaks.

ROY CAMPANELLA NEVER COMPLAINED

"There are two kinds of luck—good and bad—and every person should expect a little of each. I've had more than my share of the good, so when some of the other kind began coming my way, I couldn't very well moan about it."

Roy Campanella played in the Negro leagues for 10 years until major league baseball opened its doors to blacks. Campanella became one of the top catchers in baseball for the Dodgers and emerged as a power hitter and a fine defensive catcher.

Then on January 28, 1958, Campanella was injured in a car accident. He was left a quadriplegic and doctors were not even certain that he would live. But Campanella knew what it was like to face a tough opponent. He survived the initial crisis, then spent many hours in rehabilitation, exercising his crippled body.

"When you're in a slump, you don't feel sorry for yourself," he said. **"That's when you have to try harder. You have to have faith, hope and conviction that you can lick it."**

He also said: **"When you're paralyzed, you can't just take a pill and expect to walk. There is no such thing as a walking pill. It's all work and you have to have something right there in your heart. You just have to be mentally tough."**

Roy Campanella accepted his fate and then he worked as hard as he could to improve it. He worked his way out of the hospital and back into the ballpark, this time as a coach for the Dodgers. When they held "Roy Campanella Night," 93,000 fans came to pay tribute to a man who would not give up and who would not complain.

CARL JOSEPH DIDN'T MAKE EXCUSES

"A lot of people go through life wishing they could change this or change that. God gave me one leg, and I'm just happy and thankful to be healthy and to have done as much as I have."

Carl Joseph was the captain of his high school football team. He could dunk a basketball, was a power hitter in baseball, high jumped 5 feet 10 inches and also threw the shot and discus. Joseph was quite an all-around athlete...especially when you consider that he had only one leg.

The epitome of the All-American boy, Carl Joseph accepted the gift of life as it was offered to him with all its limitations. He lives that life to the fullest. He is the perfect example for all athletes to follow. He never worried that he couldn't do certain things. It was mind over matter; he just went out and did the things that he wanted to do.

For his achievements, Carl Joseph received numerous awards, his most cherished being the Philadephia Sports Writers 1982 Most Courageous Athlete Award.

"I just wanted a chance to compete and I didn't want anybody feeling sorry for me, cause I sure wasn't feeling sorry for myself," Joseph said. "Ever since I was a kid, I could do anything I wanted to. One leg or two, it didn't make any difference to me. It's all in the mind."

"My mind always told me I could do things, so I just went out and did them. I never thought much about it. You keep trying and you always get there."

Anyone can stand tall on the high peaks. It is the people who survive the valleys between the peaks who will emerge the strongest. These survivors will be our leaders—the ones who are mentally tough and have the perseverance to keep going.

Preston Pearson, NFL Halfback

There are times when we cannot explain the adversities both on and off the field. To feel sorry for ourselves is to prolong the situation. To blame others is the coward's way. But to press on gives us a strength and direction to rise above.

Steve Garvey, Major League First Baseman

> I'm tired of being called a loser or a choker. I know in my heart I have never once stepped on a basketball court and cheated a fan of his money...Back in my early days I was taking a beating from sports writers who hated me and a coach who literally tried to break me as a man. I had stomach problems, my nerves were shattered. I even considered suicide. But I didn't, I persevered. The Lord said, "You will endure many trials and tribulations and you will come through it a better man." Today, I'm a better man.
>
> Elvin Hayes, NBA Center

PERSEVERANCE — PERSISTENCE

You've probably heard a lot about the "drive" that the premier athletes have on their way to the top. That "drive" is perseverance and persistence. It separates winners from losers. In life. And in sports.

When winners want to achieve something in life, they set a goal and persevere. They put in 100% effort and they don't quit. They overcome all problems as they focus on their goal.

Of course, there'll be problems. Nothing in life is perfect. Successful people have the perseverance and persistence to keep struggling toward their goal — regardless of roadblocks in the way. I like to think of these roadblocks as tests to see just how badly I really want my goal. If I pass these tests, I'll be a stronger person and my goal will be worth more. If I reach a goal without a few good fights along the way, it seems too easy. Set your goals higher than you can reach — then reach them. When you do, you'll feel you've deserved them.

The true test of an athlete's character comes when he or she is literally buried under problems and obstacles, and there seems no possible way to reach the set goals. The main objective is surviving. If athletes find their inner strength in tough times, they'll persevere and come out winners.

We have a saying at St. Edward: "Quitting is NOT an option." It means precisely what you think it means. When you have a problem, have the courage to face it directly. Figure out what your options are, then solve your problem. Quitting is not one of those options. That's for losers. Another way to say it, "When you're knee-deep in the alligator swamp fighting off the 'gators, don't forget what you're going to do once you get to the other side."

You can get anything you want out of life if you just keep trying. Sound hard? Of course, it is! That's why there are so few champions. Sound impossible? No! Nothing's impossible if you want it badly enough.

When you get older, you'll look back and today's goals will be only memories. It's one of the saddest feelings in life to think back over the years to what might have been. Regret leaves you with a big empty feeling in the pit of your stomach. It drives some people crazy thinking, "What if...?" If you've already reached this point in your life, then you're a proud member of the "should have, would have, could have club": "I should have been a professional tennis player, but..."; or "I would have played in the major leagues, but..."; or "I could have been a State Champion wrestler, but..."

You always have choices. You can sit around the house in your old age, as Bruce Springsteen says, "Talking about the glory days." If that's what you want in life, fine. Your other option is to keep working until you have reached all of your goals. If you don't achieve your goals today, you need them for tomorrow, or the next day. It's that simple. It's not where you are now that counts; it's where you're going that matters. So reach for the stars and don't give up. When you're taking a break from your workout, talk about what you're going to do "tomorrow."

PERSEVERANCE—PERSISTENCE

MIKE EASLER
Major League Outfielder

People see Mike Easler of the Pittsburgh Pirates and think that's just great, but they have no idea what it took to get here. Today's fans aren't seeing the jobs I took to augment my salary—bellboy, assembly line worker, employment agency temporary jobs. Nothing has come easy and I never looked for any short cuts. I just knew that if a big league manager would stick with me long enough, I could produce for him.

JACK NICKLAUS
Professional Golfer

Most golf tournaments are not so much won by opportunistic play as not lost when opportunity presents itself. This is a great realization for breeding patience and perseverance.

ANDY VARIPAPA
Professional Bowler

Perseverance and determination usually win most of the battles and are the keys to success.

WOODY HAYES
College Football Coach

Paralyze their resistance with your persistence.

LAMAR HUNT
NFL Owner

Whatever the project, the key ingredients are persistence and determination. These two traits can overcome most every obstacle.

LOU BROCK
Major League Outfielder

I went out for my college baseball team. I couldn't get the coach to notice me, to give me a chance to bat. All he had me doing was chasing fly balls. Finally, after running around all afternoon in the hot sun, I fell from exhaustion. I came to and rested a little and as a goodwill gesture the coach let me hit. I took five swings and hit four out of the park. Then they asked me my name and where I was from.

MICHAEL BURKE
NBC President

If you enjoy your sport, do not be discouraged because you are on the third or fourth string. Keep at it. Be persistent. Your skills will improve. Upper classmen graduate and opportunities will present themselves.

CHARLES GOW
American Author/Engineer

Most successes have been built on failures, not on one failure alone but on several. A majority of the great historic accomplishments of the past have been the final result of a persistent struggle against discouragement and failure. A man is never beaten until he thinks he is.

CATHY RIGBY
Gymnast—World Silver Medalist

All athletes, or for that matter anyone with career ambitions, have times when everything seems to go wrong. They're tired; motivation slips—and they can think of 101 reasons not to do whatever they're supposed to do.

I found that at these times I would push myself the hardest—do extra routines, a few more exercises, concentrate harder. This was when I would see my biggest improvement—after the slump—maybe in two or three days or two or three months—it would happen. Also, I would set one or two long-term goals and many daily and weekly goals just to keep myself checked.

You can accomplish anything if you're persistent enough.

HERBERT KAUFMAN
American Writer

Failure is only postponed success as long as courage "coaches" ambition. The habit of persistence is the habit of victory.

Spurts don't count. The final score makes no mention of a splendid start if the finish proves that you were an "also ran."

SID LUCKMAN
NFL Quarterback

Each one of us has some goal we want to reach and we must work toward that goal, one step at a time. You can't reach for your goal and expect it on the first try. All your small steps will bring you just a little closer. You must continue to work toward this goal. You may take a few steps back or be at a standstill, but you will be learning from each step. Through hard work, self-confidence and motivation, you will find ways to move ahead. You alone can help yourself to move ahead in life and gain personal satisfaction. You only get out of life what you put into it.

MARGO JONES
American Movie Director/Producer

The answer is simple: if you want something very badly, you can achieve it. It may take patience, very hard work, a real struggle, and a long time, but it can be done.

CARL YASTRZEMSKI
Major League Outfielder/First Baseman

The travel, the night games, and the long season are tough but I do a lot of running and work out constantly during the off-season. As long as I can stay in good physical condition and take care of my body—I'll keep on playing. No matter how tired I may have been the night before—No matter how badly things may have gone—No matter how down I may have been—I'll be ready to go the next day.

MARIO ANDRETTI
Race Car Driver

My goal has been to win in every category of racing. To smoke them all where they least expect me to. I've won on 127 different kinds of track, clockwise and counterclockwise. I've experienced the passing of the engine from the front to the back. I have raced with greats who have since retired, and in places now that are parking lots. I'm an old fogy, but I want to keep driving for 10 or 20 years. I figure I was put on earth to drive race cars so no matter how tired I may be or how discouraged I may be, I'll be ready when the next race starts.

TOMMY LASORDA
Major League Manager

When things get tough, we like to refer to a little piece of paper that Dusty Baker carries in his pocket. I'd like to share it with you—it's from Romans 5:1-5: "Tribulations bring about perseverance, and perseverance brings about proven character, and proven character brings about hope, and hope does not disappoint."

J. R. MILLER
American Educator

It is not enough to begin; continuance is necessary. Mere enrollment will not make one a scholar; the pupil must continue in the school through the long course, until he masters every branch. Success depends upon staying power. The reason for failure in most cases is lack of perseverance.

PLUTARCH
Greek Philosopher

Perseverance is more prevailing than violence; and many things which cannot be overcome when they are together yield themselves up when taken little by little.

C. W. WENDTE
American Clergyman/Author

Success in life is a matter not so much of talent as of concentration and perseverance.

JACOB M. BRAUDE
English Business Executive

Life is a grindstone. Whether it grinds you down or polishes you up depends on what you're made of.

JACK KEMP
NFL Quarterback, United States Congressman and Secretary of Housing and Urban Development

I learned in football that you shouldn't try to score on every play. Get the first downs and the touchdowns will hit you in the face.

MERLIN OLSEN
NFL Tackle, Sports Broadcaster and Actor

No one gets an iron-clad guarantee of success. Certainly, factors like opportunity, luck and timing are important. But the backbone of success is usually found in old fashioned, basic concepts like hard work, determination, good planning, and perseverance.

SEBASTIAN COE
Distance Runner — Three Time Olympic Gold Medalist

Anything good is developed slowly.

THOMAS F. BUXTON
English Philosopher/Philanthropist

With ordinary talent and extraordinary perserverance, all things are attainable.

CHARLES F. KETTERING
General Motors Research President

Keep on going and the chances are you will stumble on something, perhaps when you are least expecting it. I have never heard of anyone stumbling on something when sitting down.

BJORN BORG
Professional Tennis Player

My strongest point is my persistence. I never give up in a match. However down I am, I fight until the last ball. My list of matches shows that I have turned a great many so-called irretrievable defeats into victories. You can be hopelessly down as long as you win the last point.

SAADI
Persian Poet

Have patience. All things are difficult before they become easy.

Press On

Nothing in the world can take the place of persistence.

Talent will not; nothing is more common than unsuccessful men with talent.

Genius will not; unrewarded genius is almost a proverb.

Education alone will not; the world is full of educated derelicts.

Persistence and determination alone are omnipotent.

The above has been my credo since I founded McDonald's and is just as applicable today. I am convinced that to be a success in business, you must be first, you must be daring, and you must be different. These mottoes are also applicable in the field of athletics. The San Diego Padres must be persistent and determined in order to achieve success and I am eagerly waiting for us to be first, daring, and assuredly different.

RAY A. KROC   Major League Owner and Founder of McDonald's Restaurants

JOHNNY UNITAS
JUST KEPT ON WORKING

"If you want something badly enough, and I mean badly enough, chances are that you'll wind up getting it."

Another man might have decided that he wasn't cut out to play football and quit the game. Instead, Johnny Unitas knew what he wanted to do and he went after it—tenaciously.

Coaches at Notre Dame told Unitas that, at six feet and 145 pounds, he was too small to play college football.

He failed an entrance exam when he was offered a scholarship at Pitt.

After finally getting a chance to play at the University of Louisville, Unitas became a fine college football quarterback. But when he tried to break into the pro game with the Pittsburgh Steelers, he was cut.

"I was disappointed, but not discouraged. I had enough of a taste of the big game to know I could play if I had the chance, no matter what anybody else thought," Unitas said.

He called the Cleveland Browns, but Paul Brown told him no, he wasn't looking for a quarterback.

Unitas kept his dream alive by playing semi-pro football in Pittsburgh for six dollars a game. He also worked as a piledriver on a construction gang.

"I'd get to the park about nine in the morning, do calisthenics, run four or five laps and then practice throwing to some high school kids if they were around," he said. **"If I was by myself, I'd hang an old tire between the light standards and throw at it. I'd begin at 10 yards and then gradually move back to 30. I'd throw on the run, while moving back after imaginary fakes..."**

The work paid off the following season when Unitas tried out with the Baltimore Colts. This time he made the team and the National Football League. He started slowly, but soon became one of the top quarterbacks in the history of the NFL.

"Folks are often kind enough to compliment me for sticking with football in the face of a lot of discouragement. They say it was quite a feat to come up from the sandlots at six dollars a game to all-pro quarterback with the champion Colts in three years. But there is no chance that such praise will make me oversatisfied."

"All I have to do is compare my lot with my mother's after my father died and left her with four children, the oldest only 10. She kept my father's little coal truck business going for a while. She also worked from nine to one at night, scrubbing floors in office buildings. She was always improving her jobs to make things better for us. She left the scrubwoman's job to work in a bakery, and then she sold insurance. At night, she went to school and studied bookkeeping and got the highest mark on the civil-service exam. She has been bookkeeper for the City of Pittsburgh since. She never got discouraged, and she taught us to think the same way. She taught me more about football by example of what it takes to get ahead than any of my coaches, and I've played for some good ones."

8

THE GAME OF LIFE

- Leave Something Behind
- Don't Forget About Your Education
- Common Sense
- The Same Principles Apply
- The Challenge Never Ends
- Why And How To Say No

The Bridge Builder

An old man going down a lone highway
Came in the evening cold and gray
To a chasm vast and deep and wide
Through which was flowing a sullen tide.
The old man crossed in the twilight dim;
That swollen stream held no fears for him;
But he turned when safe on the other side
And built a bridge to span the tide.

"Old man," said a fellow pilgrim near,
"You are wasting your strength with building here;
Your journey will end with the ending day;
You never again must pass this way;
You have crossed the chasm deep and wide—
Why build you this bridge at the eventide?"

The builder lifted his old gray head.
"Good friend, in the path I have come," he said,
"There followeth after me today
A youth whose feet must pass this way.
This swollen stream which was naught to me
To that fair-haired youth may a pitfall be;
He, too, must cross in the twilight dim;
Good friend, I am building the bridge for him."

Every professional athlete owes a debt of gratitude to the fans and management, and pays an installment every time he plays. He should never miss a payment.
Bobby Hull, NHL Left Wing

Set a goal and make a commitment to meet that goal. Do the best you can, but never forget your roots, never forget where you came from. After you have succeeded, look back and see if there are others that you might help to achieve what you have accomplished.
Larry Holmes, Professional Boxer

I like getting involved in a community doing youth work. I've taken so much out of this game that it often weighs on my mind. Therefore, I'd like to give something back.

Reggie Jackson, Major League Outfielder and Sports Broadcaster

LEAVE SOMETHING BEHIND

No one makes it alone. You may be by yourself when you win the championship or break the records, but look behind you to see the people who have made your success possible: Parents, coaches, friends and fans. They have given you so much and they ask for so little in return. You can leave them with memories of a true champion who cared enough for his sport to give something back.

People will soon forget the records you created. What they will remember is the way you hustled, the poise you had under pressure and the class you showed.

You can never fully pay back those who have helped you. What you can do is follow their example and help others get started. Take your knowledge, experience and enthusiasm and share it with others. Teach them everything you were taught about winning. Teach them about class. Teach them how to overcome adversity.

A few words of wisdom to someone eager to be a winner might make his road to the top a little easier. You may help him solve or even avoid some problems.

Reach out to as many people as you can. Your impact on these young people can be significant. When you touch their lives this way, you'll never go to bed discouraged, be depressed or worry about getting old. The way you feel inside about the people you have helped and about yourself is your payoff.

By helping others you also help yourself. As these young people grow emotionally, physically and spiritually, so will you. There isn't any amount of money that can replace the pure self-satisfaction of knowing, that your love and your time have helped someone else.

If you really enjoy your sport, you'll enjoy teaching it to others. One of the greatest thrills in life is working with young people, watching them improve and knowing that you played a significant part in their growth and development.

Each year at Christmas, our wrestling room is filled with graduates, home from college, working with their former teammates. They're eager to show the younger wrestlers how to improve their game. They want the tradition of success that they were part of to continue. They are proud of what they accomplished while at school. They feel it's their duty to "Leave Something Behind," to give something back to the sport they love. What better way than by passing their knowledge on to a younger generation.

They can't make our regular scheduled practices because they are working. Many of them pick out one boy and work with him in the evenings. They coach him one-on-one with the goal of making that one high school wrestler a State Champion. They show moves. They talk about dealing with the pressure and about the positive attitude you must have to become a State Champion. They relive their own experiences. What better way to "Leave Something Behind" than to put yourself in the shoes of a high school athlete, and help him live his dream just as you lived yours.

This is the stuff that makes dreams come true. The nice thing about it is that everybody benefits. The current wrestlers get to pursue their dreams of becoming a champion. The older wrestlers get to "Leave Something Behind" to a sport they love. There is no better way.

LEAVE SOMETHING BEHIND

DAVE WINFIELD
Major League Outfielder

I've gotten a lot out of baseball. I expect to get a whole lot more. I just think someone in my position should put something back into the game. Give something; don't just take.

RED GRANGE
NFL Halfback

The next best thing to playing football is coaching it—passing on to kids bursting out of their skins with health, vigor and bounce some of the things you picked up about the game as you went along.

DOROTHY FULDHEIM
American Lecturer

All those young people who have a full life ahead of them should be noble and generous so that no matter how small or large one's sphere of influence may be, when one's life is concluded he will have left a great deal of generosity and tenderness behind.

AL KALINE
Major League Outfielder and Sports Broadcaster

I never wanted to do anything that would hurt my reputation with the fans. I never wanted to do anything that would not reflect positively on myself, my family, the Detroit ballclub or baseball.

CHRIS SCHENKEL
Sports Broadcaster

In sports announcing, if you can turn one athlete into a little kid's hero, you might keep the kid from doing something he shouldn't do later.

GARY CARTER
Major League Catcher

I feel that the Man upstairs has given me a lot and for that I'm very thankful. Hopefully, I can be in a position that kids might look up to me and find a direction in life.

PELE
Professional Soccer Player

I worked very hard for many years to make the name "Pele" mean something. It not only had a very definite financial value, but it also had a certain moral value to the youth of the country.

PETE ROSE
Major League First Baseman and Manager

The thing that I would most like to leave behind is to be remembered for trying hard—hustling if you will.

WILLIE DAVENPORT
Hurdler—Olympic Gold Medalist

Because of my reputation and all that I have accomplished, I feel a responsibility to young kids. I know they look up to me and listen to what I say. I emphasize just one thing and that is the need for goals.

S. SMILES
American Writer

Example teaches better than precept. It is the best modeler of the character of men and women. To set a lofty example is the richest bequest a man can leave behind him.

AL OERTER
**Discus Thrower—
Four Time Olympic Gold Medalist**

I do not believe that it is my place to tell anyone on earth what they should or should not do. I do believe that by providing an example of what can be accomplished if you apply your thoughts and energy with great determination, more people will make the first attempt toward some distant goal.

GEORGE BRETT
Major League Third Baseman

I want to be remembered as a winner—as a good example for the young people. I want people to say, "George Brett was a winner. Regardless of what he did, he was a winner." I would like people to say, "He always busted his butt. He was very competitive. He made the most of his potential." That will be my contribution.

ROONE ARLEDGE
Sports Producer

You can only make so much money in life and only enjoy so many creature comforts. The important thing is to do something meaningful—to leave something behind.

HAL LEBOVITZ
Sports Editor

Like singers and movie actors, pro athletes have a responsibility, an obligation they may not want. When they accept all that money and perform before the public, they give up some of their privacy. The kids put their picture in their rooms, buy their bubble gum cards, and speak of them in worshipful tones. They owe these kids something in return. If you are fortunate enough to become one of the few who can earn a living through professional sports, I hope you will never forget this.

BILL REYNOLDS
NFL Halfback

In the end, when you are all through with the active part of sports, give something back to the game that gave so much to you. Don't forget that the game will go on without you just as it did before you came along.

GEORGE ALLEN
NFL Coach and Sports Broadcaster

I want to be remembered as a man who wanted to win so badly that he'd give a year of his life to be a winner.

KAREEM ABDUL-JABBAR
NBA Center

I was in all the slums of New York telling young athletes to stay in school and to make men out of themselves. I thought then, and I think now, that that job was a lot more important than winning a gold medal in the Olympics or a World Championship. I tried to give them some kind of example. They dig basketball, so they dig me.

DON SHULA
NFL Defensive Back and Coach

I would like to be remembered as fair minded, always trying to do things with class, never knowingly hurting anybody.

JOHN HAVLICEK
NBA Forward

Everyone knows the basic difference between right and wrong. If you can put more rights than wrongs on your side of the ledger, then you'll be successful. If you can achieve that, while at the same time leading by example, you'll end up influencing a lot of young people in a positive way. I hope that throughout my entire basketball career I have been able to do that.

TERRY FOX WANTED TO LEAVE SOMETHING BEHIND

"I want to show people that just because they're disabled, it's not the end."

Terry Fox was an outstanding high school athlete in Canada. His athletic career, though, ended suddenly when it was discovered that he had cancer. His right leg was amputated above the knee. But cancer didn't affect Fox's heart. He still had determination and soon, he had a dream.

Fox's dream, which he turned into a reality, was the Marathon of Hope. It was a trail 5,300 miles through Canada which Fox ran to prove that a person need not give up because of a handicap. He also raised almost two million dollars for the Canadian Cancer Society as a result of the run before cancer forced him to end the marathon.

Terry Fox died from cancer in the summer of 1981, but not before he had passed his dream onto others. He was an inspiration to thousands.

"I don't feel that this is unfair," he said. **"That's the one thing about cancer. I'm not the only one; it happens all the time to other people. I'm not special. This just intensifies what I did; it gives it more meaning; it'll inspire more people."**

RICH MAUTI HAS AN OBLIGATION

"I know this sounds corny, and I don't care, but I really think each one of us has the responsibility of making things a little better for the next guy, of using whatever talents we have to help others."

Rich Mauti, kick returner for the New Orleans Saints, raises money through pledges, challenges, golf tournaments and donations for the Mauti Foundation. The purpose of the foundation is to fight cancer, the disease that claimed Mauti's father, Dominic.

It was in 1978 that Mauti first learned that his father had cancer. Mauti's first reaction upon hearing the news was, "Why my father?" Then, instead of feeling sorry for his father and himself, Mauti decided to do something.

He began the Mauti Challenge, speaking at fund raisers and pledging to donate money for every tackle and every yard he made during the season. He asked others to match his donation. The "Rich Mauti Scramble for Cancer" golf tournament came into existence. Businesses made donations. People throughout New Orleans took the story to their hearts and offered their money to the Mauti Foundation.

Mauti's father died from cancer, but Rich Mauti continues to fight so that others may live.

"We each have an obligation. All you hear from people today is how tough things are. Too many people spend all their time worrying about what they don't have, instead of being thankful for the things they do have, making use of the talents they do possess."

Little Eyes Upon You

There are little eyes upon you
and they're watching night and day.
There are little ears that quickly
take in every word you say.
There are little hands all eager
to do anything you do;
And a little boy who's dreaming
of the day he'll be like you.

You're the little fellow's idol,
you're the wisest of the wise.
In his little mind about you
no suspicions ever rise.
He believes in you devoutly,
holds all that you say and do;
He will say and do, in your way,
when he's grown up like you.

There's a wide eyed little fellow
who believes you're always right;
And his eyes are always opened,
and he watched day and night.
You are setting an example
every day in all you do,
For the little boy who's waiting
to grow up to be like you.

A decade after graduation, almost everyone will have forgotten where and what they played. But every time they speak, everyone will know whether or not they are educated.

Reverend Theodore M. Hesburgh, C.S.C.,
University of Notre Dame President

Understand that where education is concerned, you have no choice. In other words, if you are to advance at all in life, you must acquire a solid formal education. Athletes hold the respect, even the envy, of their fellow students. They are the leaders in most instances. But they must guard against being misled by this position of prominence. Athletic prowess is not a sustaining talent. Physical ability fades, but the expansion of knowledge and intellectual strength provides timeless support for the self-sustaining individual.

Frank Borman, Eastern Airlines President

DON'T FORGET ABOUT YOUR EDUCATION

> The competition in the job market today calls for being as well-prepared as possible. Only a few progress from college football to the pros, and then most of the time, it is for a short time. You must prepare for your future and that key is education.
>
> Paul Bear Bryant, College Football Coach and Athletic Director

Read the quotations here. They're from a diverse group of individuals: A university president, a corporation president and the second winningest college football coach of all time. They live in different worlds, but they all share strong feelings on the value and necessity of an education. Remember their words.

Reading is to the mind what exercise is to the body. To be successful in life or in sports, you need the basics. If you have followed the steps in Chapter One through Seven of this book, but applied them only to sports and not to your education, you have failed. Our advice applies equally to athletics and academics.

When Vince Lombardi stressed that fundamentals are needed to win, he was talking about blocking and tackling in football. But he was also talking about math, spelling, grammar, sentence structure, public speaking, accounting, logic, psychology, etc. in preparation for adult life. What applies to the world of sports also applies to education.

Did you know that less than one-tenth of one percent of all athletes actually wind up making a living at their sport? If you're one of the few, you should be proud of yourself and consider yourself very fortunate.

However, if you're in the majority of the athletes who don't make a career out of athletics, you'll realize the value of your formal education when you enter the job market. Without an education, you have about as much chance of becoming successful in the business world, as Lombardi's teams would have had of winning without ever practicing.

If you're fortunate enough to become a professional athlete, you must realize your career will not last forever. You should not turn your back on education. It's sad to see a former pro athlete trying to make it in the business world unprepared. Don't think your name and reputation alone will be enough to get you through. Reputations only last so long. People judge you on what you can do today, not on what you did yesterday.

Each year, we talk to many college coaches concerning our wrestlers and their chances of getting college scholarships. Without fail, the very first question all the coaches ask is, "How are his grades?" followed by, "What is his ACT or SAT score?" Doesn't that tell you something?

If your grades and college entrance scores are low, you won't receive a college scholarship for sports. You have to spend your time working just as hard on your grades as on your sport. The athletes who gain the real edge in life are the ones who obtain college scholarships, because they're at the top of their sport — and of their class.

Don't go to college just to get a piece of paper to hang on your wall. You'll be wasting your time. A college degree is much more than a diploma and a couple of initials after your name. It's an opportunity to obtain the basic fundamentals that will help you succeed throughout life. It's a place where you can take in the knowledge to enable you to make a contribution as an adult, in whatever area that interests you. The key word here is "contribute." Just as you were expected to contribute to the winning efforts of your team in school, you'll also be expected to contribute to the successful operation of your "team" in the game of life.

DON'T FORGET ABOUT YOUR EDUCATION

JOHN DEWEY
American Philosopher/Educator

Education is a social process…Education is growth…Education is not preparation for life…Education is life itself.

R. I. REES
American Engineer

Formal education is but an incident in the lifetime of an individual. Most of us who have given the subject any study have come to realize that education is a continuous process ending only when ambition comes to a halt.

JERRY BUSS
NBA Owner and NHL Owner

It is my most firm belief that education is absolutely the single most important aspect of human endeavor—for adults as well as young people.

Education is an investment in yourself; it brings quality to our life. From a practical standpoint, you cannot compete against the top people unless you are educated. Self-education is only the answer after one has made the most of the formal education available to us through the school system.

It is only through education that we can realize the vast potential we have as individuals and as a world community.

L. EDWIN SMART
Trans World Corporation Chairman

Without exception, the men and women who reach the top have worked hard to achieve a series of goals. Those goals include the need to expand their educational background to the fullest. Each step along the road—the high school degree, the college degree, graduate school—all help to build a broader background for the individual which, in turn, expands the range of available career opportunities.

My message to the young athlete of today is: Take advantage of the self-discipline that made you a success in your chosen sport by applying the same dedication and commitment to your education, and the future will hold limitless opportunities.

GEORGE SAMPSON
American Engineer

The well-meaning people who talk of education as if it were a substance distributable by coupon in large or small quantities never exhibit any understanding of the truth that you cannot teach anybody anything that he does not want to learn.

HOWARD A. WHITE
Pepperdine University President

An athlete who fails to develop his mind is more crippled than if he were to lose a leg. The smart athlete will develop himself both physically and intellectually. For not only will he be happier by being more complete, he also will develop resources that will be useful when athletic ability has diminished. A fine athlete who develops his mental capacities is preparing for a long and happy life. One who is satisfied with athletics alone may think he is fulfilled for a time, but he is doomed to ultimate disappointment.

DIGGER PHELPS
College Basketball Coach

Motivation leads to a direction. It is obvious that youngsters today need guidance in values and priorities. If one is blessed with a talent to make it as a professional athlete, that is fine. Yet, he needs credentials to make it in life after his professional period. Using a sport to reach your goals outside of athletics is very important. Some people will let a sport use them and end up with nothing once their athletic career is finished. That is why it is so very important to have athletics and academics together in a positive way. One's mental and physical talents can only lead to that direction.

LOU BROCK
Major League Outfielder

I was always academically oriented; it was a matter of pride and self-esteem. I wanted to be able to hold my own in a crowd.

ELMER JAGOW
Hiram College President

In practically every case, the opportunity for a young man or young woman to excel in athletics is connected with some level of the educational system. There have been relatively few persons who have started or continued an amateur athletic career without an association with some academic institution. The two areas are solidly together.

As a student, you can have both or you can concentrate on the academics; you do not have the option of choosing only to try to concentrate on athletics. By use of simple logic, the most important area is the pursuit of knowledge in the classroom.

The wisest choice is to pursue both and try to excel in each. They are not antagonistic; they are complementary.

ALAN PAGE
NFL Defensive Tackle and Attorney

The single most important goal for a student athlete—whether male or female—should be to achieve a good education. Today's student athlete is tomorrow's leader. Without an education, it will be impossible to meet the challenge of our ever-changing world.

TONY DORSETT
NFL Halfback

I was an honor student in high school, but my first-year grades at Pitt were awful. I was just like a lot of young dudes the first semester. You know, foolin' around, messin' with women, not going to class. I just wouldn't go. But I got through with all the foolishness. You aren't going anywhere if you don't keep your grades up.

BERT JONES
NFL Quarterback

The successful athlete cannot be satisfied with physical skills alone. He must apply himself with equal enthusiasm to academic pursuits as well. Overlooking studies to concentrate solely on sports is a costly mistake. One cannot participate in professional athletics forever; you need academic preparation for a later career.

REVEREND THEODORE M. HESBURGH
C.S.C., University of Notre Dame President

The most important thing for young athletes to understand is that while athletic performance may be an important part of their early years, an even more important part is their academic achievement. Athletics tend to pass as one gets older, whereas what one achieves academically stays with one the rest of one's life. Long after athletic exploits are forgotten, one is still using the education that in some cases was made possible by athletic achievement.

Our proudest boast at Notre Dame is that all of our athletes also become well educated and that quality shows itself in their later lives.

BOB KNIGHT
College Basketball Coach and U.S. Olympic Basketball Coach

People think a sport is very important. Well, I think it's enjoyable and we have a lot of fun with it, but we have got to understand that if we did away with the School of Education or the School of Medicine, it would have a greater effect on Indiana University than doing away with the Athletic Department.

CHARLES J. PILLIOD, JR.
Goodyear Tire & Rubber Company Chairman

An athlete is blessed with exceptional opportunity to get the most out of education. Success as an athlete depends on development of one's skills to their full potential—exercise of discipline to realize effective use of these skills, determination to excel, and ability to work as a member of a team. The athlete is thus well-equipped to apply these same qualities to his scholastic pursuits. If he does this along with his athletic efforts, he will build the foundation for success in virtually any field he chooses to pursue.

TERRY DONAHUE
College Football Coach

As a coach, I'm proud of our players and I know of their years of practice and hard work to develop strong and healthy bodies, self respect and the spirit of cooperation and teamwork. Academic preparation is equally, if not more important. A good, solid foundation of educational background is essential for success in every area and vital to your future as a well-rounded, intelligent individual. I urge you to work equally hard in the classroom and on the athletic field.

DOROTHY FULDHEIM
American Lecturer

The world and the universe is a great and exciting place. I would suggest for any young person to learn as much as possible because not only is the universe expanding, but all knowledge. The mind is like any organ—the more it's used the greater its capacity becomes.

TOMMY LASORDA
Major League Manager

Get your education. You can be the greatest athlete in the world and if, God forbid, you get hurt, you'll have nothing to fall back on. But an education is something that no one can take away from you.

LEE A. IACOCCA
Chrysler Corporation Chairman

The greatest value of organized high school sports is that it teaches discipline, loyalty, and teamwork. But of even greater importance to any athlete is the need to get the best possible education that is available. Important as sports are, they are always secondary to the overriding need for a well rounded education.

STEVE BUSBY
Major League Pitcher

To me, the college degree is a big thing, something nobody can take away. College gave me a chance to mature, physically and mentally. I learned a lot about life and people. I know that college is a big factor in my being able to compete on the professional level.

PANCHO GONZALEZ
Professional Tennis Player

Education is the most important part of your school days. Therefore, you should concentrate on this and recognize that athletics is only a part of your life and should be played as such. You should realize that athletics are still sports to be enjoyed.

PHILIP CALDWELL
Ford Motor Company Chairman

At the basic level, education trains us for making a living and providing for our families. Others will recognize these abilities when we achieve certain degrees or levels of education.

But education can do much more. By teaching us how to learn, it provides the means for developing our capabilities both at work and at home. Learning how to learn is fundamental to a good education because those skills stay with us all our lives and help us with the unknowns we face.

Just as important, however, education can tell us something about ourselves. It can help us develop a sense of what is right and wrong, good and bad. And it can open new doors to those many things that give us enjoyment and make us more human—the family, friendship, religion, the arts and literature.

For me, education is still a daily experience. On the best days, I learn a lot.

JOHN MAC LEOD
NBA Coach

One of the most critical essentials for a young athlete to remember is that athletic participation is only for a short period of one's life. It is of prime importance, therefore, that academics or school work be given great emphasis. The years of high school and college are great learning years which can result in big payoffs and much happiness. This concentration on academics can only make you a better athlete. The ability to discipline the will is a major factor in one's achievement of success.

ALDOUS HUXLEY
English Author

Perhaps the most valuable result of all education is the ability to make yourself do the thing you have to do when it has to be done, whether you like it or not.

ROGER B. SMITH
General Motors Corporation Chairman

The value of a complete, well-rounded education cannot be over-stressed.

At General Motors, we place a very high priority on education when we review the qualifications of those we hire. Yet this training cannot be focused on a narrow specialty field because the world in which today's business leader must make decisions is too complex and many-faceted.

The same is true for the young athletes of today. However competent they may be in their sport, they will not succeed in a tough, competitive world unless they have used their years of formal education to their full advantage. By building a broad range of interests and widening their scope of knowledge, they can acquire the key to a successful career and an enriched life.

JOE PATERNO
College Football Coach and Athletic Director

I'm always after my players. I tell them, "Get involved. Don't let the world pass you by. Get into it. Go after life. Attack it. Ten years from now, I want you to be able to look back on your college life as a wonderful experience, not just four years of playing football."

BABE RUTH
Major League Pitcher/Outfielder

Life may begin at 40 for other people, but it ends at 40 for the baseball player unless he has something to fall back on, and that is where a trained mind helps.

W. F. MARTIN
Phillips Petroleum Company Chairman

Achievement in competitive sports can go hand-in-hand with excellence in education. Competitive sports build character, determination, self-discipline and a willingness to sacrifice. These same qualities can be applied in pursuing a good education. An athlete is missing a valuable opportunity if he does not apply the lessons he learns in sports to his scholastic work.

The thoughtful athlete plans for the future. He prepares for an alternate career should injuries, age or other changing circumstances prevent the pursuit of athletics. Certainly, achievement in athletics can provide recognition that can be of great advantage in moving into a second career. However, that career will be difficult to develop if it is not based on a solid educational background—from both secondary school and college.

It is not unusual for young people to become so involved and dedicated to sports that their education suffers. But in the final analysis, education must take priority over athletic endeavors.

BOWIE KUHN
Major League Baseball Commissioner

Participation in athletics is part of your total learning process. If it teaches you to respect discipline and value teamwork, you will have learned something. If it teaches you self-discipline, you will have learned something even more valuable. Always have foremost in your mind that ultimately you are in high school to be educated. Sports are valueless unless they contribute to your education.

HOWARD COSELL
Attorney, Sports Broadcaster and Author

Carry within you at all times the understanding that sport is a necessary outlet for physical, mental, and emotional balance in the fullness of a lifetime, but that it is secondary to academic learning and achievement.

NEWTON D. BAKER
American Public Official

The man who graduates today and stops learning tomorrow is uneducated the day after.

DOCTOR GEORGE D. STODDARD
American Educator

The democratic ideal is contradictory to both tyranny and ignorance. Men must be free not only to think, to speak and to worship, but to build within themselves through education, a preparedness for their later years. Not every man can be a leader, but every man, however limited his natural capacities, can improve in the direction of better choices for himself and his children. If our education is good, then by educating all the people we give every person a better chance.

RAY J. GROVES
Ernst & Whinney Chairman

When Aristotle was asked how much educated men were superior to those uneducated, he said, "As much as the living are to the dead."

The wonderful part of being human is that our computer-like brain allows, indeed insists, that we continue to learn to the end of our lives.

SEYMOUR E. HARRIS
American Educator

It may be that we should stop putting so much emphasis in our own minds on the monetary value of a college education and put more emphasis on the intangible social and cultural values to be derived from learning. The time may be coming when we will have to start accepting the idea that education is life, not merely a preparation for it.

JAMES L. FERGUSON
General Foods Corporation Chairman

Functioning fully and gaining the greatest personal satisfaction from all of life's interests requires the tandem development of a sound mind and a sound body. The young person who neglects either one or the other is doing himself or herself, as well as society, a great disservice.

Furthermore, the effort and dedication required to master the challenges of today may well be insufficient to master the more complex challenges of future years. Since many of the young people of today must be our leaders of tomorrow, their continuing education represents the foundation on which their future performance as citizens—and the very future of our society—will be built.

All of us are counting on them to build that foundation well.

JULIUS ERVING
NBA Forward
The biggest thing that I felt basketball could do for me was help me get a good education.

ISIAH THOMAS
NBA Guard
I know that I'll get my law degree. I know that you can only play basketball for so many years. Then you've got the rest of your life ahead of you.

During my years on the tour I've come to the conclusion that one of the biggest problems for professionals and amateurs alike is the inability to control the distance of their less-than-full or partial shots, especially those from inside 100 yards. The key to hitting any shot is to create a constant acceleration of the club through the ball. This is particularly true on partial shots. And the key to creating acceleration is to be able to make as full a swing as possible for the distance required. Knowing this, I have done a very simple thing that has helped me quite a bit with those pesky "in-between" shots. I have added a third wedge to my bag just for those shots. It was just a simple thing to do but it has helped my game tremendously.

Tom Kite, Professional Golfer

COMMON SENSE

Common sense. We all know what it is, or do we? Common sense is knowing the difference between right and wrong. It entails a personal and subjective process of analyzing a problem and finding a solution that works for you, but not necessarily for everyone. Champions know this and that's why some of their methods may seem unorthodox. As long as they work, however, champions will keep on using them.

Common sense means taking the time to stop and ask yourself — is this right or wrong for me? It's easy to go along with the crowd, to get involved with what everyone else is doing. It's safe. But it may not always be right. Use instinct and trust your gut-level feelings. They're the best indicators you have.

When it was first suggested to sprinter Evelyn Ashford that she wear a body suit similar to the one worn by speed skater Eric Heiden, she found the idea ridiculous. It was a suit that belonged on a skin diver, not a sprinter. Fortunately, she gave the idea more thought and used common sense. That suit helped her run faster than ever before.

Golfer Tom Kite analyzed his game and saw a problem. The clubs he had in his bag were not able to handle a particular shot. Using common sense, he went out and got a new wedge for those in-between shots.

How many times have you heard people say he or she may be very smart, but they don't have any common sense? Such people speak before they think, act before they consider the consequences, and never stop to realize how their decisions affect others. They are inconsiderate, whether they intend to be or not.

Pope John XXIII once said, "Prudent is he who can keep silent that part of truth which may be untimely, and by not speaking it, does not spoil the truth of what he said."

In matters of principle, stand like a rock. You know what's right and what's wrong. Do what's right. Follow your common sense. For example, we have read everything about the dangers of smoking. Yet, people continue to smoke and buy more and more cigarettes each year. Is that common sense?

Don't compromise. Keep a clear understanding of what's right and what's wrong. The difference between them is very obvious. Don't cross over the line. Stand firm. Your personal integrity is at stake here. Once you give a little, you tend to forget where the line is and who you really are.

We have a saying at St. Edward: "How hard is it?" What this means is that when you step back and take a good look at yourself, the choices should not be that difficult. Some of our wrestlers figure this out while still in high school. Some discover it in college, others not until their competitive days are over. Regardless of when they step back and put it all together, they say, "Now I understand. Now I see. It all makes sense. The choices are obvious. How hard is it?"

All the education in the world can't give you common sense. It's simply a matter of following your intuition. If you do, you'll have the edge over an awful lot of people. As George Bernard Shaw, the writer, said, "Common sense is instinct. Enough of it is genius."

When I first saw 'the suit', I said, "I'll never wear that thing. There's no way in the world." But when I saw Eric Heiden win five gold medals wearing one and found out that it weighed only three ounces, I decided to try it. It's not really tight, it's snug. It moves when I move. I can feel the wind go by when I run. It feels good. It feels fast.

Evelyn Ashford, Sprinter —
Three Time Olympic Gold Medalist

COMMON SENSE

SAMUEL T. COLERIDGE
British Romantic Poet

Common sense in an uncommon degree is what the world calls wisdom.

SIDNEY J. HARRIS
Newspaper Columnist

One of the most serious mistakes we can make is to confuse the thing we call "intelligence" with another thing called "judgment." The two do not always or necessarily go together. Many persons of high intelligence have notoriously poor judgment.

CALVIN COOLIDGE
Thirtieth President

I have never been hurt by anything I didn't say.

HENRY FORD
Founder of Ford Motor Company/Inventor

The question, "Who ought to be boss?" is like asking, "Who ought to be the tenor in the quartet?" Obviously, it's the man who can sing tenor the best.

JACK KEMP
NFL Quarterback, United States Congressman

What could be more thrilling than to take one important idea and see it through. You don't need to be a genius to do that. Just a strong desire, a lot of hard work, faith and a little common sense.

THOMAS JEFFERSON
Third President

All through your life, you'll be faced with making a decision between two things—choose the one that is right. If they are both right, then choose the one that will make you feel the best about it at the end of the day.

BENJAMIN FRANKLIN
American Inventor

All the education and all the knowledge in the world can't help the poor soul who has no common sense.

H. W. SHAW
American Humorist

Common sense is the favorite daughter of reason.

CHRIS HANBURGER
NFL Linebacker

Common sense! What's common sense? It's the difference between what's right and what's wrong—a very simple thing. The Good Lord gave it to all of us, and all you've got to do is use it. You do something wrong...you want to get involved with what the crowd's doing. It may not be the right thing, but you've got to be part of the crowd. You only get one chance in life today; that's just the way it is. Common sense! Use it! If it's wrong, don't do it. If it's right, jump in there and go like gangbusters!

BUD GRANT
NFL Coach

I came to believe that it is best to keep my mouth shut unless I have something to say. I learned not to do things just to be doing them.

W. SOMERSET MAUGHAM
English Author
Common sense and good nature will do a lot to make the pilgrimage of life not too difficult.

PERSIAN PROVERB
One pound of learning requires ten pounds of common sense to apply it.

RALPH WALDO EMERSON
American Writer/Poet
Nothing astonishes men so much as common sense and plain dealing.

CALVIN STOWE
American Author
Common sense is the knack of seeing things as they are, and doing things as they ought to be done.

ED HOWE
American Editor/Writer
Life is like a game of cards. Reliability is the ace, industry the king, politeness the queen, thrift the jack. Common sense is playing to the best advantage the cards you draw. And every day, as the game proceeds, you will find the ace, king, queen, jack in your hand and opportunity to use them.

THOMAS EDISON
American Inventor
The three great essentials to achieve anything worthwhile are, first, hard work; second, stick-to-itiveness; third, common sense.

JOHN GLENN
Astronaut and United States Senator
There are a lot of bright young people coming out of colleges today. The real test for them however, will not be one of sheer intelligence but rather how much common sense they possess.

DAMON RUNYON
American Journalist
One of these days in your travels, a guy is going to come to you and show you a nice, brand-new deck of cards on which the seal is not yet broken, and this guy is going to offer to bet you that he can make the jack of spades jump out of the deck and squirt cider in your ear. But, son, do not bet this man, for as sure as you stand there, you are going to wind up with an earful of cider.

JACK NICKLAUS
Professional Golfer
Anybody who is successful must be a decision-maker. You've got to make up your mind on what you're going to do and then go about doing it. I think it is the positive nature of the game of golf, just as it is the positive nature of life, that the successful people appear to have blinders on. Everything is straight ahead. They go forward and know exactly what they're going to do once they make up their mind to do it, and by God, they don't look sideways.

OLIVER WENDELL HOLMES
American Writer
Science is a first-rate piece of furniture for a man's upper chamber, if he has common sense on the ground floor.

BISHOP WESTCOTT
English Prelate/Theologian
How many people ever consider that the lack of certain qualities—such as balance, common sense, tranquility—affect the physical state of the human body?...Did you ever hear of people being sick because they hated someone? This is not uncommon.

The circumstances for my turnaround began in mid-'79. Until then, I thought of myself as a .500 pitcher, not durable enough to be a real winner...I realized I would have to unlearn and reprogram myself to be successful. So I began to meditate on the mound. I had to go through a self-evaluation. I had to take my personality and fit it into a system of mental preparation, to decide what I could tolerate and what I could not. I wasn't throwing a new pitch, or harder than in the past; I just reached for inner resources, I simply changed my attitude. I think a fellow putting fenders on a car in Detroit or working as a grounds keeper at the ball park can apply the same approach.

Steve Stone,
Major League Pitcher and Sports Broadcaster

If I were in business, and actually football is a business, I would use the same principles because they are sound. We know what we want to do, when we want to do it and how we want to do it.

George Allen, NFL Coach and Sports Broadcaster

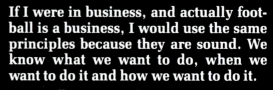

It has been often said that athletics challenge the body, mind, and spirit. They bring out the best in people, because athletic competition engenders character, dedication, determination, awareness, self-confidence, cooperation, and sensitivity to self and others. Here at USC, we believe the very same principles apply to academics. Learning requires the same degree of energy and commitment as competitive sports and yields comparable benefits for the individual. Because of this, we think athletics and learning go hand in hand to help individual men and women discover and realize their true potential in life.

James H. Zumberge,
University of Southern California President

THE SAME PRINCIPLES APPLY

We sincerely believe that what it takes to be a winner in athletics and academics is exactly what it takes to be a winner in the game of life. The principles for excellence in one are the same as in the other. The difference between a great and a mediocre athlete is the difference between one who gives up and one who doesn't. The same thing can be said about a salesman, an attorney, a doctor or a person in any other occupation.

I personally know that these same principles work in the business world. As a manager, the qualities I look for in an employee are identical to those I look for in a wrestler. I'd personally rather have five hard-working, loyal employees than 100 with little or no character who just don't care.

The same principle applies to my wrestlers. We win championships with quality, not quantity. I look for athletes who want to win so badly they can't live with losing. You can understand why I would want my salespeople to have the same competitive qualities.

Character comes first, followed closely by desire, dedication, discipline and perseverance. My salespeople, like my wrestlers, must possess all of these qualities as well as be highly competitive and mentally tough. Why? Sales is nothing more than one-on-one competition. And it's mentally tough, for sales are seldom made on the first attempt. I have found that the best salespeople are those who refuse to quit until they close. Their competitive spirit and mental toughness give them the edge.

Is it any wonder, then, why perseverance and persistence are so vital, not only for the athlete, but the businessperson as well? Success and failure are affected directly by these key personality traits. Luck has nothing to do with it, as you should know by now.

This, then is the key to success. Acquire certain personality traits — discipline, perseverance, mental toughness, desire — that will give you the competitive edge. Obtain the knowledge and skills needed to succeed. Athletics are a mirror reflection of life; they provide an excellent training ground. Combine athletics with a sound formal education and you will have a winning game plan.

Combine athletics and academics. If you're a great athlete without a sound education, you'll end up a loser in life. Likewise, a well-educated person without a competitive spirit and the necessary mental toughness will also fail.

Think about it this way. If someone you really cared about was sick and needed an operation, would you want a doctor without a competitive spirit? Would you want a doctor who loved to win or a doctor who was well-qualified, but just wanted to put in his or her time?

I would prefer a doctor who had paid the price, who had earned the right to be great, who loved to win and who was willing to make the extra effort to do so.

The American free enterprise system is beautifully expressed in athletics. The spirit that made America great is found in the competition, the drive, the pressure, the desire to achieve and the challenges of our athletic programs. The principles we've been discussing are so important. They apply everywhere.

THE SAME PRINCIPLES APPLY

NORMAN VINCENT PEALE
Clergyman/American Writer

Whatever you are doing in the game of life, give it all you've got. Don't be a "holdout".

JOHN W. GALBREATH
Major League Owner

Desire, dedication, and motivation are the things that dominate in life—whether it be in sports or in the business world.

GEORGE ALLEN
NFL Coach and Sports Broadcaster

The future is now. If we do the proper things today, we will win today and we will also win tomorrow. I think that sometimes we can be so concerned about the future that it never comes. I really believe this philosophy applies not only to football but also to everything else in life.

PETE ROZELLE
NFL Commissioner

The values of leadership, sacrifice and discipline which are acquired through high school athletics have served as useful tools for many of our NFL players. The combination of classroom academics and participation in extracurricular activities adds up to a well-rounded young adult. The same values that will make you a good athlete and a good student should stay with you, because they will help you throughout your entire life no matter what you do.

JOHN NABER
Swimmer—Four Time Olympic Gold Medalist

In swimming, success comes not in how hard you swim or how many yards you swim, but rather it depends on how many hard yards you swim.

Just as it is in life, the blending of effort and the proper technique always produces results. Success happens whenever preparation meets opportunity.

JERRY HOFFBERGER
Major League President

Be team people, whether in athletics, business, or a profession. This is a personal discipline developed early in life. Work with other people, support them, encourage them and they will support and encourage you.

VINCE LOMBARDI
NFL Coach and General Manager

Unless a man believes in himself and makes a total commitment to his career and puts everything he has into it—his mind, his body and his heart—what is life worth to him? If I were a salesman, I would make this commitment to my company, to the product and most of all to myself. A man who is trained to his peak capacity will gain confidence. Confidence is contagious and so is lack of confidence and a customer will recognize both.

BERT JONES
NFL Quarterback

If you are interested in sports, I would encourage you to strive for excellence as an individual, and become a working, contributing member of your team. Athletics teach valuable lessons. Sacrifice, dedication, and teamwork are as important in life as they are in sports.

CHUCK KNOX
NFL Coach

A successful person is one who works up to or near his full potential. The only thing you can ask any man to do is his best no matter what he chooses to do—in the game of sports or in the game of life.

BUM PHILLIPS
NFL Coach

Everyone will forget you when you leave the game and all you will have left are the things it has taught you—to sacrifice, to work hard—you will be able to use these all the rest of your life.

PHILLIP R. SHRIVER
Miami University President

It is my conviction that a young person's involvement in athletics holds a tremendous potential for learning and development. Challenged by adversity, forced to make decisions for which immediate results will be seen, provided with the opportunity to experience the "thrill of victory and the agony of defeat," and exposed to the very special relationship that many times develops among team members, I maintain that participation in athletics has the potential to teach self-discipline, cooperation, sacrifice, and countless other valuable character qualities. I would underscore my point that one's involvement in athletics holds the potential to teach qualities. Much of the success in the teaching of such attributes is dependent on the individuals involved. I believe that the coach or coaches and the athletes should recognize that the athletic field or court or diamond can and should be an extension of the classroom, a place where you and your teammates are learning more than just how to prepare to win. The field, court, and diamond should be places where athletes are constantly learning about the game in which they participate, about their coaches and teammates, and perhaps most importantly, about themselves.

TOM LANDRY
NFL Defensive Back and Coach

I don't second-guess myself. I take all the facts available and make decisions based on what I think is right at the time. I think the real mistake is to look back. This basic philosophy can be applied to everything you do in your lifetime—not just sports. Never look back.

GERRY FAUST
College Football Coach

One thing I've found out is that there isn't much difference between the business world and football, because one thing is in common—the businessman and the coach are both dealing with people, and that's the key to life—dealing with people.

JOHN WOODEN
College Basketball Coach

Those who have the team concept will be better able to step into other areas of life and contribute very effectively, both for themselves and society.

LOU GROZA
NFL Offensive Tackle and Kicker

Young athletes should establish lifetime goals in which their athletic accomplishments are only part of the whole game of life.

Regardless of what your goals may be, determine the fundamentals and become proficient in the use of them. Nothing is more complicated than the fundamental parts of a career in football or for that matter in any vocation you may choose. The same principles apply to anything you do in life.

RED GRANGE
NFL Halfback

The mental and physical discipline of college football is advance preparation for a business or a profession. The athlete learns to compete—and business today is hard competition.

JACK NICKLAUS
Professional Golfer

Commitment has always been a big word in my approach to golf, and it is equally big in my business philosophy.

JOHN NABER
Swimmer—Four Time Olympic Gold Medalist

Although they only give gold medals in the field of athletics, I encourage everyone to look into themselves and find their own personal dream, whatever that may be—sports, medicine, law, business, music, writing, whatever. The same principles apply. Turn your dream into a goal, and decide how to attack that goal systematically. Break it into bite size chunks that seem possible-and then don't give up. Just keep plugging away.

BRAGE GOLDING
Kent State University President
It is as painful to look back upon one's youth and realize that it was left in the library as to see that it was lost in the locker room. On the field, the floor, the track, in the classroom, the laboratory, the study—wherever, it is important to keep your life in balance. Test your skills against the traditions of the knowable as well as against the records of the doable, and you'll emerge from high school a stronger, wiser, better person.

ROGER NEILSON
NHL Coach
In a world where mediocrity is the mode, there is no greater challenge than giving your best in whatever you do. Vince Lombardi said that a man's finest hour is when he works his heart out in a good cause and lies exhausted on the field of battle, victorious. In the Bible, Paul implores the Corinthians to "Run your race to win." The world's greatest coach and the world's greatest Christian both have the same message...Give your best shot in everything you do! Those students who give their best at school and those athletes who always work at practice become the successful citizens of tomorrow.

JACK RAMSEY
NBA Coach and General Manager
Intensity of effort is the difference between success and failure, not only in sports but in life. In sports, that characteristic is so closely related to winning that competitors are generally quick to accept it as a basic quality of their play. It enables the shorter player to out jump the bigger one, the slower player to out-quick the faster one, and the player of lesser ability to finish ahead of the more skilled performer.

The same intensity of effort is absolutely essential in the game of life as well. It is the difference between success and failure.

BILL BUCKNER
Major League First Baseman/Outfielder
I believe that every young person who is physically capable should become involved in athletics of some kind. I think it opens the lines of communication with your fellow man as well as keeping the body and mind in top form. This is a competitive world and athletics can help you prepare yourself for later life. The same principles apply—what it takes to make one a good athlete will also enable him to become good in anything he tackles in life.

R. ANDERSON
Rockwell International Corporation Chairman
Early on, I learned that there was no substitute for hard work. It increased my native ability to execute well in the classroom or on the ball field.

As a Los Angeles high school football player, I earned a football scholarship to Colorado State University. Without that scholarship, I would have been unable to continue my education.

My business career has benefited immeasurably from those grueling practice sessions which prepared me for the unforgettable weekends when the team was working together, 110 percent of the time. Together, we could rise above our individual abilities to victory.

In my experience, I've found it is work, as in hard work, and work, as in teamwork, that will determine how well we play the game, on the field, in the classroom or in the larger game of life.

Anything less, I discovered as a young man, and you wind up getting your face pushed in the mud.

OTTO GRAHAM
NFL Quarterback and College Athletic Director
Everyone can't be the best at anything, but everyone can try to be the best at everything. If you give 100 percent effort physically, mentally and morally, you will get your share of victories in any walk of life—not just in sports but in your chosen career as well. The same principles apply.

FRAN TARKENTON
NFL Quarterback and Sports Broadcaster
In football or in business, in order to be a real winner, you have to be willing to stick your neck out. You've got to be willing to take chances.

CLARK KELLOGG
NBA Forward

Nothing good comes easy. This is clearly exemplified in the world of athletics. In order to excel in anything, it takes hard work, dedication, desire, self-discipline, sacrifice and determination. Just as you would exercise these principles trying to achieve a goal related to athletics, exercise these same principles in your studies, jobs and other activities in your life, for you only get out of something what you put into it.

RICH GOSSAGE
Major League Relief Pitcher

While many of my peers were hanging out and wasting time, I was applying myself to improving my athletic talents. As a result of my participation in sports, the qualities of discipline, loyalty, and teamwork have become important aspects of my life. Sports can teach these same values to everyone.

ROGER STAUBACH
NFL Quarterback and Sports Broadcaster

What athletics teaches is the self-discipline of hard work and sacrifice necessary to achieve a goal. Nowadays, too many people are looking for a short cut. Life is the same as athletics. You have to work to accomplish anything.

WOODY HAYES
College Football Coach
The height of human desire is what wins, whether it's on the Normandy Beach or in Ohio Stadium.

KEN DRYDEN
NHL Goaltender
In both hockey and law, there are long periods of preparation followed by relatively brief presentations.

BILL RUSSELL
NBA Center, Coach and Sports Broadcaster
I played basketball because I was dedicated to being the best. I was a part of a team, and I dedicated myself to making that team the best. To me, one of the most beautiful things to see is a group of men coordinating their efforts toward a common goal—alternately subordinating and asserting themselves to achieve real teamwork in action. I tried to do that—we all tried to do that—on the Celtics. I think we succeeded...Being part of that effort on the Celtics was very important to me. It helped me develop and grow, and I think it has helped me prepare for something other than playing basketball. One natural path for me to follow would be to continue in the field of entertainment. The same general principles of self-sacrifice and teamwork will still apply.

AL MC GUIRE
College Basketball Coach and Sports Broadcaster
I have found over and over again that the lessons I learned in the sports world also apply to the business world.

JERRY HOFFBERGER
Major League President
Winning is not the most important thing; trying to win is the highest priority. Developing the discipline to try, to study, and to work hard early in life will be the most important things an athlete can take into his classroom, his office, or his factory.

RONALD REAGAN
Fortieth President
At this moment, you are in one of the most exciting phases of your life—your teen years. The whole world lies before you. The opportunities are limitless. What you do, where you go, and what you become depends on your willingness to work toward a goal. As an athlete, you have already learned the virtue of perseverance. You have learned that you can overcome obstacles with the proper effort and practice. If you pursue other goals throughout life with the same tenacity, you will succeed. Most importantly, the real key to success is within yourself. No one can give it to you or take it from you. You hold your destiny in your hands.

The Same Principles Apply

After reviewing my athletic career, spiced with five years experience of operating my own business, I can offer the following guidelines to achieving success in both sports and the business world, because the same principles apply.

First of all, you need to have both long-range goals and short-term goals. In my case, the long-range goal was to play pro football. But in order to do this, I had to have short-term goals such as increasing agility, putting on weight, building strength, and being competitive enough to get a college scholarship. In college, I had the same basic goals, along with the development of self-discipline and making my grades. After attaining my goal of becoming a professional ball player, I set new goals—becoming an All-Pro and winning the Super Bowl.

The next ingredient in my formula for success is dedication. This includes rigorous self-discipline, consistent hard work, and maintaining a strict routine. With the right attitude of dedication, you can make every day profitable toward achieving the big goal.

Of course, to be successful, one must have good ability which is God-given. Our Creator designs each of us with specific talents, but then we have the choice to develop our potential or not. A winner will choose to make the most of his assets and even overcompensate for areas of weakness.

To be successful, one must have experience. In my case, I played in five unsuccessful seasons with the Cowboys before finally starting to win. Each losing season gave me some valuable experience which finally contributed to the winning seasons.

The final attribute I wish to list for a winner is that of self-confidence. There is a saying, "a chain is as strong as its weakest link." Lack of confidence could be the weak link in the chain, so one must believe in oneself in order to achieve success. Self-confidence comes from learning your own strengths and weaknesses. Through much experience in competing, one arrives at this knowledge. Then one can build up weak areas and focus on the strong ones.

BOB LILLY — NFL Defensive Tackle

THE CHALLENGE NEVER ENDS

When does it all end? The improvement? The dedication? The desire? The glory? The recognition?

At age 43, discus thrower Al Oerter discovered that it doesn't have to end. There are always new challenges to conquer, new goals to reach. The aging process is a constant enemy for all athletes. Most athletes can't do in their forties what their bodies let them do in their twenties. But the aging process can be seen as a challenge.

Track and field is a young person's sport according to conventional wisdom. No one ever told Al Oerter that.

Al Oerter was 47 years "young" when the Olympic Games were held in Los Angeles in 1984. While that's hardly senior citizen status, it's an age that would prevent most men from gaining a spot on the Olympic Team as a discus thrower. But Al Oerter was a four-time Olympic Gold Medal Champion who was eager to win a fifth gold medal.

In 1984, Oerter competed against some of the world's best athletes, many who were 20-25 years younger than he. He made the U. S. Olympic Team. While he didn't win the gold, he was a source of inspiration and pride for athletes of all ages. What he may have lost in quickness or strength, he made up in desire, motivation and perseverance.

Another timeless athlete who refused to accept the aging process gracefully was swimmer Lance Larson. Lance won a gold medal for the United States in the 1960 Olympic Games at age 20. Twenty-one years later, at age 41, he won another gold medal in the Masters Program against men his own age. The interesting thing is that Larson's race time at age 41 was actually faster than his race time at age 20!

While Oerter credits his latest success to desire, Larson says he was able to cut his time because he got smarter, worked harder and made better use of his practices. Realistically, there comes a time when physical progress will cease. However, we can improve our cardiovascular system or pay better attention to nutrition. The key is to maintain your desire, dedication and determination.

I have the greatest respect for the medical profession. But I strongly disagree with their reports that people should slow down their athletic activities as they age. I think that you're only as old as you feel. I'm going to lift weights, run, play golf, play ball — whatever, until I'm called to that big wrestling mat in the sky. And if I disprove a couple of medical theories along the way, so be it.

If you're not a 100 percent believer in everything we've written so far, we think you will be after you read this section. The challenge never ends, you can continue to compete and improve regardless of age. You probably have heard that it's the legs that go first on an athlete, but that's not true. It's the heart. As long as you still have your desire, anything is possible. You can do anything you want to do in life if you really want it "bad enough".

Good-bye — take care — I have to go work out now. While I'm getting in a good lift, please sit back, relax and read the next and final chapter of THE EDGE. People have told me to save the best for last and I believe that I have.

This last chapter is for you. No one else — just you. Please read it. The 30 minutes you take to read this chapter may be the most important 30 minutes of your life.

In 1976, I returned to sports after an eight-year absence from all training and competition. The world record in the discus was then more than 232 feet, and my best effort of 212 feet 6 inches, achieved in winning the Olympic gold medal in Mexico City, was rather poor by comparison. I established a schedule that if I could follow would have me within range of making the 1980 Olympic Team. I threw 181 in 1976, 205 in 1977, 214 in 1978, 221 in 1979 and a lifetime best of 227 feet 11 inches in 1980. At age 43, I had thrown the discus 15 feet further than I had 12 years earlier when I was 31 years old.

Al Oerter,
Discus Thrower—
Four Time Olympic Gold Medalist

I'm surpassing almost all of the best times I achieved over twenty years ago. Why? Because I'm training smarter now, because I have all of this experience behind me. I'm also training harder, with more intensity. I'm not screwing around at practice like a younger person might do. My time is limited and I'm going to use it to full advantage.

Lance Larson, Swimmer—Age 20, Olympic Gold Medalist
Age 41, Masters Gold Medalist

THE CHALLENGE NEVER ENDS

MURRAY ROSE
Swimmer—Age 17, Olympic Gold Medalist
Age 42, Masters Gold Medalist

Over the years, I've continued to work out, whether it's playing squash or running or doing calisthenics, but there's nothing that gives me the same feeling of well-being as swimming. I've found that since I resumed swimming, my life is a bit easier. I'm walking just a little more in tune with myself. I love to swim.

HERB ODOM
Boxer—Age 22, NCAA Champion
Age 48, Professional Welterweight

Yeah, I need to fight. It's nice to be somebody. I don't just want to be an unidentified object out there. What I love about boxing is the victory. You just don't know how good it feels when the referee grabs your hand and raises it and the announcer shouts, "The winnn-naaaaahhh." That doesn't happen often in life.

SAMUEL ULLMAN
American Writer

Youth is not a time of life; it is a state of mind. Nobody grows old by merely living a number of years, but to give up enthusiasm wrinkles the soul.

PETE ROSE
Major League First Baseman and Manager

I never think about my age. I let other people worry about it. Age is a state of mind. You can be old at 30 if you don't have enthusiasm and you can be young at 45 if you do.

JACK NICKLAUS
Professional Golfer

Back in 1978 and 1979, I was discouraged enough to think about quitting once in a while. But I didn't want to go out with two bad years. I decided it was time to get back to work. I improved my putting, flattened my swing plane slightly and regained distance off the tee. I have to find a balanced approach to my schedule that will enable me to continue playing and playing as well as possible. It's the only way I can be true to myself.

GARY PLAYER
Professional Golfer

As you grow older, you've got to make adjustments—for the body, eyes, mind, strength. I believe a man can play as well at 50 as he can at 30 if he makes these adjustments.

DOCTOR BILL YORZYK
Swimmer—Age 23, Olympic Gold Medalist
Age 48, Masters Gold Medalist

You go through all the stuff about how the training makes you feel better physically. And certainly it does, because I work better, I think better, I feel better, I feel younger. But I also like to win.

RED AUERBACH
NBA Coach, General Manager and Owner

You take a guy who's supposedly too old and if you instill his pride again and create desire, you can squeeze a good year or two out of him, maybe even more.

WOODY PEOPLES
NFL Offensive Guard

As I grow older, I have become more aware of my body and how to keep it in prime condition. I watch my weight and I train seriously. When I was younger, I didn't pay attention to the little things as I do now. I didn't think so much about what I was doing—or not doing. Today, I don't stay out late, and I don't drink alcohol.

TEDDY THOMAS
German Songwriter/Conductor

Why do they keep saying that he's too old? Have they looked at his body? Have they checked out his soul?

GEORGE BLANDA
NFL Quarterback/Kicker

I'm not crying because I know this is the end. I'm too old. If a team took me, they'd be nuts. But if they did, I'd go, I'd do it, and I'd be a winner.

CARL YASTRZEMSKI
Major League Outfielder/First Baseman

People who say ballplayers should go out on top are dealing with false pride; if you can help a club, you're valuable. Sure, I'd be the DH. But right now I feel good. I'm two pounds lighter at 178 than I was my rookie year. I haven't had any serious, wearing injuries. I never think about the day when I won't be able to play.

WILLIE SHOEMAKER
Professional Jockey

My latest success—it's been like a rejuvenation, a new beginning. I wish I could go on forever. I enjoy it. I enjoy riding today more than ever before. Because of the knowledge—what I know in bringing horses up to different races, what I've been through all these years—I know how to win. It's here that counts. Right now. Today. For me. I know my business; I know my game. And I love it.

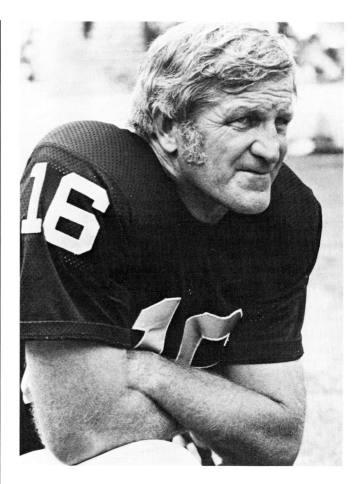

BOB YOUNG
NFL Offensive Guard

I lift weights and I play racquetball and I run wind sprints for endurance. I try to keep in shape by doing the same kind of thing I'd be doing on the football field.

My general advice for the masses of the older folk: "Look, most people in their thirties and beyond just sit back on their butts and do nothing. They have office jobs. Get active."

DOCTOR MANI SANGUILY
Swimmer—Age 23, Olympian
Age 48, Masters Gold Medalist

Swimming is valuable because it means that there is something else besides working every day, making a living, raising the children, paying the bills. It means that there is something that is mine, that I do for myself. It sounds egotistical, but doing what I do every day of the week of my life is not my own. I take care of people. In swimming, I feel that I'm doing something where I'm not used.

MUHAMMAD ALI
Professional Boxer

Age is whatever you think it is. You are as old as you think you are.

WILLIE STARGELL
Major League First Baseman and Coach

When I lose the desire to go out there every day, then I'll let some other excited youngster enjoy it. Until then, someone will have to take it away.

It's a shame that people dwell on age, because they give in to it. People said that I was washed up, but if I think I'm qualified to do something, nothing's going to hold me back. If I quit because I let someone influence me, it would eat my heart out.

DOCTOR GEORGE SHEEHAN
Cardiologist and Distance Runner

Interest in fitness has sparked a revelation of sorts. What has happened is that many middle age people have become athletes and in doing so have discovered unsuspected abilities. It is paradoxical that the time called "the age of narcissism" by some has given us the remarkable evidence of our energies, not just of the champion and the genius, but of the common man and woman.

MURRAY ROSE
Swimmer—Age 17, Olympic Gold Medalist
Age 42, Masters Gold Medalist

I'm convinced that with proper training I could break 17 minutes for the 1,500—something that I have never done in my youth.

The biggest plus now—besides improvements in the pools—would be psychological and more intense and scientific training methods. Since everyone is swimming so much faster today, you just know it's something that can easily be accomplished. Therefore, you program yourself to perform at a higher standard. Younger people are discovering that their bodies can do more, so older athletes are also more conscious of that possibility.

AL OERTER
Discus Thrower—
Four Time Olympic Gold Medalist

Age is a myth. Guys in their seventies can be just as strong as younger guys if they work at it. I no longer have the boundaries I once did. In my early thirties, I thought that I was at my peak and that it would be impossible to improve in the forties. Well, I'm in my forties and improving and now I think that progress will be difficult but not impossible in my fifties.

GAYLORD PERRY
Major League Pitcher

One of the reasons I've lasted this long is that I take care of myself. I don't smoke. And I keep in shape during the off-season doing a lot of hard work. You can play the game for a long time if you take good care of your body.

GORDIE HOWE
NHL Right Wing

I always felt that there was longevity in me. As for size, I was 204 pounds when I was 16 years old and that's the weight I played at throughout my career. You've got one body, so you better take care of it, and that takes sacrifice. You've got to love what you're doing. If you love it, you can overcome any handicap or the soreness or all the aches and pains, and continue to play for a long, long time.

I believe drug problems can be overcome. You must believe in yourself and believe that hard work pays off. I don't think a person has to use drugs. There is no substitute for hard work.

Young people need positive role models. I would like to be one. If you work hard, do all the workouts, it'll definitely show. Drugs is not where it's at. Hard work is.

You don't need to take drugs to win. If you take drugs to win, you're not a true champion.

**Florence Griffith Joyner, Sprinter —
Three Time Olympic Gold Medalist**

'Just Say No' — might be the hardest thing you will ever do at the time. But, it will be the most rewarding decision you will ever make. It will take guts to stand up to your 'friends', but it also takes guts to be a man and a leader. Only the weak will follow others' mistakes.

I honestly believe you will be a better person, both mentally and physically, by avoiding drugs of any kind. The effects of drugs might appear to help at first, but this help is very short-lived. Don't let your family and your real friends down. 'Just Say No.' You will be a far better person.

Curtis Strange, Professional Golfer

WHY AND HOW TO SAY NO

"Just Say No!" has become a very popular slogan. We all know what it means, but do we know WHY we should "Say No?" Do we really understand what cigarettes, alcohol, steroids, cocaine, crack, and marijuana do to our bodies?

In a few pages, we're going to do our best to inform you WHY you should "Say No." But before we do that, we're going to help you with HOW you can "Say No."

CONTROL YOUR OWN LIFE — BE SMART — DON'T START

It takes courage to stand up for what you believe in. Many people will try to influence you to do what they're doing — like smoking, drinking or taking drugs. Peer group pressure to conform is very strong, especially among young people. Peer pressure can be, and often is, the reason for initial use. Why? Defiance, experimentation and risk-taking are the main reasons. Plus, young people feel invincible — nothing will happen to ME, only to the OTHER person. This is a common and natural feeling. But it's a growth stage everybody goes through — until they see the real dangers of smoking, drinking or taking drugs.

If you really don't want to smoke, drink, do drugs or take steroids — then don't! If not for health reasons or for the impact they'll have on your performance, then don't do it because it's illegal. Have the courage of your convictions and "Just Say No." It's the only way YOU can control your own life and do things YOUR way.

It's very easy to just do what others are doing. It's less controversial. It's risky and it takes courage to "Say No." Too many people say, "I'll try just a little and then I'll quit." But what they don't realize is the very nature of these drugs is to diminish willpower and relax your inhibitions. Eventually, a little becomes a lot. Don't talk about moderation — no use is the only way. Ask yourself this very important question, "Am I really doing what I want to do, or am I just trying to be cool?" Answer honestly. Remember — you have to live with yourself, nobody else does.

HOW YOU CAN SAY NO

Some people want to "Say No" but don't want to offend their friends. They know what their friends are doing is wrong, but they just don't have the courage to tell them. Later on, we'll be talking about helping your friends because: (a) You care about them, and (b) they need you. I feel especially strong about this and I will tell you why.

For now, let me give you a little tip on how I've personally said "No" thousands of times in my life. I simply say, "No, thanks, I'm in training." I started doing this when I was in high school and really was in training for football, wrestling or baseball. My competitive days are over now, but since I work out every day I still consider myself to be in training.

It's MY body, MY life, and if I want to be in training — I'll be in training!

WHY AND HOW TO SAY NO

WHAT DO YOU NEED TO COVER UP?

Drug use is a cover-up for the problems and pressures you face in life. You don't solve any problems or relieve any pressure this way. What you do is create more problems and more stress in your life. The solution is to face up to these problems and get help, if needed.

Ask yourself these three questions:

- "Will smoking, drinking or taking drugs make me a better person?"
- "Are there any possible benefits for me in taking drugs, smoking or drinking?"
- "Will I become any smarter, stronger, quicker or faster if I take drugs, smoke or drink?"

The answers are obvious: NO.

Sometimes they may seem to have a temporary positive effect. But down the road, the end results are always the same — devastating.

So choose your friends carefully. It's better to stand firm in your convictions and be happy, than to go along with the crowd and be sorry. If your friends have lower standards than you, pull them up to your level; don't go down to theirs.

YOUR FRIENDS NEED YOU

Earlier in this book, we talked about leadership, teamwork and helping others. We talked about athletics and how you can be a leader, on AND off the playing field. How you can help your team win as well as help your teammates become better athletes.

But wait. Think about this. What's more important: Helping your team's running back score a touchdown by throwing a key block, or helping your teammate STAY ALIVE?

Is this a dramatic statement? Yes! Overly dramatic? No!

In the pages that follow, we'll be talking about why you should "Just Say No." Our facts, examples and stories are all dramatic. And true. I certainly can't see how anyone reading this book would ever smoke, drink or do drugs.

But that isn't enough — if you really care about your friends. We're not talking about what they can do for you, or the good times you have with them. Those things are important. But, we're talking about something a lot more important: Caring for them as a person.

True friends have the courage of their convictions to persuade each other to "Say No!" to cigarettes, alcohol and drugs. Let your friends know that alcohol and drugs destroy the ability to make rational judgments and slow one's reflexes. How can anyone perform as an athlete under these conditions?

Your friends may tell you they can quit whenever they want. That's a rationalization or excuse most people use frequently. The reality is that it's not true. The drug is more powerful than your friends' willpower or excuses.

So, when you tell your friends to "Just Say No," say it with conviction! You could be saving their lives, and that's a far better feeling than the one you get from throwing that key block.

How do I know?

I WATCHED MY BEST FRIEND KILL HIMSELF AND SAID NOTHING

My best friend was a heavy smoker. I saw him every day, but said NOTHING about cigarettes killing people. Why? I'll never know.

Maybe I thought lung cancer was for other people — not Frank — he was 6 feet, 2 inches tall and 220 pounds. He was a great athlete. Lung cancer couldn't get him.

Maybe I was ignorant of the dangers of cigarettes.

Maybe I didn't really have the courage of my convictions. I loved Frank. But did I love him enough to tell him?

This last question is one that I have to live with the rest of my life. It's been three years now, and I miss my best buddy more today than the day after he died. I respected Frank so much, and he respected me. There is no question in my mind that I could have persuaded him to kick the cigarette habit. Heck, the guy loved me. I'm a salesman. If I couldn't sell my best friend on something that would save his own life, what good am I?

If I had made the effort, Frank might be alive today. We could talk and laugh. I could rag on him, and he could tell me what an overrated coach I am. God, I miss him.

You don't have to follow your friends if you don't want to. You don't have to drop them either. What you can do is be a leader and help them. They need you.

WHO ARE YOUR REAL FRIENDS?

Some of your friends may try to influence you to do what they're doing, especially when it comes to smoking, drinking and doing drugs. What may appear to be usual peer group pressure may actually be a true test of friendship. "Real friends" will accept you for what you are, and they'll not try to change or force you to do things you don't want to do.

So, if you don't want to smoke — don't. If you don't want to drink — don't. And if you don't want to do drugs or steroids — don't. It's your life. You alone must decide.

I hope you don't think we're trying to turn this very important message into a test. But please take a minute to answer three more questions to determine how your "real" friends will treat you:

- Will those friends of mine who are always after me to compromise my convictions be around when I'm in trouble? Will they help me?
- If they have no convictions, will they have a strong character?
- If they don't have a strong character, will they be loyal?

THINK ABOUT IT.

"If you are under 18 years old, you have only lived about one-fourth of your life. That means you have the remaining three fourths of your life to accomplish anything you want. Don't blow it. Don't do drugs. If you are doing them, stop it. Get some help. If you haven't experimented with drugs, don't start. Give yourself a chance to succeed and be all the wonderful things you can be."

MICHAEL JORDAN, NBA Guard

CIGARETTES

OVER 50,000 AMERICANS...

have quit smoking cigarettes for a very good reason. Evidence accumulated in recent years has proven that what was once considered merely a bad habit is a major health threat.

Of the hundreds of chemicals found in cigarettes and "smokeless" tobacco, the most dangerous is nicotine. The Surgeon General of the United States has declared that nicotine is "an addictive drug," as addictive as cocaine.

THE HEALTH BENEFITS OF QUITTING

Surveys show that millions more smokers would like to quit but continue to smoke, because they think "the damage has already been done." This is one of the biggest myths connected with smoking.

The truth is you gain immediate health benefits when you stop smoking. Shortness of breath disappears. Your pulse and heartbeat return to normal. And your lungs and heart begin to repair themselves immediately.

SMOKERS DIE YOUNGER

The death rate of cigarette smokers is higher than that of nonsmokers for all ages. It climbs higher as the number of cigarettes smoked and the number of years smoking increases. The earlier you start, the longer you continue, the worse the damage.

Men who smoke less than half a pack per day have a death rate 60% higher than non-smokers; one to two packs a day increases it 90% higher; and two packs plus per day drives it to 120% higher than nonsmokers.

Cigarettes limit your potential as an athlete. The main reason for the deadliness of cigarettes is the many different diseases they cause.

HEART ATTACKS AND STROKES: Cigarette smokers have 50% more heart attacks than nonsmokers. Each year, nearly one million Americans die of heart attack, stroke and related disorders — more than all other causes of death combined.

LUNG CANCER: Uncommon among nonsmokers, it's the most frequent cause of death among cigarette smokers after heart attacks and strokes. It's directly related to the number of cigarettes smoked. Even mild smokers are seven times as likely to die of lung cancer as nonsmokers; moderate smokers 12 times, and heavy smokers 24 times.

SMOKING AND ATHLETES: Cigarettes drastically limit your potential as an athlete. Smoking leads to narrowing of the blood vessels which carry blood to leg and arm muscles. Constricted blood vessels allow less oxygen to get to muscle and brain cells. This gives you less endurance and less ability to concentrate.

OTHER CIGARETTE-RELATED CANCERS: Cancers of the mouth, larynx, urinary tract and pancreas are all high risk diseases caused directly by cigarettes.

FRANK WON'T EVER READ MY BOOK...HE'S DEAD

Before Frank died from lung cancer, he was many things to many people. He was one of the best wrestlers ever to come out of Ohio. He was a coach, a referee, a school teacher, a husband, a father, a grandfather and my best friend.

Frank was a best friend to a lot of people. He was a people person in the first degree. He was a great man. I guess you could say the only vice he had was his cigarettes. Those stupid cigarettes.

Frank's tremendous knowledge of wrestling, combined with his desire to help young men, is what brought him to St. Edward High School. He was my personal consultant and our wrestlers' best critic. Frank would come to our practices once every couple of weeks and tell me what our coaching staff was doing wrong. He'd come to meets and tournaments and do the same for our wrestlers. His comments were straight from the hip. He didn't always tell us what we wanted to hear, but he told us what we needed to know. Frank told it like it was, and our young men loved him for it. There was nothing phony about Frank. He was a man's man. He was as tough as they come, and he was as gentle as a lamb. He was the most honest and loyal man I have ever known.

I was with Frank just before he died. I'm glad that I was able to talk to and pray with him, but at the same time, the sight of my best friend — once six feet two inches tall — two hundred and twenty pounds — all man — lying helplessly in a hospital bed, is a sight that has stayed with me. It won't go away.

Those last days were the worst. My buddy was down to 120 pounds. His once dark hair was gone. His teeth began to turn orange. Frank's eyes, those strong, dark eyes, looked as though they were sunken six inches into his skull.

When he looked at his wife, son or me, it was a look of pleading. "Can't you guys help me? You're my buddies — please help me."

When they took Frank off pain killers, the fight was over. Despite what all the doctors had said, neither Frank nor I would admit that he was going to die. Dying was for other people, not for Frank.

But 100 pounds later, when the hair was gone — the teeth turning orange — Frank began crying out for help. The sounds were from a very strong man in a pain that was obviously worse than anything he had ever experienced.

Frank fought the battle as hard, as long, and as bravely as he possibly could. Then he died.

My buddy is gone. It's been three years now, and I still haven't accepted it. Every time we win a big wrestling match, I look for Frank's approval. But he's not there. Whenever I have a problem, I need Frank's advice. But, he's not there.

When I receive the first copy of this book, I'll want to give it to Frank. But I won't. He's not around any more. I won't ever see Frank again.

I'LL THINK ABOUT THIS.

FLORENCE GRIFFITH JOYNER

JACKIE JOYNER KERSEE

GREG LOUGANIS

MATT BIONDI

September, 1988
Seoul, South Korea

HOW MANY OF THESE OLYMPIC CHAMPIONS DO YOU THINK SMOKE?

THINK ABOUT IT

CARL LEWIS

STEVE TIMMONS

JANET EVANS

GREG BARTON

ALCOHOL

ALCOHOL IS A DRUG

Ethanol, the active ingredient in all beer, wine and liquor is a DRUG. Many people don't like to admit it, but it's true.

Alcohol is the single biggest drug problem in our country today. It kills more people than all other drugs put together. Nearly 575,000 people are either killed or injured each year in alcohol-related traffic accidents, an average of more than one per minute. Thousands more die from homicides or suicides directly or indirectly caused by alcohol. Alcohol is the leading cause of death among young people ages 16 to 24 nationwide.

WHY...

then do people drink substances that contain the deadly drug called ethanol? Do they drink because it tastes good? Don't they know how deadly it can be — how dangerous to themselves and others? Or do they know better and drink because in today's society, to some people it's "socially acceptable."

Let's discuss these three questions one at a time:

ONE — I LIKE THE TASTE

When I ask young people why they drink, the answer I receive the most often is, "I like the taste."

Unbelievable! Hog wash! The smell is obnoxious and the taste even worse. I'd like to go out on a limb and say that possibly one teenager in 1,000 actually likes the taste of his first drink.

The "I like the taste" answer simply doesn't cut it. A more honest answer would be: "I drink to be cool. To be funny. To be one of the boys (or girls). When I had my first drink, I thought it was horrible. So, I kept drinking until I ACQUIRED THE TASTE."

Imagine wanting to work to acquire the taste for a DRUG. That's sad. Really sad.

TWO — IT'S NOT DANGEROUS

Alcohol is a depressant — a drug that depresses and slows down the central nervous system. This includes the brain and nerve tissue involved in controlling thoughts, feelings and actions. When someone drinks more alcohol than the liver can filter, the extra alcohol builds up in the bloodstream, slows down the central nervous system and causes a loss of control.

Alcohol shuts off the brain centers. First your inhibitions go, then your speech and coordination, then your perception of speed and depth and eventually, all body functions. This can be fatal if you're driving a car. In addition, drunk drivers become bolder, more willing to take risks. Teenagers and young adults now cause 43% of all fatal alcohol-related automobile accidents.

THREE — IT'S SOCIALLY ACCEPTABLE

Unfortunately, many people feel this is true. But for myself and thousands of families across America that have been ripped apart — destroyed — because one member of the family was a drinker — the answer is NO!

As far as I'm concerned, there is nothing funny about anything a person who has been drinking says or does. It's just proof that the person is weak — too weak to handle his or her problems without taking a drug. Or not creative enough to have a good time, laugh or be funny without the help of drugs.

When I was young — many years ago — I made a promise that I would never embarrass my kids in front of their friends BECAUSE I USED DRUGS. And alcohol is a DRUG.

Socially acceptable? Maybe to some people, but not to your children or those you'll have someday and their friends. Not to the members of a family that was ripped apart because one of their loved ones drank. Not to the brothers, sisters, friends and parents of a teenager who was killed or crippled for life in a drinking-related accident.

I don't think any of these people think that drinking is "socially acceptable."

Neither do I.

ESCAPE FROM ALCOHOLISM FOR A BASKETBALL STAR

For Bob Lowrie, a flashy high school basketball star who helped his team win the state title, one day in 1982 will always serve as a vivid reminder of the pain alcohol can cause.

"A lot of it was peer pressure," he says. "I got involved with a crowd that at a young age appeared cool. But the alcohol overtook me."

Lowrie lost his college scholarship, dropped out of school and moved to California. "I got a job selling cars and continued to use alcohol and drugs. It got to the point where I didn't know who I was anymore.

"I was walking around this park where I played basketball as a kid. I felt so bad, so lost, that I actually contemplated suicide.

"Somehow, I made it through that day. I'll never forget it. I came home and there on TV was Tommy Kramer, Minnesota Vikings' quarterback, talking about alcohol abuse. He had just gotten out of a rehabilitation center. He was somebody I could relate to, and the very next day I called for help."

Unfortunately, Lowrie's story is not uncommon. But the fact that he survived is.

"The age at which people get involved with alcohol and drugs keeps getting younger and younger," explains Lowrie, now a counselor dedicated to helping kids overcome the same problems that destroyed part of his life. "In working with the kids, I relate my own experiences."

"It's scary," he says, "but in some cases, the parents are actually supplying the alcohol and drugs. There are so many young people who are afraid to ask for help. So they use this stuff to cover up the pain and depression."

"I have a conviction," Lowrie says. "If I can help just one kid stay away from drugs or alcohol for just one day, then I've accomplished something."

TEENS + DRINKING = TRAGEDIES

I've been coaching for 22 years now. During each one of these years, I have known about tragic traffic accidents involving teenagers under the influence of alcohol. I have either read about them, witnessed them, heard about them from a friend or watched them on television.

The most recent accident involved a member of the 1988 United States Olympic Team who was convicted of drunk driving. He has lost his career and his freedom, and two high school students lost their lives — because of his drunk driving.

Young healthy adults needlessly end up in wheelchairs or tragically lose their lives, because they drive when they have had too much to drink. The alcohol in their bodies slows down their reflexes and interferes with their judgment.

Most investigations of such accidents show that they probably would not have happened if the drivers had not been drinking.

I DIDN'T WANT TO BE DIFFERENT

When offered a ride in a tipsy friend's new car, Barb Eisenhardt did not hesitate. After all, the Kent State University freshman had driven drunk herself a few times. "I thought everybody did it." Besides, she hated to sound like a chicken. "I didn't want to be different." Now, four years later, Eisenhart is different. She rides in a wheelchair. And she plays a grim form of show-and-tell with students, bearing witness to the dangers of drinking while driving.

"The new car went only two miles before skidding off a curve and flipping upside down," Eisenhart recently told 1,700 teenagers at a day-long program sponsored by SADD (Students Against Driving Drunk). "As I lay in the car I said: Please, Lord, don't make me like the (handicapped) girls on the first floor of my dorm. "I knew how people looked at those in wheelchairs. I didn't want people looking at me that way." Today, Eisenhart lives on the floor for the handicapped.

When the rescue squad freed her arms, they flopped helplessly to her sides. Her spinal cord had been crushed. The night of the crash, doctors said Eisenhart would probably not live until morning, and that if she did, she'd be a quadriplegic. "I thought my life was over," Eisenhart recalls. "My parents and sister said, 'There's no way she's going to handle this.' " For eight weeks, Eisenhart's skull was screwed to a device that pulled with a constant 15-pound pressure. The nurses had to turn her upside-down from time to time, like a chicken on a spit. Her doctor and her family had to sit on the floor to talk with her.

Eisenhart spent 18 months in the hospital, followed by a year of outpatient therapy. She slowly regained some feeling and movement in her arms and legs. She warns teens about the false sense of security they have about drunk driving. "You read about it in the paper, about other kids at other schools. You think it isn't going to happen to me." The irony of the accident was that her friend, the driver, was only bruised. Eisenhart tries not to blame the driver: "I'm just as much at fault for getting in the car as she was for driving it."

THINK ABOUT IT.

BERNIE KOSAR
NFL Quarterback

I remember watching Dan Marino playing with the Dolphins when I was in college. I learned from watching him on the field. But I learned more things from him and other quarterbacks by watching them off the field — how they conducted themselves, how they felt about fame, the press, people's attitudes. I couldn't even think of using drugs or any other chemical substance. To me they're all the same — alcohol, drugs, steroids. I care about myself and I care about the young people who look up to me.

DAN MARINO
NFL Quarterback

You always have to be one step ahead of your opponent to win the game. Drugs and alcohol put you one step behind. How do you expect to win with such a handicap? 'Say No' to drugs and alcohol.

STEROIDS

We live in a society that enjoys and encourages instant gratification. Advertisers promise us youth, vitality, improved figures, better health and instant weight loss. We want these results, and we want them now. But where do we get these things? Can we simply buy them?

THERE ARE NO SHORTCUTS

Contrary to popular belief, a product that could produce these results is not on the market. But many athletes think it is and seek a shortcut to increased performance with anabolic steroids. In the 1988 Summer Olympics in Seoul, sprinter Ben Johnson had his Gold Medal taken away from him after he tested positive for anabolic steroids. The shame of it was, he won the 100 meter race by setting a new world record. His record was erased — a record he may never set again. And he lost his place in history.

Many people falsely believe that steroids will improve muscle tone and increase strength. While steroids may increase muscle mass, they do not necessarily increase strength. Furthermore, the health consequences include chronic illnesses such as heart disease, liver trouble, urinary tract abnormalities, sexual dysfunctions and a shortened life. Is the gamble worth it?

JACK LAMBERT DIDN'T

Jack Lambert, considered by many the NFL prototype middle linebacker, said he is proof football players do not need steroids.

"If anybody had an excuse to use steroids, it was me," said Lambert, who weighed only 215 pounds when he left Kent State.

"They told me when I was a senior in college I was a good player, but too small for the NFL."

"I had a choice. I could have taken steroids. But if I couldn't do it on my own, I figured it wasn't meant to be. Steroids are nothing but a shortcut."

Steroids "make you stronger and bigger, but whether they make you a better player, that's open to question," said Lambert.

"I was at a football camp in Cleveland and told the kids, 'I've been to nine Pro Bowls and four Super Bowls. I did it and I did it clean. Tell me why you should use steroids?'"

Lambert helped the Pittsburgh Steelers win four Super Bowls.

THE ADVERSE EFFECTS OF STEROIDS

Steroids are powerful drugs with questionable benefits that produce hazardous and potentially fatal side effects. There's no proof that respiratory or cardiovascular capacity is increased, or that performance is enhanced beyond that resulting from routine weight training and proper diet.

Steroids have long been known to promote violent, aggressive, bizarre behavior. A recent study of athletes who took steroids reveals one-eighth of them experienced a psychotic episode called "body-builders' psychosis."

They heard voices nobody else did, believed they could jump out third-story windows without harm and saw imaginary enemies. Steroid users exhibit other erratic behavior such as severe mood swings and neglect of school or work.

The most deceptive part of this frightening situation is that in male athletes, steroids may not even produce the quick gain in muscle mass they seek so desperately. They actually may be counter-productive to peak performance.

Recent research shows that steroids increase muscle mass and strength only in people who are already weight-trained, and who continue intensive training with high protein, high-calorie diets. And more significantly, any muscle gained by steroids may be offset by exposing athletes to greater risk of injury.

With the increase of steroid abuse, there comes an alarming number of dangerous side effects. Physically, these include ugly uncontrolled acne, liver cancer, cardiovascular problems, sterility, sexual dysfunction, shrinking of the testicles, enlarged and sometimes functional breasts in males, and deepening of the voice and increased growth of body hair in females.

Little is known about the effects of steroids in large doses, or the repeated use or long-term effects of steroids. We do know of more than 70 side effects linked to their use. We have covered the more serious ones here.

MR. AMERICA DID

"I knew the risk," Norman Rauch, a former Mr. America, said. "But, I thought, 'Those things only happen to the other guy. That could never happen to me.' Now I'm a walking time bomb!

I might live a long time. I might not. I don't know. But I have to live with the fact that I caused my own cancer by using steroids. The only way I can live with that is by talking to kids, warning them of the dangers, and telling them my story.

"I was a totally different person when I was on steroids. I was just terrible. I was rude. And nasty. My family was afraid of me.

"The pain I caused is what I regret the most. The pain I inflicted on the people I love most. My dad always used to say, 'There's no shortcut, kid.' Boy, was he right! Thank God my dad never knew I took steroids — he died before I went public. It would have crushed him if he knew.

"My lesson is simple: I took steroids. Don't you do it. It cost me two marriages. It cost me my sport. And, I guess, it's gonna cost me my life. It's bad news! That's my message to you."

GIVEN THE FACTS, WHY WOULD ANYONE EVEN THINK OF USING STEROIDS?

Why? Because most young people simply don't think the complications will happen to them. The steroids are available, and they are cheap. People want them, and they can get them. How are you going to tell an 18-year-old who's watching his buddies put on 30 pounds of muscle, that he's going to have heart problems when he gets older?

Hey, he's 18; he thinks he's invincible. Think you're going to convince him? Good luck!

Young people want everything and they want it right now. They don't want to wait for tomorrow. They could achieve the same gains in strength slowly, permanently, and naturally through weight training. But they don't want to hear that.

The truth is that if they're patient they will make progress. And, unlike the athlete who's using steroids, they won't have to worry about the damage they're doing to their bodies.

The bottom line is they'll win and they'll be healthy.

WINNING WITHOUT STEROIDS ADDS SATISFACTION TO ATHLETES' VICTORIES

Andre Phillips won a gold medal at the 1988 Summer Olympics and established himself as the world's premier 400-meter hurdler. Viewed in the narrow context of one race, it was a major victory.

But because Phillips resisted the temptation to supplement his training regimen with banned substances, such as anabolic steroids, he says he experienced an even stronger feeling of personal triumph.

"I've thought about using steroids. If I said I haven't ever thought about it, I'd just be wrong," Phillips says. "All I know is that I've decided I want to see my kids grow up. I don't want to die when I'm 40.

"The real question is: Do I want to screw around with steroids for a few years of great achievements? Or do I want to do what I always said I was going to do, which is to be drug-free, to be safe."

Anabolic steroids become an option for some because, when combined with training, they hasten the growth of muscle tissue, increase strength and add bulk. But steroids are not the only option.

Synchronized swimmer Tracie Ruiz-Conforto, a two-time gold medalist in Los Angeles and a silver medal winner in Seoul, drew double-takes a couple of years ago when she came out of retirement. A convert to natural bodybuilding, she was leaner and more muscular than ever.

"Basically, with good hard work, a good trainer and proper nutrition, you can look the same as these people who do it with steroids," Ruiz-Conforto says.

"Diet and nutrition are the great equalizers for athletes hoping to keep pace with steroid users," says Dr. Herbert Haupt, a St. Louis steroids expert. Haupt recommends a high-carbohydrate diet with vegetables, pasta, and fruits as primary foods; carbohydrates should account for 70 percent of the athlete's diet.

"With the proper training techniques, you can do it. You can increase size and strength naturally," Haupt says, "You don't have to rely on a drug. The process is a little bit slower, but it's permanent."

THINK ABOUT IT.

MATT BIONDI
Swimmer — Five Time Olympic Gold Medalist
Just watching Olympian Michael Gross win all those medals made me realize the steroids are not needed for success. I knew I could do it on my own. Hard work is the answer. There is no other way.

JANET EVANS
Swimmer — Three-Time Olympic Gold Medalist
I knew some people who have gone to steroids. Maybe it does make them stronger and swim faster. But for me there was no way I would use them. I just spent a little more time in the pool — worked a little harder.

HOWIE LONG
NFL Defensive End

Steroids are a long-term problem. In some cases, they're a shorter term problem than you might think. One weightlifter I knew died with a twenty-three pound liver. It's sad. I can't push enough for the testing and banning of steroid use. I don't need to take steroids. I roll out of bed at a hard-worked 275 pounds.

DR. ROBERT VOY
Chief Medical Officer, U. S. Olympic Committee

Is the prize worth the price? In some cases, you might not even be around to pick up the prize.

DR. RICHARD EASTMAN
Director of Endocrinology, Georgetown University Hospital

The thought of guys taking huge amounts of steroids and engaging in contact sports is frightening.

I have never prescribed steroids. I can't imagine any reputable physician prescribing this stuff.

JOSE CANSECO
Major League Outfielder

All the allegations of my steroid use are ridiculous. What people have failed to see is all the hard work I've had to put in to correct my limitations. I've spent hours working on my stroke, my concentration and my patience at the plate. I'm proud that my accomplishments have been because of hard work. I think that when you take drugs to help your performance, you only cheat yourself, because it isn't your ability that gets you where you are.

ALAN FRIED
Wrestler — Four Time National High School Champion

I have things to do, goals to meet. I guess you could call them dreams. I know what I have to do in order to give myself a good chance to live my dreams.

I'm going to work as I've never worked before. The college boys will be big so I'll be pumping a lot of iron. Steroids, you've got to be kidding. That's just stupid. Why would I want to work as hard as I do and put something like that in my body. Heck, I don't even drink pop.

TONY MANDARICH
NFL Offensive Tackle

Everybody's looking for the easy way out. How many guys squat till they puke? I do. I go to the breaking point and beyond.

No, I've never used steroids. All the allegations of my use is ridiculous. I'm insulted by all the rumors. I take pride in all the hard work I put in. I would be cheating myself if I let a substance (steroids) take the credit for my body.

GREG LOUGANIS
Diver — Four Time Olympic Gold Medalist

I don't understand what goes through all those athletes' minds. It doesn't make any sense. I mean — why do they do it? Why do they use steroids? Are they afraid of hard work?

COCAINE, CRACK, MARIJUANA

When cocaine killed basketball star Len Bias in June, 1986 many people probably thought, "Well, at least now we've got some straight facts on this particular drug."

It was a shock, of course. On one hand, there was Bias, a gifted, apparently clean-living, young athlete who had just signed a multi-million dollar contract with the Boston Celtics.

On the other hand, there was the drug.

Only 40 hours after he was chosen by the Celtics as their second draft pick, Bias, 22, was dead from cocaine. Larry Bird of the Celtics called the death of Bias, "the cruelest thing I've ever heard."

It was cruel because everything Len Bias had ever dreamed of had come true. His death was ironic because he was not a known drug user. In fact, Bias tried to avoid drugs. But in that one moment of weakness, he decided his own fate. There wouldn't be any more cheering crowds or championship rings — just 2,000 mourners at his funeral who couldn't believe what had happened.

For years, we had been told that cocaine was relatively "safe" and "non-addictive." It had become famous as the "recreational" drug of the rich and the movie stars.

Then, the Celtics' newly-signed young prince took a hit of cocaine. And suddenly, he was dead.

"What a waste!" people said. "But at least we know now that cocaine is a killer."

The expectation was that Bias' death would help save others from making the same mistake. People thought cocaine addicts would wake up and seek help for themselves, and occasional users would avoid it. There was a clear message to his death.

A message anyone could hear.

Or would they?

What if some people didn't hear?

What if they couldn't hear?

What if they couldn't hear because cocaine is different, a special kind of drug? What if the effect of taking cocaine is so unique that a user would go on taking it even when he knew it could cause his death?

Cocaine is that special. It's effects are that unique.

Cocaine, we're firmly convinced, is the most dangerous drug of them all. The members of the Len Bias family are equally certain.

COCAINE: THE HIGHER YOU GO, THE FARTHER YOU FALL

Cocaine comes from the cocoa bush located in the Andes Mountains of South America. Its leaves are soaked in a mixture of chemicals until they break down into the cocaine salt or crystals.

Cocaine is one of the most powerful, seductive and sought-after drugs today. It makes users feel sociable, confident and in control. The drug blocks appetite and erases fatigue. For many, it is thought of as the ideal '80s performance-booster.

Cocaine triggers intense pleasure signals in the brain of joy, alertness and talkativeness that last anywhere from five to 30 minutes. This results in a rapid increase in the heart rate and blood pressure. This "high" is short-lived, leaving the user feeling anxious, depressed, tired or exhausted. It's at this "low" point that many people use pot, valium or alcohol to ease the pain, while the heavy users seek more cocaine. Continued heavy usage brings hallucinations, suspicion, paranoia and other serious mental problems. Taken frequently, cocaine can cause convulsions and death.

Very few people understand even the most basic facts about cocaine. Chemically, cocaine is a double-acting drug:

- It's a stimulant that lights up the central nervous system like a short-circuiting pinball machine.
- It's an anesthetic that numbs whatever tissue it touches.

HOW DANGEROUS IS COCAINE? IT KILLS

Just eight days after Len Bias' tragedy, cocaine killed safety Don Rodgers of the Cleveland Browns. Rodgers was an All-American at UCLA as well as the AFC Defensive Rookie of the Year in 1984.

Like Bias, Rodgers was not considered a drug user. He, too, had a moment of weakness in which he used cocaine; and it killed him.

Kenny Easley, former teammate of Rodgers at UCLA, put this horrible event into grim words: "I was supposed to be a groomsman for his wedding on Saturday. Now I will be a pallbearer at his funeral on Thursday."

COCAINE CAN KILL YOU, TOO

Physically, cocaine sends the body into overdrive, boosting heart rate, blood pressure and body temperature. Unlike most other drugs, cocaine creates a racing heartbeat and a fierce nervous sweat. But it's more than just nerves. Cocaine unleashes a sudden jolt of stimulation that can result in serious health problems, such as:

STROKE: Nowadays, it's not unusual to see a cocaine user who is suffering from the effects of a stroke. A cocaine-induced stroke can lead to massive brain damage or permanent paralysis.

HEART ATTACK: Stimulation of the heartbeat and blood pressure can also cause users to have a classic heart attack. Many users report experiencing a pounding heart and chest pain when they are high on the drug. This indicates a problem with heart circulation that is made worse by the use of cocaine.

BRAIN HEMORRHAGE: A cocaine-triggered rise in blood pressure can rupture weakened blood vessels in the brain.

RESPIRATORY ARREST: This becomes a possibility, particularly with smokable forms of cocaine.

UNCONTROLLED BEHAVIOR: The heart beats faster. The sweat flows. The brain goes haywire. The cocaine user has no clue as to what is happening. Suicide is often the result.

BODY BURN-OUT: Long-term cocaine use causes the body to burn itself out. Insomnia, weight loss and malnutrition are early signs.

CRACK — THE NEW COCAINE

Crack — or "rock" cocaine — is the new, smokable form of the drug that suddenly seems everywhere. This extremely popular drug provides users with a relatively cheap, instant high. For good reason, it has the reputation of possibly being the most dangerous drug on the street.

Crack is similar to another form of smokable cocaine called "freebase", which is the drug that killed comic John Belushi. Because crack is smoked as a vapor, while ordinary cocaine is sniffed as a powder, its effect is immediate and much more intense than ordinary cocaine — and often overwhelming for users.

COCAINE DEPENDENCY

Psychologically, young people are at a high risk of having drug-related problems because of their immaturity and peer group pressure. Cocaine is one of the most addictive drugs of all — and one of the hardest drug habits to shake. It's so powerful that you become almost instantly addicted, due to its extreme stimulation.

Most people who try cocaine with any regularity will get hooked on the drug. In lab tests done with mice and monkeys, the animals rejected all other drugs in favor of cocaine. Once they started taking it, they couldn't stop. Every single animal tested overdosed and died. This drug is too dangerous to even try.

Symptoms of mild cocaine dependence include suspiciousness, anxiety, irritability and insomnia. Symptoms of longer-term dependence include extreme paranoia, compulsive behavior, hallucinations, loss of sense of self and lack of self-control. Problems with schoolwork, a lack of motivation, and social withdrawal are symptoms of teenage cocaine abuse. Supporting one's habit can lead to drug running, stealing and prostitution (happens with both males and females).

MARIJUANA AND POTHEADS

Marijuana has been called everything from "killer weed" to "pot", "grass" and "reefer." Of the 460 different chemicals in marijuana, the powerful, mind-changing drug, THC, is the most dangerous. We're not sure of all the effects marijuana has on our bodies. But we do know that most of the chemicals stay in the body for a month after use.

Most people use pot to get a "buzz" — just like with alcohol. It's used to cover up personal problems. But instead of solving any problems, pot just creates more. Soon you feel you need another joint. The momentum builds. You feel depressed when you're not high, so you smoke more. You become dependent. Now you're a pothead! You lose your drive and ambition. You become apathetic. You lose what it takes to be a winner.

Are we going to allow these "street drugs" to take over our society? Are we (you) that soft? It's stupid to put a drug into your body that does not have one positive effect and has been proven to be extremely harmful. In fact, IT KILLS. I guess you could say that's pretty extreme.

THINK ABOUT IT.

KAI HAASKIVI
MISL Midfielder and Head Coach

When the talk turns to drugs, do yourself a favor and give yourself a chance in the game of life. It does take a lot of courage, but say "NO" to drugs and be an instant winner.

BERNIE JAMES
MISL Defenseman

If you want to reach your goals in life even if they don't involve sports, avoid drugs and alcohol and you'll have a greater chance of achieving them.

RORY SPARROW
NBA Guard

I get tired and depressed, and sometimes it's a struggle to maintain optimism in a pessimistic society.

But then, just as quickly, I remember what I was put on this earth for. I look at life every day as a gift and a challenge. If I can help one youngster — every day of my life — to stay away from drugs, I will feel good about myself. It's an old adage, but it's a true one, what you get in life you should give back.

DALE MURPHY
Major League Outfielder

We must have the courage and strength to stand up for high standards. Have the courage to say no. Standards are essentials of success, and no apology should ever be made for living a Christian, drug-free life. If you live what you believe, you will always have the respect of others.

ISIAH THOMAS
NBA Guard

Athletes are role models. We should take advantage of that opportunity and make other people's lives better. Cigarettes, alcohol, steroids, drugs — how can any of these make anyone's life better?

DOC EDWARDS
Major League Manager

There is no way any athlete whether he's a professional or amateur can play up to his full potential under the influence of drugs. Drugs lie to him, he may think he's doing well but he's not. He just isn't and that's a fact.

CHARLES BARKLEY
NBA Forward

I rely on my God-given talents. If I fail or succeed, I do so on my own. Temptation to experiment with various substances will always be there. You have to be above it. You have to be smarter. Smart enough to realize that it can only hurt you and your body. It takes guts to be a leader and not a follower. 'Say No' and feel good about it and good about yourself.

DWIGHT GOODEN
Major League Pitcher

The hardest thing I've ever done in my life was facing my folks and telling them about my use of cocaine. My little boy was there, too. I couldn't believe that I had risked my life, the life and love of my son and the respect of my parents for a few cheap thrills.

PETER UBERROTH
Major League Baseball Commissioner

Somebody has to say 'enough is enough' about drugs. Baseball is going to accomplish this. It's a tiny, little segment of society, but we're going to remove drugs and be an example.

LARRY BROWN
NBA and College Basketball Coach

I feel the easiest way to avoid a problem with drugs is to never begin. If that door is never opened, there is no worry about recovery or damage to body or spirit. To have complete control of one's life is the greatest feeling!

BOB GRIES
Businessman, NFL Owner and Ultra Marathon Runner

Drugs must be purged from sports. Performance enhancing drugs are unfair to those who are too smart to risk the serious physical side effects. Every athlete deserves a level playing field.

GREG SWINDELL
Major League Pitcher

Drugs aren't for winners. I've been a winner by staying away from drugs. As soon as you turn to drugs you become a loser. Nobody wants to be a loser.

PAUL MOLITOR
Major League Second Baseman

I tried drugs when I was young. Why, I'm not sure. Probably the two main reasons were peer pressure — trying to fit in — and avoiding my problems. It was a big mistake. Drugs get you nowhere. Make a stand. Meet life head on, straight! Be a leader.

RON HARPER
NBA Guard

By selling or using drugs, some kids try to take a shortcut to get rich. It's easier to get rich the right way — by staying in school and working hard. If you sell or do drugs, you die early.

DOUG JONES
Major League Pitcher

I can't believe that anybody would expect to improve their performance by taking drugs. Or have any inclination towards being a better athlete through the use of drugs. If you can't do it on your own, then you don't have any business playing sports.

BARRY SANDERS
NFL Running Back

I know I have an opportunity to be a positive influence on young people. I have never used drugs. I don't drink. I try to study hard and stay out of trouble. I want to set an example.

MATT NYKANEN
Ski-Jumper — Olympic Gold Medalist

I finally realized that I had to stop drinking to avoid messing up my future.

JIM RODGERS
NBA Coach

By 'Saying No' to alcohol, cigarettes and other drugs, you're telling the world that, yes, you want to be the best that you can be!

DALE MURPHY
Major League Outfielder

I think athletes should be role models and accept that responsibility. It sounds hokey, but what else are you going to say? The reality is that kids are going to look up to us, and if you're in the public eye you do have a responsibility. Kids emulate their idols. Therefore, we have a responsibility to live a clean life and 'Say No' to drugs, including alcohol.

JANET EVANS
Swimmer — Three Time Olympic Gold Medalist

Most teenagers figure that if they don't do what other people do, they won't be accepted. If you like yourself, it doesn't matter what anyone else thinks.

KEVIN JOHNSON
NBA Guard

Many of my friends from home have been sent to jail for drugs. But I didn't want to end up like that. I wanted to make something out of my life. I would go to the gym every night to practice. Once the janitor said, 'It's Saturday night. Why aren't you out at the parties like everybody else?' I said, 'Parties won't take me where I want to go.'

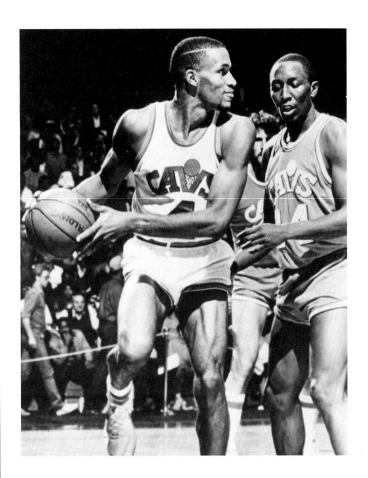

RODNEY PEETE
NFL Quarterback

Whether we want to be or not, we are role models to impressionable kids. We have to take that responsibility. I don't do drugs and I don't drink. I suppose I could have a beer once in a while but I would never want a young kid to see me drinking.

JOE CARTER
Major League Outfielder

In baseball as in real life, there are winners and losers. When you're involved with drugs or alcohol there are no winners. Eventually you will always be a loser. Drugs are a menace to society. Drugs are giving our youth a false impression of what life can really be. It's taking away all their dreams and hopes besides the reality of losing their loved ones.

JOE GIBBS
NFL Coach

Never compromise on anything that would allow you to become less than what you were put on this earth to be. There are times when being selfish about your ideals is an asset.

BOB COSTAS
Sports Broadcaster

I have never encountered a successful athlete who claimed that drugs or alcohol enhanced their lives in any long-term sense. The smart ones, the truly self-assured ones, avoid them from the start — those who get smart later, end up deeply regretting the game of Russian Roulette they played with their lives and careers. If you believe only one thing you hear from your parents, teachers and other adults, let it be this — don't do drugs. Don't abuse alcohol. Nobody's kidding you here. No one who cares about you would give you any other advice.

BOBBY KNIGHT
College and U.S. Olympic Basketball Coach

Each of us is free to make up our minds as to what's best for us as individuals. The worst thing that any one of you young people can ever say is 'I did it because the other kids did it.'

The 'absolute' best word in the English language for you kids ever to learn is 'No.' No, I won't. No, I can't. No, I don't. No, I'm not. And if that doesn't work, you can call me and I'll give you a couple of stronger words you can use.

You are a heck of a lot more important to you than anybody else is, and you have to learn to take care of you, because you can change it to yes if you should; but, it is darn difficult to change 'yes' to 'no'.

CARL F. HUGHES
Businessman

After any success, a winner gives credit to those who taught and encouraged him to work hard. Did you ever hear a winner give credit to drugs? Of course not. Drugs are a message from losers.

CARL LEWIS
Sprinter, Long Jumper — Six Time Olympic Gold Medalist

There are three things to remember about drugs. The first is that if you take drugs, you'll never know your full potential; second, there is the obvious health risk; and third, if you do drugs, you're quitting on yourself.

REGGIE WILLIAMS
NFL Linebacker and Politician

There's always time to demonstrate to other people, especially your friends, that you care. Have the courage of convictions not only to say no to drugs, but help your friends to have the courage to say no. One moment of caring can set in motion a whole series of events, that can have a positive impact on someone's life. It isn't enough to say no for yourself. Help your friends say no.

JIM CARNEY, JR.
Businessman

Success is the biggest possible high.

PAT RILEY
NBA Coach

Develop a philosophy about yourself, your attitude and the basic truths and values that should help you 'Say No.' Believe and commit yourself to that philosophy.

Demand discipline from your parents and teachers when needed. Your 'right' philosophy could be tested.

Do things right! Have a plan how to 'Say No.'

Do things well! Take pride in 'Saying No.'

Do things the same way all the time through repetition.

It's your attitude that 'Says No.'

BRIAN BRENNAN
NFL Wide Receiver

The reason I never tried drugs is simple. If you try them and like them, two things can happen. One, you go to jail, and two, you die!

DOUG WILLIAMS
NFL Quarterback

If I ever needed an excuse to be an alcoholic or a drug head, my wife's death was it. You never get used to death. But somehow I was strong enough to overcome it.

Through all the frustration in my life I've realized it could have been worse. I have a lot more than most people. I've been lucky and blessed. Thank God I found the courage to 'Say No.'

MIKE SCOTT
Major League Pitcher

Don't strike out with drugs. Remember, alcohol is a drug, too. Get the big hit. Stay away and control your life.

OZZIE NEWSOME
NFL Tight End

The death of my teammate, Don Rogers, a few years back should send the message loud and clear; but our society is still plagued by drug abuse. I have a great deal of concern for our youth who succumb to peer pressure. Losing some friendships (are they really friendships?) can only lead to victory and self-esteem. Our world will depend on our youth some day, and it's up to them to realize that drug abuse can only lead to the ruination of their lives and the lives of their loved ones.

STEROIDS — THE DRUG OF LOSERS
As Told By TOMMY CHAIKIN

I was sitting at The Roost, the athletic dorm at the University of South Carolina, with the barrel of a loaded .357 Magnum pressed under my chin. My finger twitched on the trigger. I was in bad shape, very bad shape. All from the steroids. It had all come down from the steroids, the crap drug I took to get big and strong and aggressive so I could play this game that I love.

I'd lost control of everything — it's impossible to describe the horror I felt. The fear. The anxiety over my loss of control. Suicide was always on my mind.

At first, I said no way was I going to mess with something as risky as steroids. I was going to build myself up naturally. Then I saw how well the guys on steroids were doing. They looked fine to me. They were happy; they seemed to have normal sex lives. They were a hell of a lot bigger than I was. Maybe it was time for me to join the crowd. I also felt that nothing bad could happen to me. I was young. I was invincible. So I decided to take steroids to get big and strong and aggressive.

People who say that steroids don't work, don't know what they're talking about. You've got to experience it to know what I mean. Your muscles swell, they retain water and they just grow.

But besides the muscle growth, there were other things happening to me. I got real bad acne on my back, my hair started to come out, I was having trouble sleeping and my testicles began to shrink. However, the worst thing that happened was psychological. I was becoming like an animal. Guys started calling me 'Quasi-bloato' and 'The Experiment', because they thought I'd take anything. They were right.

I was also going through a personality change. I was becoming a hard-ass, one of the meanest guys on the team. Images of violence often filled my mind. I'd drive alone and find myself thinking about sick things, like crushing people to death and tearing off their limbs. I'd be grinding my teeth and gripping the wheel so hard, that my arms would hurt. This hadn't been my way, but it had become my way. Steroids ruled my life and controlled me.

My aggressiveness was out of control. I was cheap-shotting people in practice, clotheslining them, ripping scout team quarterbacks' helmets off in non-contact drills. One night I pulled a shotgun on the pizza delivery boy, threw him down and put the gun to his face. It was loaded and I could have blown the kid all over the floor. It was the kind of thing I thought was funny then.

After the second year I was on steroids, I started to battle anxiety attacks that I knew were caused by the steroids. I sat in my room for hours just trying to hold on to reality. I was too afraid to go outside — I was so paranoid. I couldn't read because I couldn't concentrate. Thoughts of suicide started coming into my mind regularly.

Finally one day in class, I felt the room start to sway. I staggered out of the class and down the stairs, even though they seemed to be moving. I weaved past people, but I couldn't hear anything. I got outside and I lost control of my bladder and my bowels. I urinated and defecated all over myself. I was praying to God I could make it to my car. Somehow I got there, drove back to the dorm, showered and laid down in bed. That was the end. I couldn't do anything. I couldn't practice. It was over.

People ask me why I'm talking about my troubles. I just want people to know that steroids change you in many ways, and the psychological changes are the most drastic of all. I've seen so many players become brutal and mindless from steroid use. Look what happened to me.

I take no drugs now, not even aspirin. I still have problems with my vision, but the doctor says that should pass with time. The whooshing in my ears is probably there forever. I can't deal with physical stress the way I used to, and I can't exercise too aggressively or I get terrible headaches. My balance isn't what it used to be, and I still feel edgy. I can't work full time because some days I have to rest. I'm not well. Steroids screwed me up pretty good. Maybe you have to be a little crazy to play football, but you have to be crazier to take steroids — THEY'RE THE DRUG OF LOSERS!

THE FOLLOWING 12 MESSAGES ARE FROM HIGH SCHOOL WRESTLERS. NOT ONE WORD HAS BEEN EDITED FOR PUBLICATION IN THE EDGE, WHICH MAKES WHAT FOLLOWS ALL THAT MORE MEANINGFUL.

JASON — SENIOR

It isn't all that simple to 'Just Say No', even though NO is only two letters long. It is a matter of will power. Teenagers just drink to be cool. They don't drink because they like the taste. Maybe they drink for the buzz, but I've learned that fun never really came for me when I smoked marijuana or drank. It just caused trouble with my family, school and friends. I'm glad that I stopped drinking and smoking pot because now I'm myself, not just a mask of alcohol or drugs. It just isn't good for a person to use chemical, mood-altering substances. I don't see how anyone could answer this question unless they didn't drink or do drugs at one time in their life.

MIKE — SENIOR

You must decide whether you want to do something or you don't want to do it. Then you must make a stand and stick to it. If you don't want to drink and someone asks you if you want a beer, don't be weak and say, 'Maybe later'. Make a stand and say, 'No, thanks. I don't drink.'

CRAIG — JUNIOR

It's easier to 'Just Say No' than you think. If you're sure of who your friends are, and if they are the people you can depend on, then you should take the initiative to gain their respect and be an example that others can really have courage to gain from. You'll be a much happier person because it allows for greater freedom of who you are and how you want to live your life. Once you've gained and earned respect, it takes courage on the part of others to oppose what has made you a respected person.

PAT — SENIOR

Everyone wants to succeed in life, to do great things and to be the best person possible. Taking drugs will not help any aspect of a person's life, so why take them? Looking at it this way, 'Saying No' is the only answer that makes sense. It takes courage and self-confidence not to give in to peer pressure. Those persons with enough self-assurance to 'Say No' will feel better about themselves and will have the respect of their peers.

RICH — SENIOR

The main thing to remember is to be true to yourself. You can fool the whole world, but you can never fool yourself. Have the courage to stand by your convictions. If you do not want to smoke, drink or take drugs, then don't. Your true friends will not abandon you, nor will they try to force you to compromise your beliefs. They will respect you for keeping your convictions, which will allow you to have respect for yourself.

DAVE — SENIOR

You 'Say No' by not giving in to peer pressure. It's your choice to 'Say No' and you should stand up to what you believe. Don't go along with the crowd. You 'Say No' because drugs are dangerous to your health. You never know what kind of bad reaction drugs can cause. They never help you. Drugs only hurt you!

JOE — JUNIOR

The message I give to my peers deals with the fact that our ultimate goal is to succeed not only in wrestling, but in life. To succeed you have to become quicker, stronger and smarter. Drugs can not, in any way, give you these attributes. Eventually, drugs can only hurt you. Don't lose out. Learn to 'Say No' now.

JEREMIAH — SENIOR

You have to choose what you feel is right. If you cannot 'Say No' without your peers respecting that, then they are really not your friends. You should 'Say No' just out of respect. That is, respect for your body, respect for values and respect for yourself.

ADAM — JUNIOR

The number one excuse why kids don't 'Say No' is because of peer pressure. That's a copout for saying you don't have the self-confidence to stand up to those peers. Real friends won't make or pressure you into doing something you don't want to. No matter what users try to say, there is nothing good about any drug, including alcohol. Every drug can kill or seriously harm you. The risk isn't worth it. If you don't care what happens to your body and mind, just think about what it can do to the lives of others, like your loved ones who don't want to see you throw your life away just to fit in, or the person and his family whom you injure or kill because you were drunk driving. Could you live with yourself? Why take the risk? 'Just Say No.'

ALAN — SENIOR

The way to 'Say No' is simply with a smile on your face. Say 'No, thank you' and react naturally if abnormally pressured. You 'Say No' because this is your only body, and even if you are not an athlete, you should respect it and keep it healthy until the day you die, which will come much later if you control yourself now.

RAY — JUNIOR

To 'Say No' to someone who offers you beer or drugs, says you have guts and a brain. Drugs are mindless. They destroy your brain and ruin your life. If someone offers you something, look right in their eyes; so they really know you mean it and say 'No, thanks.'

BRIAN — JUNIOR

Peer Pressure is the big thing with teenagers today. I would have to say that it is the major reason why kids use controlled substances. But I don't think the kids realize (or at least some), how dangerous alcohol and marijuana are. The main reason why to 'Say No' is because of the damages these things can do to your health. It kills brain cells, causes cirrhosis of the liver or lung cancer. Why would anyone want to purposely do this to himself? How to 'Say No' comes from a person's own willpower, and how much he respects his body.

MY FINAL PLEA

HEART PROBLEMS, CANCER, VIOLENT BEHAVIOR — NOT ME, I'M TOO YOUNG — I CAN ALWAYS QUIT WHEN I GET OLDER

When I wrote this last chapter, I asked for and received a great deal of help. I asked several of my closest friends, our assistant coaches, the St. Edward wrestlers and alumni, our principal, my daughters, my nephew and my sister for their input.

I asked them to help me get these messages across to my readers. I wanted to help people. I wanted my readers to get something out of this very special chapter. I wanted my readers to really think about what they had just read. I wanted to make my own little contribution to society. I sincerely hope that I have.

If I haven't quite done the job that I set out to do, then I guess I'll have to try a little harder.

Please take just a couple of minutes to read my final plea.

CIGARETTES, ALCOHOL, MARIJUANA, STEROIDS AND COCAINE

Question: What do they have in common?

Answer: They can all kill you.

Answer: There is not one positive benefit that you can get from any one of them.

Answer: On the way to killing you, they all have a long list of extremely harmful, painful, embarrassing and ugly side effects.

Answer: They're all addictive! No, you can't just up and quit after awhile. They are powerful, habit-forming drugs. You use them for awhile and you're no longer in control of your own life. You are hooked.

If you use any of them, you're an alcoholic, a pot head, a zit face, an impotent muscle head or a druggie — whatever.

As a user, you've lost your identity. Your freedom. Your pride. Your confidence. You're hooked — which means you're DEPENDENT ON A CHEMICAL SUBSTANCE.

Think about it. Believe me, this is true. I tell my wrestlers that there are two types of people in the world — smart people and stupid people — please don't be a stupid one!

Take one half hour out of your life for YOU. No one else, just you. Flip back a few pages to the beginning of this chapter. Read what I have written. With the help of my friends and family, I worked very hard on these words. I'm not a great writer, but I care a great deal. I want you to stay alive. What we're talking about can not only be very harmful to you IT CAN KILL YOU. After you have read my words, please read the messages from the famous personalities who were exposed to every drug known to mankind, but had the courage to "Say No."

Read their messages a second time. Close your eyes and picture them winning gold medals, scoring touchdowns, hitting home runs — being champions in life!

Can they all be wrong?

THINK ABOUT IT.

INDEX OF QUOTATIONS

ARTISTS:
Henri, Robert ... 3-32
Michelangelo ... 2-6, 3-6
Rogers, J. R. ... 7-25
Simmons, Edward C. ... 3-31

AUTO RACING:
Andretti, Mario ... 2-26, 7-41
Clark, Jim ... 5-30
Fittipaldi, Emerson ... 4-38
Foyt, A. J. ... 2-32, 5-48, 5-62
Guthrie, Janet ... 5-58
Jones, Parnelli ... 3-10, 6-30
Mears, Rick ... 5-21
Stewart, Jackie ... 4-12
Unser, Al ... 5-4
Unser, Jr., Al ... 4-34

BASEBALL:
Aaron, Hank ... 3-19, 3-24, 5-59
Alston, Walter ... 2-6, 4-30, 5-28, 7-19, 7-34
Anderson, Sparky ... 5-54
Bell, George ... 5-20
Bench, Johnny ... 1-21, 5-26
Berra, Yogi ... 4-18, 6-32
Bibby, Jim ... 7-15
Black, Joe ... 6-23
Bochte, Bruce ... 1-14
Boggs, Wade ... 4-35
Boudreau, Lou ... 2-4, 4-24
Bowa, Larry ... 5-42
Brett, George ... 2-18, 3-6, 4-24, 5-52, 5-57, 8-5
Brock, Lou ... 4-22, 6-8, 7-24, 7-40, 8-10
Buckner, Bill ... 8-24
Busby, Steve ... 2-22, 8-13
Campanella, Roy ... 4-5, 5-32
Canseco, Jose ... 4-36, 8-44
Carew, Rod ... 3-31, 4-31
Carter, Joe ... 4-35, 5-20, 8-49
Carlton, Steve ... 4-13, 5-52, 7-23
Carpenter, R.R.M. III ... 2-32
Carter, Gary ... 2-11, 5-26, 8-4
Cedeno, Cesar ... 2-6, 7-20
Cey, Ron ... 7-15
Clark, Will ... 4-34
Clemente, Roberto ... 6-15
Clemens, Rodger ... 5-16
Cobb, Ty ... 5-5, 5-50, 5-58
Coleman, Jerry ... 2-12
Concepcion, Dave ... 5-26
Cooper, Cecil ... 4-26
Cruz, Jose ... 2-18
Dent, Bucky ... 3-8, 4-5, 5-59
DiMaggio, Joe ... 5-26, 5-50, 5-66, 6-16, 7-7
Easler, Mike ... 7-40
Edwards, Doc ... 5-21, 8-47
Fairly, Ron ... 6-32
Fingers, Rollie ... 4-18, 6-10, 7-13
Foster, George ... 2-22, 3-15, 4-2, 4-4, 6-10
Galbreath, Daniel M. ... 1-13
Galbreath, John W. ... 1-4, 6-23, 8-22
Garagiola, Joe ... 4-24, 5-5, 5-14
Garvey, Steve ... 2-5, 3-19, 7-38
Gehrig, Lou ... 2-25
Gibson, Bob ... 4-26, 5-4, 6-9
Gibson, Kirk ... 5-16
Gooden, Dwight ... 5-22, 8-47
Gossage, Rich ... 6-6, 8-25
Griffith, Calvin R. ... 7-15
Guidry, Ron ... 4-5, 4-24
Gura, Larry ... 5-30, 6-4
Harrah, Toby ... 5-28, 7-17
Henderson, Rickey ... 5-50, 7-25
Hernandez, Keith ... 5-30
Hershiser, Orel ... 5-21
Hoffberger, Jerry ... 8-22, 8-26
Hornsby, Roger ... 4-24
Hoyt, Lamarr ... 5-38
Jackson, Reggie ... 1-7, 2-27, 3-28, 5-14, 5-38, 5-64, 7-26, 7-32, 8-3
John, Tommy ... 3-16, 6-23, 7-33
Jones, Doug ... 4-33, 5-22, 8-48
Kaline, Al ... 8-4
Kingman, Dave ... 4-21
Kuhn, Bowie ... 8-14
Kuiper, Duane ... 3-22
Larussa, Tony ... 2-27
Lasorda, Tommy ... 2-2, 4-4, 5-32, 7-41, 8-12
Lemon, Chet ... 2-30
Leonard, Dennis ... 4-12
Lurie, Robert A. ... 2-12
Lynn, Fred ... 3-5, 3-22
Maddox, Gary ... 5-52
Mantle, Mickey ... 2-16
Maris, Roger ... 3-10, 5-66

Martin, Billy ... 5-53, 7-22, 7-32
Mattingly, Don ... 4-38
Mays, Willie ... 2-12, 2-25, 4-24, 4-33, 6-28
McGraw, Tug ... 1-18, 3-5, 7-23
McGuire, Mark ... 4-32
McHale, John J. ... 5-14
Molitor, Paul ... 8-47
Morgan, Joe ... 4-25, 5-49
Murcer, Bobby ... 1-20
Murphy, Dale ... 4-21, 8-46, 8-48
Murray, Eddie ... 7-22
Musial, Stan ... 3-15, 7-34
Nettles, Graig ... 5-41
Niekro, Phil ... 7-26
Norris, Mike ... 3-16
Ogilvie, Ben ... 3-19
O'Malley, Walter ... 3-4
Paige, Satchel ... 6-22
Palmer, Jim ... 5-28, 5-52
Parker, Dave ... 2-21, 4-26
Perry, Gaylord ... 6-14, 8-33
Puckett, Kirby ... 4-35
Quisenberry, Dan ... 6-10
Raines, Tim ... 4-25
Reuss, Jerry ... 3-23
Rice, Jim ... 2-21
Richard, J. R. ... 5-6, 6-17
Ripken, Cal Jr. ... 4-21
Rivers, Mickey ... 7-20
Robinson, Brooks ... 4-6
Robinson, Frank ... 1-6, 1-19, 3-8, 5-48, 6-10
Robinson, Jackie ... 5-6
Rose, Pete ... 3-21, 3-31, 4-24, 5-49, 5-57, 6-30, 7-23, 8-4, 8-30
Rosen, Al ... 3-22, 7-20
Ruth, Babe ... 2-17, 3-24, 4-26, 5-28, 6-22, 8-14
Ryan, Nolan ... 1-13, 7-24
Schmidt, Mike ... 4-5, 5-42, 6-8, 7-16
Scott, Mike ... 8-50
Seaver, Tom ... 2-18, 2-20, 3-22, 5-38, 5-54
Simmons, Ted ... 5-5
Singleton, Ken ... 2-5
Slaughter, Enos ... 2-16
Smalley, Roy ... 1-12
Smith, Reggie ... 5-38
Snyder, Cory ... 4-36, 5-16
Spahn, Warren ... 4-24
Stargell, Willie ... 1-14, 4-31, 5-24, 6-32, 8-32
Strawberry, Darryl ... 4-33
Steinbrenner, George ... 6-14
Stone, Steve ... 2-26, 4-13, 8-20
Sullivan, Haywood ... 1-20
Sutton, Don ... 2-4
Swindell, Greg ... 4-35, 5-18, 8-47
Torre, Joe ... 3-19, 5-43
Ueberroth, Peter V. ... 8-47
Virdon, Bill ... 2-26
Weaver, Earl ... 1-6, 1-13, 5-3, 5-27
Williams, Dick ... 1-14, 5-12
Williams, Ted ... 2-18, 6-8
Winfield, Dave ... 5-4, 5-64, 8-4
Yastrzemski, Carl ... 6-28, 6-32, 7-41, 8-31
Yount, Robin ... 4-21, 5-28
Zimmer, Don ... 5-59

BASKETBALL:
Abdul-Jabbar, Kareem ... 5-25, 5-28, 8-5
Albeck, Stan ... 5-33
Auerbach, Red ... 1-18, 3-23, 5-12, 7-15, 8-30
Barkley, Charles ... 8-47
Barry, Rick ... 5-34
Bird, Larry ... 2-8, 5-50, 6-7
Brown, Dale ... 5-40
Brown, Larry ... 4-36, 8-47
Burke, Michael ... 7-4, 7-40
Buss, Jerry ... 8-10
Carril, Pete ... 1-4, 2-31, 3-15, 5-30
Chamberlain, Wilt ... 2-24, 6-5
Colangelo, Jerry ... 7-22
Cousy, Bob ... 3-22, 5-52, 7-7
Cowens, Dave ... 5-48, 5-59, 6-4
Cunningham, Billy ... 3-22
Daugherty, Brad ... 4-33, 5-20
Dumars, Joe ... 4-38
Elliott, Sean ... 4-36
Ewing, Pat ... 5-34
Erving, Julius ... 3-32, 4-17, 4-27, 5-32, 6-4, 8-15
Fitch, Bill ... 6-24
Fitzsimmons, Cotton ... 1-19
Foster, Bill ... 5-14, 5-32
Gervin, George ... 4-24, 5-58, 7-6
Harper, Ron ... 4-32, 5-22, 8-48
Havlicek, John ... 1-14, 2-24, 4-18, 6-2, 6-18, 8-5
Hayes, Elvin ... 7-39

Haywood, Spencer ... 7-6
Heinsohn, Thomas ... 3-30, 7-8
Holzman, Red ... 5-32
Jackson, Chris ... 4-38
Johnson, Dennis ... 6-10
Johnson, Kevin ... 8-48
Johnson, "Magic" Earvin ... 2-8, 2-14
Jordan, Michael ... 4-33, 8-37
Kellogg, Clark ... 8-25
King, Stacey ... 4-38
Knight, Bobby ... 2-16, 3-12, 5-58, 5-64, 6-14, 7-4, 8-12, 8-49
Layden, Frank ... 1-8
MacLeod, John ... 8-13
Malone, Moses ... 7-13
McGuire, Al ... 6-10, 6-20, 7-9, 7-32, 7-34, 8-26
McGuire, Frank ... 1-6
Meyer, Ray ... 3-27, 4-34
Murphy, Calvin ... 1-7
Nance, Larry ... 4-34, 5-19
Phelps, Digger ... 1-26, 2-22, 5-32, 5-58, 7-21, 7-34, 8-10
Price, Mark ... 4-36, 5-19
Ramsay, Jack ... 8-24
Riley, Pat ... 8-50
Robinson, David ... 5-22
Rodgers, Jim ... 4-36, 5-20, 8-48
Russell, Bill ... 3-8, 3-9, 8-26
Sharman, Bill ... 3-30, 5-4, 5-52, 6-4
Smith, Dean ... 5-68, 7-4, 7-9
Sonju, Norm ... 5-42
Sparrow, Rory ... 8-46
Thomas, Isiah ... 7-26, 8-15, 8-47
Thompson, John ... 3-26
Valvano, Jim ... 4-32
VanArsdale, Dick ... 3-4, 4-4, 4-18
Walton, Bill ... 1-14
West, Jerry ... 3-16, 4-26
Westphal, Paul ... 1-12, 2-18
Wilkens, Lenny ... 1-5
Wilkins, Dominique ... 5-21
Wooden, John ... 1-4, 1-6, 1-10, 1-26, 2-22, 3-18, 3-28, 5-28, 5-43, 6-15, 7-22, 8-23

BOWLING:

Anthony, Earl ... 2-13
Varipapa, Andy ... 3-31, 7-40
Weber, Dick ... 5-38

BOXING:

Ali, Muhammad ... 1-20, 2-22, 2-32, 3-8, 4-23, 4-24, 5-59, 6-23, 8-32
Cooney, Gerry ... 2-7, 3-29
Corbett, James ... 6-22
Dempsey, Jack ... 2-18, 2-32, 5-4, 5-50, 7-25
Frazier, Joe ... 2-7, 4-14, 5-52, 6-4, 6-23
Hagler, Marvin ... 2-13, 2-23
Hearns, Tommy ... 2-23, 2-29, 4-20, 5-15, 5-40, 5-65
Holmes, Larry ... 8-2
Leonard, Sugar Ray ... 2-23, 4-24, 5-7, 5-47, 6-22
Louis, Joe ... 5-5, 5-15
Marciano, Rocky ... 2-24, 5-5, 6-32
Norton, Ken ... 2-12
Odom, Herb ... 8-30
Patterson, Floyd ... 4-4
Robinson, Sugar Ray ... 4-14, 6-32
Tyson, Mike ... 5-18

BUSINESSMEN:

Bagehot, Walter ... 7-17
Baker, Newton D. ... 8-14
Barnard, Chester ... 5-14
Braude, Jacob M. ... 7-42
Brennan, J. H. ... 4-14
Carnegie, Andrew ... 3-8, 5-40
Carney, Jr., Jim ... 8-50
Cottingham, Walter ... 2-18
Dodge, John F. ... 1-5
Doherty, Henry L. ... 3-19, 6-30
Fletcher, Horace ... 5-15
Friedsam, Michael ... 5-38
Gries, Bob ... 5-20, 8-47
Hughes, Carl F. ... 5-21, 8-49
Johnston, Eric ... 5-64
Kindleberger, J. ... 3-10
Kingsley, Darwin P. ... 4-13
O'Rell, Max ... 7-32
Patterson, John H. ... 7-34
Prochnow, Herbert V. ... 3-10
Rogers, Charles B. ... 7-7
Sherman, Harold ... 4-14
Simmons, Charles ... 4-13
Vail, Theodore N. ... 5-15
Walsh, Basil S. ... 2-4
Ware, Eugene F. ... 2-31
Watson, Thomas J. ... 4-4
White, F. Edison ... 5-42

CLERGYMEN:

Babcock, Maltbie ... 7-22
Beecher, Henry Ward ... 1-4, 1-18
Brooks, Phillips ... 1-4
Bucher, Henry Ward ... 1-8
Cecil, Richard ... 3-18
Clarke, J. F. ... 4-4
Gibbons, Cardinal ... 5-26
Hawes, J. ... 1-4
Holmes, J. A. Dr. ... 2-4
Murphy, Ph.D., Rev. John F. ... 4-5
Osborn, Ronald E. ... 5-15
Peale, Norman Vincent ... 2-15, 3-30, 4-4, 4-13, 7-26, 8-22
Powell, Sidney ... 5-32
Schweitzer, Albert ... 1-5
Sharp, James ... 7-26
Smith, Roy L. ... 1-5
Sockman, Ralph W. ... 2-31
St. Bernard ... 7-7
Wendte, C. W. ... 7-42
Westcott, Bishop ... 8-19

COLLEGE/UNIVERSITY PRESIDENTS:

Hiram College
Elmer Jagow ... 8-10
Kent State University
Brage Golding ... 8-24
Miami University
Phillip R. Shriver ... 8-23
Notre Dame, University of
Rev. Theodore M. Hesburgh, C.S.C. ... 8-8, 8-12
Pepperdine University
Howard A. White ... 8-10
Southern California, University of
James H. Zumberge ... 8-21
Wayne State University
Elbert Hubbard ... 1-6
Yale University
A. Bartlett Giamatti ... 4-35, 5-5

CORPORATION PRESIDENTS/ CHAIRMEN OF THE BOARD:

Bonne Bell Cosmetics
Jess Bell ... 1-7
Chrysler Corporation
Lee A. Iacocca ... 8-12
Eastern Airlines
Frank Borman ... 8-8
Ernst & Whinney
Ray J. Groves ... 8-14
Ford Motor Company
Philip Caldwell ... 8-13
Ford Motor Company
Henry Ford ... 7-22, 8-18
General Foods Corporation
James L. Ferguson ... 8-14
General Motors Corporation
Charles F. Kettering ... 7-42
General Motors Corporation
Robert B. Smith ... 8-13
General Motors Corporation
Charles E. Wilson ... 5-50
Goodyear Tire & Rubber Corporation
Charles J. Pilliod, Jr. ... 8-12
Hilton Hotels Corporation
Conrad Hilton ... 1-5
North American Systems
Vincent G. Marotta ... 2-10
OKC Corporation
Cloyce Box ... 1-13
Phillips Petroleum Company
W. F. Marten ... 8-14
Rockwell International Corporation
R. Anderson ... 8-24
Success Motivation Institute
Paul Meyer ... 2-10
Trans World Corporation
L. Edwin Smart ... 2-26, 8-10

ENGINEERS:

Douglas, Donald ... 2-32
Noble, Charles C. ... 2-5
Rees, R. I. ... 8-10
Sampson, George ... 8-10
Weinberg, George ... 6-22
Wheeler, Elmer ... 6-22

CYCLIST:

LeMond, Greg ... 5-22

ENTERTAINERS:

Alda, Alan ... 5-32, 5-40
Eastwood, Clint ... 2-16
Goldwyn, Sam ... 2-18
Hoffman, Dustin ... 1-18
Jones, Margo ... 7-40
Matthau, Walter ... 2-22
Moore, Mary Tyler ... 5-14
Newman, Paul ... 3-4
Paderewski, Ignace ... 3-10
Poitier, Sidney ... 1-18
Pryor, Richard ... 4-6
Rogers, Will ... 3-10
Stewart, Jimmy ... 1-18
Wayne, John ... 6-22

FOOTBALL:

Aikman, Troy ... 4-38
Allen, George ... 1-19, 5-4, 5-53, 6-4, 7-24, 8-5, 8-20, 8-22
Allen, Marcus ... 6-10
Anderson, Ken ... 5-29
Bahr, Matt ... 6-11
Bartkowski, Steve ... 1-19, 4-6, 7-4
Baugh, Sammy ... 3-8
Benirschke, Rolf ... 1-20
Bennett, C. Leeman ... 2-11, 5-6
Blanda, George ... 4-19, 6-8, 7-14, 8-31
Bleier, Rocky ... 2-10, 3-17
Bradshaw, Terry ... 4-30, 5-24, 5-38, 5-43, 5-65, 6-16
Brennan, Brian ... 8-50
Brown, Jim ... 1-7, 5-40, 6-5
Brown, Larry ... 5-18
Brown, Paul ... 1-6, 1-26, 2-12, 3-6, 3-28, 5-33, 5-43, 7-27
Bryant, Paul "Bear" ... 2-32, 5-4, 5-58, 7-32, 8-9
Butkus, Dick ... 2-22, 6-31, 7-16
Campbell, Earl ... 1-3, 2-27, 7-18
Carson, Harry ... 4-14, 5-52
Carter, Anthony ... 4-34
Clark, Monte ... 1-7, 7-21
Collier, Blanton ... 5-30
Collinsworth, Cris ... 3-11
Cousineau, Tom ... 2-27, 5-67, 7-20
Craig, Roger ... 5-17
Cribbs, Joe ... 3-22, 5-67
Csonka, Larry ... 2-30, 4-20, 5-5, 7-8
Daugherty, Duffy ... 2-30
Davis, Al ... 5-6
Dawkins, Pete ... 1-18
DeLamielleure, Joe ... 2-12
Dickerson, Eric ... 4-39
Dierdorf, Dan ... 2-10
Donahue, Terry ... 2-5, 7-21, 8-12
Dorsett, Tony ... 3-5, 5-4, 5-31, 7-13, 7-25, 8-11
Easley, Ken ... 5-50
Elway, John ... 5-21
Faust, Gerry ... 1-8, 3-30, 4-4, 4-13, 6-8, 7-24, 8-23
Ferguson, Joe ... 6-23, 7-33
Flores, Tom ... 2-25
Fouts, Dan ... 2-16, 4-12, 4-26, 5-5, 6-15, 7-22
Gibbs, Joe ... 4-32, 5-16, 8-49
Gifford, Frank ... 5-30, 5-40, 7-15
Golic, Bob ... 4-36
Graham, Otto ... 8-24
Grange, Red ... 7-6, 8-4, 8-23
Grant, Bud ... 6-24, 7-16, 8-18
Green, Hugh ... 3-22
Greene, Joe ... 2-27, 5-48, 6-30, 7-33, 7-34
Gregg, Forrest ... 2-24, 3-12
Griese, Bob ... 5-39
Griffin, Archie ... 5-31
Groza, Lou ... 8-23
Ham, Jack ... 5-28
Hampton, Dan ... 1-12, 2-26, 5-58
Hanburger, Chris ... 8-18
Hannah, John ... 3-32
Harris, Franco ... 3-7, 4-13
Hayes, Lester ... 4-24, 4-26
Hayes, Woody ... 1-4, 2-3, 3-8, 4-12, 4-18, 5-10, 7-26, 7-40, 8-26
Hill, Calvin ... 1-4
Hirsch, Elroy ... 1-12, 3-5
Holtz, Lou ... 1-4, 2-24, 3-10, 3-30, 5-4, 7-31, 7-32
Huff, Sam ... 3-15
Hunt, Lamar ... 7-40
Jackson, Bo ... 4-39, 5-21
Jaworski, Ron ... 1-18, 2-16, 4-10, 4-24, 6-9, 7-32
Jefferson, John ... 4-30, 5-39
Jones, Bert ... 5-29, 8-11, 8-22
Knox, Chuck ... 1-12, 3-18, 3-30, 3-31, 4-18, 6-32, 7-8, 7-31, 8-22
Kosar, Bernie ... 4-34, 5-18, 8-41
Kramer, Jerry ... 6-15
Kush, Frank ... 6-4
Lambert, Jack ... 2-10, 4-31, 6-31, 7-6
Landry, Tom ... 2-25, 3-13, 4-3, 4-18, 4-20, 5-27, 5-32, 5-38, 5-64, 7-26, 7-32, 8-23
Largent, Steve ... 3-11, 5-16, 7-20
Layne, Bobby ... 4-24, 5-6
LeBaron, Edward Jr. ... 2-32
Little, Floyd ... 6-14
Lofton, James ... 6-32
Logan, Dave ... 4-30, 7-26
Lombardi, Vince ... 2-22, 3-6, 3-15, 4-18, 5-26, 5-28, 5-30, 5-48, 5-66, 6-4, 6-12, 6-16, 8-22
Long, Howie ... 8-44
Luckman, Sid ... 5-26, 7-40
Madden, John ... 1-5, 1-18, 5-10, 5-32, 6-30, 6-32, 7-4, 7-33, 7-34
Mandarich, Tony ... 4-38, 8-44
Marino, Dan ... 4-35, 5-22, 8-41
Martin, Harvey ... 4-27, 5-50
Maynard, Don ... 1-13
McInally, Pat ... 3-10
McKay, John ... 1-11
Michaels, Walt ... 1-8, 3-10
Montana, Joe ... 4-20, 4-35, 7-6
Montgomery, Wilbert ... 5-53
Namath, Joe ... 1-12, 1-26, 3-31, 4-4, 4-30, 5-26, 6-17
Newsome, Ozzie ... 8-50
Nitschke, Ray ... 5-42
Noll, Chuck ... 3-18, 4-18, 5-13, 5-27, 6-8, 7-14, 7-26, 7-33
Olsen, Merlin ... 2-4, 3-6, 3-18, 5-14, 5-38, 5-48, 5-58, 7-42
Osborne, Tom ... 3-4, 7-22
Page, Alan ... 2-25, 8-11
Pagna, Tom ... 1-4
Pardee, Jack ... 5-32
Parseghian, Ara ... 1-26, 2-2
Paterno, Joe ... 1-17, 1-19, 1-20, 2-18, 2-26, 3-28, 4-14, 4-30, 5-6, 5-14, 5-15, 5-48, 5-50, 5-65, 6-32, 7-8, 7-16, 7-25, 7-34, 8-14
Payton, Walter ... 3-5
Pearson, Preston ... 7-38
Peete, Rodney ... 8-49
Peoples, Woody ... 8-30
Phillips, Bum ... 1-6, 3-5, 3-22, 3-31, 4-30, 7-4, 8-22
Plunkett, Jim ... 4-20, 6-14, 7-17
Powell, Marvin ... 7-16
Pruitt, Greg ... 5-31
Pruitt, Mike ... 3-7, 6-4
Ralston, John ... 2-24, 4-14, 7-26
Rashad, Ahmad ... 6-11
Reynolds, Bill ... 8-5
Rice, Jerry ... 5-17
Robbie, Joseph ... 5-53
Rockne, Knute ... 5-28, 7-6
Rogers, George ... 5-54, 6-8
Rooney, Arthur J ... 1-26, 3-6
Royal, Darrell ... 5-4
Rozelle, Pete ... 8-22
Rutigliano, Sam ... 1-8, 2-24, 2-31, 7-8, 7-31
Sanders, Barry ... 5-22, 8-48
Sayers, Gale ... 2-6, 5-50, 6-32
Schembechler, Bo ... 2-16, 5-2, 5-48, 6-24
Schlichter, Art ... 5-67
Schramm, Texas E. ... 7-20
Selmon, Dewey ... 6-17
Sherk, Jerry ... 7-15, 7-33
Shula, Don ... 1-5, 2-12, 3-10, 3-26, 3-32, 5-6, 5-64, 7-5, 7-24, 7-31, 7-34, 8-5

Sims, Billy ... 5-63
Singletary, Mike ... 4-33
Sipe, Brian ... 5-40, 5-43, 7-14
Sloan, Steve ... 7-32
Starr, Bart ... 2-30, 4-14
Staubach, Roger ... 1-26, 3-4, 4-18, 6-6, 8-25
Still, Art ... 1-20
Stram, Hank ... 1-20
Tarkenton, Fran ... 5-32, 5-58, 6-14, 8-24
Taylor, Charley ... 2-26, 5-28
Theisman, Joe ... 2-31
Tittle, Y. A. ... 4-20, 5-5, 5-28
Unitas, Johnny ... 2-26, 3-10, 4-2, 4-18
Upshaw, Gene ... 6-4
VanBrocklin, Norm ... 3-15
Vermeil, Dick ... 2-16, 3-4, 3-18, 6-4, 7-34
Walker, Doak ... 2-12, 4-30
Walker, Herschel ... 7-35
Walsh, Bill ... 7-27
Waters, Charlie ... 3-31
White, Danny ... 5-14, 5-40
White, Randy ... 4-14
Wilkinson, Bud ... 3-19
Williams, Doug ... 8-50
Williams, Reggie ... 8-50
Winslow, Kellen ... 4-31, 6-15
Young, Bob ... 8-32

Youngblood, Jack 7-22
Zorn, Jim 5-30

GOLF:
Boros, Julius 5-43
Boswell, Charley 3-30, 5-6
Burns, George III 2-6
Caponi, Donna 5-38
Crenshaw, Ben 7-24
Daniel, Beth 2-5
Faldo, Nick 4-32
Floyd, Raymond 2-4
Green, Hubert 4-20
Hogan, Ben 5-40, 5-66
Geiberger, Al 7-24
Irwin, Hale 1-12, 2-25, 5-65, 6-8
Kite, Tom 8-16
Lietzke, Bruce 5-65
Lopez, Nancy 3-6, 5-66, 6-8, 7-5
Miller, Johnny 4-30, 7-35
Nelson, Byron 3-16
Nicklaus, Jack 1-26, 2-16, 2-22, 3-23, 3-28, 3-32, 4-29, 5-41
                      5-62, 5-68, 6-4, 6-8, 6-10, 6-30, 7-5, 7-40
                      8-19, 8-23, 8-30
Norman Greg 5-16
Palmer, Arnold 5-5, 6-20
Pate, Jerry 5-50
Player, Gary 1-26, 2-10, 3-3, 4-19, 6-4, 8-30
Reid, Mike 1-4, 2-18
Snead, Sam 2-6
Strange, Curtis 4-34, 5-20, 8-35
Trevino, Lee 3-3, 3-17
Tway, Bob 5-22
Venturi, Ken 5-14, 7-4
Watson, Tom 5-65
Weiskopf, Tom 5-43
Whitworth, Kathy 1-26, 2-17

GYMNASTICS:
Comaneci, Nadia 3-9
Fujimoto, Shun 6-14
Rigby, Cathy 7-40
Thomas, Kurt 2-4, 4-16

HOCKEY:
Berry, Bob 5-32
Bossy, Mike 4-5, 6-10, 7-6
Brooks, Herb 5-42, 5-58
Craig, Jim 3-8
Dryden, Ken 5-14, 5-64, 7-35, 8-26
Eruzione, Mike 5-30
Esposito, Phil 5-32, 6-9, 7-14
Esposito, Tony 5-38, 7-18
Fuhr, Grant 4-32
Gretzky, Wayne 3-4, 4-28, 5-30
Howe, Gordie 1-14, 2-18, 7-33, 8-33
Hull, Bobby 1-26, 5-42, 8-2
Lemieux, Mario 4-35
Mikita, Stan 7-6
Neilson, Roger 8-24
Orr, Bobby 6-6
Parent, Bernie 2-7
Potvin, Denis 1-7, 1-19

HORSE RACING:
Arcaro, Eddie 5-50, 5-68
Cauthen, Steve 4-24, 5-53
Hartack, Bill 4-26, 5-4, 7-32
Krone, Julie 5-22
Shoemaker, Willie 1-5, 2-7, 8-31
Turcotte, Ron 4-5

INVENTORS/SCIENTISTS:
Bell, Alexander Graham 7-20
Butler, Edward B. 2-18
Carver, George W. 7-34
Edison, Thomas 2-5, 3-4, 6-22, 8-19
Franklin, Benjamin 1-5, 3-28, 5-43, 7-6, 7-7, 8-18

KAYAKER:
Barton, Greg 4-35

LABOR LEADERS:
Debs, Eugene V. 2-30
Lewis, John L. 2-31

MEDIA:
Arledge, Roone 8-5
Burke, Michael 7-4, 7-40
Chandler, Nev 2-7
Cosell, Howard .... 1'-13, 1-17, 8-14
Costas, Bob 8-49
Fuldheim, Dorothy 8-4, 8-12
Gumbel, Bryant 5-42, 7-24

Lebovitz, Hal 8-5
McKay, Jim 3-5
Mueller, Jim 5-52
Newcombe, John 1-26, 5-5
Phillips, Wendell 7-26
Schenkel, Chris 5-64, 8-4
Shanley, Gib 1-5
Snyder, Jimmy "The Greek" 4-14, 5-43
Whitaker, Jack 5-28, 5-50, 5-59

MOUNTAIN CLIMBING:
Hillary, Edmund Sir 5-68

PHILOSOPHERS/EDUCATORS:
Aristotle 1-4
Bryson, Lyman 3-32
Burnett, Adam W. 7-7
Buxton, Thomas F. 7-42
Confucius 2-31, 7-33
Dewey, John 1-13, 8-10
Eliot, Charles W. 1-8
Epictetus 7-26
Gregg, Alan 7-4
Harris, Seymour E. 8-14
Jacobi 4-4
Lao-Tzu 7-7
Miller, J. R. 7-42
Papyrus 2-17
Plutarch 7-42
Sawyer, Charles 2-6
Stoddard, George D. Dr. 8-14

PHYSICIANS:
Eastman, Richard 8-44
Osler, William Sir 2-18
Voy, Robert 8-44
Winette M. 3-23

POLITICIANS/MILITARY LEADERS:
Aurelius, Marcus 7-25
Bulwer, Edward Sir 6-30
Byrnes, James F. 5-15
Churchill, Winston Sir 2-32, 6-21
Clay, Henry 3-8
Coolidge, Calvin 8-18
Disraeli, Benjamin 2-5, 5-48
Eisenhower, Dwight D. 5-18
Farley, James A. 1-12
Ford, Gerald R. 2-10, 3-4
Garfield, James A. 1-20
Glenn, John 8-19
Humphrey, Hubert H. 5-65
Jackson, Andrew 2-32
Jefferson, Thomas 4-12, 7-22, 8-18
Kemp, Jack 7-42, 8-18
Kennedy, John F. 2-29, 2-32, 7-24
Lincoln, Abraham 4-12, 7-14, 7-25
MacArthur, Douglas 3-6
Reagan, Ronald 8-26
Roosevelt, Eleanor 2-30
Roosevelt, Franklin D. 5-28, 6-23
Roosevelt, Theodore 1-4, 5-68
Roosma, John S. 6-17
Stevenson, Adlai 1-18
Truman, Harry 1-5, 2-16, 2-31, 4-14, 5-26
Washington, George 1-5
Wilson, Woodrow 1-6, 2-7, 7-7

SKATING:
Blair, Bonnie 5-21
Boitano, Brian 4-32
Hamill, Dorothy 3-23
Heiden, Eric 4-10, 4-20, 6-17, 7-33
Flemming, Peggy 2-15
Salomon, Janet Lynn 3-19
Thomas, Debi 5-20

SKIING:
Cochran, Barbara Ann 5-53
Killy, Jean-Claude 4-16, 5-42, 5-66, 7-33
Klammer, Franz 5-37
Mahre, Phil 2-17, 5-53, 6-13
Nykanen, Matt 8-48
Saarinen, Veli 4-18
Schaeffler, Willie 6-14, 6-23
Stenmark, Ingemar 4-11, 4-26, 5-6, 5-50
Tomba, Alberto 4-34, 5-22
Zurbriggen, Pirmin 5-20

SOCCER:
Chinaglia, Giorio 2-13, 6-3
Haaskivi, Kai 8-46
James, Bernie 8-46

Pele 3-5, 3-21, 4-28, 5-48, 5-64, 8-4
Rote, Kyle, Jr. 1-13, 4-6

SWIMMING:
Biondi, Matt 4-33, 5-23, 8-43
Caulkins, Tracy 2-17, 3-29
Evans, Janet 4-36, 5-23, 8-43, 8-48
Fraser, Dawn 2-6, 2-18
Goodell, Brian 4-26, 5-66
Larson, Lance 8-29
Lee, Sammy Dr. 7-26
Louganis, Greg 5-16, 5-50, 8-44
Naber, John 8-22, 8-23
Rose, Murray 8-30, 8-32
Sanguily, Mani Dr. 8-32
Schollander, Don 1-12, 5-65, 6-16, 7-5
Spitz, Mark 5-54
Vanderbush, Carin Cone 5-6
Yorzyk, Bill Dr. 8-30

TENNIS:
Agassi, Andre 4-32, 5-18
Ashe, Arthur Jr. 4-18
Austin, Tracy 3-16
Borg, Bjorn 5-42, 5-47, 6-32, 7-8, 7-33, 7-42
Connors, Jimmy 6-29
Gonzalez, Pancho 2-17, 8-13
Goolagong, Evonne 7-14
Graf, Steffi 4-37, 5-22
King, Billie Jean 1-14, 6-10
Kramer, Jack 4-26
Lendl, Ivan 3-29, 5-6, 6-29
Evert, Chris 4-27, 5-4, 5-36, 5-38, 5-40, 7-5, 7-33
McEnroe, John 1-18, 4-19, 5-7, 5-64, 6-17
Navratilova, Martina 4-20
Newcombe, John 1-26, 5-5
Smith, Stan 4-5
Wade, Virginia 2-26
Wilander, Mats 4-37

TRACK & FIELD:
Ashford, Evelyn 1-21, 8-17
Bannister, Roger 2-22, 5-40, 5-59, 6-15
Beardsley, Dick 6-16
Coe, Sebastian 2-28, 6-8, 7-4, 7-42
Davenport, Willie 8-4
Decker, Mary 2-18, 2-25
Elliott, Herb 2-4
Floyd, Stanley 5-51
Jenner, Bruce 3-9, 4-12, 4-14, 5-68
Joyner, Florence Griffith 5-18, 8-35
Kersee, Jackie Joyner 4-32, 4-38
Kingdom, Roger 4-35
Lewis, Carl 8-49
Moses, Edwin 3-14, 5-36, 6-30, 7-5
Nehemiah, Renaldo 5-51
Oerter, Al 2-16, 5-68, 8-5, 8-29, 8-32
Ovett, Steve 5-51
Prefontaine, Steve 6-14
Richards, Bob 2-6, 2-25, 2-31, 3-15, 3-23, 4-6, 5-64, 7-20
Rodgers, Bill 3-19, 5-59
Ryun, Jim 5-14
Salazar, Alberto 2-5, 3-28, 6-12
Sheenan, George Dr. 8-32
Shorter, Frank 6-22
Thompson, Daley 4-33, 5-18
Waitz, Grete 5-68, 6-15
Zatopek, Emil 2-7

WEIGHT LIFTING:
Alexeyev, Vasili 3-8

WRESTLING:
Drago, Mike 8-52
Dziedzic, Stan 7-34
Fox, Brian 8-52
Fried, Alan 8-44, 8-52
Gable, Dan 1-26, 3-4, 6-2, 6-32
Hackett, Jason 8-52
Hlywiak, Joe 8-52
Johnson, Pat 8-52
Kemp, Lee 5-2, 6-17
Lemmeier, Ray 8-52
Leonti, Dave 8-52
Lieberman, Mark 3-6
Mills, Gene 4-13, 5-58
Millson, Adam 8-52
Rupanovic, Rich 8-52
Sawyer, Jeremiah 8-52
Schalles, Wade 4-13
Smith, John 5-20
Tome, Craig 8-52
University of Iowa Wrestling Team 7-14

WRITERS / AUTHORS / POETS / PLAYWRIGHTS:
Adams, Charles Kendall 5-58
Adams, George Matthew 1-13
Addison, Joseph 3-6
Amiel, Henri Frederic 1-19
Anderson, Bob 1-8
Author Unknown 5-48
Bennett, Arnold 4-14
Benson, Edward F. 1-12
Bovee, Christian Nestell 5-59
Brown, George 5-14
Buckner, Thomas A. 4-12
Buxton, Thomas Sir 3-10
Carlyle, Thomas 1-12, 7-22
Carnegie, Dale 2-31, 7-17
Casson, Herbert N. 1-7
Chesterfield, Lord 2-24
Coleridge, Samuel T. 8-18
Colton, Arthur 7-24
Curtis, Cyrus H. K. 4-4
De La Rochefoucauld, Francois 7-24
Dreier, Thomas 2-7
Dresser, H. W. 5-53
Edmonds, Bernard 2-30
Eggleston, Louise W. 4-12
Elliott, L. G. 2-6
Ellis, Havelock 1-12
Emerson, Ralph Waldo 1-8, 2-32, 8-19
Fertig, Lyman 7-20
Fitzgerald, F. Scott 5-15
Forbes, B. C. 2-17, 5-30, 5-52
Gide, Andre 1-20, 2-31
Giovanni, Nikki 7-34
Goethe, Johann 1-8
Gow, Charles 7-40
Graham, Gordon 7-20
Griffith, John L. 3-5
Grove, Frederick Philip 2-7
Guiterman, Arthur 7-17
Harris, Sidney J. 1-13, 8-18
Hazlitt, William 1-7
Holmes, Oliver Wendell 8-19
Hose, E. W. 5-42
Howe, Ed 7-17, 8-19
Hubbard, Elbert 5-59, 7-16
Huxley, Aldous 8-13
Jansen, H. E. 6-22
kaufman, Herbert 7-40
Kingsley, Charles 1-8
Kipling, Rudyard 5-30, 7-32
Liddon, H. P. 3-15
MacAulay, Thomas 1-4
Matthews, William 5-38
Maltz, Maxwell 2-32
Maugham, W. Somerset 8-19
Mencken, H. L. 2-31
Moliere 5-66
Montgomery, Robert 7-4
Persian Proverb 8-19
Proctor, J. J. 7-20
Quarles, Francis 3-5
Ray, Marie Beynon 5-15
Riger, Robert 3-22
Robinson, James Harvey 2-30
Runyon, Damon 8-19
Saadi 7-42
Salak, John Charles 5-14
Schultz, Susan Polis 2-4
Shakespeare, William 1-5, 1-8, 7-6
Shaw, George Bernard 2-30, 2-31
Shaw, H. W. 8-18
Simms, Lewis 7-17
Skinner, B. F. 7-22
Smiles, S. 7-33, 8-5
Stevenson, Robert Louis 3-22
Stowe, Calvin 8-19
Sullivan, Mark 1-14
Syrus 3-32
Thackeray 3-32
Thomas, Teddy 8-30
Toland, W. D. 5-64
Ullman, Samuel 8-30
Von Schiller, Johann Christoph 3-28
Wilde, Oscar 7-5, 7-15
Wilson, Earl 7-34
Yutang, Lin 1-13

PHOTO CREDITS

COLOR — SPORTS ILLUSTRATED

1-2	Earl Campbell	John Iacono
1-2	O. J. Simpson	Neil Leifer
1-10	John Wooden	Rich Clarkson
1-10	John McKay	Sheedy & Long
1-16	Howard Cosell	Tony Triolo
1-16	Joe Paterno	Rich Clarkson
1-22	Chris Evert Lloyd	Stephen Green—Armytage
1-22	Bjorn Borg	Russ Adams
1-22	Jack Nicklaus	Walter Iooss, Jr.
1-22	Sugar Ray Leonard	Manny Millan
1-23	Julius Erving	Heinz Kluetmeier
1-27	Kathy Whitworth	George Tiedemann
1-27	Arnold Palmer	Tony Tomsic
1-27	Roger Staubach	Carl Iwasaki
1-27	Tom Seaver	Walter Iooss, Jr.
1-27	Carl Yastrzemski	Dick Raphael
1-27	Larry Bird	George Tiedemann
2-2	Tommy Lasorda	Tony Triolo
2-2	Ara Parseghian	Sheedy & Long
2-2	Woody Hayes	Tony Tomsic
2-14	Peggy Fleming Jenkins (2)	John G. Zimmerman
2-14	Earvin "Magic" Johnson	Andy Hayt
2-14	Earvin "Magic" Johnson	Manny Millan
2-19	Lee Trevino	Walter Iooss, Jr.
2-19	Sebastian Coe	Rich Clarkson
2-19	Terry Bradshaw	Heinz Kluetmeier
2-19	Willie Mays	Neil Leifer
2-19	Evonne Goolagong	Tony Triolo
2-19	Muhammad Ali	Manny Millan
2-19	Nancy Lopez	Harry Benson
2-19	A. J. Foyt	Eric Schweikardt
2-20	Tom Seaver	Walter Iooss, Jr.
2-20	Dave Parker	Heinz Kluetmeier
2-20	Jim Rice	Heinz Kluetmeier
2-28	Sebastian Coe	Steve Powell
2-28	Tommy Hearns	Manny Millan
3-2	Gary Player (2)	Walter Iooss, Jr.
3-2	Lee Trevino	Walter Iooss, Jr.
3-2	Lee Trevino	Andy Hayt
3-12	Bobby Knight	Rich Clarkson
3-12	Forest Gregg	John Iacono
3-13	Tom Landry	George Tiedemann
3-20	Pete Rose	Heinz Kluetmeier
3-20	Pele	Eric Schweikardt
3-26	Don Shula	John Iacono
3-26	John Thompson	Lane Stewart
3-27	Ray Meyer	Heinz Kluetmeier
3-33	Ted Williams	Fred Kaplan
3-33	Tony Dorsett	Walter Iooss, Jr.
3-33	Roger Staubach	James Drake
3-33	Bart Starr	Heinz Kluetmeier
4-2	Johnny Unitas	Walter Iooss, Jr.
4-2	George Foster	Heinz Kluetmeier
4-3	Tom Landry	Heinz Kluetmeier
4-10	Ron Jaworski	Paul Kennedy
4-10	Eric Heiden	Heinz Kluetmeier
4-11	Ingemar Stenmark	Jerry Cooke
4-16	Kurt Thomas	Raphael Beer
4-16	Jean-Claude Killy	Eric Schweikardt
4-17	Julius Erving	Heinz Kluetmeier
4-22	Lou Brock (2)	Heinz Kluetmeier
4-23	Muhammad Ali	Jane Stewart
4-28	Pele	Jerry Cooke
4-28	Wayne Gretzky	Tony Triolo
4-29	Jack Nicklaus	Walter Iooss, Jr.
5-2	Lee Kemp	Roy Hobson
5-2	Bo Schembechler	Neil Leifer
5-3	Earl Weaver	James Drake
5-12	Dick Williams	John McDonough
5-12	Red Auerbach	Jane Stewart
5-13	Chuck Noll	Rich Clarkson
5-16	Willie Stargell	Manny Millan
5-16	Terry Bradshaw	Heinz Kluetmeier
5-17	Kareem Abdul-Jabbar	Peter Read Miller
5-28	Edwin Moses	Peter Read Miller
5-28	Chris Evert Lloyd	Walter Iooss, Jr.
5-29	Franz Klammer	Helmut Gritscher
5-37	John Stallworth	Walter Iooss, Jr.
5-37	Kareem Abdul-Jabbar/Julius Erving	Manny Millan
5-37	Paul Newman	Ellen Griesdieck
5-37	John McEnroe	Walter Iooss, Jr.
5-37	Ben Hogan	Sheedy & Long
5-37	Johnny Bench	Walter Iooss, Jr.
5-37	Joe Namath	Neil Leifer
5-37	Larry Bowa	Heinz Kluetmeier
5-38	Bjorn Borg (2)	Walter Iooss, Jr.
5-38	Sugar Ray Leonard	John Iacono
5-38	Sugar Ray Leonard	Walter Iooss, Jr.
5-47	Tracy Austin	Peter Read Miller
5-47	Bill Walton	Hank deJespinasse
5-47	Fernando Valenzuela	Heinz Kluetmeier
5-47	Walter Payton	Walter Iooss, Jr.
5-47	Johnny Miller	Peter Read Miller
5-47	Fran Tarkenton	Neil Leifer
5-47	Oscar Robertson	James Drake
5-47	Nolan Ryan	John G. Zimmerman
5-48	Pete Rose (2)	Heinz Kluetmeier
5-48	George Brett	Walter Iooss, Jr.
5-48	George Brett	Richard Mackson
5-53	Marty Liquor/Jim Ryun	James Drake
5-53	Mark Spitz	Heinz Kluetmeier
5-53	Vasily Alexeyev	Neil Leifer
5-53	Earl Campbell	Rich Clarkson
5-53	Dave Wottle	Neil Leifer
5-53	Willie McGee	Jerry Wachter
5-53	Elvin Hayes	Manny Millan
5-53	Lynn Swann	Heinz Kluetmeier
5-54	Jack Nicklaus	Tony Triolo
5-54	A. J. Foyt	Tony Tomsic
5-55	Billy Sims	Ronald C. Modra
6-2	Dan Gable	Jerry Cooke
6-2	John Havlicek	Manny Millan
6-3	Giorgio Chinaglia	George Tiedemann
6-6	Bobby Orr	Heinz Kluetmeier
6-6	Rich Gossage	John Iacono
6-6	Roger Staubach	Neil Leifer
6-7	Larry Bird	Richard Mackson
6-12	Vince Lombardi	Phillip Leonian
6-12	Alberto Salazar	Jerry Cooke
6-13	Phil Mahre	Helmut Gritscher
6-20	Arnold Palmer	Hy Peskin
6-20	Al McGuire	Rich Clarkson
6-28	Carl Yastrzemski	Art Shay
6-28	Willie Mays	Hy Peskin
6-28	Ivan Lendl	Russ Adams
6-29	Jimmy Connors	Tony Duffy
6-35	Rod Carew	Peter Read Miller
6-35	George Brett	Neil Leifer
6-35	Frank Robinson	Herb Scharfman
6-35	Mickey Mantel	Arthur Daley
6-35	Roberto Clemente	Tony Triolo
6-35	Reggie Jackson	Walter Iooss, Jr.
6-35	Mike Schmidt	John Iacono
6-35	Hank Aaron	Herb Scharfman
7-2	Pat Ewing	Heinz Kluetmeier
7-2	Herschel Walker	Andy Hayt
7-2	Marcus Allen	Richard Mackson
7-3	Ralph Sampson	Manny Millan
7-11	Al Unser	Heinz Kluetmeier
7-11	Brian Goodell	Heinz Kluetmeier
7-11	Nadia Comaneci	Heinz Kluetmeier
7-11	Edwin Moses	Walter Iooss, Jr.
7-11	Bill Walsh	Walter Iooss, Jr.
7-11	Kareem Abdul-Jabbar	Peter Read Miller
7-11	Olga Korbut	Tony Triolo
7-11	Giorgio Chinaglia	Enrico Ferorelli
7-12	Moses Malone	James Drake
7-12	Rollie Fingers	Richard Mackson
7-12	Tony Dorsett	Walter Iooss, Jr.
7-18	Tony Esposito	Heinz Kluetmeier
7-18	Earl Campbell	Ronald C. Modra
7-19	Walter Alston	George Long
7-30	Chuck Knox	John Iacono
7-30	Don Shula	Neil Leifer
7-30	Sam Rutigliano	Heinz Kluetmeier
7-30	Lou Holtz	Rich Clarkson
7-38	Preston Pearson	Heinz Kluetmeier
7-38	Steve Garvey	Ronald C. Modra
7-39	Elvin Hayes	Manny Millan
8-2	Bobby Hull	Neil Leifer
8-2	Larry Holmes	Tony Triolo
8-3	Reggie Jackson	John Iacono
8-9	Paul "Bear" Bryant	Walter Iooss, Jr.
8-16	Tom Kite	Carl Iwasaki
8-16	Evelyn Ashford	Heinz Kluetmeier
8-20	Steve Stone	Dan Baliotti
8-20	George Allen	Tony Triolo
8-28	Al Oerter	Eric Schweikardt
8-28	Lance Larson	Andy Hayt

TIME/LIFE PICTURE SERVICE

2-28	John F. Kennedy	Alfred Eisenstaedt

BLACK AND WHITE • SPORTS ILLUSTRATED

2-13	Marvin Hagler	John Iacono
2-23	Marvin Hagler	Tony Triolo
2-23	Sugar Ray Leonard	Carl Skalak
2-34	Dan Gable	John Jagua
3-14	Edwin Moses	Peter Read Miller
3-14	Edwin Moses	Al Satterwhite
3-16	Jerry West	Walter Iooss, Jr.
3-24	Hank Aaron	Neil Leifer
4-21	Robin Yount	Ronald C. Modra
4-21	Cal Ripken, Jr.	Ronald C. Modra
4-25	Joe Morgan	Heinz Kluetmeier
5-22	Keith Hernandez	Ronald C. Modra
5-27	Earl Blaik	Richard Meek

5-33	Graig Nettles	Paul Kennedy
5-43	Steve Ovett	Heinz Kluetmeier
5-57	Tommy Hearns	John Iacono
5-60	Grete Waitz	Walter Iooss, Jr.
6-10	Frank Robinson	Tony Tomsic
6-14	Steve Prefontaine	James Drake
6-18	Willis Reed	Walter Iooss, Jr.
6-33	Ted Williams	Hy Peskin
7-9	Al McGuire	Rich Clarkson
7-15	Ron Cey	Heinz Kluetmeier
8-23	John Naber	Heinz Kluetmeier
8-33	Gordie Howe	Dan Baliotti

NFL PROPERTIES, INC.

1-5	Don Shula	Dave Cross
1-7	Monte Clark	L. D. Fullerton
1-8	Walt Michaels	Rod Hanna
1-12	Dan Hampton	Don Lansu
1-20	Hank Stram	Rod Hanna
1-24	Gale Sayers	Herb Weitman
2-11	C. Leeman Bennett	David Boss
2-11	C. Leeman Bennett	Scott Cunningham
2-12	Doak Walker	George Gellably
2-24	Sam Rutigliano	Robert Harmeyer
2-25	Tom Flores	Russ Reed
2-27	Earl Campbell	Nancy Hogue
2-31	Joe Theismann	Peter Read Miller
3-5	Walter Payton	Don Lansu
3-7	Mike Pruitt	Pete J. Groh
3-7	Franco Harris	Andy Hayt
3-7	Franco Harris	Tak Makita
3-11	Steve Largent	Corky Trewin
3-11	Steve Largent	Seattle Seahawks
3-18	Dick Vermeil	M. V. Rubio
3-18	Chuck Knox	Robert L. Smith
3-19	Bud Wilkinson	Herb Weitman
3-31	Charlie Waters	Vernon Biever
3-31	Charlie Waters	Herb Weitman
3-22	John Hannah (2)	Tom Croke
4-8	Dallas Cowboys (3)	Russ Russell
4-8	Dallas Cowboys	Fred Anderson
4-14	Randy White	Russ Russell
4-19	George Blanda	Takaski Makita
4-27	Harvey Martin	Russ Russell
4-31	Kellen Winslow	A. N. Anderson
4-31	Jack Lambert	George Gaadt
5-6	Al Davis	Michael Zagaris
5-8	Tony Dorsett	Al Messerschmidt
5-8	Joe Greene	John E. Biever
5-8	John Jefferson	John E. Biever
5-10	John Madden	Peter Read Miller
5-19	Tom Landry	Arthur Anderson
5-23	Tony Dorsett	Russ Russell
5-31	John Jefferson	Vernon J. Biever
5-32	Danny White	Tak Makita
6-5	Jim Brown	N.F.L.
6-9	Ron Jaworski	Russ Russell
6-11	Matt Bahr	Bill Amatucci
6-11	Ahmad Rashad	Vernon Biever
6-16	Terry Bradshaw	Nancy Hogue
6-17	Joe Namath	N.F.L.
6-26	Rocky Bleier	Tak Makita
6-26	Rocky Bleier	Herb Weitman
7-8	Sam Rutigliano	David Boss
7-14	Chuck Noll	Malcolm Emmons
7-16	Bud Grant	Peter Read Miller
7-27	Bill Walsh	George Gojkovich
7-28	Rolf Benirschke	A. N. Anderson
7-42	Merlin Olsen	Dave Boss
7-44	Johnny Unitas	Herb Weitman
7-44	Johnny Unitas (2)	Malcolm W. Emmons
7-44	Johnny Unitas	Dick Raphael
8-11	Alan Page	Bill Smith
8-11	Bert Jones	David Boss
8-24	Fran Tarkenton	Tim Culek

THE RING PUBLISHING CORP.

2-23	Tommy Hearns	

LIFE PICTURE SERVICES

2-33	Jackie Robinson	Ralph Morse

PRO FOOTBALL HALL OF FAME

1-18	John Madden	Malcolm Emmons
3-6	Arthur Rooney	

JOE G. GLICK

1-19	Steve Bartkowski	5-46	George Rogers
1-21	Johnny Bench	6-23	Tommy John
2-26	Mario Andretti	6-23	Joe Ferguson
2-27	Joe Green	6-31	Jack Lambert
3-5	Bum Phillips	7-14	Brian Sipe
3-7	Mike Pruitt	7-22	Dan Fouts
4-13	Franco Harris		
5-21	Bert Jones		

JANIS RETTALIATA

8-46	Kai Haaskivi	

WIDE WORLD PHOTOS

1-6	Earl Weaver	4-31	Willie Stargell	7-8	Bjorn Borg	5-35	Brian Sipe
1-14	John Havlicek	4-31	Rod Carew	7-9	Dean Smith	5-43	Stanley Floyd
1-24	Gale Sayers	5-4	George Allen	7-9	Al McGuire	6-5	Wilt Chamberlain
2-4	Kurt Thomas	5-5	Y. A. Tittle	7-15	Jim Bibby	6-26	Rocky Bleier
2-5	Steve Garvey	5-7	Sugar Ray Leonard	7-21	Digger Phelps	7-6	Joe Montana
2-6	Sam Snead	5-7	John McEnroe	7-23	Steve Carlton	7-17	Toby Harrah
2-8	Earvin "Magic" Johnson	5-8	Joe Montana	7-25	Rickey Henderson (2)	7-33	Tommy John
2-8	Larry Bird	5-10	Woody Hayes	7-28	Rolf Benirschke	8-11	Tony Dorsett
2-16	Dick Vermeil	5-25	Stan Albeck	7-29	Floyd Layne	8-25	Roger Staubach
2-17	Babe Ruth	5-26	Pat Ewing	7-35	Herschel Walker		
2-24	Forrest Gregg	5-31	John Jefferson	7-35	Johnny Miller	**VERNON J. BIEVER**	
2-33	Jackie Robinson	5-31	Bob Griese	7-37	Carl Joseph	1-24	Gale Sayers (2)
2-34	Dan Gable	5-34	Herb Brooks	7-41	Mario Andretti		
3-4	Gerald Ford	5-35	Terry Bradshaw	7-41	Carl Yastrzemski	**DENNY LANDWEHR**	
3-9	Bruce Jenner	5-36	Bjorn Borg	7-41	Tom Lasorda	3-11	Cris Collinsworth
3-9	Nadia Comaneci	5-41	Pete Rose	8-4	Al Kaline		
3-10	Roger Maris	5-41	Joe Morgan	8-4	Willie Davenport	**BRUCE CRIPPEN**	
3-11	Cris Collinsworth	5-43	Renaldo Nehemiah	8-5	John Havlicek	1-21	Johnny Bench
3-17	Lee Trevino	5-45	Steve Cauthen	8-15	Julius Erving	3-15	George Foster
3-23	Bob Richards	5-46	Mark Spitz	8-15	Isiah Thomas	3-30	Gerry Faust
3-24	Hank Aaron	5-46	Sparky Anderson	8-18	Jack Kemp	4-4	Gerry Faust
3-25	Rocky Marciano	5-56	Dave Winfield	8-19	John Glenn	5-8	Forrest Gregg
3-28	Alberto Salazar	5-59	Joe Cribbs	8-25	Rich Gossage	5-18	Johnny Bench
3-29	Gerry Cooney	5-60	Bruce Jenner	8-30	Pete Rose	5-44	Gary Maddox
3-29	Tracy Caulkins	5-61	Charlie Boswell	8-31	Carl Yastrzemski	5-46	Tom Seaver
3-30	Lou Holtz	6-5	Wilt Chamberlain	8-32	Willie Stargell		
4-5	Mike Schmidt	6-8	Gerry Faust			**MINNEAPOLIS TRIBUNE**	
4-6	Brooks Robinson (4)	6-9	Bob Gibson	**CARL SKALAK**		8-18	Bud Grant
4-8	Dallas Cowboys (2)	6-11	Matt Bahr	1-6	Bum Phillips		
4-19	Gary Player	6-15	Dan Fouts	1-13	Nolan Ryan	**PAUL H. ROEDIG**	
4-20	Joe Montana	6-19	Lou Gehrig	2-5	Steve Garvey	4-5	Mike Schmidt
4-20	Eric Heiden	6-31	Dick Butkus	2-8	Larry Bird	7-23	Tug McGraw
4-21	Dave Kingman	7-5	Nancy Lopez	2-10	Jack Lambert	7-23	Pete Rose
4-21	Dale Murphy	7-5	Chris Evert Lloyd	2-30	Bart Starr		
4-25	Tim Raines	7-7	Joe DiMaggio	4-25	Joe Morgan	**DAVE REPP**	
4-30	Terry Bradshaw	7-7	Bob Cousy			8-15	Isiah Thomas

ACKNOWLEDGEMENT OF MOVIES

THE FUTURE IS NOW by George Allen
TEN FOR GOLD by Bruce Jenner
GO FOR BROKE, A GAME OF INCHES AND TEAMWORK by Jack Whitaker
TAKE A BIGGER LEAD by Joe Garagiola
NEW GOLD FOR OLD GLORY by Herb Brooks and Jack Whitaker
THE WINNING EDGE by Herb Brooks, Bill Foster and Tom Osborne
THE DIFFERENCE IS YOU by Reggie Jackson

ACKNOWLEDGEMENT OF BOOKS

THE HEART OF A CHAMPION by Bob Richards (Fleming H. Revell Company, 1959)
THURMAN MUNSON, AN AUTOBIOGRAPHY WITH MARTIN APPEL by Thurman Munson and Martin Appel (Coward, McCann & Geoghegan, Inc., 1978)
YOGI, THE AUTOBIOGRAPHY OF A PROFESSIONAL BASEBALL PLAYER by Yogi Berra and Ed Fitzgerald (Doubleday & Company, Inc., 1961)
I AM THIRD by Gale Sayers and Al Silverman (The Viking Press, Inc., 1970)
THE MAN INSIDE...LANDRY by Bob St. John (Word Books, 1979)
ON AND OFF THE FAIRWAY by Jack Nicklaus with Ken Bowden (Simon & Schuster, 1978)
PB, THE PAUL BROWN STORY by Paul Brown with Jack Clary (Atheneum, 1979)
THE WINNING EDGE by Don Shula with Lou Sahadi (E.P. Dutton & Company, 1973)
JOHN WOODEN, THEY CALL ME COACH as told to Jack Tobin (Word Books, 1972)
BUCKEYE, A STUDY OF COACH WOODY HAYES AND THE OHIO STATE FOOTBALL MACHINE by Robert Vare (Harper's Magazine Press, 1974)
ROAD TO NUMBER ONE, A PERSONAL CHRONICLE OF PENN STATE FOOTBALL by Ridge Riley (Doubleday & Company, Inc., 1977)
SATCHEL PAIGE, ALL-TIME BASEBALL GREAT by Robert Rubin (G. P. Putnam's Sons, 1974)
JOE NAMATH, A MATTER OF STYLE by Joe Namath with Bob Oates, Jr. (Little, Brown and Company, 1973)
DIGGER PHELPS AND NOTRE DAME BASKETBALL by Richard "Digger" Phelps and Pat Scanlon (Prentice-Hall, Inc.)
THE POWER OF POSITIVE THINKING by Norman Vincent Peale (Prentice-Hall, Inc. 1952)
JOHN F. KENNEDY: WORDS TO REMEMBER by John F. Kennedy (Hallmark Editions)
KNIGHT WITH THE HOOSIERS by Bob Hammel and Rich Clarkson (Josten's Publications, 1975)
MY LIFE AND THE BEAUTIFUL GAME: THE AUTOBIOGRAPHY OF PELE by Pele with Robert L. Fish (Doubleday & Company, Inc., 1977)
WALTER ALSTON, A YEAR AT A TIME by Walter Alston with Jack Tobin (Word Books, 1976)
BJORN BORG MY LIFE AND GAME by Bjorn Borg as told to Eugene L. Scott (Simon and Schuster)
IT'S GOOD TO BE ALIVE by Roy Campanella (Signet Book)
JACK NICKLAUS' PLAYING LESSONS by Jack Nicklaus with Ken Bowden (A Golf Digest Book)
THE INNER GAME OF TENNIS by W. Timothy Gallwey (Bantam Books, 1974)
PETE ROSE'S WINNING BASEBALL by Pete Rose with Bob Hertzel (Contemporary Books, Inc., 1976)
ROCKY BLEIER FIGHTING BACK by Rocky Bleier with Terry O'Neil (Warner Books, Inc.)
WOODY HAYES AND THE 100-YARD WAR by Jerry Brondfield (Random House, Inc.)
GERRY FAUST — NOTRE DAME'S MAN IN MOTION by Denny Dressman (A. S. Barnes & Company, Inc.)
MY 55 WAYS TO LOWER YOUR GOLF SCORE by Jack Nicklaus (Simon and Schuster)
RUN TO DAYLIGHT by Vince Lombardi with W. C. Heinz and Robert Riger (Prentice-Hall, Inc. 1963)
THE GREATEST: MY OWN STORY by Muhammad Ali with Richard Durham (Random House, Inc., 1975)
PLAY TO WIN—A PROFILE OF PRINCETON BASKETBALL COACH PETE CARRIL by Dan White (Prentice-Hall, Inc., 1978)
THE OFFICIAL PETE ROSE SCRAPBOOK by Pete Rose (Signet Special, 1978)
JOE PATERNO: FOOTBALL MY WAY by Mervin D. Hyman and Gordon S. White, Jr. (Collier Books)